Caroline Sumpter's monograph *The Victoria[n ...] / [an]* inspiring example of the fruitful combinatio[n of ...] media history and literary history. — Kirsti [...] *Authorship, Reading & Publishing*

As the first significant academic work to a[ddress ...] press culture, *The Victorian Press and the Fairy Tale* takes u[...] Sumpter's book is impressive both in its overarching scope and in its focused readings of 1860s and 1890s periodicals. Further value lies in its gestures towards an enormous range of periodical resources that remain largely untapped and which will surely inspire further studies. — Beth Palmer, *Victorian Periodicals Review*

[Sumpter's] book should draw the attention of those with interests in topics such as education, marriage and sexuality, with which the more overt issues of labor and urbanization were intimately connected ... this book makes signal reading for specialists in *English Literature in Transition* fields. — Benjamin J. Fisher, *English Literature in Transition*

Book No. 3931258

Palgrave Studies in Nineteenth-Century Writing and Culture

General Editor: **Joseph Bristow**, Professor of English, UCLA

Editorial Advisory Board: **Hilary Fraser**, Birkbeck College, University of London; **Josephine McDonagh**, Linacre College, University of Oxford; **Yopie Prins**, University of Michigan; **Lindsay Smith**, University of Sussex; **Margaret D. Stetz**, University of Delaware; **Jenny Bourne Taylor**, University of Sussex

Palgrave Studies in Nineteenth-Century Writing and Culture is a new monograph series that aims to represent the most innovative research on literary works that were produced in the English-speaking world from the time of the Napoleonic Wars to the *fin de siècle*. Attentive to the historical continuities between 'Romantic' and 'Victorian', the series will feature studies that help scholarship to reassess the meaning of these terms during a century marked by diverse cultural, literary and political movements. The main aim of the series is to look at the increasing influence of types of historicism on our understanding of literary forms and genres. It reflects the shift from critical theory to cultural history that has affected not only the period 1800–1900, but also every field within the discipline of English literature. All titles in the series seek to offer fresh critical perspectives and challenging readings of both canonical and non-canonical writings of this era.

Titles include:

Laurel Brake and Julie F. Codell (*editors*)
ENCOUNTERS IN THE VICTORIAN PRESS
Editors, Authors, Readers

Colette Colligan
THE TRAFFIC IN OBSCENITY FROM BYRON TO BEARDSLEY
Sexuality and Exoticism in Nineteenth-Century Print Culture

Dennis Denisoff
SEXUAL VISUALITY FROM LITERATURE TO FILM, 1850–1950

Laura E. Franey
VICTORIAN TRAVEL WRITING AND IMPERIAL VIOLENCE

Lawrence Frank
VICTORIAN DETECTIVE FICTION AND THE NATURE OF EVIDENCE
The Scientific Investigations of Poe, Dickens and Doyle

Jarlath Killeen
THE FAITHS OF OSCAR WILDE
Catholicism, Folklore and Ireland

Stephanie Kuduk Weiner
REPUBLICAN POLITICS AND ENGLISH POETRY, 1789–1874

Kirsten MacLeod
FICTIONS OF BRITISH DECADENCE
High Art, Popular Writing and the *Fin de Siècle*

Diana Maltz
BRITISH AESTHETICISM AND THE URBAN WORKING CLASSES, 1870–1900

Catherine Maxwell and Patricia Pulham (*editors*)
VERNON LEE
Decadence, Ethics, Aesthetics

David Payne
THE REENCHANTMENT OF NINETEENTH-CENTURY FICTION
Dickens, Thackeray, George Eliot and Serialization

Julia Reid
ROBERT LOUIS STEVENSON, SCIENCE, AND THE *FIN DE SIÈCLE*

Anne Stiles (*editor*)
NEUROLOGY AND LITERATURE, 1860–1920

Caroline Sumpter
THE VICTORIAN PRESS AND THE FAIRY TALE

Ana Parejo Vadillo
WOMEN POETS AND URBAN AESTHETICISM
Passengers of Modernity

Phyllis Weliver
THE MUSICAL CROWD IN ENGLISH FICTION, 1840–1910
Class, Culture and Nation

Palgrave Studies in Nineteenth-Century Writing and Culture
Series Standing Order ISBN 0–333–97700–9 (hardback)
(*outside North America only*)

You can receive future titles in this series as they are published by placing a standing order. Please contact your bookseller or, in case of difficulty, write to us at the address below with your name and address, the title of the series and the ISBN quoted above.

Customer Services Department, Macmillan Distribution Ltd, Houndmills, Basingstoke, Hampshire RG21 6XS, England

The Victorian Press and the Fairy Tale

Caroline Sumpter
Lecturer in English, Queen's University, Belfast

© Caroline Sumpter 2008, 2012

All rights reserved. No reproduction, copy or transmission of this publication may be made without written permission.

No portion of this publication may be reproduced, copied or transmitted save with written permission or in accordance with the provisions of the Copyright, Designs and Patents Act 1988, or under the terms of any licence permitting limited copying issued by the Copyright Licensing Agency, Saffron House, 6–10 Kirby Street, London EC1N 8TS.

Any person who does any unauthorized act in relation to this publication may be liable to criminal prosecution and civil claims for damages.

The author has asserted her right to be identified as the author of this work in accordance with the Copyright, Designs and Patents Act 1988.

First published 2008 in hardback
First published in paperback in 2012 by
PALGRAVE MACMILLAN

Palgrave Macmillan in the UK is an imprint of Macmillan Publishers Limited, registered in England, company number 785998, of Houndmills, Basingstoke, Hampshire RG21 6XS.

Palgrave Macmillan in the US is a division of St Martin's Press LLC, 175 Fifth Avenue, New York, NY 10010.

Palgrave Macmillan is the global academic imprint of the above companies and has companies and representatives throughout the world.

Palgrave® and Macmillan® are registered trademarks in the United States, the United Kingdom, Europe and other countries.

ISBN 978–0–230–51805–6   hardback
ISBN 978–0–230–36149–2   paperback

This book is printed on paper suitable for recycling and made from fully managed and sustained forest sources. Logging, pulping and manufacturing processes are expected to conform to the environmental regulations of the country of origin.

A catalogue record for this book is available from the British Library.

Library of Congress Cataloging-in-Publication Data

Sumpter, Caroline.
The Victorian press and the fairy tale / Caroline Sumpter.
p. cm.—(Palgrave studies in nineteenth-century writing and culture)
Includes bibliographical references and index.
ISBN 978–0–230–51805–6 (cloth) 978–0–230–36149–2 (pbk)
1. English fiction—19th century—History and criticism. 2. Fairy tales in literature. 3. English periodicals—History—18th century. 4. English periodicals—History—19th century. 5. English fiction—18th century—History and criticism. 6. Literature and folklore—England—History—18th century. 7. Literature and folklore—England—History—19th century. 8. Fairy tales—Great Britain—History and criticism. 9. Fairy tales—Adaptations—History and criticism. I. Title.

PR878.F27S86 2008
823'.809—dc22   2008016148

10 9 8 7 6 5 4 3 2 1
21 20 19 18 17 16 15 14 13 12

Printed and bound in Great Britain by
CPI Antony Rowe, Chippenham and Eastbourne

For my parents, John and Frances Ann

Contents

List of Illustrations	ix
Acknowledgements	xi
Preface to the Paperback Edition	xiii
Introduction	1

1 Serialising Scheherazade: An Alternative History of the Fairy Tale — 11
   Antiquarianism, Romanticism, nationalism: The chapbook and the press — 15
   Originals and counterfeits: Inventing the 'classic' fairy tale — 25

2 Myths of Origin: Folktale Scholarship and Fictional Invention in Magazines for Children — 34
   'Highmindedness and refinement' versus 'cheap and nasty literature': Defining the middle-class juvenile monthly — 35
   The Romantic child and recapitulation — 39
   Max Müller, the Indo-European thesis and juvenile periodical fantasy — 42
   'Savage survivals' and the fairy tale — 49
   'Life is the most beautiful fairy tale': Class and gender fantasies — 52
   Readers write back: Fairy tales and storytelling communities in *Aunt Judy's Magazine* — 62

3 Science and Superstition, Realism and Romance: Fairy Tale and Fantasy in the Adult Shilling Monthly — 67
   The 'magic wand of language': Comparative mythology, Celticism and savagery — 68
   Servants, sweeps and Cinderellas: Darwinian fairy tales — 75
   Sleeping beauty and the prince's progress: 'The woman question' — 82

4 'I wonder were the fairies Socialists?': The Politics of the Fairy Tale in the 1890s Labour Press — 88
   'A precarious existence': Strategies for survival in the 1890s socialist press — 89
   The ideological contexts of reading — 92
   Cinderella and socialism — 101
   Evolutionary frameworks: Childhood, the fairy tale and rural utopianism — 105
   Making socialists — 113

	New tales from old: Context and meaning	115
	'Joining the crusade against the giants': Keir Hardie, child readers and interactive fairy tales	118
5	'All art is at once surface and symbol': Fairy Tales and *fin-de-siècle* Little Magazines	131
	'Too highbrow to be popular': Little magazines, elitism and commerce	132
	Beauty and use: Arts and Crafts and the fairy tale	135
	Innocents and epicures: Decadence, Symbolism and the child	140
	Alternative masculinities: The fairy tale and coded gay discourse	156

Conclusion: Myth in the Marketplace	175
Abbreviations Used in Notes	179
Notes	180
Bibliography	220
Index	239

Illustrations

2.1 A. W. Bayes, 'The Hillman and the Housewife',
Aunt Judy's Magazine, 1870. © The British Library Board.
All Rights Reserved. PP59922i   56

2.2 George Cruikshank, 'Timothy's Shoes',
Aunt Judy's Magazine, 1871. © The British Library Board.
All Rights Reserved. PP59922i   58

2.3 Cover illustration, *Chatterbox*, 1880. © The British Library
Board. All Rights Reserved. PP5992g   59

2.4 Randolph Caldecott, cover illustration,
Aunt Judy's Magazine, 1882. © The British Library Board.
All Rights Reserved. PP59922i   60

4.1 Jordie, 'An Empty Feast', *Labour Leader*, 18 May 1895.
© The British Library Board. All Rights Reserved. NPL LON 420   97

4.2 Jordie, 'Little Red Riding Hood', *Labour Leader*, 10 Aug. 1895.
© The British Library Board. All Rights Reserved. NPL LON 420   99

4.3 Alexis, 'Sleeping Beauty', *Labour Leader*, 25 Dec. 1897.
© The British Library Board. All Rights Reserved. NPL LON 1000   128

5.1 Sidney Meteyard, 'Rapunzel', *Quest*, 1896. Used by
permission of the University of London Library   138

5.2 [John] Byam [Liston] Shaw, 'Beauty and the Beast', *Dome*,
1898. Used by permission of the University of London Library   159

5.3 Laurence Housman, illustration to Jane Barlow,
The End of Elfin-Town, 1894. © The British Library Board.
All Rights Reserved. KTC.35.a.4. Used by permission of
the Random House Group Ltd.   165

5.4 Laurence Housman, 'The Reflected Faun', *Yellow Book*, 1894.
Used by permission of the University of London Library
and the Random House Group Ltd.   168

5.5 Laurence Housman, 'Blind Love', *Pageant*, 1897.
Used by permission of the University of London Library
and the Random House Group Ltd.   173

Acknowledgements

Thankfully, I have not yet succumbed to the delusion that this book was guided by the fairies, but I have been extremely lucky in the help that I have received along the way. I first began to think about the relationship between the press and the fairy tale at the University of Leeds, where I was privileged to be supervised by experts so willing to share their time. Sincere thanks to Gail Marshall for her insights into Victorian literature, and to Andrew Wawn, whose impressive knowledge of the fairy tale was matched by a much-appreciated warmth and wit. Laurel Brake and Richard Salmon offered invaluable advice on the project at this early stage, and Laurel has offered a particularly shrewd engagement with my subsequent work on the press. Nicola Bown read a draft of chapters 2, 4 and 5: I have benefited from her perceptive comments then, and her generosity since. Peter Stoneley very helpfully read Chapter 5, and our conversations about fairies, the ballet and gay culture have always been fun as well as informative. I was particularly fortunate with my readers at Palgrave Macmillan. It is a pleasure to thank Joseph Bristow, whose editorial comments were encouraging, perceptive and pertinent, and the equally encouraging anonymous reader (since identified as Jack Zipes) for his extremely constructive advice.

My editorial team have been patient, helpful and efficient throughout, and I owe particular gratitude to Paula Kennedy and Christabel Scaife. This type of project relies on the resources of numerous libraries, and thanks are due to the institutions plagued with my visits over the years: the British Library and British Newspaper Library, the Brotherton Library at the University of Leeds, the Queen's University Library (Belfast), the Leeds Subscription Library, the Sheffield Archives, the University of London Library, and the British Library of Political and Economic Science. Significant thanks are due to the AHRC, for the semester of study leave that allowed me to complete the final typescript and for the Postgraduate Fellowship that helped to make an academic career possible in the first place.

The enthusiasm of the students who have taken my specialist option at Queen's University, Belfast, has worked wonders when I've thought that I couldn't face another fairy tale. Josephine Guy, Robert Colls and Joanne Shattock were inspiring early influences, and I am lucky to still benefit from Joanne's intellectual rigour and encouragement. I am particularly grateful to Bob Owens and the Open University, for the Research Fellowship that enabled me to explore the history of reading, and to Leon Litvack, who welcomed me to Victorian literature teaching at Queen's. I have benefited from sharing ideas with my excellent MA and PhD students, including Peter Eakin, Clare Gill, Peter Millar and Beth Rodgers.

Queen's not only provided me with a semester of study leave in 2007, but has also introduced me to colleagues who have since become great friends. Heartfelt thanks to all of you who have shared your intelligence and hospitality over the last five years. I am particularly grateful to David Dwan, Shaun Regan, Adrian Streete, Robert Ward and Ramona Wray, who suffer my comic pessimism with wit, intelligence and kindness. Many others have helped in academic and personal ways at different times during the project, including Eadaoin Agnew, Nick Bandu, Mark Burnett, Suzannah Camm, Stephen Colclough, Rosalind Crone, Debbie Lisle, Melanie Ord, Aisling Mullan, Andrew Pepper, Mark Ruddle and Colin Winborn.

I am grateful to Catherine Trippett from Random House for permission to quote from and reproduce visual material by Laurence Housman and to the University of London and the British Library for permission to reproduce images. Material from Chapter 4 has appeared in *Culture and Science in the Nineteenth-Century Media*, edited by Louise Henson et al. (Aldershot: Ashgate, 2004), and in *Literature and History*, 15 (Autumn 2006). A section of Chapter 5 has also appeared in altered form in *Nineteenth-Century Contexts*, 28 (Sept. 2006). I am grateful to Ashgate Publishing, Manchester University Press and Taylor & Francis for their permission to reproduce this material. If I have failed in any case to trace a copyright holder, the author and publisher apologise for any apparent negligence, and will make the necessary arrangements at the first opportunity.

Helen, Mike, Katy, Betsy and Mabel Sumpter have reminded me that many things are more important than academia. Over many years, John Braime shared his obsession with Monkeyworld, as well as his love, intelligence and humour, and this project would have been impossible without him. I dedicate the book to my parents, John and Frances Sumpter, without whose love, generosity (and sloe gin) it would also have been unimaginable. To Garrett Carr, writing Prince of Donegal, all my love, and thank you for the adventure.

Preface to the Paperback Edition

The nineteenth-century writers who cast print as a destroyer of the fairy tale might wonder at its recent transformation from villain to fairy godmother. W. B. Yeats was convinced that newspapers had helped to exile the English fairies, but even he could not have predicted the further death blow that they would gleefully deliver a century later. 'Scholar denies oral roots of fairy tales', proclaimed the *Guardian* in 2009, while the *New York Times* posed the dramatic question: 'The story of fairy tales: a fairy tale?'[1] Since the publication of this book in 2008, the argument for the fairy tale's urban, print-based origins, made by Ruth B. Bottigheimer in *Fairy Godfather: Straparola, Venice and the Fairy Tale Tradition* (2002), but much more widely popularised in her 2009 book *Fairy Tales: A New History*, has generated significant media coverage. Bottigheimer's claim that such tales began, not with oral tradition, but with the literary works of Giovanni Francesco Straparola in the early modern period, has been the subject of controversy in scholarly circles, as well as engaging writers in the mainstream press.[2] A few months after national newspapers circulated Bottigheimer's claims that 'folk invention and transmission of fairy tales has no basis in verifiable fact',[3] the British daily the *Telegraph* reported the work of evolutionary anthropologists that promoted a very different thesis. Here, it was argued that 'Little Red Riding Hood' could be traced back to a narrative ancestor circulating in 2,600 BC, and that the fairy tale had evolved, just like a 'biological organism', from a truly ancient oral tradition.[4]

We are still fascinated, it seems, with the process of formulating and contesting grand narratives about the fairy tale's beginnings – a practice, this book suggests, that owes much to our Victorian forebears. Whether imagining fairy tales as the metaphorical flights of fancy of long lost Indo-European tribes, or as the mythic productions of a universalised 'savage' stage of development, nineteenth-century philologists, anthropologists and creative writers were indefatigable in their attempts to track the fairy tale to its source. It is not just in the twenty-first century, of course, that the press has played a major role in igniting these debates. If the recent controversy about the fairy tale's oral or literary origins can be seen to have engaged a range of quite different audiences (from specialists in scholarly contexts such as the *Journal of American Folklore* to the broader academic readers of the *Chronicle of Higher Education*, and the general browsers of the online content of British and American dailies), it has been invested with rather different significance by all of these reading communities.[5] In the nineteenth century, I argue, things were not so different. Here, I explore the seminal role of newspapers and periodicals in bringing fairy tales and folkloric debates to mass and minority audiences, and in firing the imaginations of Victorian readers and writers.

If contention over definitions of the fairy tale (and over the relative significance of the oral and the literary in its development) looks set to continue, engaging with these debates in the nineteenth-century press might enable us to reflect more critically on the assumptions of scholars' different disciplinary traditions. If Victorian periodicals were often happy to perpetuate the claim that print was a deadening force in folk culture – a belief, as we shall see, that left its mark in twentieth-century fairy-tale scholarship – it is also possible to read a different narrative in their pages, one that reveals mass culture's role in fostering creative relationships between the spoken and the written, the individual and the communal. Since hardback publication, I have become increasingly humbled by my own linguistic and geographical limitations, and more aware of the work of European scholars who have offered fascinating insights into the relationships between creative writing, the newspaper format and tale-telling traditions in other national contexts.[6] This book is a very modest contribution to an emergent international debate.

One recent discipline with which this book attempts to engage – one that is rarely in the foreground of research on the Victorian fairy tale – is the history of reading.[7] While I explore the press's neglected role in the fairy tale's development, calling into question some familiar accounts of its nineteenth-century history, I make no ambitious claims about the genre's beginnings. Instead, I focus on what tales meant to particular reading communities in specific historical moments. Since this book first appeared, it is perhaps less my engagement with better-known writers of the fairy tale than my focus on the creation of fairy tales in the socialist press, and amongst a periodical subculture of aesthetes and homosexual readers, that has generated attention. The working-class, primarily urban, socialist writers and readers of the fairy tale that I discuss in Chapter 4 were far from the rural 'folk' romanticised in nineteenth-century antiquarian scholarship, but they certainly made the fairy tale their own, as a vehicle for very specific political aspirations. One key aim of this book is to show that we generalise about nineteenth-century readers of the fairy tale, whether child or adult, at our peril. Indeed, broad claims about the cultural meanings of Victorian fairy tales are increasingly difficult to sustain when we come face to face with the idiosyncrasies of actual readers and contexts of reception. Periodical fairy tales were read alongside articles about science, race and nation, democracy, childhood, and women's rights, but they also participated in those debates.[8] Here I show the ways Victorian fairy tales were shaped by those rich political and publishing contexts.

The limitations of this book, however, are obvious. Within the British and Irish press (as well as within international periodicals) many more writers and readerships still deserve attention. Other scholars may pursue this course, but a bigger methodological question will still remain. How we move between micro and large-scale histories – that is, how we reconcile broad theses concerning the fairy tale's origin and development with evidence for localised experiences of the genre – remains a challenge for both nineteenth-century specialists and broader fairy-tale scholars.[9] In future research, intimate and culturally situated histories of the fairy tale will no doubt continue to engage with and question some of the grand narratives. Historians of the fairy tale in print may increasingly look beyond the chapbook and the book. For readers of this book, I hope the experiences of these particular fairy-tale writers and audiences are historical tales that seem worth the telling.

Caroline Sumpter
Belfast, 2011

Notes

1 Alison Flood, 'Scholar denies oral roots of fairy tales'. <http://www.guardian.co.uk/books/2009/may/19/oral-roots-fairy-tales> [Accessed 19/05/2009]. Tom Kuntz et al. 'Idea of the Day: The Story of Fairy Tales: A Fairy Tale?' <http://ideas.blogs.nytimes.com/2009/05/20/the-story-of-fairy-tales-a-fairy-tale/> [Accessed 20 May 2009].

2 Specifically, Bottigheimer claims that Straparola was the inventor of 'rise' fairy tales, defined as secular tales in which a 'poor boy or girl suffers tasks and trials, marries royalty through the aid of magic, and becomes rich here on earth'. She excludes 'fairyland fictions', which traverse fairy and human realms, from her definition of the fairy tale. See *'Fairy Godfather*, Fairy-Tale History, and Fairy Tale Scholarship: A Response to Dan Ben-Amos, Jan M. Ziolkowski, and Francisco Vaz da Silva', *Journal of American Folklore*, 123 (Fall 2010), 447–96 (457). For the most recent challenges to Bottigheimer's definitions and arguments, see the articles by Ben-Amos, Silva and Ziolkowski in the same edition of *Journal of American Folklore*, 373–446, and Christina Bacchilega's review of *Fairy Tales: A New History* in *Children's Literature Association Quarterly*, 35 (Winter 2010), 468–71.

3 Bottigheimer, *Fairy Tales: A New History* (Albany: State University of New York Press, 2009), 1. On folk genesis and transmission of the fairy tale, Bottigheimer states: 'literary analysis undermines it, literary history rejects it, social history repudiates it, and publishing history [...] contradicts it' (*Fairy Tales*, 1). She maintains that 'folk knowledge of fairy tales followed upon their book distribution' (*Fairy Tales*, 75).

4 Richard Gray, 'Fairy Tales have ancient origin'. <http://www.telegraph.co.uk/science/science-news/6142964/Fairy-tales-have-ancient-origin.html> [Accessed 5 September 2009]. The article reports on the research of the evolutionary anthropologist Jamie Tehrani, but there have been a number of recent literary scholars of the fairy tale who have argued for the genre's distant historical origins: see, for example, Ziolkowski, *Fairy Tales from Before Fairy Tales: The Medieval Latin Past of Wonderful Lies* (Michigan: University of Michigan Press, 2006) and Graham Anderson, *Fairytale in the Ancient World* (London: Routledge, 2000).

5 Both the *Guardian* and the *New York Times* picked up on this debate from the preview of an article by Jennifer Howard in the *Chronicle of Higher Education*. See 'From "Once Upon a Time" to "Happily Ever After"', *Chronicle Review*, 22 May

2009 <http://chronicle.com/article/From-Once-Upon-a-Time-to/44402> [Accessed 23 May 2009]. A key difference between the nineteenth century and the twenty-first, of course, is the role of the internet in the distribution of newspaper and periodical content.
6   While she does not focus on the fairy tale, Kirsti Salmi-Niklander's research on manuscript newspapers amongst early twentieth-century Finnish readers reveals an intimate relationship between the press, writing, reading and oral tale-telling: see 'Manuscripts and Broadsheets: Narrative Genres and the Communication Circuit among Working-class Youth in early 20th-Century Finland', *Folklore: Electronic Journal of Folklore*, 33 (2006), 109–26 <http://www.folklore.ee. folklorevol33/salmi.pdf> [Accessed 1 August 2010].
7   Such approaches have been more prominent in the context of analysis of fairy tales in other European contexts and periods: relevant research is discussed in the introduction.
8   Since the publication of this book, an important work has appeared that is relevant to my own discussions of the child in the context of comparative science: see Sally Shuttleworth, *The Mind of the Child: Child Development in Literature, Science and Medicine, 1840–1900* (Oxford: Oxford University Press, 2010).
9   I first made this point in *Elore* 17 (2010), 127–37 <http://www.elore.fi/arkisto/2_10/sumpter_2_10.pdf>. On microhistory as a concept, see John Brewer, 'Microhistory and the Histories of Everyday Life', *Cultural and Social History*, 7 (2010), 87–109 and Filippo de Vivo, 'Prospect or Refuge? Microhistory, History on a Large Scale', *Cultural and Social History*, 7 (2010), 387–97.

Introduction

> As the hand points to two o'clock on the illuminated dial of St. Paul's, Covent Garden, there is not much business doing in the great market. [...] But as I turn away down Wellington-street the gleaming of the lights and the roar of the engines make me aware that I am on the threshold of Pressland – the domain of Queen Journalia – a much bepraised and well-abused potentate, who knows not high day nor holiday, to whom gaslight is as good as daylight, whose work goes on ceaselessly from day to day, from week to week, from year to year.[1]

On Christmas Day in 1875, readers of *All the Year Round* were encouraged to reflect on the marvel of modernity that they held in their hands. 'How we get our Newspapers' reveals the endless industry that produces familiar dailies and weeklies, and the spectacle inspires awe and wonder. Pressland has become a new Fairyland, whose monarch, unlike Scheherazade, never stops or sleeps. Yet the lament that Queen Journalia was displacing Queen Mab – exiling the fairy tale, as well as folk beliefs – was also well known to nineteenth-century readers. The most persistent of Journalia's critics hailed from Pressland itself.

Whimsical and self-referential, Dickens's own two-penny weeklies were nevertheless ambivalent about relations between 'fancy' and the press. In George A. Sala's 'The Complaint of the Old Magician' (published in *All the Year Round's* predecessor, *Household Words*, in 1854), the Old Magician, though 'unembodied', takes an 'interest in the doings of the material world'. Indeed, he claims to 'peruse, not unfrequently, the hebdomadal productions of the press', and is a regular reader of Sala's own journalism. The Magician can therefore remind Sala that

> [i]nflated with conceit, and blinded by opiniation, you lately undertook to commiserate and to point out a Case of Real Distress, one Mab or

Mabel, a shiftless jade, calling herself Queen of the extinct kingdom of Fairyland – a kingdom recently blotted out from the map by the united efforts of the March of the Intellect, Transatlantic Go-a-headism, and the Society for the Diffusion of Useful Knowledge.[2]

Critiquing one of Sala's previous articles for *Household Words*, the Magician complains that the Queen of Fairyland has been wrongly credited with powers that fall within his own domain. Nevertheless, by citing the 'March of Intellect' and the publishers of the *Penny Magazine* as destroyers of Mab's fairy kingdom, Sala and his Magician make an all too familiar claim. *Chambers's Journal* makes clear in 1858 that while water fairies had lived twenty years previously in rural Yorkshire, it was 'notwithstanding railways, and what is called the march of intellect, and in spite of all the newspapers had written against them'.[3] In 1877, the tellers of popular tales and legends in the Western Highlands of Scotland are assumed by *Belgravia* to be 'rapidly becoming an extinct race, through the pressure of those new creations of the railway era that hunt them in their far-away nooks': creations that include 'tourists, telegrams, daily newspapers'.[4] In 1882, *Chambers's* decides that 'tales of wonder' can no longer survive the influence of the press, asserting, '[f]rom the maturer popular belief, [fairy tales] are fast fading away. Weakly and puny infants are no longer supposed to be fairy changelings, except in districts so remote that the newspapers cannot reach them, nor the new broom of the School Boards sweep them clean'.[5] Yet in these nostalgic farewells to both fairies and fairy tales, an obvious fact is persistently overlooked. While the press is assumed to be extinguishing fairy belief, it is newspapers and magazines that frequently make those claims, and that keep fairy tales in continual circulation. Some journalists signal an enlightened distance from (supposed) folk belief, but others, as we have seen, mourn the fairies as a loss.[6] In fact, in the nineteenth century, the form often associated with the 'march of intellect' brought literary fairy tales and fairy superstitions to truly mass readerships, including the rural lower classes Romanticised as 'the folk'.

In the present study, I argue that Pressland did more than keep Queen Mab in the news. By continually bringing the genre into the contemporary moment, the press also helped to reinvent the fairy tale, and secured its cherished place at the heart of Victorian culture. For while the nineteenth century saw major developments in the fairy tale as a literary form, it also witnessed dramatic changes in the cost and accessibility of print, resulting in an explosion of newspapers and magazines. These developments, normally regarded as discrete areas of interest, are analysed here in terms of their dynamic relationship. Authors and readers used the fairy tale to grapple with a surprisingly wide range of controversies, from the impact of industrialism, socialism and evolution, to debates over race and nationalism, masculinity and women's rights. By recovering the fairy tale's place in media history and the history of reading, it is possible to bring those political engagements back into focus. Nineteenth-century magazines and newspapers shaped the fairy tale as we know it, but fairy tale and fantasy also helped to create new communities of readers, in dailies and penny weeklies, children's periodicals, middle-class monthlies and experimental magazines. It is this largely forgotten history – of the press as well as the fairy tale – that I seek to uncover. Whether used to debate models of evolution and progress, to forge coded gay discourse, or to anticipate a socialist utopia, these fairy tales reveal the ingenious ways that writers, artists and readers used the press, not to kill the genre, but to make it their own.

Fairy-tale scholars have given newspapers and magazines much less attention than they deserve: a fact that may owe something to the evasions of our nineteenth-century predecessors.[7] There is certainly no denying the number of writers who depicted the 'genuine' fairy tale as the antithesis of the newspaper – as timeless, untouchable, and beyond the reach of politics and commerce. Dickens's pronouncement in *Household Words* is perhaps the most famous. In 'Frauds on the Fairies' (1853), he was clear that fairy tales should be regarded as 'nurseries of fancy', fictions that should 'be as much preserved in their simplicity, and purity, and innocent extravagance, as if they were actual fact'.[8] In *All the Year Round* in 1865, however, Andrew Halliday suggested that amateur newspaper production and magazine reading were activities that set modern youth apart from the imaginative innocence of their forbears. The author offered his own personal reminiscence:

> When I was a boy, my stock of play literature consisted of some half-dozen sixpenny books, such as Jack the Giant Killer, Puss in Boots, the History of Cock Robin, and an Abridgment of the Arabian Nights. I remember that I kept them locked up in a deal box, and was exceedingly chary of lending them, or even letting any one look at them. But boys now-a-days take in their monthly and weekly magazines, correspond with the editor, answer riddles and rebuses, contribute puzzles and engage in chess tournaments by correspondence; nay, they club subscriptions to Mudie's, and read all the new sensation novels as they appear.[9]

Halliday was far from the first writer to link the fairy tale to nostalgia for older forms of print. In Chapter 1, I point to the still pervasive influence of Romantic and Victorian histories of the fairy tale, which often view the chapbook as a more authentic voice of childhood and the folk. Uneasy responses to newer print cultures – particularly to the expansion of the press and the rise of the penny magazine in the 1830s – helped to create the antiquarian interest in chapbook fairy tales and romances. Yet the fairy tale and folklore revival took root, not just in expensive quarterlies, but also in Irish and Scottish (as well as English) cheap magazines – the very medium that was seen to be driving the fairy tale out.

I track these debates through to the 1890s, when Yeats offers his own nationalist twist on the newspaper and journalist as killers of the (English) fairies. Unlike the newspaperman, Yeats claims, the Celt is a 'visionary without scratching'; 'great art' as well as folklore is 'perhaps dead' in England, where a 'hidden sergeant' drills minds with journalistic 'formulas and generalisations'. Yeats, of course, wrote extensively for magazines and newspapers. Parts of his anthology *Fairy and Folk Tales of the Irish Peasantry* were culled from popular magazines, including the English titles *All the Year Round*, *Belgravia* and the *Monthly Packet*.[10] In championing the peasant roots of the tales in this collection, Yeats was responsible for some powerful myth-making of his own, but he was far from unusual in indicting the medium on which he was reliant for his folk sources. In order to understand why the fairy tale became central to nineteenth-century culture, we must go beyond both the myth of the folk and the medium of the book.

In 1890, in the preface to his anthology *English Fairy Tales*, Joseph Jacobs (editor of the journal *Folk-Lore*), claimed that indigenous English folk and fairy tales had not been 'brought to light' earlier due to 'the lamentable gap between the governing and recording classes and the dumb working classes of this country – dumb to others but eloquent to themselves'. In his patriotic task of recovering the English folktale for 'all classes', Jacobs had to turn a blind eye to the fact that the working classes had been reading and recording for some time. In his notes, Jacobs elegantly sidesteps the uncanny similarity of some of his oral English tales to those well known from popular print – including one originally claimed for German patriotism by the Grimms.[11] We owe the myth of orality as a marker of authenticity to the nineteenth century, but it is a myth that is gradually being eroded by scholars working on a number of periods in the fairy tale's history. The contributions of Ruth Bottigheimer and Ann Wanning Harries are discussed in Chapter 1, but Jennifer Schacker's exploration of nationalism in four nineteenth-century folktale collections also deserves mention, not least for its attempts to situate these books within contemporary publishing history. Suggestive as such studies are for my work, I view periodicals and their readers as an equally vital part of fairy and folktale history, one largely overlooked in fairy-tale scholars' discussions of chapbooks, books and the 'communications circuit'.[12]

By focusing explicitly on the press, I not only probe those nineteenth-century tendencies to mystify links between print and oral culture, but also foreground contemporary definitions of the fairy tale, which were contested, contradictory and often very capacious. As my first chapter reveals, in the nineteenth century 'fairy tale' could be used to describe both modern, authored literary works, and orally collected 'popular tales', 'nursery fictions' or 'folks-story' – wonder tales deemed cultural survivals and source materials for the science of origins.[13] It will be clear in subsequent chapters – for example, in the analysis of literary work by Charles Kingsley, Anne Thackeray Ritchie, Keir Hardie and Laurence Housman – that Victorian writers regularly experimented with both form and audience. As Nancy L. Canepa and Antonella Ansani have recognised, the fairy tale has never been 'a monolithic genre', but 'a vital, changing form, firmly entrenched in cultural history'; innovation, rather than stasis, guarantees it's survival.[14] Moreover, as all readers of *Jane Eyre* or *Great Expectations* know, fairy and fairy-tale motifs were not confined to Victorian fantasy. They were appropriated in realist novels, in ballet and pantomime, and in poetry and painting. While these issues have received attention elsewhere, my own discussion foregrounds some less familiar visual and fictional material, which, buried in the Victorian press, has been largely hidden from view.[15]

The press both created a canon of 'classic' fairy tales, and found new aesthetic and political possibilities for the genre. While my opening chapter covers broad chronological ground, ranging from the eighteenth century to the end of the nineteenth, the rest of my study offers more in-depth analysis of two landmark eras for both fairy tales and the press. It was certainly no coincidence that shilling monthlies, including the *Cornhill* and *Macmillan's* (the focus of Chapter 3), became prominent in the 1860s, the same decade that saw the rise of the middle-class children's titles that feature in my second chapter. Such developments were part of the mid-Victorian publishing boom, which harnessed the potential of cheaper printing and paper-making technologies (and increasing middle-class prosperity) to shape newly lucrative markets.[16] In these years, major publishers also established children's departments: Macmillan, for example, published key works such as Lewis Carroll's *Alice's Adventures in Wonderland* (1866) and Dinah Mulock's *The Fairy Book* (1863).[17] Macmillan had previously published Charles Kingsley's *The Heroes; or Greek Fairy Tales for My Children* (1856); it now brought out a significantly revised version of Kingsley's *The Water-Babies* (1863), hot on the heels of its *Macmillan's Magazine* serialisation (1862–3). Indeed, in publishers' attempts to broaden readerships for fairy tale and fantasy, magazine and book publication were often intimately linked. As Chapter 2 reveals, George Macdonald's *At the Back of the North Wind* (1868–70), *The Princess and the Goblin* (1870–1) and the *Princess and Curdie* (1877), as well as Charles Kingsley's *Madam How and Lady* (1868–9), enticed young readers in *Good Words for the Young*, before their better-remembered book editions. Chapters 4 and 5 shift the focus to the 1890s, which registered changes in the literary landscape that were every bit as dramatic. This was the first era shaped by newspapers for the million, when cheap mass production and the New Journalism brought papers and illustrated magazines within the reach of unprecedented audiences. This decade of near universal literacy also saw the emergence of some less-discussed readerships who sought to assert an aesthetic or political distance from commercial newspaper culture. These included two very distinctive reading communities: the self-styled bohemians who subscribed to experimental little magazines and the readers of the socialist penny press.

Placing an emphasis on the press therefore encourages us to think again about who was reading the fairy tale, and why. Jack Zipes has argued that Victorian authors writing in this genre 'always had two ideal implied audiences in mind: the middle class parent *and* child', but this only tells part of the story.[18] While authors such as Anne Thackeray Ritchie wrote specifically for adults, and Keir Hardie's implied audience was working class, the success of the best-known European author of fairy tales was premised on a much wider circulation across nations and classes. This fact became particularly evident to the writer in question. Strolling through London in 1847, Hans Christian Andersen experienced the thrill of modern celebrity – the curious pleasure of seeing his own face on the cover of a magazine. Buying and sending a copy of the weekly to Henriette Collin, he declared, 'I am strangely happy! I cannot realise it. I am actually famous, so much so as neither I myself or Denmark is aware of'.[19] As Andersen discovered, anyone with two pence to spare could purchase *Howitt's Weekly Journal*, admire the author's portrait and read Mary Howitt's eulogy. Some readers had already encountered Andersen through a fairy tale in *Chambers's Journal*, while others would wait for further tales in *Howitt's* and the *London Journal* to see if he deserved his fame.[20] These cheap weeklies, which openly targeted working-class readerships, hardly feature in many histories of the fairy tale, but Andersen had a shrewder understanding of their significance. Although he never tired of boasting of his reputation with the nobility, it was to Danish and British magazines, newspapers and reviews that he looked – quite obsessively – to secure his reputation.[21]

The publication of three English language editions of Andersen's fairy tales in 1846 is widely regarded as a seminal moment for fantasy literature in Britain, the point at which the literary fairy tale achieved an unprecedented popularity.[22] Yet Andersen's tales, targeting adults as well as children, reached much wider audiences than those who saw these books. In 1846, gentlemen browsing the two-shilling *Bentley's Miscellany* in the clubroom were among the first British readers of Andersen's 'The Little Mermaid'.[23] Those who missed this text could catch the laudatory reviews elsewhere: W. M. Thackeray's in *Fraser's Magazine*, for instance, or the earlier *Athenæum* review where Thackeray had discovered Andersen.[24] In the mid-Victorian period, Andersen was caricatured in *Punch* and discussed in *The Times*, while his tales were reproduced in Irish reviews and English children's periodicals. In the 1890s, they were reclaimed for a multiplicity of new readerships, from the audiences of avant-garde magazines to consumers of the socialist press.

The role of readers, and the significance of reading contexts, is therefore key to the present study. From engagements with 'serial time' and the periodical as a form with 'open and closed' traits to attempts to explore reading spaces and the serial consumption of communities and individuals, periodical scholars have played a distinctive role in the emergent debates within the history of reading.[25] Those wider debates, however, have yet to be fully registered by many historians of fairy tales and children's literature. Michel de Certeau's theorisation of the reader as 'poacher' – as creative, individual, resisting and unpredictable – is perhaps overused within book history, but it at least needs to be persuasively countered by those fairy-tale scholars who make more straightforward links between reading and social indoctrination. When Rudolf Schenda argues that 'the passive reception of narrative texts, no matter what their quality, is in the long run a sterile affair', the suggestion is that reading can function as a one-way process, rather than a social contract that requires the reader's engagement.[26] Here, in exploring some of the ways that Victorian readers of the fairy tale wrote back, I have also sought to put reading practices back in the picture.

In the *Intellectual Life of the British Working Classes*, Jonathan Rose includes an autobiographical account of the early reading of a working-class poet, born in the 1820s. Rose argues:

> Lancashire millworker Ben Brierley read penny fairy tales and horror stories as a boy, but they did not contribute to his work as a dialect poet: 'I must confess that my soul did not feel much lifted by the only class of reading then within my reach. It was not until I joined the companionship of Burns and Byron that I felt "the god within me"'.[27]

Rose explores much fascinating material, but we must also acknowledge that there is no unmediated way of recovering such historical reading experiences. Working-class autobiographies were shaped by their own generic conventions, which, in some exceptional individuals' narratives of literary, religious or political reawakening, could include the disavowal of such low-status reading as a way of asserting the author's (hard won) right to literary culture. We can, however, read such accounts against other narratives of readerly self-construction, and other explorations of the social contexts in which reading took place. Periodical correspondence columns were subject to much editorial shaping and stage-management, but surprising dialogues sometimes emerge. Parts of Chapters 2 and 4 use such columns to foreground voices that are frequently overlooked in Victorian cultural analysis – those of teenaged girls, in *Aunt Judy's Magazine*, and working-class children in the *Labour Leader*. In the latter exploration of Labour papers, I resituate fairy tales by Keir Hardie (and others) within the context of a distinctive political and print culture. Children's as well as adult fiction was used to critique industrial capitalism, and reading itself could be seen as a step on the road to a socialist future. Chapter 5 looks at a very different reading context, *fin-de-siècle* little magazines. As will become clear, many consumers of the fairy tales within their pages drew on a knowledge of experimental movements, including Arts and Crafts, the Celtic Revival, decadence and Symbolism. Others interpreted these works through a more specific frame of reference, shared only by that select group of little magazine readers who belonged to an emergent (and clandestine) gay subculture.[28]

At the outset, I wish to acknowledge the value of affordable anthologies of Victorian fairy tales (such as those edited by Nina Auerbach and

U.C. Knoepflmacher, Michael Patrick Hearn and Jack Zipes).[29] These publications have brought some previously neglected works back into scholarly discussion and have also helped to strengthen undergraduate teaching in this area. Nevertheless, I am also interested in the methods that we use to package and interpret these tales, because, as Tony Bennett has argued, 'the text the critic has on the desk before her or him may not be the same as the text that is culturally active in the relations of popular reading'.[30] If a fairy tale was published in the press, the way it was read might also depend on the magazine's politics and implied audience, the 'progress and pause' that shapes serial reading, and the tale's physical proximity to other textual and visual contributions: contexts that are lost if anthologists rely on subsequent book editions.[31] Moreover, different (academic) relations of reading explain the different conclusions drawn by Zipes (influenced in part by a Frankfurt-School inflected Marxism) and Auerbach and Knoepflmacher (drawn to feminist and psychoanalytic approaches). It is no surprise that these critics activate the same fairy tales in different ways, and that many of the authors who Zipes believes 'reconcile themselves and their readers to the status quo of Victorian society' are perceived to be subversive by Auerbach and Knoepflmacher.[32]

It would be naïve, of course, to suggest that my own approach is without its political investments, or is indeed unshaped by its own set of interpretative conventions. I argue that media history and the history of reading offers a critically productive and historically enriching way of engaging with debates about class and gender in the fairy tale, as well as bringing some wider political contexts into focus. For example, from its launch in 1859, *Macmillan's Magazine* sought to foster debate over religion, science, and social reform, no difficult task in a year that saw the publication of Samuel Smiles's *Self-Help*, John Stuart Mill's *On Liberty* and Charles Darwin's *On the Origin of Species*. In Chapter 3, I argue that Charles Kingsley's *The Water-Babies* was one of a number of texts in *Macmillan's* and the *Cornhill* that drew on fairy tale and fantasy to respond to these contemporary developments. In periodicals such as *Macmillan's*, fairy tales were linked not only to evolutionary and mythological science, but also to debates about child poverty, Irish and British identity, race, women's education and transatlantic politics.

As that frame of reference might suggest, the creative relationships between folktale scholarship, literary fairy tales and journalistic non-fiction inform my inquiries in the chapters that follow. If we view non-fictional writing on folklore as the preserve of historians and folklorists, and authored fairy tales simply as the concern of literary critics, we will fail to see the significance of Victorian readers' familiarity with both genres. For mainstream magazines did not just publish literary fairy tales – they also played a seminal role in the rise of folktale study as discipline. As Chapter 1 reveals, in the 1820s magazines and reviews popularised the tales collected by the Grimms, linking these (supposed) 'tales from the folk' to a wider quest for racial and national roots. In 1846 the term 'folklore' was famously coined in the *Athenæum*.[33] Later, when 'comparative mythology' was deemed a science (and a field over which philologists and anthropologists fought to gain mastery), magazines once again inspired their readers to use the folktale to reflect on their own prehistory. Children's titles as well as adult periodicals popularised folktale research, a practice that was linked to wider attempts to imagine class, race and Empire. Those folkloric debates both influence and function as an interpretative context for some of the key works from the 'golden age' of fantasy, including those by Charles Kingsley, George MacDonald and J. H. Ewing.

Whether conceived as the early cultural products of spiritual, creative primitives, or the relics of a brutal, 'savage' ancestry, folktales became a source of powerful myths about cultural, religious and racial origins. This study reveals that the influence of scientific studies of myth was apparent in some unexpected contexts, including constructions of childhood and national identity, theorisations of avant-garde writing and the culture of 'back-to-the-land' socialism. For if the 'science of fairy tales' was a politicised discourse, it was never politicised in straightforward ways: it could be used to defend or disavow the political status quo, to question as well as buttress dominant racial hierarchies. Victorian folktale scholarship did not simply 'filter down' from scholarly authorities to working-class adults, middle-class girls and artistic coterie readerships. It came to mean very different things for each of these audiences.

Richard M. Dorson argued that '[t]he idea that folklore is dying out is itself a kind of folklore'.[34] In one respect, casting the Victorian newspaper as the killer of the fairy tale was merely a modern take on a centuries-old theme. If the myth of the 'fairies' farewell' has been current since the time of Chaucer, print's role in the supposed death of folklore has also been lamented since (at least) the late seventeenth century.[35] As Nicola Bown and Carole Silver have shown, in the nineteenth century, too, the fairies are always on the point of departure. Perhaps the press became such a potent symbol of their decline because it was intimately linked to other developments frequently associated with the fairies' exile: mass education, the popularisation of science, urbanisation and industrialisation.[36] My opening quotation, however, should remind us that both fairies and fairy-tale metaphors also shaped representations of industrial modernity. The fairy could be used (as Bown's analysis makes clear) to explore evolutionary science and the wonders industry, as well as to mourn their disorientating arrival. Moreover, Sinéad Garrigan Mattar's shrewd re-evaluation of comparative science's impact on the Irish Revival, and Silver's exploration of links between the fairy and racial science, show the need for a more critical and nuanced approach to the relations between late nineteenth-century primitivism and earlier Romantic stereotypes.[37] While it is the cultural figure of the fairy (and not the fairy tale) that concerns both Bown and Silver, my own explorations of the fairy tale and the press extends that wider dialogue about constructions of science, savagery and primitivism, and is in the interdisciplinary spirit of such work.

While some of the writers and magazines under discussion sought to challenge mainstream culture and politics, I do not claim that their fairy tales were unshaped by commerce. Jack Zipes has argued that, in the Victorian period, 'Fairy tales for profit and fairy tales of conventionality were disregarded by English writers of the utopian direction'. Yet Zipes's 'utopian' writers (including George MacDonald, Lewis Carroll, J. H. Ewing and Oscar Wilde) were also acutely conscious of writing for the market.[38] Macdonald, Ewing and Wilde each edited magazines that sought mainstream audiences; these three authors published regularly in commercial periodicals. While Zipes does not focus on the relationship between MacDonald's editorship of *Good Words for the Young* and his 'struggles against [...] commercial capitalism', Macdonald certainly did not disregard his publisher's need to turn a profit.[39] Rather than suggesting that certain writers could simply reject that capitalist literary marketplace, I explore the uneasy compromises and challenges that were enacted from within its confines. The close of the nineteenth century saw the triumph of the press baron and the rise of the New Journalism, but it also saw the birth of the socialist penny press. That political press turned to more commercial formats in its own struggles to survive; the little magazines that sought to annoy the bourgeoisie were engaged in a dance of complicity with the markets they claimed to despise. This study tracks those complex negotiations.

As the century drew to a close, former Folklore Society president Edward Clodd was happy to proclaim that while 'the great harvest of fiction which each generation of caterers provides for Mudie's subscribers is but for a season, there is one class which is not for an age, but for all time, and for every zone'. Yet the supposedly 'timeless' fairy tale found its biggest audiences in a commercial form that continually wrote to the moment. In 1877, the *Church Quarterly Review* article 'Magazine Literature' suggested that there was both an allure and an immaturity in magazine reading: 'as the sheaf of periodicals comes in, we treat them as a naughty child does a dish of apples, taking a bite out of each in haste'. The attempt to settle 'into some solid book' instead of 'being swept from it by the tide that sets in on the first of every month' was apparently doomed to failure: 'we find ourselves left behind in household talk, in social conversation, and altogether out of the current affairs'.[40] Individuals and communities found their own ways of engaging with the products of Pressland, with the papers and magazines that shaped and structured social life. In exploring how a literature for 'all time' adapted to serial time, and was reinvented for (and by) different reading communities, this book examines the fairy tale's role in Victorian current affairs, and recovers its intimate relationships with politics, science and culture.

1
Serialising Scheherazade: An Alternative History of the Fairy Tale

'The custom, in periodicals, of sustaining interest by happily-conceived divisions of the plot, may perhaps be traced to this subtle artifice of Scheherazade', James Mew observes in the *Cornhill Magazine* in 1875.[1] Mew was not the first writer to make the analogy between the skills of the fairy-tale narrator and those of the magazine novelist: for Dickens, Mrs Gaskell was famously 'my Scheherazade', spinning artfully rationed weekly instalments for the readers of *Household Words*.[2] In fact, both echoed enterprising editors from the previous century, who made literal links between Scheherazade and serialisation. While the first English novel serialised in a newspaper, Daniel Defoe's *Robinson Crusoe*, was still running in the *Original London Post*, the *Churchman's Last Shift* was entertaining its readers with 'The Voyages of Sinbad'. Three years later, in 1723, the *Arabian Nights* began appearing thrice-weekly in *Parker's London News*. Making good use of its heroine's mastery of pleasurable postponement, the serialisation took over three years to come to completion.[3]

In his *The Blue Fairy Book*, the Victorian folklorist Andrew Lang revealed that Perrault's *Contes de ma Mère l'Oye* (1697) had been 'Englished' by 1729, for a 'version is advertised in a newspaper of that year'.[4] While eighteenth-century newspapers alerted readers to the appearance of future classics of the genre, its boundaries were still far from defined. When the *Universal Spectator* published one of the French court tales, Mlle Marie-Jeanne L'Héritier's 'The Wary Princess, or the Adventures of Finette' in 1743, it was subtitled a 'novel' rather than a fairy tale.[5] Such classifications reveal the still emergent nature of both literary forms in mid eighteenth-century Britain and the significant traffic between fairy tale, novel and romance. The variety of works with fantastic elements circulating in eighteenth- and early nineteenth-century periodicals – from the dream narrative and tale of alternative worlds to the oriental tale, the 'novel of circulation', the fable and the satire – reveal that fairy tales were shaped by a much wider literary dialogue. Indeed, Hans Christian Andersen's 'rare and surprising' art for anthropomorphism seems less surprising in relation to some of these tales from the previous century, in which coins, pins and lapdogs narrate their own tales.[6]

Histories of the fairy tale in Britain before the first English translation of the Grimms' tales (1823–6) often chart the appearance of some key book editions. These include Antoine Galland's French translation of *The Thousand and One Nights* (1704–17) and the first English translations (1706 onwards): Robert Samber's 1729 translation from Perrault, *Histories, or Tales of Past Times* (also known by its frontispiece as *Tales of Mother Goose*); the first English translations of Madame d'Aulnoy's tales (1699 onwards); and the eighteenth-century versions for children, *Tales of Mother Bunch*. These are often joined by realist texts that featured interpolated fairy tales – Sarah Fielding's *The Governess* (1749) and the French and English versions of Madame Prince de Beaumont's *The Young Misses Magazine* (1756/1757), which included a version of 'Beauty and the Beast'.[7]

At the same time, critics have long acknowledged that legends and tales such as 'Jack the Giant-Killer' and 'Tom Thumb', as well as condensed versions of medieval romances, enjoyed a much longer and varied life (and much larger audiences) as chapbooks, which were sold by travelling chapmen throughout Europe and the British Isles. While such texts seem to have circulated widely from at least the sixteenth century, in the eighteenth century the *Arabian Nights* and French court tales joined the chapbook repertoire. This mode of circulation remained popular in Britain into the early decades of the nineteenth century. As Ruth B. Bottigheimer has shown, the wide and early circulation of chapbook romances challenges those Romantic histories of the fairy tale that locate the origins of the genre (and authenticity within the tradition) within an oral culture completely untouched by literacy.[8] Those myths might be exploded once and for all when we look at a rather different form of print.

In *Before Novels*, J. Paul Hunter offers an account of the fairy tale's disappearance from popular culture in the seventeenth century. He argues:

> On the Continent (and in Ireland and the Scottish Highlands) the tradition of fairy tales remained intact into the nineteenth century when the writing down of such material began to be systematic. But in England the tradition was interrupted between the seventeenth century and the mid eighteenth; for some reason the tales were no longer passed down from generation to generation, and the joy once associated with their telling turned to fear and distrust.[9]

Elizabeth Wanning Harries has rightly questioned the evidence for this narrative of exile – for the evaporation of a 'joyous' oral tradition that evolved entirely beyond the influence of print. The notion that this oral tradition remained 'intact' on the Continent and in Ireland and Scotland has also come under interrogation. As Peter Burke (among others) has argued, that systematic writing down – the discovery of folk culture – might equally be described as an invention by a 'group of German intellectuals at the end of the eighteenth-century'. Burke usefully draws attention to the assumptions of 'primitivism', 'communalism' and 'purism' that underpinned Herder and the Grimms' constructions of the folk, while subsequent critics have produced a wealth of analysis to show the significant roles played by print culture, as well as editorial intervention, in the Grimms' orally collected tales, the *Kinder und Haus Märchen* (1812–14).[10] Interestingly, while Harries uses the chapbook to point to Hunter's neglect of the fairy tale in print, neither writer makes links between the fairy tale and the newer print cultures that Hunter's book captures so evocatively. For counter to Hunter's claims, fairy tales were clearly circulating in Britain before the 1750s: in newspapers and magazines as well as in chapbooks. They evolved alongside, rather than cleared the way for, that newest of genres, the novel – a dialogue that was to continue throughout the nineteenth century.

If many historians and folklorists have been keen for some time to signal distance from nineteenth-century celebrations of primitivism, communalism and purism, we still need to look beyond the canon created by the Romantics and Victorians to see the true variety of fairy tales that circulated in Britain in the late eighteenth century.[11] In fact, tales published in magazines included fantastic authored works inspired by the *Arabian Nights*, translations from German Romantics such as Wieland and Musäus, French court tales, and some unexpected authored texts. One of the latter, 'Annette: A Fairy Tale', which purported to be by 'Master George Louis Lenox, Aged only 12 years', is as far as can be imagined from a tale from the folk. Modelled on an elaborate French courtly romance tradition, it is suspiciously sophisticated for an author not yet in his teens. Whether Master Lenox was a journalistic hoax or a genuinely precocious schoolboy, the tale clearly reached a significant periodical public: from its first publication in *The British Magazine and Review* in 1782, it was republished in at least four more magazines (including the cheaper serials) in the next 25 years.[12] While Lenox's text seems to target adult audiences, children were also beginning to be recognised as readers of fairy tale and fantasy. John Newbery is often credited with the first experiment in serial publishing for children, with *The Lilliputian Magazine* in 1751. In the early 1770s, a competitor of the same name appeared, which promised the adventures of 'King Tom Thumb of Lilliputia' in monthly instalments.[13]

While eighteenth-century magazines reveal a history of adult fairy-tale reading that has often been overlooked, periodicals also help us to engage more critically with another familiar account of the fairy tale's disappearance – this time from middle-class children's literature at the beginning of the nineteenth century. In this history, taken up by much twentieth-century criticism, Lamb, Coleridge and Wordsworth are presented as defenders of the imaginative freedom of the fairy tale in defiance of didactic and rationalist educators, while the Romantics are seen to be ultimately vindicated by the triumph of Victorian fantasy and fairy tale. Alan Richardson has made the most convincing attacks on this '"Whiggish" version of the history of English children's reading', revealing that those oppositions between fantastic and didactic literature were far less sustained than has frequently been assumed.[14] This is indeed apparent in one of few periodicals, Sarah Trimmer's *Guardian of Education* (1802–6), that does receive a mention in most histories of the fairy tale in Britain. Only recently, however, has the critical reliance on the same highly selective quotations, used as evidence for a widespread middle-class backlash against the fairy tale, been challenged by more nuanced readings of the periodical as a whole. In fact, Trimmer may have refused to review chapbooks and cheap publications, but she was not always entirely hostile to fairy tale and fantasy.[15] In 'Observations on the Changes That Have Taken Place in Books for Children and Young Persons' (1802), she claims:

> When the idea of uniting amusement with instruction was once started by such a writer as Mr. Locke, books for children were soon produced of various sorts: Fables, Fairy Tales, &c &c. [...] Some of the books written in what may be called the *first period of Infantine and Juvenile Literature* in this country, we well remember, as the delight of our childish days, viz *Mother Goose's Fairy Tales*; *Esop* [sic] and *Gay's Fables*; the *Governess, or Little Female Academy*, by Mrs Fielding, &c &c.

While Trimmer echoes Locke in her condemnation of tales such as 'Bluebeard' for their perceived ability to terrify young minds, 'valuable French books' such as Madame le Prince de Beaumont's are viewed as far superior to the novels from circulating libraries: novels which Trimmer notes also fell into the hands of young people in the same period.[16] In November 1802, the *Adventures of Musul; or, The Three Gifts* is deemed a book that is entitled 'to rank among instructive ones, though the Tales are full of the marvellous'.[17] It is works that unite 'amusement and instruction' – that conform to the narrow strictures of Trimmer's own Christian morality, and counter the radical 'torrent of infidelity' – that are lauded in the early volumes of the *Guardian of Education*, whether they employ fantasy or realism. In 1802, Trimmer is concerned that 'such a rage for new publications is excited in the nation, that even *children* are taught to expect *a daily supply of literature*'.[18] Trimmer could always be relied upon for hyperbole, but she was also right to perceive an expanded audience for print since her youth: newspaper circulation had also doubled between 1753 and 1792.[19] As new firms such as Tabart brought fairy tales to child audiences, Trimmer proved that magazines were not just contexts in which fairy tales were read, but also sites where they were reviewed, championed and censured – indeed where such works became a subject of public debate.

Even such a necessarily brief snapshot of this earlier period suggests a more complicated history of the fairy tale than its complete exile by rationalist educators and its subterranean survival as the 'literature of the people', in the chapbooks of popular culture. It is now becoming less controversial to argue that to privilege orality over print in the fairy-tale tradition is to take Romanticism on its own terms. However, it was not just the oral tale, but the chapbook that became central to that British folktale revival – that underwent, to use Susan Stewart's term, its own nineteenth-century process of 'artifactualization'.[20] Here, I argue that the celebration of the chapbook as authentic folk culture was related to the emergence of reading audiences undreamt of in the eighteenth century and to the growth of newer forms of print.

Antiquarianism, Romanticism, nationalism: The chapbook and the press

In his 1819 *Quarterly Review* article on the 'Antiquities of Nursery Literature', Francis Cohen notes with regret that *Fairy Tales: or the Lilliputian Cabinet* (a reissue from Tabart) is far inferior to the fairy tales told by his nurse in his youth. Cohen laments:

> Scarcely any of the *chap books* which were formally sold to the country people at fairs and markets have been able to maintain their ancient popularity; and we have almost witnessed the extinction of this branch of our national literature. Spruce modern novels, and degenerate modern Gothic romances, romances only in name, have expelled the ancient 'histories' even from their last retreats. The kitchen wench, who thumbs the Mysteries of Udolpho, or the Rose of Raby, *won't grieve at all* for the death of Fair Rosamund.[21]

Cohen does not merely celebrate the oral tale, but the literate lower-class reader and an older print tradition that has been purged of its traditional associations with the crude, the licentious and the vulgar and has been reborn as authentic in the wake of the novel and its popular subgenres. While Gothic fiction circulated through sixpenny and shilling novelettes as well as circulating-library novels, the late eighteenth and early nineteenth centuries also saw the emergence of new cheap magazines which clearly targeted some of the old chapbook audiences. These hybrid forms (which Robert Mayo has termed 'serial chapbooks' and 'serial anthologies') included the *New Novelists' Magazine*, *Tell-Tale* and the *Marvellous Magazine*, which brought tales from the *Arabian Nights* as well as redactions of Gothic novels (including Radcliffe's) to less wealthy literate publics.[22]

Cohen does not acknowledge the continued circulation of older fairy tales and romance through these newer forms of serial culture.[23] In fact, he suggests that it is not just the novel, but serial reading of a more radical kind that is killing off the kitchen wench's links to the fairy tale and the spirit of the folk:

> Politics and sectarianism complete the change which has taken place in the budget of the flying stationer. The old broadside-ballads have given way to the red stamp of the newspaper; and pedlars have burnt their ungodly story-books like sorcerers of old, and fill their baskets with the productions sanctified by the Imprimatur of the Tabernacle.[24]

Alan Richardson argues that concern about the spread of political pamphlets via chapbook sellers may explain Wordsworth's celebration of the less volatile fairy-tale chapbook.[25] Similar concerns may be lurking in Cohen's account too, for beyond the 'red stamp' and prohibitive four-penny tax on the official newspapers (which nevertheless doubled in circulation from 1800 to 1830), there was a cheaper, unstamped political press that was not so easy to regulate.[26] In Cohen's metaphor, the political fare of the newspaper is a new kind of sorcery that engenders the death of the fairy tale: the chapman is now a 'flying stationer' whose wares have the power to cast off the old gods of superstition. Yet the newspaper signifies more than the birth of political consciousness among the folk. It is directly linked to Cohen's championing of scholarly antiquarianism, a practice that promises to tabulate and record the last vestiges of folk innocence. Wryly suggesting that the now obsolete penny chapbooks of the publisher Marshall will soon fetch high sums under the auctioneer's hammer, Cohen reveals a clear link between lower-class engagements with news and new print cultures and the middle-class 'artifactualization' of the chapbook, which is reinvented as the true voice of the folk.

Cohen's article, which asks readers to lend a sympathetic ear to 'the ingenious theories of the historian, the mythologist, or the philologer', prefigures the substantial growth of those fields in a British context. Linking the fairy tale to a racial and cultural infancy ('the imagination of man in the childhood of his race'), Cohen also explores an originary thesis that would come to exert a profound influence over nineteenth-century imaginations. Championing 'the important addition to nursery literature' in Germany by 'John and William Grimm [sic] two antiquarian brethren of the highest reputation', Cohen elaborates the Indo-European thesis, which had been sketched by Sir William Jones in the 1780s, was further developed by the German new philology, and was popularised in relation to the folktale by the Grimms in their *Kinder und Haus Märchen*. Cohen argues not only that English and German folktales emerged from a shared Teutonic mythology, but also that the similarities between German, Danish, English and Indian tales revealed a distant linguistic source to which all these mythologies could be traced, back to the 'the first seat of the Caucasian tribes'.[27]

When Edgar Taylor published the first volume of *German Popular Stories*, his immensely successful translation of the Grimms' tales in 1823, he acknowledged a deep debt to Cohen's article for revealing 'how wide a field is open, interesting to the antiquarian as well as the reader who only seeks amusement'.[28] Before producing this translation, however, Taylor had helped to shape a receptive audience of both kinds of reader through his own periodical journalism, in his four articles on 'German Popular and Traditionary Literature' in the *New Monthly Magazine* (1821–2). Noting that many beast fables were common to Persia, India and Germany, Taylor, echoing Cohen, asks whether such animal fables are not

> remnants of some great mass of amusing moral instruction, which has at the remotest periods and in all countries found its way for the edification of man, flowing from some fountain-head of wisdom, whence Calmuck, Russian, Celt, Scandinavian and German, in their various manifestations, have imbibed their earliest and simplest lessons of improvement?

In presenting the possibility of an 'Oriental hypothesis of the origin of [...] fairy fictions', Taylor joins a number of writers in the *New Monthly Magazine* in the 1820s who focus on European and Asian myth from comparativist and Romantic perspectives.[29] 'The Smith Velant' (1822), noting the parallels between a supernatural tale found in Scandinavia, a supernatural tale found in Berkshire and a work by Walter Scott concludes: 'we are brought back at length to a common country of the greater number of most ancient traditions – to India, which may be regarded as the cradle of truths and fables'.[30] In one of his *New Monthly Magazine* articles, Taylor argues that 'traditionary tales' are the 'curious momentos of simple and primitive society, the precious glimmerings of historic light' – and that they offer an invigorating escape from the present.[31] In the *Five-Book Prelude* (1804), Wordsworth had famously lamented the 'deep experiments' of the child 'prodigy' valorised by Enlightenment rationalism, holding empire with 'telescopes and crucibles and maps':

> Oh! Give us once again the wishing cap
> Of Fortunatus, and the invisible coat
> Of Jack the giant-killer, Robin Hood,
> And Sabra in the Forest with St George!
> The child whose love is here at least does reap
> One precious gain – that he forgets himself.[32]

Taylor also hopes for the child's liberation from rationality and modernity through chapbook romance. In the *New Monthly Magazine*, he looks forward to a time when the gay dreams of fairy innocence shall again hover around them, and scientific compendiums, lisping botanics, and leading-string mechanics, shall be postponed to the Delights of Valentine and Orson, the beautiful Magalona, or Fair Rosamond.[33]

A very similar quotation appears in the introduction to Taylor's *German Popular Stories*. The epigraphs to these volumes are taken from the prefaces of seventeenth-century chapbooks: the first from 'Thom Thumbe the Little' (1621) and second from the romance of 'Valentine and Orson' (1677). While the subtitle to Taylor's volume assures readers that the Grimms' tales are collected 'from oral tradition', the English tradition was perceived to be rather more difficult to trace. Supposedly deprived of their own unbroken stream of oral tales, the chapbook tradition also becomes English readers' way back to the past – a print form that seems to preserve remnants of that 'fountain-head of wisdom'.

In the *New Monthly Magazine*, Taylor, like Cohen, addresses his comments largely to a readership of upper-middle-class, educated adult males, within the discourse of an expensive, small-circulation periodical.[34] The celebration of both British folk traditions and German literary Romanticism was widely evident in such periodicals from the 1820s to the 1840s. *The New Monthly Magazine* published articles on Schiller and Goethe, while *Fraser's Magazine* republished a recent translation of Goethe's 'The Tale' in 1832. In the same year it offered 'Dorf Juystein', an original tale clearly shaped by German Romantic predecessors; an article discussing Welsh fairy superstitions; and serialised tales based on Scottish folklore by the 'Ettrick Shepherd' – the former *Blackwood's* stalwart James Hogg.[35] *Blackwood's* published a short story inspired by Chamisso's *Peter Schlemihl* in 1839, and also published Ludwig Tieck's fantasy 'Pietro D'Abano: A Tale of Enchantment' in the same year.[36] In fact, Tieck was the subject of numerous reviews in the monthlies and quarterlies throughout the Victorian period. These literary texts were also intimately connected to Romantic constructions of the folk, including the German *Volksbuch* or chapbook tradition. As Tieck argued:

> The common reader should not make fun of the popular stories (*Volksromane*) which are sold in the streets by old women for a Groschen or two, for *The horned Siegried, The sons of Amyon, Duke Ernst* and *Genoveva* have more true inventiveness and are simpler and better by far than the books currently in fashion.[37]

While Tieck produced his own versions of chapbooks, his literary tales were praised for their supposed connection to folk roots: a writer cited in the *Athenæum* in 1841 claims that they seem to be written '*by* fairies', and have 'the engaging naïvité and the daring invention of the old stories that lived in the hearts and on the lips of the people'.[38] When writers appropriated the chapbook in a British context, they often continued to move (like Taylor before them) between higher journalism, antiquarianism and commercial children's fiction. In 1846, W. J. Thoms, using the pseudonym 'Ambrose Merton', wrote a letter to the *Athenæum* in which he proposed 'a good Saxon compound, Folklore', in place of the current terms in usage, 'Popular Antiquities and Popular Literature'.[39] As Thoms helped to establish a developing scholarly discipline by contributing columns to the *Athenæum* (which in turn led to the establishment of the more specialist *Notes and Queries*), he was also engaged in the production of a far more popular series of texts, 'Ambrose Merton''s *Gammer Gurton Story Books*. These books exhibited antiquarian interest in the chapbook culture from which they took their sources, while simultaneously sanitising their contents. British legendary tales were 'newly revised and amended' for middle-class pockets and tastes.[40]

Thoms's legends formed part of the *Home Treasury* series, commissioned by the publisher Joseph Cundall in conjunction with the *Felix Summerly* collection of fairy-tale books. In presenting old fairy tales anew to middle-class readers, Henry Cole undertook a similar process of revision. When he came to produce a new edition of 'Little Red Riding Hood' in the 1850s, Henry Cole again turned to chapbook sources, revealing he had before him 'not less than five *penny* editions of a very primitive sort, printed almost on brown paper' which did not look 'more than fifty years old'.[41] Cohen's prediction – that the chapbook would become the prized possession of the middle-class antiquarian's library – had clearly already come to pass.

When Edward Clodd introduces a new edition of Hans Christian Andersen's tales in 1901, he strives to link Andersen's literary work to a folk tradition that existed in print as well as oral form. Claiming the Odense of Andersen's childhood had been culturally static for 200 years, and 'was rich in unspoilt folk-tales such as the Grimms collected', he also notes that '[t]he home cupboard had its shelf of chap books and the like'.[42] Yeats also draws on similar impulses when he claims that, in late nineteenth-century Ireland, chapbooks are still a vital part of folk culture. In 1888, he suggests that they are

> to be found brown with turf smoke on the cottage shelves, and are, or were, sold on every hand by the pedlars, but cannot be found in any library in this city of the Sassanach. 'The Royal Fairy Tales', 'The Hibernian Tales', 'The Legends of the Fairies' are the fairy literature of the people.[43]

That 'are, or were' is crucial. There are reasons why Yeats tentatively acknowledges that the sale of chapbooks in Ireland may be a thing of the past, while wanting to assert that it is very much of the present. In the same book, *Fairy and Folk Tales of the Irish Peasantry*, Yeats also acknowledges some very different sources. Although he mentions the publications of the

Folk-Lore Society, the *Folk-Lore Record* (established in 1878) and the *Folk-Lore Journal* (1883), he claimed in private correspondence that they were 'useless', and had turned instead to more popular miscellanies. In *Fairy and Folk Tales*, Yeats lists the *Dublin and London Magazine* (noting 'Sir William Wilde calls this the best collection of Irish folk-lore in existence'), the *Dublin University Magazine* and a host of cheaper Irish titles. He claims: 'Old Irish magazines, such as *The Penny Journal, Newry Magazine*, and *Duffy's Sixpenny Magazine* and *Hibernian Magazine*, have much scattered through them. Among the peasantry are immense quantities of ungathered legends and beliefs.'[44]

Yeats's last two statements, presented as unrelated, beg some obvious questions. What are the links between those Irish magazines (including the penny weeklies established in the 1830s) and that store of 'ungathered' peasant legends? Brian Earls has explored the ways in which improving literacy rates, an emergent nationalism and more numerous outlets for literary production coalesced in Ireland from the 1820s onwards, making supernatural legends widespread in new serial contexts. He notes that such legends, the most common of which included tales of fairy figures such as the Púca and the Sidhe, became immensely popular, in part because their length was ideally suited to these new magazine formats.[45] Interestingly, as soon as they emerged, such newspapers and magazines became the subjects (as well as the disseminators) of fairy legends. In 1825, the *Dublin and London Magazine* opens with the fifth article in its series entitled 'Superstitions of the Irish Peasantry'. In County Wicklow, on a Sunday in 1822, the reader encounters Jerry O'Toole, encircled by villagers and 'labouring to spell his way, with the help of spectacles, through an old newspaper, lent him by his neighbour Father Kavanagh, the parish priest'. Although he struggles through the bankruptcy notices and political news, Jerry's listeners draw close 'with looks of intense curiosity' when he reads aloud 'An Account of the Luprechaun, lately seen near Carlow'. The newspaper account is the springboard for villagers to offer their own oral accounts of Luprechaun (or Leprechaun) sightings and tales.[46]

A footnote from the editor reveals that the same newspaper article is discussed that month by another contributor, 'The Hermit'. In the latter text, the writer visits Carlow, where a friend and native of the place asks him if he remembers hearing of the visit of the Leprechaun. The narrator indeed recollects 'having seen something in the Carlow Morning Post at one time, about a small shoe that was found, and a strange little being that was seen near it'. The tale, as retold, features a Mrs Doran, who captures a Leprechaun, is tricked out of a promised pot of gold and deposits the Leprechaun's shoe for public appraisal at the office of the *Carlow Morning Post*.[47] In these intriguingly self-referential accounts, the newspaper becomes a source of supposed folkloric authenticity; oral tale-telling is assumed to be reinvigorated by its appearance. Like images of Mother Goose, of course, this tale-telling frame is a conceit, part of the colourful authorial fiction. Yet such frames are nevertheless revealing about assumptions concerning the reach of print in Ireland in the 1820s, and about the ways in which oral tellers (including the illiterate) are assumed to be audiences for, as well as contributors to, fairy legends in newspapers and magazines.

While the *Dublin and London Magazine*, nationalist in sympathy, sought to present itself as a cheaper Irish competitor to the *New Monthly Magazine*, the *Irish Penny Magazine* sought a much wider audience. Borrowing elements from the cheap weeklies launched in 1832, Charles Knight's *Penny Magazine* and Robert and William Chambers's *Chambers's Edinburgh Journal*, it targeted readers who ostensibly included men such as Jerry O'Toole. An 1833 contribution, 'Sketches from the Country II: Bringing a Wife to Reason', offers a similar framing device to the *Dublin and London Magazine*, but one which functions far more explicitly as self-promotion. The writer (in all probability Samuel Lover) informs his readers that, in Wexford, a group of seven or eight peasants meet twice weekly in a back parlour of an alehouse, each taking turns to buy a copy of the *Irish Penny Magazine*. Larry Hennessy, who is always called upon to read aloud the 'grotesque and ludicrous' stories from the magazine, tells his companions that he once tricked some magazine editors into thinking one of his invented tales was an ancient local legend. When chastised for his deceit, he tells the editors a supposedly true anecdote about a possessive wife. He repeats this tale for his oral listeners at length in the alehouse. When the story is concluded, Larry tells the club's members

> That's the way *I'll* compose – I'll tell my story – another picks it up, an claps it down in black an' white, with what illustrations he likes for the 'Magazine,' – nay, I'll bet ye a cherry-cheeked apple against a turnip, that this story of '*bringing a wife to raison*', is in one of them this moment.

In this most metafictional of articles, the magazine is presented as a forum where folklore meets fiction – and both are reinvented by readers as well as writers. Larry, the peasant taleteller, may have offered an invented tale to credulous editors, but it would be a credulous reader indeed who would take the humourised Larry as an authentic voice of the peasantry. The employment of the device of peasant readers and listeners in the rural alehouse seeks to displace the myth of print as the killer of communal lore, but it also seeks to displace something else, as the opening of the article makes apparent:

> All success to the PENNY MAGAZINES! They deserve it. Their editors have gone spiritedly and sensibly to work, and already the good effects are visible. Many a rough *fist* that erst had clutched the shillelagh, or worse still – the paltry and ribald ballad in which nonsense and sedition frequently strive for mastery, now thumbs the Penny Magazine.[48]

It is not oral tale-telling, but a different kind of cheap print – the ballad and chapbook – that the *Irish Penny Magazine* sought to supplant. While Earls is right that Irish magazines with both Tory-Unionist and nationalist politics could unite in their condemnation of the chapbook, to view chapbooks as part of 'an autonomous popular culture' also risks disguising this older form's commercial status and the intimate relationships between publishers of chapbooks, newspapers and books. As Earls himself notes, James Duffy made extensive use of fairy legends in the numerous nationalist magazines that he published from the 1840s onwards, but his career began with an earlier form of print: he was a chapbook hawker and printer before he began to publish magazines.[49] It was in the commercial interest of cheap magazines to continue to employ the type of material that had entertained chapbook audiences, while fostering the notion that chapbooks were of dubious cultural value.

In 1833, *Chambers's* was proud to reveal to its readers the revolutionary technological innovations – from the steam press and stereotyping to the paper-making machine – that had enabled it to provide a magazine for a penny and a half. Such developments have been described by one twentieth-century commentator as 'the greatest step forward in book production since Caxton'.[50] As R. K. Webb notes, it was this mechanisation, combined with transport improvements, that 'facilitated the expansion and centralization of newspapers, magazines, serial stories, and novels in parts'. Yet to assert that new habits of reading 'made the cruder and simpler tales of an earlier generation fall away' may overlook the ways in which even self-consciously 'improving' papers such as *Chambers's* capitalised upon, as well as condemned, the storytelling traditions of the chapbooks.[51] *Chambers's*, which claimed a sale of sixty-six thousand copies a week by 1838 (from printers in Dublin and London as well as Edinburgh), published a plethora of ballads, fairy tales, superstitions and fairy poems, as well as articles about international folklore.[52]

In fact, *Chambers's* employed the very same self-promotional strategies as the *Irish Penny Magazine*. In 1833, it cites an account in the *Dumfries and Galloway Courier* from a bookseller who claims that he no longer stocks 'trashy ballads' and 'trashy pamphlets', for 'almost every urchin' among the milk boys of rural Scotland is now 'thumbing *Chambers*' instead'. The 1855 article 'Chap-Book Literature' designates chapbooks 'vile and worthless trash', but claims that such literature is largely obsolete: '*Chambers's Edinburgh Journal* and similar publications have superseded the literature of our forefathers'. Predictably enough, *Chambers's* treats such material in the spirit of nostalgia rather than condemnation by the 1860s, when chapbooks are viewed as entirely an 'antique class of literature'. In 1862, fairy-tale chapbooks such as 'Blue-Beard' and 'Jack the Giant-Killer' are praised for their 'firm, manly, old-English style, like the ballads' and extensive quotations are provided from the humorous and superstitious publications that *Chambers's* had earlier condemned. In the 1880s, the paper is again quoting liberally from chapbooks as the quaint and harmless entertainment of the past, while assuming the very concept is unknown to *Chambers's* readers: they are now valuable collector's items which 'very rarely come within the ken of ordinary readers'.[53]

The newspaper, *Chambers's* proclaims in 1844, is 'the ephemeral record of the exciting *now*': unlike the endlessly reprinted chapbook, it belongs to the contemporary moment.[54] As Earls has noted, many of the writers attracted to fairy legends in Ireland between the 1820s and 1840s were middle-class Catholics fighting for the repeal of the Union; they made extensive use of local newspapers as well as magazines. Yet in magazines too folklore was incorporated into those nationalist debates. In the article by 'the Hermit' in the *Dublin and London Magazine*, the Leprechaun is seen as an auger of trouble, anticipating the visit of the 'Bible-men', who oppose the people's claims 'as subjects of a free state', and begin to separate Protestant and Catholic.[55] In the 1820s, the decade in which campaigners won the fight for Catholic Emancipation, the legend was a possession that was reinvented anew, with the fairies claimed in different papers for Irish nationalism and Britishness.[56] In the English magazine *The Leisure Hour* in 1890, Yeats claims that he is often doubted when he insists that the Irish peasantry still believe in fairies, for people think it impossible that 'any kind of ghost or goblin can live within the range of our daily papers'.[57] Yeats's critics may have raised sensible questions about his sentimental endorsement of folk belief, but in fact magazines and newspapers were just where the ghosts and goblins multiplied. Yeats's wry tale in the *Celtic Twilight*, in which a peasant is chased by a copy of the *Irish Times* which metamorphoses into a devilish seducer, suggests that he was less confident about Irish folk culture's imperviousness to the press than he sometimes claimed.[58] In the 1820s and 1830s, a period that saw investments in literacy in Ireland that were significantly higher than those in England, such magazine and newspaper tales undoubtedly found their way into oral tale-telling, shaping those 'immense quantities of ungathered legends and beliefs' that Yeats discovered among the Irish peasantry.[59]

The great success among English readers of Thomas Crofton Croker's *Fairy Legends and Traditions of the South of Ireland* (1825–8), which claimed to be taken down from the 'mouths of the peasantry', cannot be separated from these political or print debates. If fairy beliefs in Croker's tales were sometimes rationalised and humourised as the delusions of drunk and over-exuberant peasants, Croker was also keen to insist that the folk themselves were still firm believers. In the preface to the second volume, he turns to some intriguing evidence: not oral testimony, but newspapers reports. Croker quotes from two murder trials, where fairy involvement had been claimed by the accused, lifted from *The Dublin Evening Mail* and the *Morning Post*. He both insists and laments that such 'delusions' still exist among Irish peasants; if perpetuated fairy superstitions will 'retard the progress of their civilization'.[60] As Angela Bourke has shown, in the 1890s such rare and sensationalised cases could still be invoked in defence of the Union. During the debate over Home Rule, the burning of Bridget Cleary by her husband (who claimed that his wife had suffered a fairy abduction) became a *cause célèbre* courtesy of both Irish and English newspapers, nationalist titles countering the implications drawn by the Tory-Unionist press.[61] As Chapter 5 reveals, Yeats's own nationalist, symbolist and spiritualist leanings in the 1890s ensured that he saw the Irish peasantry through a very different primitivist lens to Croker's. Commenting on Croker's Anglo-Irish origins and sympathies, Yeats notes that his humour had done its own political work: Croker's writing 'had the dash as well as the shallowness of an ascendant and idle class'. Croker and Lover had 'created the stage Irishman': 'The impulse of the Irish literature of their time came from a class that did not – mainly for political reasons – take the populace seriously'. Yet while Yeats suggests that the famine had 'burst their bubble', he also ensures that a number of Croker's tales live on: they appear, following this introductory caveat, in (and as) *Fairy and Folk Tales of the Irish Peasantry*. Sinéad Garrigan Mattar is right to claim that Yeats's collection is a 'tertiary text masquerading as an original', but it sometimes reveals part of that masquerade.[62] In both asserting and undermining straightforward distinctions between editors and the 'folk' and between orality and print, Yeats echoes strategies used by Croker himself as well as by the Irish press.[63]

In 1882, John Ashton claims that in England chapbooks had 'flourished, for they formed nearly the sole literature of the poor, until the *Penny Magazine* and Chambers's penny Tracts and Miscellanies gave them their deathblow, and relegated them to the book-shelves of collectors'. It is the cheap magazine, not the newspapers identified by Cohen, that Ashton sees as ending the reign of the chapbook. Despite his own antiquarian interests, Ashton views the expansion of the press as progress: the time when 'newspapers were rare indeed, and not worth much when obtainable' is hard to imagine in a 'day of cheap, plentiful, and good literature'.[64] Others were more ambivalent about equating the expansion of the press with progress.

To avoid the newspaper tax in the 1830s, *Chambers's* also needed to carefully avoid news: this may be another reason for its frequent focus on the (supposedly) timeless subjects of folklore and fairy tale. Parallel developments can be seen in other national contexts. As Satu Apo has noted, the Tsarist administration in nineteenth-century Finland censored printed matter, and stories and folktales made up a significant part of Finnish newspapers. One well-known oral, regional tale bore a very close resemblance to a newspaper serialisation from the 1860s, discovered by chance by a folklorist among his grandfather's papers.[65] Folktale collectors in Hawaii in the 1860s and 1870s may have been surprised by the local knowledge of tales which bore an uncanny resemblance to the Grimms' 'Twelve Brothers', the *Arabian*

Nights, 'Snow White' and 'Bluebeard'. All had been translated in a Hawaiian language newspaper.[66]

In 1878, the *Folk-Lore Record* argues that a history of 'popular fictions' has 'never yet been written, nor can it be undertaken with any completeness until the vast mass of materials on which it must be based – the fragments that are scattered through innumerable journals – are, if not collected and printed, at least recorded and indexed'. The article (which was reprinted from the *Pall Mall Gazette*) cites the author's own book of clippings from 50 years earlier, which includes Somerset and Lincolnshire folktales in the *Quarterly Review* and the *Mirror*, and articles in the *Literary Gazette* and in *Blackwood's*.[67] Yet the notion that the press could shape oral tradition rather than merely recording it was less easy for the folklorist to countenance. In 1889, Edward Clodd suggests that the value of the folktale 'Tom Tit Tot' lies in its 'being almost certainly derived from oral transmission through uncultured peasants', despite the fact that he first discovered it in an old copy of *The Ipswich Journal*.[68] While much work remains to be done in British and international contexts, the reach of the press in the nineteenth century – including local papers and cheap magazines – encourages us to rethink assumptions about audiences for the fairy tale in print, as well as to accord greater significance to that long history of creative interchange between voice and text.

Originals and counterfeits: Inventing the 'classic' fairy tale

In *All the Year Round* in 1860, Dickens recalls a terrifying tale that had haunted him as a child – a tale, he claims, told repeatedly by his nurse before he was six years old. This daughter of a shipwright had, our narrator reveals, 'a fiendish enjoyment of my terrors, and used to begin, so I remember – as a sort of introductory overture – by clawing the air with both hands, and uttering a long low hollow groan'. These chilling gestures prefaced the bloodthirsty story of Captain Murderer, a cannibalistic serial husband whose wives unknowingly make the piecrusts that their own human flesh will fill. Dickens retells the tale for his periodical readers with his own fiendish enjoyment of their terrors – an enjoyment that has its literary equivalents to the nurse's gestures and groans. [69]

Like the creations of the Irish press, Larry Hennessy and Jerry O'Toole, Dickens's autobiographical reminiscence is also a fictional conceit, a rhetorical device to bring readers together as a magazine community. In his attempts to capture the immediacy and the thrill of oral culture, Dickens claims links to a storytelling tradition that will outlast the commercial moment. However, as Dickens told John Forster, such haunting tales came from print as well as oral contexts: from his regular childhood purchase of the 'penny blood' the *Terrific Register*.[70] In fact, the tale of cannibalism recalled in 'Nurse's Stories' bears more than a passing resemblance to an urban myth that originated in a more recent penny magazine: the tale of the barber Sweeney Todd, which appeared in 1846 in Edward Lloyd's *The People's Periodical*. In the 1840s, publishers such as Lloyds made both Gothic fictions and fairy tales widely accessible to lower-class readers. While the 'String of Pearls', featuring Sweeney Todd, was in serialisation, the *People's Periodical* also published the 'The Twelfth-Cake Goblin: A Story for Christmas', and carried regular advertisements for a new penny-part work, Lloyd's 'Splendidly Illustrated Edition' of the *Arabian Nights Entertainments*.[71] In the early 1860s, George Vickers, who published the *Halfpenny Journal: A Weekly Magazine for All Who Can Read* offered another enticingly cheap fairy-tale edition: *Grimm's Goblins*, a loosely translated and profusely illustrated version of the tales was available in sixpenny monthly parts or for a penny a week.[72]

In his well-known article 'The Unknown Public' (published in *Household Words* in 1858), Wilkie Collins makes ethnological specimens of the readers of the penny press. He is eager to assert the middle-class consumer's distance from such popular reading, a distance that Dickens's own childhood reading belied.[73] However, if the two-penny *Household Words* sought middle-class audiences, it also professed more inclusive aims. Dickens famously claims in his opening 'Preliminary Word':

> To show to all, that in all familiar things, even in those which are repellant on the surface, there is Romance enough, if we will find it out:- to teach the hardest workers at this whirling wheel of toil, that their lot is not necessarily a moody, brutal fact, excluded from the sympathies and graces of imagination; to bring the greater and the lesser in degree, together, upon that wide field, and mutually dispose them to a better acquaintance and a kinder understanding – is one main object of our *Household Words*.[74]

This was not the only occasion on which Dickens would encourage *Household Words*' readers to 'tenderly cherish that light of Fancy', presenting the fairy tale as central in that project of class rapprochement. In *Hard Times*, serialised in the periodical in 1854, Sissy Jupe has been taught to renounce her days in the circus, when she read to her father from the 'wrong books', but she also knows that they have 'kept him, many times, from what did him real harm. And often and often of a night, he used to forget all his troubles in wondering whether the Sultan would let the lady go on with the story, or would have her head cut off before it was finished'.[75] In Coketown, Blue Books have replaced Bluebeard. If fairy tales have helped to make Sissy the 'good fairy' of the narrative, the narrator also offers a darker warning about keeping 'fancy' and 'romance' from the lower classes:

> Utilitarian economists, skeletons of schoolmasters, Commissioners of Fact, genteel and used-up infidels, gabblers of many little dog's-eared

creeds, the poor you will have always with you. Cultivate in them, while there is yet time, the utmost graces of the fancies and affections, to adorn their lives so much in need of ornament; or, in the moment of your triumph, when romance is utterly driven out of their souls, and they and a bare existence stand face to face, Reality will take a wolfish turn, and make an end of you![76]

The fairy tale in *Hard Times*, and in *Household Words* itself, is not simply a celebration of freedom of imagination: it is sometimes a consolation for seemingly intractable social problems, and protection from the wolves of class unrest that seem to lie in wait. Henry Morley had also turned to the same fairy-tale metaphor in 'Little Red Working Coat', published in *Household Words* in 1851, but the 'good fairy' here is not fancy but the 'Ragged School Shoeblack Society', saving poor children through productive labour from 'the wolf that fattens in our London alleys'. Such children are clearly future wolves as well as prey, unless rescued from streets 'which they pollute, and where they are polluted'. Blacking shoes by day, while attending a Sunday and evening Ragged School, such boys are shown to be 'very much satisfied with the existing order of things'; they 'look up to the good fairy generally with an earnest gratitude'. Morley concludes that '[it] is by practical schemes like these that the best fairy-transformations of our own day are effected. Little-Red Working Coat can tell a story quite as interesting to our hearts as any pleasant legend of the nursery'.[77] If the working child is not the Romantic archetype who appears elsewhere in *Household Words*, Morley sidesteps such problems through appeals to the 'heart': to sentiment, 'romance' and 'fancy'. Staunch in its condemnation of factory abuses and in the call to working men to protest, yet sometimes equally anxious about trade-union demagoguery, fairy-tale analogies elide tensions at the heart of *Household Words* from the beginning.[78]

In 'Frauds on the Fairies', Dickens famously claims '[w]hosoever alters [fairy tales] to suit his own opinions, whatever they are, is guilty, to our thinking, of an act of presumption, and appropriates to himself what does not belong to him'.[79] Dickens frequently used *Household Words* to do exactly that: his own 'The Thousand and One Humbugs' offered a satirical reworking of the *Arabian Nights*' Tale of the Barber's Sixth Brother, in which Palmerston offers an empty dish of 'reefawm' to the long-suffering 'Guld Publeek'.[80] If Dickens's position in 'Frauds on the Fairies' seems perplexing, it is perhaps because we are so used to casting this well-known debate in the terms used by critics such as Michael Kotzin, with Dickens as one of the 'pro-fancy forces' in the fairy tale 'war'.[81] We might, however, see this as a rather different debate: not as an argument over the relative merits of didacticism and imagination, but as a defence of an established middle-class canon of works. For the 'act of presumption' to which Dickens was responding had been made by George Cruikshank, who, having rendered the Ogre with such 'extraordinary justice' in Taylor's Grimm, was now inseparable from *German Popular Stories* in many middle-class minds. When Cruikshank revised the Grimms' tale of 'Hop O' My Thumb' – later to form part of his *Fairy Library* – in line with his own teetotalism, Dickens (after reading Forster's positive review in the *Examiner*) conceived, 'half playfully and half-seriously', his own damning response.[82]

While Dickens's article is by far the best known, it forms part of a much wider middle-class periodical debate which sought to preserve the place of Taylor's Grimm as Cruikshank's 'true' fairy-tale edition. In the *Inquirer*, William Caldwell Roscoe suggests that before the travesty of the *Fairy Library*, Cruikshank had been 'associated with the purest and most delightful real fairy-stories'; he was the man from 'whom we learnt what an elf really was by the picture of that one putting on his breeches in the shoemaker's shop'. In an 1863 *Spectator* review of Dinah Mulock's *Fairy Book*, which included an extensive selection of familiar tales, R. H. Hutton gives the book an enthusiastic reception, but questions why the editor has been 'so hardhearted as to withhold that story of "The Golden Bird",' which 'Cruikshank has immortalised for children by his unrivalled picture of that curious feat of foxmanship?' By mid-century, Cruikshank's illustrations have achieved their own authenticity: for Hutton they have 'almost identified themselves in children's imaginations with the tales themselves'.[83]

In 1869, Charlotte Yonge is delighted to note in *Macmillan's Magazine* that 'the true unadulterated fairy tale', provided by Taylor and Cruikshank, is back in circulation: 'we rejoice to see that the whole book, illustrations and all, has been reproduced by Mr. Hotten, with a preface by Mr. Ruskin'.[84] Ruskin's influential introduction echoes many of Dickens's earlier concerns, warning that there is a deep 'collateral mischief in this indulgence of licentious change and retouching of stories to suit particular tastes, or inculcate favourite doctrines'.[85] Yet despite Ruskin's wish that this beloved text should remain timeless, Taylor and Cruikshank's two volumes were clearly not the same: as a commodity, they now had a new cultural place as a valuable collector's item, as a publisher's advertisement at the front of the reissue reveals:

> Both series passed through two or three editions soon after publication; and when Messrs. Robins the publishers retired from business, the work became very scarce. At the present day, when the collectors of the works of Cruikshank are greatly increased in number, the two volumes, originally sold for 12s., are worth at least £5 or £6!

Ruskin uses his introduction to dedicate the book to 'children of open hearts and lowly lives'; yet lower-class readers, urban or rural, could not have afforded to buy this text, in its original 12 shilling or contemporary reprint editions.[86] Reviews in middle-class periodicals played an important role in establishing this text as 'the true unadulterated fairy tale', ensuring that it would be Taylor and Cruikshank's Grimm, not Vickers's *Grimms' Goblins*, that would be remembered as the Victorian nursery classic.

If this particular fairy-tale collaboration was unparalleled in its perceived cultural significance, there was nevertheless a wider canon of books that were promoted and established, like Taylor's Grimm, largely through periodical reviewing. In 1846, W. M. Thackeray's article for *Fraser's Magazine*, 'On Some Illustrated Children's Books', finds him in raptures over a new series of legends and fairy tales:

> The mere sight of the little books published by Mr Cundall – of which some thirty now lie upon my table – is as good as a nosegay. [...] I envy the feelings of the young person for whom (after having undergone a previous critical examination) this collection of treasures is destined. Here are fairy tales, at last, with real pictures to them. What a library! – what a picture gallery! [...] I can fancy that perplexity and terror seizing upon the small individual to whom all these books will go in a parcel, when the string is cut, and the brown paper is unfolded, and all these delights appear.[87]

Thackeray's hopes for a thrilled response were not disappointed. In 1877, in an unpublished memoir for her niece, Laura Stephen, Thackeray's daughter Anne reminisces about her childhood and that of her sister, stating:

> One of the nicest things that ever happened to us when we were children at Paris was the arrival of a huge parcel, which my Grannie cut open and inside there were piles and piles of the most beautiful delightful wonderful fairy tale books all painted with pictures – I thought they would never come to an end but alas! in a week we had read them all. They were called the *Felix Summerly* series.[88]

Thackeray's parcel to his daughter had some unexpected consequences. The antiquarian and commercial interests that fed into the *Felix Summerly* series inspired something quite different in the 1860s: Anne Thackeray Ritchie's complex, wry, realist short stories, based around the motifs of those classic fairy tales. Many of the middle-class readers who had bought or grown up with *Felix Summerly* were to become readers of Thackeray Ritchie's tales in one of the most innovative publishing ventures of the 1860s, the *Cornhill Magazine*.

In the *Cornhill*, Thackeray Ritchie's short stories appeared in a magazine that published articles on Venetian folktales, the *Arabian Nights* and comparative mythology – in a context where the fairy tale was the subject of philological and ethnological as well as literary debate. In fact, before professionalisation and the arrival of specialist journals, it was miscellaneous titles with wider readerships that registered those disciplinary shifts from antiquarianism to folklore, and folklore to comparative mythology. Seminal in establishing the popularity of the latter was the work of the celebrated Sanskrit scholar and philologist [Friedrich] Max Müller. In his 1856 essay 'Comparative Mythology', Müller championed the Indo-European thesis, but also elaborated his own thesis of mythological origin: higher myths (and their degraded forms, folktales) could be traced back to the early ages of Aryan cultural development, to mankind's awe and linguistic creativity in response to the wonder of the sun. Müller's thesis and its remarkable influence are explored in detail in Chapters 2 and 3. Here, I merely wish to note the role of the press in establishing its popularity. Those unable to join the fashionable crowd who flocked to Müller's lectures could do the next best thing – they could read the lectures, or commentary on them, in the papers and magazines. Over eighty articles by Müller appear in the *Wellesley Index to Victorian Periodicals* alone.[89] He was embraced in cheap papers and children's periodicals, as well as in the higher journalism.

In his introduction to *The Red Fairy Book* (1890), Andrew Lang muses that 'to exhaust the knowledge – literary, anthropological, religious, antiquarian, moral – of our nursery tales' could 'be the occupation of a career'. Wryly commenting on the hobby horses of the folklorist, he adds:

> As specialism advances, we may see young men, spectacled form the cradle, and bald from their birth, voyage into middle age and extreme eld, still poring over 'Cinderella' or 'Puss in Boots'. They will trace these narratives to Aryans and barbarians; they will find lunar, solar, stellar myths in them; or will prove that 'Puss in Boots' was originally the spirit of vegetation, or a prehistoric parable of the Gulf Stream.[90]

Lang's gentle mockery of Müller's solar mythology thesis is not surprising. After the publication of E. B. Tylor's *Primitive Culture* (1871), when anthropological approaches began to challenge Müller's thesis, it was Lang who offered the most famous attack, and the press in which those battle lines were drawn. Lang's 1873 article in the *Fortnightly Review* was described as 'epoch-making' by the folklorist Joseph Jacobs: in his introduction to Margaret Hunt's edition of Grimms' *Household Tales* (1884), Lang revealed that the arguments between celestial mythologists (including Müller and George Cox) and the anthropologists (including Tylor, Clodd and Laurence Gomme) had been played out by their protagonists in the higher journalism, including in the *Nineteenth Century*, *Fraser's Magazine* and the *Contemporary Review*. In his *Fortnightly Review* article, Lang insisted that folktales were not the 'detritus of the higher mythology' of Müller's spiritual Aryans, but the remains of a much earlier stage of development, productions of the 'savage' consciousness that characterised all human origins. Supernatural elements in folktales (and the religious beliefs of the ancestors to the Aryans) had indeed developed from what were regarded as the 'disgusting customs of savages' – from animal-worship, cannibalism, shamanism and belief in 'bestial transformations'. Richard M. Dorson claims that in 'one brilliant essay Lang reversed the whole trend of mythological criticism', but in many popular magazine contexts that reversal was not always so apparent, and Müller's thesis retained imaginative power well beyond the 1870s.[91] In articles in children's magazines, little magazines and in the formative reading of purchasers the socialist press, anthropological theorisations of a universalised savage mind continued to battle it out with Müller's Romantically inflected primitivism.

By now, the ambiguities in nineteenth-century usages of the term 'fairy tale' will be obvious. Despite R. A. Gilbert's recent claim, it is far from the case that nineteenth-century fairy tales were simply defined as 'tales about the fairies'. While the term, adapted from the French, was established in Britain by 1750 (when it appears in the title of a periodical tale as well as a book collection), the question of whether fairy tales should contain fairies at all was the subject of much Victorian debate.[92] In the *Illustrated London News* in 1892, Lang uses the examples of the Grimms' tales and Dasent's *Tales from the Norse* to argue that '[e]very student of the genuine old nursery tales knows that in them fairies are conspicuous by their absence'. Moreover, Lang claims that while 'the ladies who followed Perrault [...] made a great deal of the fairies, inventing for them a Court and etiquette like that of the Grand Monarque', these literary fairies were very different from the barbarous fairies of peasant tradition, those 'survivals, perhaps in legend, of a vanished prehistoric race'. If Yeats shared Lang's prejudice against the ladies who followed Perrault, and his fascination with peasant 'survivals', it was in service of a different national agenda, with a different definition of the authentic fairy tale. For Yeats the English fairies were mere literary 'bubbles from Provence'. Ireland was the home to authentic fairy tales, whose vitality sprung from their status as true cultural survivals. Whether the fairies were believed to be degraded gods or fallen angels, Yeats was insistent that, in the 1890s, they were still part of living peasant belief.[93]

To seek a definition of the nineteenth-century fairy tale that smoothes over these contradictions is to ignore the political investments that made them culturally important in the first place. While Victorian folklorists often viewed collected oral 'traditional tales' or folktales as altogether different to authored works, in reality these distinctions were rather more blurred. Many supposed supernatural 'traditional tales', including Croker's, show clear signs of literary creation, while notions of folkloric authenticity shaped the writing and reception of authored tales.[94] While Edwin Sidney Hartland includes only orally collected material in his definition for his 1891 monograph *The Science of Fairy Tales*, a more familiar (and inclusive) range of works is discussed under the umbrella of the fairy tale by Charlotte Yonge in *Macmillan's Magazine* in 1869. Yonge includes collections such as Taylor's and Croker's, which were (packaged, at least) as tales from 'the folk', authored wonder tales by d'Aulnoy and Perrault, and more modern literary works by writers such as Hans Christian Andersen. The book-length contributions of Kingsley and Lewis Carroll – that are seen to deal with contemporary creatures 'and just dip them into the realms of Dreamland' – are also described as fairy tales, 'for want of a better name'.[95]

Other writers refused even such capacious formal definitions. When asked to define a fairy tale, George MacDonald responded, 'I should as soon think of describing the abstract human face'.[96] Yet despite these competing mystical, scientific and literary categorisations, there was nevertheless a list of mid-Victorian books that many writers assumed could be recognised as the genuine article. While Dickens spoke of 'simplicity' and 'purity', Yonge states in *Macmillan's* that it is 'the genuine – we had almost said authentic – fairy tale, taken in moderation, that is the true delight of childhood'. Lamenting the recent appearance of a burlesque note in children's literature, in which fantastic scenes are 'lowered to make Cockneys laugh', Yonge protests against parodies that are 'vulgarizing every sweet nook of fairyland'.[97] While Yonge refers to literary burlesque, her comments have interesting parallels with Dickens's earlier claims in *Frauds on the Fairies* that the theatre has 'done its worst to destroy these admirable fictions'.[98] If popular pantomimes and parodies are not 'genuine' fairy tales, Yonge has a clear sense of what should be included in their stead: with Taylor's *German Popular Stories*, Croker's *Fairy Legends*, Dasent's *Tales from the Norse*, Mary Frere's Indian tales *Old Deccan Days* and Mulock's *Fairy Book*, 'young people would be provided with the real classics of fairy lore, and would soon learn to regard them with the same sort of respect as the conclave of Olympus, with whom no one now-a-days thinks of taking liberties'. For Yonge, Mulock's book is 'an excellent collection of old English fairy-tales' despite the fact that its introduction reveals that most of the tales have been taken from Perrault, d'Aulnoy and Grimm.[99] In the mid-Victorian marketplace, it was the familiarity of the tales in Mulock's collection to middle-class readers that gave them the stamp of 'Englishness' and authenticity.

Yet as the cheap press expanded with the steady rise of literacy throughout the century, it became apparent that this intimate network of middle-class readers, with their possession of a shared history of treasured childhood editions, were far from the 'everyone' that they claimed to represent. While Andew Lang's series of coloured fairy books, which brought international tales to better-off children, are remembered as Victorian classics, W. T. Stead's 'Books for the Bairns' have been largely forgotten. Yet Stead's penny publications, issued each month in a series that ran for 25 years, sold a hundred and fifty thousand copies a month. In the preface to the issue for September 1896, *Cinderella and Other Fairy-Tales*, Stead claims to have made the fairy tale 'the Priviledge of the Poor' rather than the 'Perquisite of the Rich', while in the abridged edition of *The Water-Babies* (published in May and June 1905) he notes that 'this story has never before been published at such a cheap price; so for most children it will be quite a new fairy tale'.[100] Following in the footsteps of Vicker's *Grimm's Goblins* and Lloyd's *Arabian Nights*, Stead's series also reveals the significance of the monthly cheap issue, which existed in a curious hinterland between periodical and book. Indeed, in 1914, Stead's daughter Estelle briefly turned *Books for the Bairns* into a miscellaneous magazine, before returning to the previous booklet format. The fragility of such cheap publications has ensured a limited survival: most have crumbled like the chapbooks before them. Yet their disappearance is also an absence in the history of the fairy tale. Rather than killers of fairy tale and romance, newspaper editors brought international and British fairy tales, as well as penny poems and novels, to what was, by the end of the nineteenth century, an overwhelmingly literate public.[101]

Yonge argues that 'a real traditional fairy tale is a possession', while in 'Frauds on the Fairies', Dickens cautions that 'with seven Blue Beards in the field', a 'generation or two hence would not know which was which, and the great original Blue Beard would be confounded with the counterfeits'.[102] Yet fairy tales were also appealing precisely because there were no originals, and the tradition continued to be re-imagined as the century drew to a close. While Stead chose to claim the Grimms for pacifism, Oscar Wilde and Laurence Housman appropriated the Grimms' and Andersen's tales in the spirit of both homage and parody, inverting their motifs and wryly mocking their morality.[103] In the same period, Keir Hardie's recruitment of 'Jack the Giant-Killer' for socialism is proof that it was not just the fairy tale, but the lower social classes cast as its preservers that refused to remain fixed. The aesthetic failures of his *Fairy Library* might incline us to forget that it was Cruikshank, rather than Dickens, who ultimately won the argument. Any writer could 'take the liberty of altering a common Fairy Tale'.[104] While the fairy tale was never to function as Dickens had hoped, as a utopian space beyond politics and history, it was used in ingenious ways to rewrite that history, and took its own place in emergent political debates.

2
Myths of Origin: Folktale Scholarship and Fictional Invention in Magazines for Children

> The beginning of all nations must be ever buried in obscurity, or, at all events, blended with fables and legends.[1]
>
> I prick up my ears like an old horse at sound of the hunt, whenever there is the slightest reference to what is called folk-lore.[2]

'As the "boy is the father of the man," it may not be amiss to draw the attention of our young readers to the boyhood, if we may so term it, of England', the *Boys of England* announces in 1866. Picturing a liberal history of continual ascent, the author marvels 'What magic has transformed the howling young savage of the wilderness – the wolf-hunter of English woods and hills – into the brave yet refined, muscular yet withal gentle boy reader of this Journal?'[3] It was not just cheap boys' weeklies that presented English youth as the apex of evolutionary development, and marvelled at the process that had brought them there. Many juvenile magazines were fascinated by that same quest for origins – with tracing national, racial, cultural and linguistic roots.

This chapter offers sustained analysis of three middle-class monthlies – *Aunt Judy's Magazine*, *Good Words for the Young* and the *Monthly Packet* – which provide surprising insights into the significance of that quest for young Victorian readers. All three titles were fascinated with folklore, with a distant history accessed through the 'fossil poetry' of the past.[4] All three drew on recent developments in comparative philology and 'savage' anthropology, displaying an interest in the fairy tale that was not simply reducible to commercial or didactic motives. These titles were the first to publish major work by some of the best-known writers of Victorian fairy tale and fantasy, including George MacDonald, Charles Kingsley and J. H. Ewing. Those classic works, I argue here, were partly inspired by the folkloric researches that their first child audiences shared as common knowledge.

Rather than proffering a 'top-down' model of scientific popularisation, I suggest that the findings of philology and anthropology were used in new ways in magazines for children. These periodicals' appropriations of comparative mythology have much to tell us about middle-class engagements with childhood, gender, class and race. For if fairy tales could be used to prepare children for their roles within domestic and public, and national and imperial spheres, they were also assumed to capture the 'timeless' essence of childhood, linked to an idealised Romantic child who led back to the childhood of the race. In these magazines, the child could be simultaneously cast as an impressionable individual in need of instruction, a critical reader, and the passive object of a powerful myth of origins. However, in correspondence columns, those readers also answered back – from the perspective of aspirant writers as well as that of consumers.

'Highmindedness and refinement' versus 'cheap and nasty literature': Defining the middle-class juvenile monthly

The 1860s marked a key stage in the rise of the juvenile magazine: as Sheila Egoff has revealed, at least seventy new titles were launched between 1860 and 1870 alone.[5] The new sixpenny children's monthlies employed marketing strategies that set them apart from the cheap denominational children's titles, which had assumed guaranteed niche markets since the beginning of the century.[6] As Mark W. Turner notes, Norman Macleod, editor of Strahan's adult title *Good Words* (1860), helped to move the magazine away from the cheap weekly religious market into an arena where it competed with secular monthlies such as the *Cornhill* (which it had overtaken in circulation by 1863).[7] *Good Words* rejected a denominational religious positioning and adopted high-profile signed contributions, strategies later adopted by Macleod in his editorship of the juvenile sibling launched in 1868, *Good Words for the Young*. In October 1869, when Macleod announces George MacDonald as *Good Words for the Young*'s new editor, he foregrounds MacDonald's commercial prestige:

> The Boys and Girls who read this Magazine – and every Boy and Girl of sense does so – may now rest assured that, like a splendid racing yacht, *Good Words for the Young* will beat all competitors, having such a fine 'Old Boy' at the helm, and a steady 'North Wind' at his back.[8]

Although the periodical targeted both genders (often running a serialised domestic fiction and an adventure story simultaneously), the use of such metaphors of masculine adventure was in marked distinction to the opening address of *Aunt Judy's Magazine*, which compares the magazine to a bouquet of spring flowers.[9] There were, however, many similarities between the two titles. They were sixpenny monthlies that employed eminent illustrators and had extensive leanings towards fantasy literature and natural history. Both magazines featured domestic fiction and poetry, and articles on history and exotic travel. Their publishers sought editors who were well-known writers for children with recognisable profiles: in the case of *Aunt Judy*, Margaret Gatty, whose reputation was established by her *Parables from Nature*, Christian homilies that were familiar Sunday reading in respectable homes.[10] The assumption that *Aunt Judy's Magazine* was female-orientated was made by correspondent 'Blanche Cremorne' in 1870, to whom editor Margaret Gatty replied, 'The magazine is by no means intended for girls only, but for all young people from six years old upwards. You may carry the *upwards* as far as you please, for we flatter ourselves we contain good for grown-up minds as well as infants'.[11] Such comments reveal a degree of commercial wishful-thinking, and were contradicted by Charlotte Yonge, who felt the magazine was ideally suited to readers between the ages of seven and fourteen.[12] It is clear, however, that many periodical contributions assumed a sophisticated audience, and a number of *Aunt Judy's* readers seem to have remained faithful into their late teens. From the evidence of the correspondence columns, the vast majority of these older readers appear to have been female.[13]

In this respect, *Aunt Judy's Magazine* has some interesting overlaps with an older, less commercial, more overtly religious periodical – Charlotte Yonge's *Monthly Packet* (subtitled *Readings for Younger Members of the English Church*) which ran from 1851 to 1898. Without illustrations, and targeting a female reader in later adolescence, the *Monthly Packet* identifies in its opening address 'young girls, or maidens, or young ladies' who are 'above the age of childhood' and are 'looking back on school-days with regret'. This implied audience is consistent: by 1866, Yonge (noting that the magazine has itself obtained its 'teens') again suggests that it is adapted to 'the young – not to mere children – but to those who have begun […] to think and study for themselves'.[14] Although it encouraged piety and self-improvement, in common with some of the cheap religious weeklies aimed variously at child, adult female or 'family' readerships, this monthly (priced at a shilling by the mid-1860s) was far more exclusive in class terms.[15] The *Church Quarterly Review* perceived that the *Monthly Packet* had 'adapted itself from the first to the needs of young girls of the well-educated classes'; the magazine's (possibly manufactured) correspondence dialogue of 1866, in which clergymen's wives, born to 'a higher sphere', were encouraged to practice forbearance towards uncouth lower-middle-class women seems to corroborate Kirsten Drotner's assertions that its ideal readership was 'rectors' and professors' elder daughters'.[16]

Although Low Church rather than Tractarian in religious affiliation, Margaret Gatty, *Aunt Judy's* editor until her death in 1873, was herself proudly aligned with Yonge's 'higher sphere', as the daughter of Alfred Scott, Chaplain to Nelson, and the wife of the vicar of Ecclesfield. The two periodicals enjoyed a distinct intimacy in their professional relations, which endured throughout *Aunt Judy's* brief co-editorship by J. H. Ewing and her sister H. K. F. Gatty (1874–6) and the extensive period during which the latter edited alone (1876–85). Yonge published the work of Margaret Gatty prior to her editorship of *Aunt Judy's Magazine* and also gave J. H. Ewing (then Juliana Gatty) her first outlet for publication. The *Monthly Packet* and Yonge's novels were regularly recommended in *Aunt Judy's* correspondence pages, while the *Monthly Packet* sometimes reviewed *Aunt Judy's* fictions.[17]

While *Aunt Judy's Magazine* and *Good Words for the Young* were the more attractively packaged of these titles, all three carefully weighed pleasure for the young against parental desires. Margaret Gatty pledges in her opening address that factual information will be supplied to allay adult fears about an 'overflowing of mere amusement'.[18] Macleod also promises 'more serious talks' as well as 'fun and frolic' in *Good Words for the Young*, but it is Yonge and Gatty who most explicitly embrace the editor's role as censor and moral guardian.[19] In Margaret Gatty's 'Editorial Address' of 1867, she invokes the 'mothers of families who have welcomed *Aunt Judy* to their hearths, as a wise and safe, as well as amusing, companion; a fit associate for those who have yet to be trained – over whom, therefore, literature has so powerful an influence for good or for evil'. In her efforts to raise a dwindling circulation, Gatty continues that *Aunt Judy*

> grudges no labour, and the publishers do not grudge expense, either in adequate payment of contributors, or the tasteful issue of the publication. But the absence of 'sensational' tales – the endeavour to instruct in virtue, without drawing loathsome pictures of vice – while it makes *Aunt Judy* a treasure in the eyes of judicious parents, restricts her circulation to the judicious and the domestic.[20]

Gatty's gendered metaphors are revealing: while she plays on established associations between a domestic female identity and moral superiority, such an editorial stance is also associated with small circulations and literary neglect. The juvenile serials which garnered by far the greatest sales in this period were the penny weeklies from publishers such as Edmund Brett, Charles Fox and the Emmett brothers: 'blood and thunder' magazines which published lurid tales of adventure and gained a strong following of working and lower-middle-class readers. Significantly, the most high profile of these publications, the *Boys of England*, was shrewdly marketed as an escape from the mechanisms of class as well as parental authority: 'We wish you to receive this Journal as one intended expressly for your *amusement*; and it gives us great satisfaction to imagine you returning from school, from the office, the work-room, or the shop, and taking up your weekly number of the "BOYS" to soothe and enliven your "caretired thoughts."'[21] Launched in the same year as *Aunt Judy's Magazine*, it became the most successful juvenile publication for a decade. To Gatty's obvious chagrin, it was weeklies such as these, rather than her own 'tasteful and judicious' publication, that consistently dominated the best-seller lists.[22]

While Gatty did not attempt to court lower-class audiences, the Rev. Erskine Clarke actively tried to subvert the penny dreadful trend with his half-penny weekly *Chatterbox*, a periodical established in the same year as *Boys of England*, and resolute in its aims to remind working-class readers of their humble place in shop, office and school.[23] However, while the *Boys of England* wished readers to believe that 'many letters' had been received from 'the Ladies of England', the sensational lure that Gatty perceived to lie in wait for her older, female readers appears to be connected with a different type of publication.[24] Charlotte Yonge's indignant defence of *Aunt Judy's Magazine* in the *Monthly Packet* in 1877 highlights that other source of concern:

> It does not look well for our schoolrooms that the circulation cannot continue at so low a price as sixpence. It would be far better if the elders gave up one of the trashy, sensational novel-mongering magazines for the sake of giving children anything so really useful and suggestive.[25]

The 1867 *Monthly Packet* article 'Novel Reading' also identifies sensation fiction as 'simply wicked'. One danger is the distracting pleasure that such texts are assumed to afford to lower-class women, leading to servants forgetting their place. 'What wonder', asks the author, 'if children are left to "grow" like Topsy, in the hatching ovens of nursemaids who have cousins in the guards, and give suppers on the sly at their mistresses' expense to friendly policemen'.[26] The movement of dangerous literature in a different social direction is Alexander Strahan's concern ten years later, when he discusses the penny dreadfuls then supposedly 'flourishing in vile luxuriance'. While it could not be expected that the 'sons and daughters of parents who read *The Police News* and *The London Clipper*' should appreciate good literature, '[t]he alarming and dispiriting part of the case is the gradual spread, upwards in what is called the social scale, of this sort of trash'.[27] When J. H. Ewing wrote to George Bell in 1881, expressing her regret that he no longer found *Aunt Judy's Magazine* a viable concern, it was the loss of 'highmindedness and refinement' in 'the fast rising generation' that she regretted. The blame was laid at its perceived nemesis: 'cheap and nasty literature'.[28]

Margaret Gatty claims defiantly in her 1867 'Editor's Address' that *Aunt Judy* looks to 'a permanent popularity [...] if to popularity at all'. Although the magazine survived for 19 years, this was not achieved by the buying public alone.[29] As a publisher Strahan clearly courted commercial success, but had his own concerns about his title *Good Words for the Young*. Writing to his wife in 1871, George MacDonald claims that his current work for the periodical is some of the best that he has ever produced. He adds, however, as editor of the magazine:

> I have had a bit of bad news. The Magazine, which went up in the beginning of the volume, has fallen very much since. Strahan thinks it is because there is too much of what he calls the fairy element.[30]

Strahan's comment initially seems perplexing. From its inception in 1868, *Good Words for the Young* traded heavily on the commercial appeal of fairy tale and fantasy. MacDonald's 'At the Back of the North Wind' and Charles Kingsley's 'Madam How and Lady Why' were the first number's star contributions, and in the 1870s, a new fairy-tale novella from MacDonald still attracted purchasers. In fact, the initial increase in sales noted in MacDonald's letter coincided with the opening part of his new work 'The Princess and the Goblin'.

Yet the 'fairy element', as Strahan was aware, covered wider ground than MacDonald's serialised fantasies. Two months after MacDonald's letter, the periodical included the second part of 'King Arthur's Boar Hunt: An Ancient British Fairy Tale' with detailed scholarly annotations.[31] The previous year, Dinah Mulock Craik's 'Last News of the Fairies' had explored oral testimony of a fairy sighting at Ilkley Well, introducing an informant and tale that would later appear in the *Folk-Lore Record*.[32] *Good Words for the Young* was not the only title to cast an eye at the adult reader. While *Aunt Judy's Magazine* capitalised on the commercial lure of a new short fantasy by Lewis Carroll, 'Bruno's Revenge' (1867), it also published Margaret Gatty's 'Cat "Folk-Lore"', an article the author was obliged to admit was not 'strictly juvenile literature' at all.[33] In fact, these editors did not merely regard fairy tales as children's literature, but as relics that offered insights into cultural origins – insights into the 'childhood' of the race.

The Romantic child and recapitulation

In 1887, the *Chambers's* article 'Childish Things' chooses an arresting metaphor to illustrate changes in attitudes to childhood over the previous 50 years. Claiming that 'Mrs. Ewing's genial teachings have superseded Mrs. Sherwood's grim severities', the author is pleased to note that the 'rod of castigation' has been replaced with a 'fairy wand of enchantment'.[34] Charting the movement away from the child as exemplar of original sin towards a notion of childhood as a state of imaginative purity, such articles owe an obvious debt to a Romantic legacy. Much useful work has been done on Victorian appropriations of the Romantic child, but the implied audiences that such models assume still needs further attention.[35] Towards the end of the nineteenth century, Alfred Ainger argues that J. H. Ewing's *Jackanapes* and *The Story of a Short Life* (both published in *Aunt Judy's Magazine*) are in fact adult fictions: 'beautiful tales *about* children, which are not meant for *their* reading at all'.[36] Ainger sidesteps the ambiguities of fictions that offer two distinctive angles of vision: that of the child as magazine reader, and that of the reading adult for whom the child is a symbol of loss.

Like the juvenile periodical, authored fairy tales frequently incorporated these two ways of seeing, attempting to cater for the often contradictory desires of adult and child consumers. U. C. Knoepflmacher has argued that Victorian fairy tales' double audience was frequently acknowledged in the authorial construction of multi-levelled narratives:

> the act of public transmission involved, by necessity, a consideration of an audience composed of parents, older family members, or governesses, an adult readership as related to the implied author's identity as a grown-up, socialised being as the child-auditor was related to the author's reawakened youthful self.[37]

Knoepflmacher's distinction between the author's socialised adult persona and his/her reawakened youth usefully draws attention to the construction of childhood in the fairy tale (or the juvenile periodical) as a dynamic process, dependent on the subtle interplay of opposing textual personae. One might argue, however, that the author's 'reawakened youthful self' was related to the adult as much as to the child auditor, for only adults could share in the nostalgia implicit in this construction of childhood. Both MacDonald and Charles Kingsley in *Good Words for the Young* were prone to flights of fancy that they frequently confessed to be beyond the comprehension of child readers. In an 1870 instalment of *Ranald Bannerman's Boyhood* in the magazine, MacDonald breaks off his narrative with a typical interjection to an implied adult audience:

> But I find I have been forgetting that those for whom I write are young – too young to understand this. Let it remain, however, for those older persons who at an odd moment, while waiting for dinner, or before going to bed, may take up a little one's book, and turn over a few of its leaves. Some such readers, in virtue of their hearts being young and old both at once, discern more in the children's books than the children themselves.[38]

In particular, it was suggested that all adults could 'reawaken' their youthful self through the fairy tale. This was precisely the promise made in an advertisement for MacDonald's *Dealings with Fairies*, which appears in *Good Words for the Young* in 1869. It cites a *British Quarterly Review* critic who has experienced an apparently blissful regression through MacDonald's writing:

> the charming little volume, if it did not make us wish to be young again, did more, for while we were reading, so great was the magic from the

Enchanter's Wand, we became young once more, and clapped our venerable hands over the tears of the Light Princess, and the groans of Mr. Thunderthump.[39]

While this reviewer's return to youth may appear no more than a fanciful metaphor, many of his readers would have been familiar with scientific models that explicitly linked the fairy tale to childhood. In the mid- and late-Victorian period, such assumptions were buttressed by the widespread cultural knowledge of Haeckel's biogenic law, or the recapitulation thesis. Usefully paraphrased by Stephen Jay Gould as 'the repetition of ancestral adult stages in embryonic or juvenile stages of descendants', the biological theory of recapitulation was widely appropriated in social contexts, and was particularly influential among folklorists and anthropologists.[40] The progress of the child was perceived to replicate early stages of national, cultural or geological evolution; children became psychologically analogous to early man, both groups existing in a state of mental immaturity that was adapted to the creation and reception of simple art forms such as the fairy tale. In *Good Words for the Young* in December 1868, Hugh Macmillan instructs his young readers about coal with a striking analogy:

> The page of the earth's story-book that tells us the history of coal is a very extraordinary one. It is to the familiar appearance of the world at the present day what the fairy-story books of childhood are to the sober duties and enjoyments of grown-up men. The earth has its ages just like a human being. It has its childhood and youth.[41]

While new metaphors of social evolution blossomed in the wake of Darwin and Spencer, Macmillan turns specifically to earlier geological research for his own developmental analogy. The physical youth of the child parallels early stages of the earth's evolution; physical and cultural evolution are also conflated, the fairy tale becoming an early strata in both the individual's cultural development, and the world's cultural evolution from primitive society to civilisation. While this invokes a linear model of progress, to view development through the prism of Macmillan's geological metaphor also requires a psychological and cultural return. Only by rediscovering the child's implicit understanding of the fairy tale is it possible to read the earth's 'story-book'. Macmillan draws not only on evolutionary metaphors, but also on Romantic conceptions of nature as a book of symbols, and Wordsworthian ideas of the child's essential connection to the natural world.

Such analogies also echo the writings of Max Müller, who claimed in his second series of lectures on the 'Science of Language' that languages could be treated 'in exactly the same spirit as the geologist treats his stones and petrifactions'. In 'Philology as One of the Sciences' (which was published in *Macmillan's Magazine* in 1862, alongside Müller's lecture), F. W. Farrar also argued for significant connections between geology and philology, between uncovering fossils and 'extinct words and forms'.[42] While Hugh Macmillan concludes his article in *Good Words for the Young* by claiming that 'there are wonders in the fire stranger than in any fairy-story', in an instalment of 'Madam How and Lady Why', serialised in the periodical four months later, Charles Kingsley suggests that the wonders of nature should indeed be described as the 'true fairy tale'. Kingsley is convinced that '[a]ll those feelings in you which your nursery tales call out, – imagination, wonder, awe, pity, and I trust, too, hope and love – will be called out, I believe, by the Tale of all Tales, the true "Märchen allen Märchen," so much more fully and strongly and purely'. While Kingsley suggests that all man-made fictions pale in comparison to 'the great green book, of which every bud is a letter, and every tree a page', fairy tales are nevertheless perceived to call forth feelings of the sublime.[43] While the fairy tale was used by Macmillan and Kingsley to inspire childish imaginations with the wonders of a Divinely ordered nature (echoing Coleridge and constructing the ideal reader as a 'child of feeling'), it also invoked notions of a more profound cultural return.[44] In fact, the writings of Kingsley, MacDonald and Macmillan in *Good Words for the Young* dovetail in intriguing ways with a branch of contemporary folktale scholarship that perceived fairy tales to be the record of man's earliest spiritual impulses; that saw them as creative evidence of man's first reading of 'the book of nature'.

Max Müller, the Indo-European thesis and juvenile periodical fantasy

In the *Monthly Packet* article 'Andalusian Folk Lore' of 1865, J. G. Hincks notes:

> still the old fairy-tales are as great favourites as ever they were. Men of learning and research are also now directing their attention towards them; [...] they have raised fairy-lore to be almost a subject for scientific enquiry, and have shown an affinity between the legends of Northern and Southern Europe, and even betwixt those of our own continent and those of Asia.[45]

For the readers of the *Monthly Packet* article 'Fairy Tales' in 1878, the link between European and Asian fairy tales is assumed to be already known: a disquisition on the 'Indo-European family of nations' is only necessary for those few readers not 'sufficiently acquainted with the harvest of knowledge concerning the early history of mankind which has been yielded to the students of comparative philology during the last few years'.[46]

The article goes on to reference two texts by Max Müller: *Lectures on Language* and *Chips from a German Workshop*. In his 1856 essay 'Comparative Mythology' (reprinted in *Chips*), Müller, comparing linguistic parallels in the names of gods in the ancient Indian Vedas with those of Greek myth, further advanced the thesis propounded by the 'new philology' – that the Indo-European dialects had developed from a single language, shared by an Aryan people who had once dwelt together in the east, but had separated at an early point in mankind's history.[47] The Rev. S. Goldney, in his article 'Fables and Fairy Tales' (1885) in *Aunt Judy's Magazine*, assumes that most young readers are already acquainted with such research, aware 'that we originally came from the table-land of Iran in central Asia'.[48]

The *Monthly Packet* article 'Fairy Tales' also engages with the most distinctive component of Müller's folktale scholarship, suggesting:

> Perhaps all these stories originally sprang from an allegorical way of describing the actions of nature; [...] Of those which are most clearly what are called *nature-myths*, we may mention Thorn-rose (or, as it is often called in English, 'The Sleeping Beauty'), which simply arises from an allegory of the Spring kissing the Earth into new life.[49]

Müller believed the origins of such tales lay in a distant 'mythopœic' epoch, when the Indo-European language developed the capacity to describe natural phenomena through gendered poetic metaphors. In Müller's theory, those metaphors (expressive of a spiritual awe and wonder) were woven into mythological tales by later generations through a phenomenon known as the 'disease of language' – a gradual process of linguistic forgetting in which the original meaning of the terms was lost. There were considerable Romantic impulses at work in Müller's evocation of this mythopœic (or 'Mythic') stage.[50] He compared the linguistic descriptions of nature made by early man to the poetry of Wordsworth:

> When [Worsdworth] speaks of 'the last hill that parleys with the setting sun,' this expression came to him as he was communing with nature; it was a thought untranslated as yet into the prose of our traditional and emaciated speech; it was a thought such as the men of old would not have been ashamed of in their common every day conversation.[51]

Müller's conception of primitive man, whose 'unconscious poetry' springs from an intimacy with nature which allows glimpses of the Divine, reinterprets myth as the earliest religious literature.[52] In Müller's advocacy of linguistic recapitulation, this 'unconscious poetry' is shared not only by the poet and early man, but also by the rural labourer and the child. In his revised 1872 edition of 'Comparative Mythology', Müller adds a footnote from the *Printer's Register* to endorse his argument:

> It is with the world, as with each of us in our individual life; for as we leave child-hood and youth behind us, we bid adieu to the vivid impressions

things once made on us, and become colder and more speculative. To a little child, not only are all living creatures endowed with human intelligence, but *everything is alive*. [...] The same instinct that prompts the child to *personify* everything remains unchecked in the savage, and grows up with him to manhood. Hence in all simple and early languages, there are but two genders, masculine and feminine [...] We see the same tendency to class everything as masculine or feminine among even civilized men, if they are uneducated. To a farm labourer, a bundle of hay is '*he*,' just as much as is the horse that eats it.[53]

For Müller, as for Wordsworth, the child and the peasant retain elements of a Romantic primitivism; both groups are characterised not by barbarity, but instinctive creativity. The first volume of *Good Words for the Young* opened with two serialised texts that show the influence of such notions of linguistic recapitulation: George MacDonald's 'At the Back of the North Wind' and Charles Kingsley's 'Madam How and Lady Why'. In their thematic concerns and through their physical juxtaposition, these tales encourage intertextual readings. While Kingsley uses the powerful fairies Madam How and Lady Why to explain the immensities of nature to an implied boy reader, MacDonald's tale relays the mystical experiences of the small working-class boy Diamond, who witnesses the sublime powers of the similarly awe-inspiring (and gendered) North Wind.

When Diamond undergoes the symbolic move from city to country towards the end of MacDonald's text, he becomes the true Worsdworthian child, his communion with nature resulting in a spontaneous, primitive poetry.[54] The cover of *Good Words for the Young* utilised a Wordsworthian epigram 'The Child is Father of the Man', an aphorism that becomes curiously appropriate in the context of the recapitulation thesis.[55] Kingsley's and MacDonald's works in the magazine display similar impulses to (and significant affinities with) Müller's etymological study of myth, which not only blended Romantic notions of spiritual development with the science of philology, but also constructed its own powerful mythology, in which the child's language leads the adult back to the 'childhood of the race'.[56]

As the *Monthly Packet* reveals, fairy tales were conceived not just as the literature of childhood, but of 'infant nations'.[57] The frequently assumed proximity of the peasant and child to such early cultural forms (and therefore to linguistic and racial origins) may go some way towards explaining the fixation in juvenile periodicals with supposedly 'authentic' European peasant folklore: Caroline Peachey's translations of the Andalusian folktales collected by 'Fernán Caballero' in *Aunt Judy's Magazine*, the scholarly article and tales from the same region in the *Monthly Packet* or the Breton tales in *Good Words for the Young*. In Dinah Mulock Craik's 'Last News of the Fairies', the narrator asks her self-educated working-class informant John if there are 'any fairies in this part of Yorkshire': he replies, 'The folks hereabouts used to think so – at least they did before we had Mechanics' Institutions and those sort of things to tell us it wasn't possible.'[58] If a pure folk spirit that exists outside modernity was conjured up in Müller's mid-Victorian celebration of the mythmaking capacities of the child and the rural labourer, it was to re-emerge in new ways in the 1890s, in the back-to-the-land socialism of Allan Clarke's *Labour Leader* fairy tales, and in the veneration of the Irish folk mind expounded by Yeats.

John Ruskin's 1868 introduction to Grimms' *German Popular Stories* asserts that 'every fairy tale worth recording at all is the remnant of a tradition possessing true historical value'; that it has 'naturally arisen out of the mind of a people'. Yet Ruskin also voices an underlying fear that such cultural links to the roots of identity are rapidly being lost; that genuine fairy tales are giving way to modern fantasy, produced for 'children bred in school-rooms and drawing-rooms, instead of fields and woods'.[59] Ruskin's own venture into the fairy tale, *The King of the Golden River*, mounts a critique of Victorian commerce by transposing such a consciousness to a pre-industrial setting heavily indebted to the tales of the Grimms.[60] In a letter to Margaret Gatty, written in 1869, J. H. Ewing discusses her own plans to write a series of 'Old-fashioned Fairy Tales' for *Aunt Judy's Magazine*. Echoing Ruskin's sentiments, Ewing tells her mother: 'You know how fond I have always been of fairy stories of the Grimm type. Modern fairy tales always seem to me such *very* poor things by comparison'. Ewing intends to model her tales on what she perceives to be the 'old traditional ones'; her diaries during this period show a regular recourse to the Grimms' tales for inspiration. Her theory is that 'all real "fairy tales" shld be written as if they were oral traditions taken down from the lips of a "story teller"', and she is insistent that her tales should initially appear anonymously, despite her status as a children's author of considerable reputation.[61]

While Charles Kingsley was a brother-in-law (and intimate friend) of Max Müller, Ewing's letters reveal that she was also well acquainted with the Indo-European thesis.[62] In *Aunt Judy's Magazine*, *Good Words for the Young* and the *Monthly Packet*, the Grimms' tales and Jacob Grimm's scholarship functioned as mutually informing discourses. Romantic myths of origin and philological researches were inextricably linked: when George Dasent translated Norwegian folktales collected by Asbjørnsen and Moe for a British audience in 1858, he invoked Jacob Grimm in the spirit of Aryan pride. Like Hincks in the *Monthly Packet* article 'Andalucian Folklore', Dasent suggested that Jacob Grimm's study of myth led directly to racial origins:

> His Teutonic Mythology, his Reynard the Fox, and the collection of German Popular Tales, which he and his brother William published, have thrown a flood of light on the early history of all the branches of our race, and have raised what had come to be looked on as merely nursery fictions and old wives' fables – to a study fit for the energies of grown men, and to all the dignity of a science.[63]

Dasent asserted that 'the first authentic history of a nation is the history of its tongue'. If language was 'fossil poetry', as Müller (borrowing from Emerson and Trench) suggested, survivals from Scandinavian mythology could appear to offer the ossified remains of a shared Aryan history: cultural, racial and spiritual.[64] Grimm, Müller and Dasent's engagements with comparative philology can indeed be seen to have influenced the Rev. J. C. Atkinson's long-running series 'Comparative Danish and Northumbrian Folk Lore', which was published intermittently in the *Monthly Packet* from February 1865 to March 1866. Atkinson, like Cohen and Taylor before him, traces northern British folklore back to the Viking invasions, suggesting that it would be difficult to prove that

> the North England folk lore, generally, is not as much a descendant of the folk lore of the old Danes of nine hundred or one thousand years ago, as the mass of the Northumbrian population is, in the main, of those same Scandinavian conquerors and colonists.[65]

Atkinson's engagement with the complex differentiations between the supernatural figures of folkloric mythology, as well as the parallels between Danish and Northumbrian linguistic variants, seems rather daunting even for a teenaged readership. A direct link can be traced, however, between Atkinson's scholarly researches and J. H. Ewing's fantasy fictions. In September 1865, in an article on 'Hobs', Atkinson collects a formidable range of folkloric sources on the 'Brownie', or house spirit. He tells his readers that, in the 'more northerly districts of ancient Northumbria, we find faith in, and legends of, the Brownie more and more current; in fact, wherever the Northmen penetrated, there the Brownie seems to have companied them'.[66] The Brownie's characteristics, including its habit of faithfully working for a family at night in return for a dish of cream or porridge, and its banishment if a suit of clothes is left out for it by the fire, are discussed through extracts from Scott's *Minstrelsy of the Scottish Border* (1802–3), Keightley's *Fairy Mythology* (1828) and other authorities.[67]

Three months later, J. H. Ewing's 'The Brownies: A Fairy Story' was published in the *Monthly Packet*, a tale which took Atkinson's folkloric source material and shaped it into bourgeois domestic fiction. Within its metafictional narrative structure, the child Deordie tells the doctor, a family friend, of his reading of 'The Shoemaker and the Elves' in Grimm. The doctor then tells Deordie the extemporised tale of Tommy Trout, a tailor's son, who is in turn told by his grandmother about a Brownie that once lived with their family. Tommy seeks the 'wise owl' of his grandmother's narrative to discover more, but realises with great disappointment that there are 'no Brownies but children', although the owl acquaints him with the legend as handed down by her 'grandmother's great-grandmother'. Tommy and his siblings decide to take on the role of Brownies in their own home, his sister making '(as girls are apt to make) the best house-sprite of all'; actions which are then replicated in the outer narrative by the middle-class Deordie and his siblings.[68]

While this tale's reshaping of folkloric materials into a celebration of middle-class domestic virtue found widespread approval (later even giving a name to the younger Girl Guide movement), 'The Brownies' is no simple didactic fiction.[69] In this sophisticated aggregate of narratives, complex enough for the *Monthly Packet*'s teenaged readers, a famous German folktale in a celebrated collection, British folklore and a spontaneous oral fairy tale from a middle-class storyteller, all coalesce as contributory elements in the fairy-tale tradition. The *Monthly Packet* relied on a regular audience, who were able to follow links between monthly issues. Atkinson's folklore and Ewing's fantasy offer complementary meanings through subtle textual interplay, an interplay that was particularly striking when these works were bound together in the periodical's six-monthly volume.[70]

'The Brownies' was not the only one of Ewing's periodical tales over which researches in Scandinavian folklore appear to have exerted an important influence. A number of Ewing's 'Old-fashioned Fairy Tales' in *Aunt Judy's Magazine* utilise its familiar folkloric archetypes – and indeed 'The Neck' was partly inspired by Keightley.[71] Ewing's 'Old-fashioned Fairy Tales' 'The Hillman and the Housewife' and 'Under the Sun' castigate human greed and meanness by faithfully replicating the traits ascribed to the hill-dwelling dwarfs or trolls of folklore – particularly the Northumbrian and Danish folkloric tradition previously explored by Atkinson in the *Monthly Packet*.[72] In an 1875 tale by Ewing, 'The Kyrkegrim Turned Preacher', in *Aunt Judy's Magazine*, the narrator turns a folkloric archetype into a figure of religious rectitude, noting that 'In Norway every church has its own Niss, or Brownie', and that 'the church Niss is called Kyrkegrim'.[73] In this tale, rather than the traditional accusation that the building of churches has driven away such supernatural figures, the Christian Kyrkegrim chastises a farmer who thinks about turnips rather than his own soul. In these tales (in a similar manner to 'The Brownie'), it is figures of pagan folklore that teach Christian gratitude and generosity. While Ewing creates new texts which participate in a Christian homiletic tradition, they also draw on the comparative mythologists' scholarly researches into pre-Christian origins.

Ewing took an amateur interest in the 'fossil poetry' of the vernacular folktale; her interest in dialect use was expressed in the preface to the republished *Old-fashioned Fairy Tales* (1882) as a 'scrupulous endeavour to conform to tradition in local colour and detail'.[74] In texts such as the Scottish dialect tale 'the Laird and the Man of Peace' (1871) or the Irish 'Murdoch's Rath' (1872), Ewing even produced a footnoted glossary of Gaelic terms, making the texts' status as literary fairy tale or folktale transcription ambiguous.[75] The folkloric aspiration of the 'Old-fashioned Fairy Tales' was always a literary conceit, achieved through the appropriation of a series of mediated textual materials: the Scottish dialect novels of George MacDonald, the Grimms' tales, a series of Andalucian folktales published in *Aunt Judy's Magazine* and the literary fairy tales of Ludwig Bechstein and Andersen.[76]

In the Indo-European thesis, however, it was not just European folklore that became a source of renewed fascination. Juvenile magazines' engagements with comparative philology led to assertions that might initially appear to destabilise their wider endorsement of colonial ideologies. In a thesis that linked Indians and Europeans in a common racial ancestry, with Sanskrit as the oldest surviving language, it was impossible to ignore the ancient provenance of Indian civilisation. While Eastern culture was perceived as static (as Goldney tells the readers of *Aunt Judy's Magazine*, premised on thought rather than action), there was no escaping the fact that it both preceded and shaped Western civilisation. Goldney, echoing Taylor, concludes that 'our popular fables and fairy tales were brought to us by our Indian ancestors'. Norman Macleod's 'Talks with the Boys about India' (1870) in the same periodical goes further in acknowledging the extent of Indian cultural development. He asserts that 'the Hindoos, who are of the same stock as the Europeans', from the first 'possessed a high civilisation. The Sanskrit language, in which all their great works are written, is perhaps the most perfect and beautiful that ever existed. Their poetry, earlier than that of Homer, and their religious hymns (Vedas) [...] are full of sublime ideas of God'.[77]

It might seem surprising that such assertions were made in *Aunt Judy's Magazine*, the *Monthly Packet* and *Good Words for the Young*, periodicals that not only expected their readers to support missionary work, but anticipated that some of them would spend their lives in India as 'great merchants', 'great missionaries' and 'great soldiers or statesmen, the rulers of millions', bringing supposed economic advancement and Christian enlightenment.[78] Typical of these magazines' generally staunch endorsement of the imperial mission is the *Aunt Judy's Magazine* article 'Little Brown Girls' (1876), in which philanthropy is solicited to bring imperialist homogeneity, to help the pupils of the 'Lahore Native Christian Girls School' express a delight in 'everything that would please and amuse white school-girls'.[79] An article on 'The Bengalees at School' (1872) in *Good Words for the Young* regrets that the civilising process with 'European methods of instruction' is not advancing more quickly.[80] In an obvious sense, colonial ideologies and the science of philology had been intertwined from the beginning: when F. W. Farrar, in his *Macmillan's* article 'Philology as One of the Sciences' traces the Indo-European thesis back to Sir William Jones and the foundation of the Asiatic society in 1786, he argues that 'Comparative Philology would not even yet have existed but for the mighty Providence which bestowed upon us the government of India, and guided to that country such scholars and Orientalists'.[81] Yet while colonial policy facilitated the rise of comparative philology, there was still the need to accommodate its findings: to reconcile the proven early presence of a venerable 'high civilisation' in India with the perceived need for British colonial rule. Macleod's 'Talks with the Boys about India' made that uneasy reconciliation by also drawing on nascent developments in anthropology. He argued that the real 'savages' of India were not the Aryan descendants, but the aboriginal race 'the Khonds', who dwelt in peripheral mountain regions and practised human sacrifice. It was this race whose supposedly fearful barbarity was perceived to have been curbed by a 'necessary' British rule.[82]

'Savage survivals' and the fairy tale

Macleod not only suggested that the Hindu population was subject to a slower rate of advance than the British, but drew on the notion of savage 'survivals' in civilisation, a theory propagated by the ethnologist E. B. Tylor in *Researches into the Early History of Mankind* (1865) and *Primitive Culture*. In the study of folktales, it developed its most celebrated (and prolific) advocate in Andrew Lang, who initially explored the thesis in his seminal *Fortnightly Review* article in 1873. Both drew on the comparative method of anthropological progress, in which all peoples were perceived to pass (at different rates) along a single developmental ladder, from savagery to civilisation.[83]

Tylor's developmental classifications viewed contemporary African races as savages whose supposedly arrested state brought the past into the present, shedding light on early human cultural development. Yet as Macleod's comments concerning the Khonds suggest, in this progress/stasis model, uneven rates of development were perceived to occur within as well as between nations, and were revealed by mythmaking capabilities of varying sophistication.[84] The endorsement of the comparative method in juvenile periodicals, foregrounding both the arrested savage race and the spectre of the savage survival in civilisation, could produce a far less Romantic construction of primitivism than that propagated by Müller. This construction drew less on pre-industrial nostalgia and more on entrenched fears of racial and class unrest.

When 'Norman' wrote in *Aunt Judy's Magazine* in 1867 that 'Ogres are terribly out of fashion now, and, like the Red Indian, stand a fair chance of being improved off the face of creation', he allied the extinction of a supposedly 'savage' race with the extinction of a primitive folkloric imagination.[85] Folktales and savagery were more literally united in Charles Kingsley's 'The True Fairy Tale' in *Good Words for the Young*. Kingsley suggests that the information he has to impart to his readers ought to be called 'the fairy tale of all fairy tales, for by the time we get to the end of it I think it will explain to you how our forefathers got to believe in fairies, and trolls, and elves, and ocrullings, and all strange little people who were said to haunt the mountains and the caves'. In this euhemerist argument, Kingsley suggests that such folkloric figures had originally developed from the reactions of the more civilised invading tribes to the sight of the aboriginal peoples of Britain. In this familiar thesis, the perfect validation of colonial expansion and 'progress', weaker, savage races are perpetually being driven to peripheral locations by the invasion of 'stronger and bolder people': when 'our own forefathers, the Germans and the Norsemen, came, these poor little savages, with their flint arrows and axes, were no match for them, and had to run away northward, or be all killed out'.[86]

Atkinson also gives possible credence to this argument (which had been discussed by Edgar Taylor in the 1820s) in his article on 'Trolls' (1866) in the *Monthly Packet*. Folkloric incidents of a troll speaking 'a partially unintelligible jargon' could indeed be

> a scrap of genuine authentic tradition – on the hypothesis which makes the Trolls or Dwarfs to have been the remnants of a dispossessed earlier and barbarous race of inhabitants. What more natural than that some, at least, among them should long preserve in their lone, remote, or almost inaccessible hiding places, [...] remains, more or less considerable, of their own old original language?[87]

The influence of euhemerist theories are apparent in George MacDonald's 'The Princess and the Goblin', published in *Good Words for the Young* in 1870, the year after Kingsley's 'The True Fairy Tale.' In the mythical kingdom ruled by Princess Irene's father, in underground caves, there live:

> a strange race of beings, called by some gnomes, by some kobolds, by some goblins. There was a legend current in the country, that at one time they lived above ground [...] But for some reason or other [...] they had all disappeared from the face of the country. According to the legend, however, instead of going to some other country, they had all taken refuge in the subterranean caverns.[88]

MacDonald appears to invoke the notion of savage survivals, the goblins complaining that the people above 'look upon us as a degraded race'.[89] In this text, MacDonald depicts a developing friendship between the boy miner Curdie and the Princess Irene: in this alternative fantasy realm, the significance of class difference appears to be ameliorated by the individual's possession of moral purity, honesty and bravery.[90] MacDonald's fiction creates a definite tension, however, with surrounding fictional contributions in *Good Words for the Young* (texts which he had approved as editor), where the real industrial working class are rarely treated so empathetically. In one article, miners are constructed in terms that invoke parallels, not with MacDonald's boy hero, but with his sinister goblins – suggesting not only arrested development but also barbaric reversion. Edward Howe's 'The Pit

Boys and their Dog', a short story published in *Good Words for the Young* while 'The Princess and the Goblin' was in serialisation, is a realist text that depicts a contemporary miner's strike which results in a primitivism that is the antithesis of Curdie's construction as fairy-tale hero: 'far more money than was necessary could still somehow be found for drink, and drunken riots took place in the half-starving villages'. Even the best of the colliers become 'sourly savage'.[91] In 1877, when MacDonald's 'The Princess and Curdie' was serialised in the periodical (now entitled '*Good Things for the Young of All Ages*'), he appears to acknowledge these fears. Revealing clear parallels with the fate of the 'Do-As-You-Likes' in Kingsley's *The Water-Babies*, Curdie is told by Irene's mystical great, great grandmother that 'all men, if they do not take care, go down the hill to the animals' country'. Curdie is 'not surprised to hear it' when he thinks 'of some of our miners'.[92]

The fairy tale's potential to embrace the comparative method as a model of racial and class development is illuminated in fascinating ways in William Gilbert's 'Sinbad in England' [sic], a book-length serialised tale which appeared in *Good Things for the Young of all Ages* from November 1872 to October 1873. While the author (the father of W. S. Gilbert) had already provided several short stories based around the humorous rewriting of classic fairy-tale texts for the periodical ('The Seven-Leagued Boots' and 'Mrs Blundebore's Trials'), 'Sinbad in England' was a far more complex text, creating a contemporary adventure narrative within the framework of a classic fairy tale.[93] Its ingenious conceit was a shift in perspective that defamiliarised the reader. If Western audiences were fascinated by the *Arabian Nights*, a work which constructed an alternative Eastern realm of exotica and magic, Gilbert merely reversed the premise, creating a textual audience of Baghdad listeners who marvel over 12 nights at the tales of a storyteller who has experienced the wonders of Britain.

The accumulated stories of the Cairo-born Schena, who describes his adventures in England and Europe as the servant of an aristocrat, both buttress conceptions of differential rates of development, and celebrate the achievements of Western progress. While many of his Baghdad listeners believe the tales of the *Arabian Nights* to be true, they cannot believe the everyday facts of English life: steam trains, telegraph wires and hot air balloons, all described through the wondering eyes of the reflective Easterner.[94] In Gilbert's fiction, each of the 12 tales forms a monthly serialised instalment. His narrative frame not only manipulates the sequential conceit of the *Arabian Nights*, but draws attention to a periodical exchange between a writer and a reader who share the same national values. Ultimately, Gilbert's shift in vision returns readers to the security of a familiar perspective, reinforcing the expected temporal place of the philosophical Easterner (in the ancient world of superstition rather than the modern world of science).

Notions of progress, however, are also more complex. A notable feature of Gilbert's text is the fact that racial hierarchies are undercut by class. It becomes apparent that the group perceived to exhibit the most savage behaviour are not Schena's Eastern listeners (who are at least sober, imaginative and sophisticated in their narrative entertainment) but the male, English, working class. Schena narrates the tale of his master's attempts to rescue a working-class family who have become enslaved by the father's servitude to the demon 'Kordicus' (alcohol). Under the influence of drink, the husband attacks his wife with an axe; the abstemious Eastern listeners are amazed that he escapes with a light punishment under British law. It is in Europe, not the East, that Schena encounters servants who are willing to steal from the dead.[95]

Such analogies between the English urban poor and 'primitive' tribes were not confined to fiction: they became a cliché of journalism and urban anthropology, from Thackeray's 'Half a Crown's Worth of Cheap Knowledge' (1838) to Mayhew's *London Labour and the London Poor* (1851–2) and General Booth's *In Darkest London and the Way Out* (1890).[96] George W. Stocking has noted that the methodological approaches formulated by Victorian anthropologists such as J. F. McLennan might indeed be read as an appropriation of the recapitulation thesis, fostering the illusion that 'the race-differentiated progress of the human species over the last hundred millennia' recapitulated 'the class-differentiated progress of British civilization over the last hundred years'.[97] The role of the fairy tale in foregrounding these perceived developmental parallels between the Easterner and the English urban poor is encapsulated in a series of 1883 issues of *Chatterbox*. A short article entitled 'The Arabian Night's Entertainments' discusses these tales' ambiguous ancient Eastern provenance. In subsequent weekly issues, full page illustrations of 'An Indian Sweeper-Girl' and 'A Mahomedan Fakir' are mixed with illustrations such as 'Rags and Bones' (of the 'bone-grubbers' in British cities) and 'The Street Arab' (a British homeless child). These contemporary figures, viewed with anthropological wonder, appear to have stepped from the very pages of the *Arabian Nights* itself – like this text, they appear to demonstrate the past arrested in the present and exert a similar fascination as primitive exotica.[98]

'Life is the most beautiful fairy tale': Class and gender fantasies

Hans Christian Andersen's 'What the Whole Family Said', published in *Good Words for the Young* in July 1870, ends with a homily: 'the older one grows the clearer one sees, in adversity and prosperity, that Our Lord is in it all, that life is the most beautiful fairy tale'.[99] In his article 'Hans Christian Andersen' for *Aunt Judy's Magazine*, Edward Bell translated a passage from one of Andersen's autobiographies, *The Story of My Life* (sometimes translated as *The Fairy Tale of My Life*), which was remarkably similar:

> 'My life', says Andersen, 'is a beautiful fairy-tale, so full of brightness and good fortune. When, as a boy, poor and lonely, I went out into the world,

had I met a powerful fairy and had she said to me, "Choose thy pathway and thy goal, and in accordance with the development of thy mind, and with what is reasonable in yonder world, I will protect and guide thee," my destiny could not have been happier, or more wisely and well chosen. The story of my life will say to the world what it says to me: There is a loving God who directs all things for the best'.[100]

In his autobiography, Andersen turned his own life into the archetypal quest narrative, refashioning himself as a fairy-tale hero. In his article, Bell endorses Andersen's fusion of memoir, fairy tale and *Bildungsroman*: his autobiography becomes a narrative which demonstrates that everything is for the best in the best of all possible worlds, that the poor can rise to greatness, and that Christian faith and a good heart can overcome class structures. Yet, while seeming to extol imaginative and social freedom, these appropriations of Andersen in middle-class children's periodicals also projected a Christian framework that supported rather than challenged the status quo. While social mobility appears both fantastic and possible, both Andersen's tale and his autobiography present some troubling ambiguities. Is it talent and aspiration, or obedience and humility that bring the poor reward?[101]

The second interpretation was often particularly appealing to the religious periodicals that targeted working-class juveniles. A particularly unsubtle example is *Chatterbox's* 1883 text 'Less Inequality than We Suppose', taken from Mary Frere's series of Indian fairy tales, *Old Deccan Days*. A Rajah lives in a palace and takes excessive care of himself, but is often ill. A shepherd lives an ascetic lifestyle at the top of an exposed mountain, but remains well. The curious Rajah decides to change places; after some months, the shepherd's hardened constitution is weakened by the Rajah's luxurious lifestyle, and he catches a cold and dies. The Rajah is instructed 'You see now what dangers we [the rich] are exposed to, from which the poor are exempt. It is thus that Nature equalises her best gifts; wealth and opulence tend, too frequently, to destroy health and shorten life'.[102] In *Chatterbox*, Frere's tale collection, inspired by Aryan folkloric researches, is re-appropriated in the service of class ideology. Social mobility is less elegantly refuted in an 1875 *Chatterbox* tale. A king disguised in common clothing offers to mind geese: he is so unsuccessful that the goose herd is caused to remind him of his rightful sphere. 'Whoever you are, you are a good gentleman, but don't deceive yourself that you are a goose-herd. Remember the proverb, "Shoemaker, stick to your last."'[103]

It is important to note, however, that the social positions with which readers were encouraged to be content in *Aunt Judy's Magazine* were very different from those in *Chatterbox*. In the former, differences between the upper-middle and working classes were often articulated through the editorial construction of readers as philanthropists. *Aunt Judy's* charitable pursuits aimed at older female readers can be seen to intellectually dovetail with notions of morality and social responsibility implicit in many of the periodical's fairy tales, for both stressed individual action rather than social change, and perpetuated simplified, sentimental notions of poverty. In her preface to the book edition of the *Old-fashioned Fairy Tales*, Ewing asserts that fairy tales 'cultivate the Imagination [...] – hand maid of Faith, of Hope, and, perhaps most of all, of Charity!'.[104] An obvious consolidation of such rhetoric occurs in the 'Old-fashioned Fairy Tale' 'The Widows and the Strangers', in which two widows are asked by a monk to spare goods for people who have lost their homes in a storm. The generous widow gives everything, the selfish a worn shawl; in an ensuing storm, their houses burn down, and the portentous stranger reveals the widows to be the recipients of their own charity.[105]

Both *Aunt Judy's Magazine* and the *Monthly Packet* urged their readers to pursue charitable activities, occupations that were seen as defining elements in mid-Victorian middle-class female identity. Educated at home, philanthropy formed an important part of J. H. Ewing and H. K. F. Gatty's social development. When her children were approaching adulthood, Margaret Gatty commented, '[w]e are doing all we can over the boys' education, looking upon it as money laid out to interest. The girls are pretty well; they teach and visit the sick and are as good as four curates!'[106] Her own periodical reflected this gender-differentiated veneration of charitable works, as H. K. F. Gatty's 'Farewell Address' of October 1885 makes clear.

Gatty addresses *Aunt Judy's* readers in thanks 'for all the good work' they have done through the magazine. She recalls in particular her mother's suggestion that readers endow a bed in Great Ormond Street Hospital in 1868, a successful appeal that provided funds for a number of beds and led to the launch of the 'Hospital Work Society', which encouraged readers to produce clothes for hospital patients.[107] There are some interesting intertextual connections with the periodical's fictional texts. Hans Christian Andersen's European reputation was established in part by the great popularity of his sentimental poem 'The Dying Child', a text which was reproduced in many periodicals (including *Aunt Judy's Magazine*, in April 1868).[108] Ewing's own tale of a stoic dying child, 'Laetus Sorte Meâ, or, The Story of a Short Life' was published in the periodical from May to October 1882. In *Aunt Judy's Magazine*, readers were offered reports on the progress of the real patients in the bed that the periodical had sponsored. Like Andersen and Gatty's fictional texts, these narratives sometimes terminated with the child's death and a consoling religious platitude.

Mary Cadogan and Patricia Craig argue that '[a]lthough both *The Monthly Packet* and *Aunt Judy's Magazine* went in for social comment as well as "elevating" fiction, their girl readers were encouraged only to support reforms which allowed them to remain on the tightrope of respectability. Contributors and readers were more concerned with counting their blessings than with changing the *status quo*.[109] Their claims certainly seem to be supported by the anonymous 1878 *Monthly Packet* short story 'Workhouse Visiting', which maintains a clear distinction between the deserving and undeserving poor. Three female narrators write accounts of their visits to a workhouse; the first distinguishes between her preference for the infirmary patients over the 'day-room' women. In this text, the first type of patients suffer humbly, while the second group are described as 'the supine poor', for 'it is obvious if a woman is *only* elderly, and has good health, she may, generally speaking, keep out of the workhouse, with the help of out-door relief'.

The first speaker describes sympathy with the poor as 'the fairy gift I should wish for', and there are wider fairy-tale allusions, particularly in the last account.[110] In this final tale, an archetypal symbol of the deserving poor, a small child, is allowed to freeze to death outside a respectable woman's home. The parallels with Hans Christian Andersen's 'The Little Match-Girl' are obvious. While Andersen's heroine ascends to heaven, the *Monthly Packet* text offers a more pragmatic resolution that is nevertheless a form of fairy-tale ending, in which individual action ensures the restitution of the status quo. To save the dead girl's sister from the same fate, the chastened woman asks her to come and work for her as a maid. Fairy-tale morality, domestic fiction and social reality were indeed conflated in the *Monthly Packet* in striking ways. The same month's correspondence page included a genuine request to find a home for a girl of seven to be trained for domestic service.[111]

In an unpublished commonplace book, J. H. Ewing recorded her own visit to a church in a slum district of Manchester. Here, the industrial poor, and her own attitude towards them as charitable benefactor, fail to fit the harmonious social model that was projected in *Aunt Judy's Magazine*. Ewing describes the children's faces as 'terrible and sickly looking *as a whole* & with a hideous likeness to grown-up women in slums'; they are among 'the lowest, coarsest, ugliest type of gutter children'.[112] This sense of disgust is never felt of the poor in Ewing's 'Old-fashioned Fairy Tales', inhabitants of a mythical agrarian past who can easily be made to conform to the stock characteristics of the folkloric poor: either quaintly mischievous, or clean, humble, and trusting in their maker. For this series of texts, Ewing was anxious to escape both the contemporary setting and the circumscribed pictorial and linguistic codes which were used to construct 'real life' in domestic children's fiction. She selected her illustrator carefully: A. W. Bayes had also illustrated an edition of Andersen's tales, which *Aunt Judy's Magazine* had described in a book review as 'excellent, occasionally quite weird and remarkable'.[113] Bayes's illustrations foster a sense of timelessness and evoke a comforting rustic nostalgia – an attempted return to folkloric innocence (Figure 2.1).

However, in Ewing's texts, which fused contemporary domestic settings with fairy-tale motifs, folkloric nostalgia collided with the codes of bourgeois realism and more overt tensions were sometimes visible. 'Amelia and the Dwarfs', a two-part serialised fantasy published in the periodical in February

Figure 2.1 A.W. Bayes, 'The Hillman and the Housewife', *Aunt Judy's Magazine*, 1870. © The British Library Board. All Rights Reserved. PP59922i

and March 1870, was closely based on the Irish folktale 'Wee Meg Barnileg', in which a wilful child learns obedience. Yet unlike the 'Old-fashioned Fairy Tales', 'Amelia' replaces the mythical agrarian past with a recognisably Victorian present: with servants and the trappings of the upper-middle-class parlour. While 'Amelia', as U. C. Knoepflmacher notes, 'converts an old folktale into a comedy of manners', Ewing's 'Timothy's Shoes' pays homage to Andersen's 'Red Shoes' (and possibly *Goody Two-Shoes*) by replacing Andersen's symbols of vanity and disobedience with a pair of shoes that are a convenient tool of parental instruction and social control.[114] This text's mixed modes, however, combining the styles and motifs of folktale, literary fairy tale and public school story, make the issue of 'manners' more troubling. Margaret Gatty, commenting on George

Cruikshank's illustration for 'Timothy's Shoes', suggests that he has misread the text's class codes:

> What think you of the illustration? It is pretty, but not, I think, equal to *Amelia*. He has surely got hold of the *wrong class*. You didn't mean cottage life surely [...] The schoolmaster Dr. Dixon Airey settles this, as well as [...] the mention of *silver mugs* etc [...] It is Cruikshank's sin that he must be either grotesque or in low life. Of "high art" he has no notion.[115]

Cruikshank's tripartite image has as its centrepiece a quaint rural cottage which could easily have formed one of his revered illustrations for Edgar Taylor's *German Popular Stories* (Figure 2.2). Gatty remains convinced, however, that, while suitable for the folk narrative, in the domestic text with 'fairy tale machinery' (in which Timothy attends Dr Dixon Airey's establishment for young gentlemen), 'cottage life' is distinctly out of place.[116] Conflating artistic and social status (the incompatibility of 'low life' and 'high art'), Gatty illuminates the class-specific perception of what constituted 'realism': in middle-class children's fiction in general, and in the closed world of *Aunt Judy's Magazine* in particular. In contrast, the illusion of a wholehearted return to the 'uninstructive' folktale which Ewing attempted to maintain in some of the 'Old-fashioned Fairy Tales' appears, at least superficially, to avoid these complications. The periodical's retreat into the folktale fostered a myth of social unity. Middle-class ideologies appeared as universal truths, embodying the 'timeless' values of faith, hope and charity.

In the 1880s, the covers of *Chatterbox* and *Aunt Judy's Magazine* reveal different appropriations of fairy-tale motifs for particular target audiences. *Chatterbox* presents an elderly storyteller, reminiscent of Perrault's 'Mother Goose', surrounded by boisterous child listeners. While these children hint obliquely at the real working-class readers at whom the periodical was aimed, they are linked through the surrounding tableaux with a more comforting nostalgia for a cohesive pre-industrial culture and a bygone peasant class (Figure 2.3). When *Aunt Judy's Magazine* obtains a new cover design by Randolph Caldecott in 1881, the image also features an elderly bespectacled female storyteller, but one who is distinctly modern and self referential: she reads from a copy of *Aunt Judy's Magazine* just delivered by the retreating postman. In contrast to *Chatterbox*'s cover, the well-dressed and mannered child listeners, the lacrosse racket, and the carefully ordered garden make it clear that this maiden aunt is not only a contemporaneous, but a distinctly upper-middle-class variation of Mother Goose (Figure 2.4). This illustration, fusing the myth of the 'old-fashioned' fairy tale with the 'high class' child audience, seems to perfectly capture the magazine's nostalgia and modernity. It grasps not only its fascination with the oral storytelling tradition, but also its solidly middle-class aspirations. [117]

58 *The Victorian Press and the Fairy Tale*

TIMOTHY'S SHOES.

Figure 2.2 George Cruikshank, 'Timothy's Shoes', *Aunt Judy's Magazine*, 1871. © The British Library Board. All Rights Reserved. PP59922i

Those gestures towards modernity were also apparent elsewhere: in its approaches to female education, *Aunt Judy's Magazine* was not always old-fashioned. In the anonymous 'Princess Bluestocking or, the Rival Brothers', a 'Musical Extravaganza for young players', which appeared in the periodical in December 1870, Prince Harmony complains of 'stuck-up girls' who 'Go in for women's wrongs and women's rights; / Know Hebrew, Greek, and Latin, dress like frights', but warms to Princess Bluestocking, who, in her eagerness to marry, is the perfect mix of modern education and traditional domestic values.[118] In 'The Galoshes of Happiness', 'freely adapted from

Myths of Origin: Magazines for Children 59

Figure 2.3 Cover illustration, *Chatterbox*, 1880. © The British Library Board. All Rights Reserved. PP5992g

Hans C. Andersen' (1875), the conservative Justice Knab complains of modern daughters who celebrate 'Freedom of speech, and votes, and art in dress / High education'. Interestingly, this text, by Margaret's son S. H. Gatty, makes the judge's wish for the 'good old days' when wives 'knew how to spin / And cook and make a cosy home' seem hopelessly retrograde: Knab wishes to turn back evolution (both social and Darwinian) and 'roam primaeval forests as an honest chimpanzee'.[119]

Female education in fact emerges as a wider subject of debate in *Aunt Judy's* fairy-tale fiction. In H. Buxton Forman's fairy tale 'King Wiseacre and the Six

Figure 2.4 Randolph Caldecott, cover illustration, *Aunt Judy's Magazine*, 1882. © The British Library Board. All Rights Reserved. PP59922i

Professors'(1867), King Wiseacre has nine daughters, but finds no one suitable to educate them. Six professors arrive in descending ages (Mathematics, Astronomy, Physics, Chemistry, Biology and Sociology) and offer to share their wisdom with the princesses. Finally rejected by the King, they turn into a giant which encapsulates scientific knowledge, who spurns the kingdom altogether.[120] The female scientific education which this fairy tale endorses was certainly reinforced in non-fictional contexts, and not only in Margaret Gatty's 'Parables from Nature'. Four months earlier, an advertisement appeared in the periodical for a 'Young Ladies Establishment' run by the 'Misses Carter' of Surbiton, whose course of instruction included astronomy and chemistry.[121]

J. H. Ewing's commonplace book reveals that she was reading not just the Grimms, but also John Stuart Mill during the composition of some of the

'Old-fashioned Fairy Tales'.[122] In their complex and satiric use of extra-textual referencing to allude to gender relations, some of these texts clearly deviate from the intended simplicity of spontaneous oral tales. In Ewing's 'The Blind Man and the Talking Dog', the mayor's son tells his playmate Aldegunda: 'I won't marry you when you grow big, unless you agree with what I do, like the wife in the story of "What the Goodman does is sure to be right."'[123] The experienced fairy-tale reader would have been able to decode the ironic use of Andersen's text (sometimes translated as 'Pa Always does the Right Thing' in modern editions). In this tale, a wife leaves all decisions to her husband; a variant on the Grimms' 'Hans in Luck', in Andersen's text it is a foolish husband who barters his horse for products of ever-decreasing value, and is left at the end with a sack of rotten apples.

'The Magician's Gifts', published in *Aunt Judy's Magazine* in 1872, manipulates Sleeping Beauty motifs, but in Ewing's fairy tale the agent of destruction is not a retributive fairy, but a bad-tempered husband. A prince is given three gifts at birth: the ability to have whatever he wishes for, a hasty temper and the inability to revoke what he has wished. After losing his temper with his dog and wishing it were hanged, its lifeless body is placed in a glass coffin as a reminder of his temper. When he begins to lose his temper with his wife she reminds him of the dog's fate, but to no avail:

> 'I know that I wish you were with him, with your prating!' cried the prince, in a fury; and the words were scarcely out of his mouth when the princess vanished from his side, and when he ran to the glass coffin there she lay, pale and lifeless, with her head upon the body of the hound.[124]

While the prince learns humility and his wife is eventually restored to life, this tale replaces the stark oppositions between good and evil in 'Sleeping Beauty' with a more subtle critique of contemporary marital relations.

Female obedience to domestic demands emerges in these tales (and the wider periodical) as an interesting site of contention. While some readers obediently sewed their blankets for the 'Hospital Work Society', some tales revealed the negative side of Justice Knab's wish that wives could 'spin / And cook and make a cosy home'. In Ewing's 'Old-fashioned Fairy Tale' 'The Ogre Courting', an ogre, who always chooses women who are small and good housewives, is tricked by 'Managing Molly' into believing she can spin a whole cupboard of linen in a month, make wine out of rotten apples and fine stew out of rats. In this text, the unending domestic virtues (and economies) insisted upon by unreasonable husbands are parodied by Molly's cunning.[125] This tale again highlights the productivity of an intertextual periodical context. It shows the clear influence of one of the 'Tales from Andalucia', published in the periodical three years earlier. The Andalusian text, 'Friends in Need', also allows a female to gain the upper hand over her unreasonably demanding prospective husband.[126] These tales are understandably of interest to feminist scholars, yet *Aunt Judy's Magazine* reveals the limitations of attempts to place Ewing in a camp of subversive writers. If Ewing contributes to a wider magazine dialogue on gender, it is equally necessary to acknowledge Ewing's own contribution to *Aunt Judy's* less progressive class ideologies.

Readers write back: Fairy tales and storytelling communities in *Aunt Judy's Magazine*

To conclude on such a note, however, is to suggest that there is only one way of reading *Aunt Judy's* fairy tales – and is indeed to ignore the importance of their contemporary readers. In fact, shifting the focus to the magazine's correspondence columns produces some interesting revelations. While these readers must be acknowledged as mediated voices (*Aunt Judy's* editors published replies to correspondents rather than direct questions), the dialogue between editor and respondent was often unusually frank. As Margaret Gatty herself notes in 1869, '[s]uch free correspondence as Aunt Judy has encouraged certainly lays her open to the expression of most contrary opinions'.[127] It is these contrary opinions that are a testament to the dialogic potential of the reading experience.

One of the most surprising aspects of this dialogue was the editors' willingness to publicise comments which were highly unfavourable. In the correspondence pages for July 1869, Margaret Gatty announces superbly that

> Aunt Judy has for long believed self-assertion to be one of the special sins of the present generation, and 'Sophonisba' confirms her in the opinion. One would think it needed a long experience in plain speaking to address an author by letter and tell her she has been writing 'intolerable rubbish.' But the 'girl of the period' is equal to anything. She is good enough to give her advice to the Editor upon the conduct of the Magazine, and to warn her against the vain attempt of adapting it both to 'girls and babys' [*sic*].[128]

While Gatty, with an approving nod to Eliza Lynn Linton, imperiously dismisses such presumptuous feminine 'self-assertion', she nevertheless gives such comments a published forum, as she does to those of 'A very rude set of children at Tunbridge' whose 'wholesale impertinence' is castigated but still recorded.

In fact, both negative and favourable correspondence to *Aunt Judy's Magazine* reveals a persistent interest among readers in the power relations within the periodical. The magazine was premised on a complex convergence of editorial, authorial and periodical identities, a process by which the Gatty family became the subject of their own folk mythology. 'J. H. Ewing is the real Aunt Judy, is she not?' ask 'Amy, Bertha and Kate' in the correspondence pages for December 1870. Margaret Gatty replies evasively that 'a more difficult question could scarcely be put to the editor of "Aunt Judy's Magazine," for it has a yes and a no side to it'.[129] As Gatty's equivocation suggests, the confusion was partly intentional: if the title 'Aunt Judy' invoked the professional identities of mother and daughters, it also conflated private and public (and oral and commercial) storytelling personae. First appearing in print in the title of a volume of children's tales by Margaret Gatty, 'Aunt Judy' was also the pet name for Juliana Gatty as a nursery storyteller and remained attached to her professional writing identity when she became J. H. Ewing.[130]

The confusion over the persona of 'Aunt Judy', revealing the unusual intimacy of the familial and professional relationships that defined *Aunt Judy's Magazine*, also foregrounds the ways in which domestic storytelling could be perceived as a step on the road to professional writing. In her youth, Margaret Gatty contributed regularly to manuscript magazines. The amateur juvenile writer later became the professional writer's subject matter, when the 'Black Bag' writing club was featured in her children's book *Aunt Judy's Letters* (1862).[131] Gatty's children continued the manuscript magazine tradition, with J. H. Ewing playing a central role in the family magazines *Anon!*, *Le Cachet* and *The Gunpowder Plot*, hand-written texts which are still in existence. These magazines show the teenaged Gatty children self-consciously parodying and appropriating periodical journalism, through the construction of hyperbolic editorials and playful fake advertisements.[132] Ewing was still contributing material to *The Gunpowder Plot* two years into her professional writing career for *Aunt Judy's Magazine*, and that overlap between professional and domestic writing is articulated in fascinating ways in *Aunt Judy's* correspondence columns.

Correspondents who were interested in developing their writing skills included readers in their late teens.[133] In her 1874 article 'In Memoriam, Margaret Gatty', J. H. Ewing noted this varied degree of skill in the periodical's readership. Suggesting of her mother that 'no consideration of the value of her own time could induce her to deal summarily with what one may call her magazine children', Ewing added that they ranged from 'nursery aspirants barely beyond pothooks' to a professional author who still called Gatty his 'literary godmother'.[134] That tradition was continued by Gatty's daughters, who saw solicitation for publication as no threat to female readers' respectability. Although 'Thomasina' is told frankly in 1876 that 'you will find it difficult to make any publisher believe that one who writes so unformed a hand, and expresses herself in so childish a way, can produce what is as well worth reading as books that older heads have accomplished', the editor finds her desire 'praiseworthy', and does not forbid Thomasina from offering her manuscript to any firm that she thinks 'is in the habit of bringing out books of the same description'.[135]

In 1870, Margaret Gatty had told correspondent 'B.F.', 'I cannot give you much encouragement to send fairy tales, as I have plenty, and am very critical about them; but I never refuse to look at anything that is sent.'[136] While the Gatty children wrote fairy tales for their manuscript magazines, fairy tales indeed appear to have been sent to *Aunt Judy's Magazine* by aspirant writers hoping for publication. In June 1867, the 'Magic Whistle' awaited 'application at the Publishers', while in November 1867 and January 1868, 'The Fairy Spiteful' and 'The Faun Prince' were 'declined with thanks'.[137] While *Aunt Judy's Magazine* was indeed highly critical in the standards expected from fairy tales, and appears to have published no literature by readers who were obviously juveniles, the seriousness with which it treated its young correspondents is significant. There are some interesting parallels with the *Monthly Packet*, in which creative writing and folkloric mythology were also combined. Yonge became a 'Mother Goose' to young relatives and friends who contributed to the amateur magazine *The Barnacle*; she recast the group as '"Arachne" and her Spiders' when a number began to contribute to the *Monthly Packet*.[138] One of the most commercially successful middle-class magazines, *Little Folks*, encouraged substantial fictional contributions from its readers through a range of competitions, while *Boys of England* was also shrewd enough to recognise the appeal of correspondence with the editor. *Good Words for the Young* was rather different: while it began a section called 'The Letter-Box' in late 1872, this was a fictional conceit rather than a forum for real readers' letters. It even published a fantasy which specifically discouraged young readers from aspiring to professional writing.[139]

If *Aunt Judy's* editors' close interaction with their 'magazine children' helped readers to conceptualise textual consumption, correspondence, and domestic and professional creative writing as complementary pursuits, it also created a spirited dialogue about the meaning of fairy tales. As Kirsten Drotner has noted, 'while the social range of religious reading matter is commonly acknowledged, the variability of its reception is often overridden by proclamations decrying its menacing indoctrination of children at all social levels'.[140] In the discussion in the correspondence columns about the fairy tale 'Marty's Escape', it is salutary to realise that this variability was acknowledged by readers and editors alike. This anonymous text, subtitled 'A Story for Naughty Boys and Girls', appeared in the periodical in May 1869, and is one of the most didactic tales to appear in *Aunt Judy's Magazine*. Its religious schema is unsubtle: 'There once lived a little girl, called Marty; and in the country where she dwelt, all the naughty people went black, but the good ones remained white.' Disobedient children are seized by 'Giant Grab-all' and their mouths stuffed with clay before being thrown into a sack. The text is fairly gruesome; at the Ogre's 'Castle Despair':

> The Giant Grab-all and his wife the Ogress stood by a roaring fire, grinning over all. To Marty's intense horror, this fearful couple lost no time; and seizing one after another of their unhappy victims, tore off their

clothes, and tossed them into an immense pot of water that was bubbling on the fire.

Marty is saved because she starts singing a hymn when the ogre wants to eat her, and by repeating such pious acts she gradually turns white. Finally she is rescued and returned to her parents, and the reader is left with a concluding morality: 'Such is the fate of those who obstinately rafuse [sic] to take warning and advice from others, and will not believe in the existence of a danger they cannot see until it comes upon them.'[141]

Punitive in tone and bald in its Christian morality, this text is a rather atypical contribution to *Aunt Judy's Magazine*, and critical reactions differed widely at the time of its publication. In the correspondence pages two months later, Margaret Gatty notes: 'it is a singular circumstance that on several occasions what has been most vehemently protested against has been as warmly praised'. She adds:

> This has been the case with the little tale 'Marty's Escape.' 'M. B.' writes of it in enthusiastic delight; wants to know the writer's name; and entreats for another tale from the same hand, adding that a friend has been so much pleased with it as to buy twelve copies of the number for distribution, sending one out to India. Whereas, alas! it has so greatly pained and distressed 'An Old Subscriber and Constant Reader' that she is almost alarmed for the character of the Magazine. Aunt Judy is very sorry. She is not fond of horrors herself, so there is small fear of her encouraging the 'Fee-Fo-Fum' style of literature. But still it is impossible to cater for exceptional cases of sensitiveness. 'Marty's Escape' may perhaps belong rather to the period when 'Jack and the Bean-stalk', 'Little Red Riding Hood' and 'Bluebeard' were almost the only staple nursery food. But when will these cease to be popular? And surely it is but one child in a thousand who receives hauntingly painful recollections of their horrors.[142]

These published responses are revealing about the complexity of approaches to the fairy tale within a single periodical readership. For 'M. B.' fairy tales are a valuable mode of child socialisation, at home or in a colonial context; for the 'Old Subscriber' the gruesome nature of some fairy-tale conventions threatens to haunt childish imaginations, echoing both Locke's and Mrs. Trimmer's concerns. If Gatty sidesteps the tale's overt didacticism, however, she also distances herself from assumptions that children read in literal ways, and are unable to distinguish reality from the codes of fictional works. By foregrounding a three-way dialogue between editor, adult and young readers, Gatty gives visibility to the power relations within the magazine, and foregrounds, in Margaret Beetham's terms, its 'open' as well as its 'closed' traits.[143]

While the *Monthly Packet* lived on until the end of the century, the termination of *Good Things for the Young* and *Aunt Judy's Magazine* (in 1877 and 1885 respectively) occurred during a new era in juvenile periodical publication, in which gender-specific titles with a broader class appeal, such as the Religious Tract Society's *Girl's Own Paper* (launched in 1880) gained unprecedented adolescent audiences. The middle-class titles of the 1860s reached fewer readers, but they deserve attention for other reasons. If, as *The Boys of England* argued, 'the beginning of all nations must be ever [...] blended with fables and legends', it is also true that the search for origins inspired new fables and fairy tales. Taken out of context, it is easy to miss the ways fantasies by MacDonald, Ewing and Kingsley created a mythologised history that was indeed the 'fairy tale of all fairy tales', inspired by comparative science's attempts to re-imagine the past.

3
Science and Superstition, Realism and Romance: Fairy Tale and Fantasy in the Adult Shilling Monthly

> There must be fairies, for this is a fairy tale; and how can one have a fairy-tale if there are no fairies?.[1]
>
> Alas! there are no real fairies in stories such as mine.[2]

In 1864, *The Times* suggested that 'quiet sober people favoured *Macmillan*, and were a good deal puzzled and a little scandalized when *The Water-Babies* began to tumble about in it like so many porpoises'.[3] The magazine's publisher, Alexander Macmillan, saw his readers rather differently. Writing to Charles Kingsley in 1862, Macmillan told him that his '*very* quaint and choice piece of grotesquery' would suit the magazine 'admirably', claiming that it would achieve a harmony in *Macmillan's* impossible within *Good Words*.[4] In fact, while *Macmillan's Magazine* was associated for some with 'a sort of douce sobriety', finding *The Water-Babies* amid articles on science, philosophy and political economy was perhaps not quite the shock for readers that *The Times* reviewer claimed.[5] In its first number, *Macmillan's* styled itself as a successor to King Arthur's Round Table. Like the *Cornhill*, which followed two months in its wake, it was fascinated with myth and fairy tale. In his first *Cornhill* 'Roundabout Paper', W. M. Thackeray invoked the *Arabian Nights* in defence of the magazine's serialised novels.[6] Readers of the *Cornhill* in the 1860s to 1870s, who turned to titles such as 'Cinderella' and 'Beauty and the Beast', found curious short stories which questioned the boundaries between fantasy and realism.

This chapter explores the role of the fairy tale in the first shilling monthlies of the 1860s, two pioneering magazines that helped to usher in a new era of middle-class magazine reading. Offering two serialised novels for half the price of the established miscellanies, the *Cornhill* discovered, in 1860, a winning formula and a 'phenomenal' circulation.[7] *Macmillan's*, courting much smaller audiences, promoted liberal dialogue over religion, evolution and social reform, signalling its modernity through an emersion in debates that the 'squeamish' *Cornhill* eschewed.[8] Attention to these periodicals' experiments with fairy tale and fantasy, however, might complicate this seemingly straightforward opposition between the social, scientific and political engagement of *Macmillan's* and the *Cornhill*'s more circumspect family reading. In different ways, both broached class relations, as well as issues of national and racial identity. Both responded to Darwin's *Origin of Species*; both traced broader evolutionary narratives, through explorations of the fairy tale and the 'science' of comparative mythology.

Writing in *Macmillan's* in 1869, Charlotte Yonge claims that there have been 'three really original fairy-tales' in the previous 20 years, and of these Kingsley's is the best: 'the latent though not consistent meanings that run through the "Water-Babies"' seem to 'render it more attractive than even the exquisite bits of fun in "Alice"'.[9] Subsequent critics have often disagreed and have been perplexed as well as attracted by *The Water-Babies*' form and possible meanings. For Louis MacNiece, it was 'one of the most uneven and ragbaggy books in the language'; for Valentine Cunningham, writing in the 1980s, Kingsley's mix of fairy tale, fantasy, Rabelaisian wit and realism makes *The Water-Babies* both a 'hermeneutic sponge' and an 'overdetermined' text.[10] If *The Water-Babies* remains unclassifiable and wilfully contradictory, this chapter argues that it makes a different kind of sense in *Macmillan's*, a periodical with which Kingsley was intimately connected from the beginning.[11] When *The Water-Babies* is read in the context of wider *Macmillan's* and *Cornhill* debates over theology, race, class, language and evolutionary science, forgotten dialogues emerge. The first shilling monthlies, champions of domestic realism, also provide a few surprises, for they were equally reliant on the seductions of romance.

The 'magic wand of language': Comparative mythology, Celticism and savagery

In his article 'The Fairy Land of Science', published in the *Cornhill* in 1862, James Hinton argues:

> We have often been reminded (in popular lectures and elsewhere) how curiously the achievements of modern industry embody, while they often even surpass, the imaginations of the youthful world. Who has not been invited to compare Chaucer's horse of brass, the shoes of swiftness of the *Niebelungen Lied*, or the seven-leagued boots of the renowned Giant-killer with the railway train, to the manifest advantage of the latter; Aladdin's ring by rubbing which he could instantaneously communicate with the genii at the ends of the earth, with the electric telegraph; or the magic mirror in which were portrayed the actions of distant friends with the reflecting telescope? Science has realized, and more than realized, some of these early dreams, and seems to cast on them almost a prophetic lustre.

This metaphor was a familiar one across a range of periodicals that popularised science, including the cheaper weeklies such as *Household Words* and *Chambers's*. As Chapter 2 reveals, it was also used in texts for children such as William Gilbert's 'Sinbad in England', in which superstitious Eastern storytellers wonder at the same Western inventions, which are seen as more marvellous than their own supernatural tales. In Hinton's article, like Gilbert's, such tale-telling is associated with the early stages of human progress before the scientific mind has evolved from the mythmaking 'youthful world'. Yet, as in Kingsley's 'The True Fairy Tale', this is not a Comtean progression from superstition and religion to science. For Hinton, as for Kingsley, the capacity for wonder and religious belief remains integral to the modern scientific mind: 'No justification of those poetic instincts which insist on finding spiritual significance in all material things, could be more complete than that which is given thus by science'.[12]

If fairy-tale metaphors were often used to capture the grandeur of scientific discovery, mythmaking was also helping to shape a science of its own. When Julia Wedgwood writes in *Macmillan's* in 1863 of 'that Aryan race which Professor Max Müller [...] has taught us to call up from the shadowy past with such wonderful distinctness, by the magic wand of language', she uses just such a metaphor to evoke the wonders of philology, in which myth is revealed as a key to spiritual as well as linguistic origins.[13] In the *Cornhill* article 'Comparative Mythology' of 1869, James Briggs Carlill echoes Wedgwood in praising Müller and his follower George Cox for disseminating 'this simple, elegant, and refined theory' which has allowed 'the dry bones of mythology' to 'live again'.[14]

Reviewing folktale collections that owed a significant debt to Müller – George Dasent's *Popular Tales from the Norse* and J. F. Campbell's *Popular Tales of the West Highlands* in *Macmillan's* in January 1861 – *Macmillan's* editor David Masson discusses their contributions to the 'science of Mythology' (which Campbell termed 'the science of Storyology'). Masson elaborates the Indo-European thesis, as popularised by Müller, Dasent and Campbell, with a sense of breathless wonder. In 'Gaelic and Norse Popular Tales; An Apology for the Celt', Masson reminds his readers:

> The tales and legends which we find common among the Celtic, the Gothic, the Slavonian, the Latin, and the Greek nations of the present Europe, and which we find also among the Indians, are, as it were, the water-rolled drift which has come down traditionally among the nations, through their several channels, from that primeval and pre-historic time when they had not yet disengaged themselves from the great Aryan or Indo-European mass to which they are traced back also by the evidence of common vocables in their several languages![15]

The 'magic wand of language' did more than unlock the legends of the past: such philological claims of Indo-European linguistic unity had significant implications for the conceptualisation of race. If the place of Celtic peoples in that 'Indo-European mass' had been championed by James Prichard in *The Eastern Origin of the Celtic Nations* (1831), its significance would later be explored in a more popular context – in Matthew Arnold's well-known articles 'On the Study of Celtic Literature', which appeared in the *Cornhill* in four instalments during 1866.[16] Arnold notes here that the 'science of origins' has already had 'salutary practical consequences', suggesting that the 'radical estrangement' from the Irish people has 'visibly abated amongst all the better part' of his audience:

> Fanciful as the notion may at first seem, I am inclined to think that the march of science, – science insisting that there is no such original chasm between the Celt and the Saxon as we once popularly imagined, that they are not truly, what Lord Lyndhurst called them, *aliens in blood* from us, that they are our brothers in the great Indo-European family, – has had a share, an appreciable share, in producing this changed state of feeling.[17]

As Sinéad Garrigan Mattar has shown, Arnold may have helped to inaugurate the study of Celtic as a branch of comparative literature, but his approach fell short of the scientific standards expected by those subsequent scholars of comparativism. Due to his reliance on secondary texts, Arnold was unable to entirely transcend Romantic and chivalric stereotypes.[18] Within Arnold's model, Celtic genius is characterised by emotion, imagination and an intimate connection to nature's 'fairy charm'. Losers in 'the race of civilisation', the Celtic race is of interest as a relic from the past: for 'what it *has been*, what it *has done*', not for what 'it will be or will do, as a matter of modern politics'. It is the Celts' supposed failure to materially advance – their lack of 'patience for science' – that makes them subjects rather than masters of the 'science of origins' (and fitting subjects of British rule).[19]

However, Arnold also argues for the positive results of the intermixture of Celtic elements in English as well as British identity and literature, and in so doing echoes Masson's much less familiar 'Gaelic and Norse Popular Tales', published in *Macmillan's* five years earlier. If Masson (a Scot) claims that 'the historical superiority of the Gothic race' would be 'difficult to contest', and that the Celt's place is to serve 'imperial unity', he also resists some of the stereotypes later employed by Arnold, producing wide evidence for a Celtic 'aptitude for systematic thought'. Earlier than Arnold, Masson also notes that 'the speculations in ethnology that have been going on for so many years' have led to certain quarters proclaiming 'the intellectual and historical worthlessness of the Celt':

> The wild hysterics of the Celt, his restlessness, his want of veracity, his want of the power of solid and persevering labour, his howling enthusiasm

about nothings and his neglect of all that is substantial, the perpetual necessity of some stern alien labour to keep him in order – these are everyday themes in our tales and our literature. On the other hand, the Saxon features as the tip-top of present creation.

In revealing Campbell's Gaelic folktales to be close counterparts to Dasent's Norse collection (as 'exactly the same kinds of stories about […] giants, fairies, enchantments'), Masson also points to the shared cultural and historical origins of Celt and Teuton, Arnold's 'brothers in the great Indo-European family'.[20] Some months after Masson's article appeared in *Macmillan's*, however, the periodical published a very different contribution to these debates. It was not a scholarly article on the fairy tale but a fiction that sought to be seen as a new addition to that genre: Charles Kingsley's *The Water-Babies: A Fairy Tale for a Landbaby*. When Tom arrives at a salmon river in the October 1862 instalment, the narrator wonders if it is an Irish river, presided over by the 'sly, soft, sleepy, good-natured, untrustable' Dennis. He warns:

> you must not trust Dennis, for he is in the habit of giving pleasant answers; but instead of being angry with him, you must remember that he is a poor Paddy, and knows no better, and burst out laughing; and then he will burst out laughing too, and slave for you, and trot about after you, and show you good sport if he can – for he is an affectionate fellow, and as fond of sport as you are – and if he can't tell you fibs instead, a hundred an hour; and wonder all the while why poor old Ireland does not prosper like England and Scotland and some other places, where folk have taken up a ridiculous fancy that honesty is the best policy.[21]

Although docile and childlike rather than prone to 'wild hysterics', Dennis embodies most of the racial stereotypes that Masson had earlier attacked. Kingsley is far from echoing Masson's defence in the magazine of Irish 'wit, brilliant sociability' and 'intellectual acquisition'.[22] While Kingsley was strongly influenced by Müller, his own theories of race also owed significant debts to other sources: not just to his enthusiastic reading of Darwin but those earlier 'speculations in ethnology'. As Chapter 2 makes clear, in *Good Words for the Young*, Kingsley describes progress from pre-historic times as a 'true fairy tale' enacted through a cycle of conquests; conquests achieved through the invasion of racially 'stronger and bolder people', imposing their will on less developed races. In his 1864 Cambridge lectures *The Roman and the Teuton*, he also uses a fairy-tale metaphor to conceptualise historical progress: the Romans were 'cunning and wicked' Trolls whose 'fairy palace' was finally destroyed by the Teutonic 'children of the forest'. Kingsley argues that Gibbon, who drew 'a parallel between the Red Indian and the Primaeval Teuton', had 'done so at the expense of facts': the Teutons had originated as childlike primitives, while the former were savages. For Kingsley, the Celts in the sixth century were in the latter camp. 'Poor, savage, half-naked' and sometimes cannibalistic, with 'glibs of long hair hanging over their hypogorillaceous visages', they are presented as in desperate need of salvation and St Bridget.[23]

In the January 1863 instalment of *The Water-Babies*, the fable of the Do-As-You-Likes, a human tribe whose idleness leads to starvation and eventual degeneration into apes, combines natural selection with older theories of racial extinction: the tribe degenerates partly because 'the stern old fairy Necessity never came near them to hunt them up, and make them use their wits, or die'. While they resemble 'those jolly old Greeks in Sicily', there are also obvious allusions to post-famine Ireland. When Tom notes that the Do-As-You-Likes in the waterproof book are becoming 'no better than savages', Mrs Be-Done-by-As-You-Did agrees: 'when people live on poor vegetables, instead of roast-beef and plum-pudding, their jaws grow large, and their lips grow coarse, like the poor Paddies who eat potatoes'.[24] In the previous chapter, Tom is told of St Brandan's difficulty in civilising the 'wild Irish' who prefer to 'knock each other over the head with shillelaghs' than to hear the word of God: those who refused to listen 'were changed into gorillas, and gorillas they are until this day'.[25]

Although Kingsley was a monogenist, his claim in *The Water-Babies* that 'people's souls make their bodies, just as a snail makes its shell' (a view which Kingsley endorses in his correspondence) means that moral progress or degeneration are perceived to have physical manifestations.[26] Natural selection is not random but morally directed by the Creator: as Mrs Be-Done-by-As-You-Did states, there is 'a downhill as well as an uphill road; and if I can turn beasts into men, I can by the same laws of circumstance, and selection, and competition, turn men into beasts'.[27] Kingsley's tendency to animalise race and racialise class is linked to such beliefs: it is not just the 'wild Irish' who resisted St Brandon but the heathen English sweep Tom who resembles a 'small black gorilla' and a 'little black ape' at the beginning of the narrative.[28] Yet the same contradictions appear as in 'The True Fairy Tale'. Progress is linked not only to spiritual development, but also to a survival of the fittest, the conquest of weaker by stronger races. Those racial differentials, shaped by natural selection, also seem to be God-given.[29]

Holidaying with Anthony Froude in Ireland in July 1860, Kingsley wrote a letter to his wife that has since become infamous. He describes the poor of Sligo in terms that suggest both savage survivals and a degeneration from the expected place of white races in that God-given hierarchy:

> I am haunted by the human chimpanzees I saw along that hundred miles of horrible country. I don't believe they are our fault. I believe there are not only many more of them than of old, but that they are happier, better, more comfortably lodged and fed under our rule than they ever

were. But to see white chimpanzees is dreadful; if they were black, one would not feel it as much.[30]

Kingsley's words still disturb, but to read *The Water-Babies* in *Macmillan's* is also to see Kingsley's racialism as just one perspective among many: as part of a much wider dialogue about race, language and the origins of myth and folktale, as well as about the *Origin of Species*. There is another significant context: *The Water-Babies* was serialised during the American Civil War, which, as George J. Worth notes, features in the magazine every month during 1862–3. Sometimes articles by 'Our Special Correspondent in America' directly follow instalments of *The Water-Babies*: here, the writer Edward Dicey echoes contributors such as Harriet Martineau and J. M. Ludlow in defending the Union. While Masson and most of *Macmillan's* regular contributors voiced a strong moral and religious opposition to slavery, giving consistent if qualified support for the North, the periodical also published a dissenting voice. A few months after *The Water-Babies* ended, Thomas Carlyle's highly controversial 'Ilias in Americana Nuce' questioned the difference between slavery and indentured labour, and outraged a number of the magazine's fellow contributors.[31]

Kingsley took the history of America as the subject of his Cambridge history lectures for 1862. To Sir Charles Bunbury in December 1861, he wrote that he had thought of 'nothing else' but the American question for some time, noting:

> I cannot see how I can be a Professor of past Modern History without the most careful study of the history that is enacting itself around me. But I can come to no conclusion, save that to which all England seems to have come – that the war will be a gain to us.[32]

As Larry Uffelman and Patrick Scott have shown, Kingsley modified a number of references to the Civil War in the subsequent book revision of *The Water-Babies*. Although his support for the Confederacy has largely been inferred from letters and second-hand accounts of his lectures, some revealing racial references nevertheless pepper *The Water-Babies*.[33] In the November 1862 instalment, Tom encounters a seal which 'looks exactly like a fat old greasy negro'.[34] In the part for January 1863, which includes the fable of the Do-As-You-Likes, there is finally just one member of the tribe left:

> one tremendous old fellow with jaws like a jack, who stood full seven feet high; and M. Du Chaillu came up to him, and shot him, as he stood roaring and thumping his breast. And he remembered that his ancestors had once been men, and tried to say 'Am I not a man and a brother?' but he had forgotten how to use his tongue. [...] So all he said was 'Ubboboo!' and died.[35]

In May 1861, Alexander Macmillan commented that Paul Du Chaillu's book, *Explorations and Adventures in Equatorial Africa*, which described the author's gorilla hunt, would be 'read by the thousand – all the world wonders after the Beast'.[36] Yet it is not just the question of the species barrier – famously debated by Huxley and Owen, as well as foregrounded by Du Chaillu – but the barrier between races that is questioned by the Do-As-You-Likes' appropriation of the old abolitionist slogan. As Amanda Hodgson notes, Kingsley's fable echoes the *Punch* cartoon 'Monkeyana' (1861), in which a Gorilla holds a placard posing a similar question. Yet there are also suggestive parallels with more explicit racist jokes in other contemporary *Punch* contributions. In 'The Missing Link' (1862), 'a tribe of Irish savages', found in 'some of the lowest districts of London and Liverpool by adventurous explorers' is assumed to bridge the species gap between 'the Gorilla and the Negro'.[37]

As Gillian Beer argues, 'the double issue of man's language and of his place in nature was at the centre of mythography and anthropology in the 1860s and 1870s – and they were bound up with the conflict between degradationist and evolutionist views'.[38] They were certainly questions at the heart of *Macmillan's* in the 1860s: as Julia Wedgwood suggested in her article 'Sir Charles Lyell on the Antiquity of Man' (1863), the distinction between 'the theological and the scientific view of man' rested on the question of whether man had fallen from perfection 'or was slowly and painfully working his way upward to that state'.[39] In an earlier article for *Macmillan's* in November 1862, Wedgwood revealed the significance of language in those debates. She quoted Müller's claims that man's language set him apart from the rest of creation. He had possessed (in Müller's words) from his 'most primitive and perfect state [...] the faculty of giving more articulate expression to the rational conceptions of his own mind'.[40]

Müller was able to state his case directly when one of his lectures was published in *Macmillan's* four months later, asserting that the science of language confirmed that 'the whole natural creation tends towards man'.[41] All these articles appeared while *The Water-Babies* was in serialisation. It is no revelation to suggest that Kingsley's text was shaped by his warm correspondence with Darwin, his attentive reading of Lyell and his intimate friendships with T. H. Huxley and Müller.[42] More revealing, perhaps, is the fact that many of *The Water-Babies*' first readers would have known all of these writers too, simply through browsing the pages of *Macmillan's*.[43] Regular readers would be able to see the fable of the 'Do-As-You-Likes' in the context of the magazine's wider explications of philological and ethnological, Christian and scientific constructions of mankind. In debating whether man was truly separate from beast, and in questioning if his future would be marked by descent or ascent, Kingsley's mythmaking, as E. B. Tylor was aware, went to the very heart of what it meant to be human.[44]

Servants, sweeps and Cinderellas: Darwinian fairy tales

In 1860–1, *Macmillan's Magazine* published one of many responses to Darwin's *Origin of Species* – a two part contribution structured as a Platonic dialogue. In Julia Wedgwood's article, Philocalos is troubled by the implications of a nature in which 'selfishness and progress are linked'; in which care for the sick and infirm might be viewed as an evolutionary impediment. Philolethes, however, argues that evolution can be viewed as morally as well as physically progressive:

> [the Creator] furnishes a clue to a higher state of being, in the principle which rewards every step in the right direction with the predominance of the successful type over its rivals in the struggle for existence [...]. What a depth of meaning de we find in such a view of creation as this – of such mighty changes accomplished through such faint and dim gradations, such innumerable failures for one success, such a slow and such an unpausing movement in the stream of creation, widening towards the mighty ocean! Then, indeed, we hear the voice of a teacher in nature. 'My child,' she seems to say, 'you must work as I have worked'.[45]

Wedgwood's evolutionary metaphor – a stream widening into a 'mighty ocean' – and her female teacher in nature, who resolves natural selection and natural theology, reappear, more memorably, in *Macmillan's* two years later, as Charles Kingsley narrates the underwater journey of his chimney sweep Tom in *The Water-Babies*. The tensions in Wedgwood's dialogue are present in Kingsley's fiction too. If the voice of nature oversees moral as well as physical 'steps in the right direction' – the individual's spiritual journey as well as the gradual transmutation of species – what are we to make of 'those innumerable failures for one success'?

The Christian Socialist origins of *Macmillan's* were obvious from the beginning: Alexander Macmillan and David Masson had both been active in the movement, while the magazine drew regular contributors from among its former guiding lights (Thomas Hughes, Charles Kingsley, J. M. Ludlow and F. D. Maurice). If these influences were never far from the surface, the promotion of dialogue across disciplines was also a professed aim from the first. In *Macmillan's* pages, discussions of the *Origin* appeared side by side with articles on the urban poor, and religious, biological and social debates were intimately related. Exploring some of the theories of evolution discussed in the early years of *Macmillan's*, it is also possible to see the conflict between its spirit of open intellectual inquiry and the more directive impulses at work in the magazine. For despite that liberal championing of dialogue, *Macmillan's* founders and key contributors often tried to accommodate *all* theories of evolution within a master narrative, a symbolic framework that revealed a Creator in the universe.

That framework is clearly assumed in *Macmillan's* review of Samuel Smiles's *Self-Help* in March 1860, which both welcomes Smiles's text and signals a note of caution. The writer, Richard Chermside, notes that it is mutual help, as much as self-help, that is at the heart of many of Smiles's success stories, arguing that individuality is revealed to each person by God through the agency of others. It is only to an extent, Chermside argues, that helping men – or classes – takes away the stimulus of doing for themselves.[46] In *Macmillan's* writings on the poor, such unease is often apparent, as writers struggle to come to terms with the relationships between economic liberalism, biological determinism and religious notions of moral duty.

In some contributions, poverty is linked directly to financial improvidence – to a failure of self-help. In 'The Artisan's Saturday Night' of August 1860, Percy Greg uses terminology that directly echoes Darwin's 'struggle for existence'. He notes the 'picturesque and interesting effect' created by humanity waging 'a hard and earnest struggle [...] in the Battle of Life'. That struggle is to be witnessed on a Saturday night in the working-class districts of London, as the poor make their purchases after collecting their Saturday wages. Noting that 'the effective desire for accumulation is very weak with them', Greg compares such English artisans to the Indian converts of Paraguay:

> And this, not because the men were idle, or stupid, or sensual; but because they were incapable of taking tomorrow into account; because they were, in a literal sense of the word, improvident – unforseeing. Our English artisans resemble these Indians not a little in the economy of their domestic arrangements.[47]

In a later article for *Fraser's*, 'the Failure of Natural Selection in the Case of Man' (1868), this liberal economist explicitly divides society into 'fit' and 'unfit' sectors, seeing an evolutionary impediment in an unproductive landed aristocracy, as well as an overly fertile working class.[48] Charles Alston Collins displays debts to Spencer as well as Darwin when he slips into a vocabulary that seems to conflate social reform with a racial survival of the fittest. In his article 'Beggars', published in *Macmillan's* in January 1862, Collins notes:

> I have always regarded the silent beggar with immense dislike and suspicion, believing him to be a terrific savage in his family, and a wild and violent reveller in the dark slums of London. [...] The days must surely be at hand when these things are better looked after than they are at present; and when the devouring tribes are no longer known amongst us, it will be interesting to have a record of their existence, as of any other obsolete species.[49]

Collins reveals that many of the beggars are children: 'hordes of young ragamuffins' who extort money from passers by turning summersaults and cartwheels by the side of cabs and omnibuses. Collins's article is clearly meant to create a provocative dialogue with a contribution published in the same issue of *Macmillan's*: Knightly Howman's 'The Fauna of the Streets', which shows the most sustained (if playful) application of evolutionary theory to the London poor. Howman references Chambers's *Vestiges of the Natural History of Creation*, Gosse's *The Romance of Natural History* and Darwin's *Origin*, making a direct analogy between Darwin's example of cave-dwelling animals that have gradually become blind and the London child of the alleys, streets and slums.[50] Noting the compensatory characteristics that Darwin argued such animals could sometimes develop through natural selection, Howman claims that

> There seems to be no good reason for restricting this kindly law to the brute creation. [...] for where an abnormal state of existence has been the birth-lot of any creature, Nature, in pity, makes the best amends she can, or at least schools the sufferer into a patient endurance of evils, which she is otherwise powerless to control [...]
>
> But for the influence of some such gentle discipline, how shall we account for the uncomplaining fortitude (greater than mere Stoic endurance) of the aborigines of the London streets? [...] What a study in natural history is the genuine London child [...]

Here, nature is constructed as both blind and directionless, with no powers to avert suffering, and yet endowed with some moral foresight: an ability to make minimal amends through the benevolence of a 'kindly law'. The limited and ameliorative powers granted to nature mirrors the conception of social reform propounded by a number of *Macmillan's* contributors. In describing the same child beggars, turning cartwheels on London thoroughfares, that were pictured by Collins, Howman makes a fanciful biological analogy. Crossing Waterloo Bridge, he suggests that a visitor from the country will find:

> His progress will be heralded by an apparition, which he might take as a well-grown specimen of the *Volvox globator*, or wheel insect; an acrobat, whose performances may be witnessed on the stage of the microscope – in a theatre whose drop scene is supplied by the fluid of any Metropolitan water Company [...]. On closer inspection, the phenomenon will resolve itself into a ragged urchin.[51]

Readers of George Henry Lewes's contributions to the *Cornhill* would know all about the *volvox globator*, one of the pond dwellers discussed in his second chapter of 'Studies in Animal Life'.[52] Howman's article is urban anthropology as biological romance, the working-class street child appearing in a form as mysterious and wonderful as the revelations of Darwin – and provoking the same sense of strangeness and discovery. In the first part of

The Water-Babies, published seven months later, readers are introduced to Tom, a northern child sweep who, like the London street children, could 'keep up for a couple of miles with any stagecoach, if there was the chance of a copper or cigar-end, and turn coach wheels on his hands and feet ten times following'.[53] In the second serialised instalment, Tom dies and is transformed into an underwater creature more amazing than the *volvox globator*: a four inch Water Baby with his own external gills.

In fact, Kingsley's 'fairy-tale for a land baby' – which he began writing a few months after these articles appeared – seems no more fantastic than much of *Macmillan's* non-fictional writing on child poverty published in the same year. In his own article, Howman maintains that it is not God's will that one of these children should perish; there is an implied critique of Malthus and Spencer, when he laments that such children are currently consigned to 'that little coffin which the creed of certain political economists would teach us to regard as the dust-bin of surplus population'.[54] Yet, for both Howman and Kingsley, religious and moral duty towards such children is mixed with fascination for a class so strange that it is almost another species. Empathy sits uneasily with wonder and distance, evolutionary romance with social critique.

Darwinian fantasy was not the prerogative of *Macmillan's* alone. In the *Cornhill* article 'A Vision of Animal Existences', published five months before *The Water-Babies* began its serialisation, the narrator encounters a seemingly respectable woman at a zoo who transpires to be something rather more sinister: her card reads 'Natural Selection! – Originator of Species!!' and she is accompanied by her son 'Struggle-for-Life'. While this is revealed to be a dream vision, inspired by the sight of a female author reading the *Origin*, the narrator's concerns remain – that it seems to be 'the way of the world in human society as well as with brute animals' for the strong to trample on the 'prostrate bodies' of the weak.[55] The *Cornhill*, like *Macmillan's*, also recast class relations as a form of Darwinian fantasy. In Anne Thackeray Ritchie's 'Betsinda and her Bun', published in the magazine in 1877, she divides the inhabitants of London into 'those who live above and those who live below the ground', her observation of class polarisation anticipating the species differentiation of H. G. Wells's *The Time Machine*:

> I could imagine a Darwin belonging to some future age and race describing the habits of the different occupants of our ant-heap, and telling us how the smaller and more shabby ants wait upon the large white race, who allow themselves to be fed and tended by the inferior creatures, and are utterly at a loss without them.

In the main body of the article, however, Thackeray Ritchie jettisons this arresting dystopian image in favour of a metaphor from a modern fairy-tale fiction: her father's Christmas book *The Rose and the Ring* (1855). In W. M. Thackeray's comic burlesque, the penniless Betsinda is taken in as a maid in the royal household of King Valoroso XXIV. She is later revealed to be Princess Rosalba, the lost daughter of a neighbouring kingdom. By linking the buns offered by middle-class women to servant girls at charitable teas with the Princess Angelica's offer of her own (unwanted) bun to Betsinda, Thackeray Ritchie brings a more playful tone to her article: but she also suggests some ambivalence towards complacent middle-class philanthropy. As she describes the real maidservants at a charitable tea party, stunted 'like a little company of dwarfs', their histories of starvation and abuse become a macabre '"Arabian Nights" entertainment', gesturing uncomfortably towards the 'attraction of repulsion' that their life stories offer the *Cornhill*'s middle-class readers.[56] Thackeray Ritchie's suggestions for reform are certainly ameliorative – she encourages support for an organisation which uses a system of voluntary inspectors to check the worst abuses. Yet 'fancy', rather than simply evoking sympathy, defamiliarises the reader, disorientates and disturbs.

Writing to Tennyson in November 1859, Alexander Macmillan directed him specifically to T. H. Huxley's article 'Time and Life: On Mr Darwin's *Origin of Species*' in *Macmillan's* second number. Macmillan remarked that

> Darwin's book which it mentions is remarkable certainly. I thought of 'Nature red in tooth and claw' as I was glancing over it. I wish someone would bring out the other side. But surely the scientific men ought on no account to be hindered from saying what they find as facts.[57]

In fact, from the beginning, *Macmillan's* did bring out another side. This was accomplished not by questioning the scientific foundation of the *Origin*, but by embracing evolutionary biology as Divine revelation. In Julia Wedgwood's first article, Philalethes argues that the work of agnostic scientists is still of value for believers: those scientists are in fact 'translating for you a symbol'.[58] A month before the publication of the first part of *The Water-Babies*, *Macmillan's* published Alexander Campbell Fraser's article 'The Real World of Berkeley', in which Fraser argues that Berkeley's philosophy might offer a way of resolving the antagonism between faith and science. Fraser endorses Berkeley's belief that 'The language of vision is part of that language of God, of which all physical science is an attempted interpretation'. And, he suggests:

> If this be so, may we not further ask, why men disturb themselves in theology with vexed scientific questions about the creation and development of that material world, which, for all that reason can determine, may be a language in which the Supreme is eternally revealing himself? [The pious mind] is ready to consign to science all questions of evolution

and development [...] Perpetual moral *Providence* in the material system, and not the absolute *creation* of matter, is the object of religious faith.

There are further echoes of Wedgwood's article in Fraser's claim that for Berkeley, the act of seeing involves 'tracing the relations of arbitrary signs. We are, to all extents, interpreting a language. We are reading a book'.[59] In *Macmillan's*, then, improvidence was linked to a spiritual as well as a material lack of foresight – to a failure to decipher the signs that signify God's presence in the universe. At the beginning of *The Water-Babies*, Tom is unable to recognise a picture of Christ on Ellie's wall.[60] During his underwater journey, he must use scientific observation to interpret the symbols of nature, moving closer to the revelation of the mind of a God who does not make species but makes beasts 'make themselves' – who sets evolution in train.[61] And it is through help from others, as well as Smilesian self-help, that Tom moves closer, in moral terms, to a knowledge of God's perfection. That such a process is impossible for Tom when he is alive is the text's biggest problem (and most obvious irony): no spiritual journey on earth is possible for a child consigned to the dustbin of surplus population.

Suggesting that *Macmillan's* was a magazine that 'no child was likely to encounter', Brian Alderson argues that *The Water-Babies*' repeated address to 'my little man' is less an implied reader and more 'an innocent screen' for an adult-orientated polemic.[62] It is certainly true that *The Water-Babies* in *Macmillan's* is a darker work than the 'attractive seaside companion' published a few months later.[63] Much criticism of *The Water-Babies* has drawn attention to the fact that Tom is 'watched over always by the Irishwoman', a face of the Divine who seems to undercut Kingsley's racial descriptions elsewhere, and who, from the very beginning, safeguards Tom on his moral and spiritual journey.[64] Yet there is no such Irishwoman – or benign fairy – to guide Tom in the serial text. In the chapter in which Tom's body is found – 'a black thing in the water' – the work's uncertain narrative tone is most apparent ('Don't you know that this is a fairy tale, and all fun and pretence, and that you are not to believe a word of it, even if it is true?').[65] Tom's transmutation into a Water Baby may be a fairy tale offered in the face of society's moral failures, but it is still an uneasy consolation.

Like 'The Little Match-Girl', Tom ultimately goes to a better place, and there are other fairy-tale echoes in Kingsley's fiction. Valentine Cunningham argues that *The Water-Babies*' appropriation of Cinderella motifs to explore the fate of the socially marginalised tapped into 'collective neuroses': 'as a model for the Victorian working-class, especially its children, in relation to the Victorian bourgeoisie the figure of the ash-brother could not be more apt'.[66] Cunningham is quite right about the metaphor's widespread appeal: in the *Chambers's* article 'Cinderella Downstairs' (1882), readers were assumed to feel pity for the female child servant who had never had a childhood, yet were also expected to regard her as inevitable: as 'one of the necessities of our crowded cities'.[67] In the 1860s, however, the motif was also used to explore class relations from a different angle. In Thackeray Ritchie's *Cornhill* short story 'Cinderella' (June 1866), 'Ella' is not a child worker but a respectable upper-middle-class girl whose deprivations are caused by her jealous stepmother. Her fairy godmother, Lady Jane Peppercorn, has no supernatural powers, but something just as effective: maids appear 'as if by magic', and she takes Ella to the Crystal Palace through the service of her lower-class entourage. Peppercorn's servants are workhouse boys, who come to her 'as thin as church mice': while she 'feeds 'em up and gives 'em situations', Lady Jane is eager to signal her distance from both universal suffrage and Gladstone.[68]

In fact, the fairy tale becomes a tool with which to conceptualise class relations across a range of Thackeray Ritchie's writing for the *Cornhill*. In her non-fictional article 'Maids-of-All-Work and Blue Books' (1874), she compares the exploited maid-of-all-work to the 'benevolent race of little pixies who live underground in subterranean passages and galleries' described by Walter Scott. In her earlier *Cornhill* short story 'Beauty and the Beast' (June 1867), the narrator, Miss Williamson, muses:

> Fairy times, gifts, music and dances are said to be over, or, as it has been said, they come to us so disguised and made familiar by habit that they do not seem to us strange. H. and I, on either side of the hearth, these long winter evenings could sit without fear of fiery dwarfs skipping out of the ashes, or black puddings coming down the chimney to molest us [...] As for wishing-cloths and little boiling pots, and such like, we have discovered that instead of rubbing lamps, or spreading magic tablecloths upon the floor, we have but to ring an invisible bell (which is even less trouble), and a smiling genius in a white cap and apron brings in anything we happen to fancy.

Fairy-tale metaphors offer new ways of seeing social relations that are 'disguised and made familiar by habit' (both in everyday life and domestic realism). Yet by replacing supernatural agency with realist plot development ('there are no real fairies in stories such as mine'), these adult-orientated short stories sometimes foreground the conventions – and the evasions – of fairy tales too. When poverty and wealth are structural, there is a compromised form of wish-fulfilment: marriage and the stock market may effect limited upward or downward mobility, but the low-born cannot easily rise. In 'Beauty and the Beast', Miss Williamson wryly questions the expected moral agency of the fairy-tale protagonist: 'Circumstance orders events sometimes, when people themselves, with all their powers and knowledge of good and evil, are but passive instruments in the hands of fate'.[69]

Sleeping beauty and the prince's progress: 'The woman question'

Thackeray Ritchie was not the only writer to foreground the fairy-tale heroine's lack of agency. Three months after the final part of the *Water-Babies* in *Macmillan's*, the periodical published Christina Rossetti's 'The Fairy Prince Who Arrived Too Late' (May 1863). Only six stanzas in length, the poem includes little of the pre-Raphaelite imagery, and none of the Prince's complex quest narrative that would later be incorporated into the 'The Prince's Progress', the narrative poem that would form the title work of Rossetti's second collection of poems (1866). The *Macmillan's* version begins with the later poem's bleak denouement, the censure of the prince by the princess's lamenting attendants:

> Too late for love, too late for joy,
> Too late, too late!
> You loitered on the road too long, you trifled at the gate:
> The enchanted dove upon her branch
> Died without a mate;
> The enchanted princess in her tower
> Slept – died behind the grate;
> Her heart was starving all this while
> You made it wait.

The princess, whose tones were 'sweet / And modulated' and who never spoke 'in haste', waits decades in perfect stillness for a prince who she will never see. Without the framework of the subsequent revision, it is less easy to see the prince's journey in this poem as a religious allegory about a soul in peril, a failed Pilgrim's Progress: we never see from the prince's perspective, and are aware of none of the trials or temptations that shape the later poem's quest.[70] Whether the princess's self-renunciation and passive suffering should be exulted or questioned is left for the reader to interpret. There can be no doubt about the failure of the prince.[71]

This dark inversion of 'Sleeping Beauty' was just one of 21 poems by Rossetti published in *Macmillan's* between 1861 and 1868.[72] If Ruskin hadn't cavilled at her 'quaintnesses' and 'irregular measure', Rossetti's most famous poem may also have made its debut in a shilling magazine. Dante Gabriel Rossetti initially gave 'Goblin Market' to Ruskin in the hope that he might 'say a good word for something of Christina's to *Cornhill*'.[73] By October 1861, however, the poem was in the hands of Alexander Macmillan, who introduced it to a rather different audience:

> I took the liberty of reading the *Goblin Market* aloud to a number of people belonging to a small working-man's society here [Cambridge]. They

seemed at first to wonder whether I was making fun of them; by degrees they got as still as death, and when I finished there was a tremendous burst of applause[74]

Goblin Market and other Poems was published as a Macmillan Christmas volume in 1862. By the time it was reviewed by Caroline Norton in *Macmillan's Magazine* in September 1863, the title poem's reputation for ambiguity – its capacity to confuse, startle and enthral – was already well established. Rossetti's poem had something in common with Kingsley's *The Water-Babies* after all, for, as Norton noted:

> The 'Goblin Market', by Miss Christina Rossetti, is one of the works which are said to 'defy criticism.' Is it a fable – or a mere fairy story – or an allegory against the pleasures of sinful love – or what is it? Let us not too rigorously inquire, but accept it in all its quaint and pleasant mystery, and quick and musical rhythm – a ballad which children will con with delight, and which riper minds may ponder over, as we do with poems written in a foreign language which we only half understand.

'Goblin Market' was paired in Norton's review with another Macmillan volume of a 'very different nature': Coventry Patmore's *The Angel in the House*. Patmore's title poem, which concerns, in Norton's words, 'the wooing and winning of a life-companion in the shape of a virtuous wife' was eulogised. Readers were encouraged to read the poem and 'study the lesson that reads so like a romance'. The same review reproduced close to two hundred lines of 'Goblin Market', including the most sexually suggestive passages. The few lines of interpretation ('One thing is certain; we ought not to buy fruit from goblin men') suggest a moral stance, but eschew deeper inquiry. Readers were left to find their own interpretations of Rossetti's most arresting lines: Laura 'trod and hustled' by goblins, devouring the pleasures of goblin fruit, and finally redeemed by Lizzie in charged Eucharistic imagery: 'Hug me, kisss me, suck my juices'; 'eat me, drink me, love me'.[75]

Perhaps more than any other poem, 'Goblin Market' (an adult text that has appeared in both children's anthologies and *Playboy*) provides an example of the ways in which the contexts of reading can shape meanings that cut against authorial intention.[76] Yet 'The Fairy Prince Who Arrived Too Late' also raises questions about what it means to read Christina Rossetti in context. If the masculine 'beer and tobacco parliament' of *Macmillan's* opening colloquy obscured women's significant role as contributors, the policy of signing did not: there were a significant number of high profile female (and feminist) contributors to the magazine in the 1860s, including Harriet Taylor, Elizabeth Garrett, Millicent Garrett Fawcett and Frances Power Cobbe. Andrea Broomfield has noted at least 25 articles that advocated women's rights in the pages of *Macmillan's* between 1859 and 1883.[77] While the *Cornhill* was more circumspect than *Macmillan's* when engaging with political controversies (and its female contributors were normally veiled by anonymity), it also published articles on female education, including Harriet Martineau's 'Middle Class Education in England: Girls', which appeared in the *Cornhill* the year after Rossetti's 'Fairy Prince' in *Macmillan's*. While Martineau is eager to emphasise the importance of domestic accomplishments, she also champions female higher education, including the provision of Latin and Greek. While in favour of education organised independently by the middle classes rather than centrally by the state, she suggests that no examinations are 'more valuable' than those obtained by 'women proposing to be educators, or professional workers', singling out Elizabeth Garrett's medical training for praise. Martineau argues:

> Not all the ignorance, the jealousy, the meanness, the prudery, or the profligate selfishness which is found from end to end of the middle class, can now reverse the destiny of the English girl, or retard the ennobling of the sex which is the natural consequence of it becoming wiser and more independent, while more accomplished, gracious and companionable. The briars and brambles are cleared away from the women's avenue to the temple of knowledge. Now they have only to knock, and it will be opened to them'.[78]

Writing on attitudes to female education in the *Cornhill* in the 1860s, Jennifer Phegley suggests that articles that advocated women's educational advancement frequently merged 'fact with fiction in an attempt to ease the potentially jarring nature of their proto-feminist rhetoric'. In Martineau's article, it is not merely fact and fiction, but fact and fairy tale that are fused.[79] Indeed, the use of 'Sleeping Beauty' analogies in debates over female education appeared elsewhere in the *Cornhill* in the years that followed. In Thackeray Ritchie's short story 'The Sleeping Beauty in the Wood', published in May 1866, Cecelia is an unlikely heroine, beautiful but intellectually stultified by her upbringing. Accustomed to 'embroidering interminable quilts and braided toilet-covers and fish-napkins', she 'considered that being respectable and decorous, and a little pompous and overbearing, was the duty of every well-brought-up lady and gentleman'. Cecilia's sleep is a metaphoric one; her dormant state is the product of social ignorance, her entrapment within outmoded codes of feminine respectability.

The narrator, Miss Williamson, regards Cecilia's upbringing as 'unutterably dull, commonplace, respectable, stinted, ugly and useless'. Yet Thackeray Ritchie's tale is not merely a critique of the sequestered female, but a wry reflection on the fairy-tale and realist codes that valorise her passivity. When she meets her cousin (Victorian realism's answer to the fairy-tale prince), Cecilia has been so infantilised that she does not know how to react. Even her great aunt (pointedly named Mrs Dormer) realises that the ideal of the passive heroine has its drawbacks:

> 'The girl is a greater idiot than I took her for,' cried the old lady. 'She has been kept here locked up, until she has not a single idea left in her silly noddle. No man of sense could endure her for five minutes'.

Although Cecilia marries her cousin (the middle-class 'prince') and escapes the parental home, the marital resolution is treated hastily and with some irony: 'Certainly the story would not have been worth the telling if they had not been married soon after, and lived happily all the rest of their lives'. In Thackeray Ritchie's tales, the clichéd inner resolutions are frequently at odds with the framing narrative. The contented elderly spinster Miss Williamson has evaded her own marital resolution, the expected happy ending of the fairy tale and realism alike.[80]

Thackeray Ritchie's 'Sleeping Beauty in the Wood' offers some suggestive parallels and contrasts with Barbara Bodichon's 'A Dull Life', published in *Macmillan's* a year later. Bodichon's non-fiction article, a reminiscence about a visit to Louisiana in 1858, also centres on a 'Cecilia', who is in many respects similar to Thackeray Ritchie's fictional protagonist: under the sway of an overbearing grandmother, she is infantilised and unreflective, 'listless, and without any feeling, or desire, or restlessness'; dull, in part, 'because she was a young lady with nothing to do and very little education'. But this Cecilia is the daughter of New Orleans slave owners, and a corollary of her isolation and ignorance is her failure to reflect on the horror and injustice of the institution. Bodichon's article draws together *Macmillan's* wider debates over education, the American Civil War and race, yet the conclusions of this notable feminist are somewhat surprising:

> I sat silently wondering at this dull life, and thinking of all the avenues to activity open in any little town in England for a young lady like Cecilia – the church, the chapel, the little social societies for charity, all of which occupy those who are too poor or too pious for balls, picnics and country gaieties.[81]

In contrast, Thackeray Ritchie's fictional Cecilia seems to suggest that such 'a dull life' could be all too possible at home.

In 1861, Thackeray Ritchie used her *Cornhill* article 'Toilers and Spinsters' to offer an account of the privations of lower-class female workers as well as a defence of professional opportunities for women. While she revised the article in the early 1870s to include a footnote giving cautious support to women's suffrage, she did not make this call in the pages of the *Cornhill*.[82] In *Macmillan's* in the 1860s, however, a few writers confronted this question head on. One supporter of female suffrage was Charles Kingsley, who used his article 'Women and Politics' (1869) to strongly endorse Mill's *The Subjection of Women*, a book he assumed was already known 'to every reader' of *Macmillan's*.[83] Christina Rossetti famously set herself apart from such views. Declining Augusta Webster's request that she endorse women's suffrage, Rossetti argued that such social movements did not 'tend on the whole' to uphold Christianity, therefore she could not 'aim at "women's rights"'.[84] Yet one of the achievements of 'The Fairy Prince Who Arrived Too Late' is its ability to provoke very different kinds of readings to those its author may have intended. In *Macmillan's*, some regular subscribers may have seen the poem in new ways after reading those later articles on the 'woman question'. Others, employing the Christian interpretative strategies in which *Macmillan's* readers were expected to be adept, may have bypassed secular meanings in search of spiritual truths.

By the beginning of the next century, the educational possibilities for women looked very different, but Sleeping-Beauty metaphors continued to live on. In her non-fictional *Cornhill* article 'Egeria in Brighton' (1901), the parallels with, and differences from, Thackeray Ritchie's fictional 'Sleeping Beauty in the Wood' quickly become apparent. It is now education, not marriage, that promises to awaken middle-class women from their socially inflicted dormancy. Thackeray Ritchie aligns the Fairy Blackstick (from her father's *The Rose and the Ring*) with Elizabeth Garrett Anderson. The fairy prince is now female self-development, which promises to wake the slumbering 'Princess of Education':

> Princess! Princesses would be more to the point. […] Wherever one turns one sees them rubbing their beautiful eyes. They are in the north, and on the southern cliffs; they are in the old collegiate cities, in the London suburbs, in the heart of England's green-enclosing groves. All these Sleeping Beauties may have lain dormant for a time; but lo! they start up with wide-open eyes when that charming prince, Enthusiasm, calls them from their slumbers with a kiss.[85]

Thackeray Ritchie's short stories, dismissed by a number of recent critics, create rather different meanings in relation to her *Cornhill* non-fiction, and perhaps deserve a second look.[86]

Thackeray Ritchie's elderly spinster narrator Miss Williamson and her female listener H. may wink at fairy-tale predecessors, but they also nod towards the narrative frame of a more recent realist serial text: Elizabeth Gaskell's 'Cranford', published in Dickens's *Household Words* (1851–3).[87] Employing, like Gaskell, an episodic and open-ended structure, Thackeray Ritchie's tales also have an unexpected connection with Kingsley's text, for both postpone and question a final resolution. *The Water-Babies*' attempt – and ultimate inability – to balance open-endedness and moral judgement is in many ways characteristic of *Macmillan's* itself. For while the periodical sought to present science untrammelled by religious orthodoxy – notably demonstrated by numerous contributions from T. H. Huxley – there were limits to its liberal debate. Both Philocalos and Philolethes in Wedgwood's dialogue are believers: if one condemns the *Origin*'s materialist implications, the other can confidently reconcile a Creator with natural selection. While Kingsley's fiction consistently undercuts its own fairy-tale rhetoric, he is also insistent that there 'must be fairies'. Kingsley's own faith in a Divine plan (which shapes Tom's moral agency as Protestant Englishman) suggests that the latent meanings of *The Water-Babies* may not have been so inconsistent to their author: the fairy tale as a symbol for belief and the Divine is expected to be taken as 'true'.

Gillian Beer has argued that 'mythologizing may be as much a way of keeping problems in suspense as of solving them. It makes endurable the contemplation of irreconcilable contraries'.[88] The Sir John of Kingsley's narrative bears an uncanny resemblance to the Sir John who appears among the meeting of minds and classes at *Macmillan's* opening Colloquy – eager for the hunt, and the defeat of humbug, he is a symbol of aristocratic and feudal English tradition (he even recites a ballad about the son of 'Old King Cole'). Kingsley's heroic squire is also part of the fairy tale: when Darwin joined his sister in 1852 in protesting against the 'scandalous violation of the Act against children climbing chimneys', he had noted that 'the brutal Shropshire squires are hard as stones to move'.[89] As the next chapter reveals, labour newspapers in the 1890s would appropriate the fairy tale for less politically ambiguous ends than Kingsley's, campaigning for a socialist government as well as subscribing to a free 'religion of socialism'. The term 'Christian Socialism', used to describe the early affiliations of Kingsley and his *Macmillan's* contemporaries, now seems something of a misnomer, for their writings were of a very different stamp to those of the socialists that followed.[90] In both *Cornhill* and *Macmillan's*, the fairy tale was used to disturb and to expose social injustice, but not necessarily to find lasting political solutions. For the enigma of class relations, there seemed to be no satisfactory happy ending: fantasy as well as realism could keep that problem very much in suspense.

4
'I wonder were the fairies Socialists?': The Politics of the Fairy Tale in the 1890s Labour Press

> They always wore a red cap, and were sometimes called 'the little red caps'. I wonder were the fairies Socialists, for Socialists believe in the 'red cap of liberty', as they call it.[1]

> 'Look here,' said Mon-o-Poly, 'you know these dogs we keep, I mean the Press Curs, let's set them onto Jack. They'll soon tear him to pieces, see if they don't'.[2]

In Keir Hardie's 1895 fairy tale, 'Jack Clearhead', the reader first encounters the maiden 'Social-Ism' imprisoned within a dungeon, with the 'Press Curs' attempting to tear a piece out of her dress. As the tale's publication in the *Labour Leader* demonstrates, however, such movements were developing a media voice of their own: the 1890s, key years in the genesis of British socialism, was also a seminal period in the development of the labour press. As Oscar Wilde published his fairy tales for middle-class and coterie audiences, the *Labour Leader*, the *Clarion* and the *Labour Prophet* were also rewriting this genre. The afterlives of these texts could hardly be more different. Wilde's fictions remain familiar to twenty-first-century audiences, while Keir Hardie's fairy tales are neglected curiosities even within labour history.

This chapter contextualises these forgotten attempts to claim the fairy tale for socialism, examining this genre's ideological appropriation within left-wing periodicals of the 1890s. These papers provide a window on a largely unexplored reading audience, and the interaction between such fictions and their wider publication contexts not only offers insights into the continual politicisation of the fairy tale, but reveals a fascinating point of intersection between Victorian children's literature, working-class culture and socialist educational practices. While Robert Blatchford's *Clarion* inevitably features here, more sustained analysis is offered of two less familiar socialist periodicals: Keir Hardie's weekly *Labour Leader* and John Trevor's monthly *Labour Prophet*.[3] In the 1890s, these penny papers used children's columns as experimental sites of child education, placing a significant focus on the fairy tale.

Here, I explore the way original, adapted and translated fairy tales dovetailed with these papers' wider evolutionary and political teleologies, tracing the unexpected affiliations between this genre and the ethical positions at the heart of a *fin-de-siècle* 'religion' of socialism.

'A precarious existence': Strategies for survival in the 1890s socialist press

Marked by the formation of Marxist organisations such as the Social Democratic Federation (1884), the rise of ethical socialism culminating in the Independent Labour Party (ILP, 1892–3) and the growth of Fabian socialism, the mid-1880s to early 1890s has been memorably described by Stephen Yeo as 'the religion of socialism' phase: a period in which activists from a variety of socialist schisms prepared for a new political dawn with considerable fervour.[4] In a period in which the success of the New Unionism (most visible in the Dock Strike of 1889) appeared to augur success for a mass labour movement, political organisations across the spectrum of socialism made the publication of a consciousness-raising organ an integral part of their mission. Of all the socialist papers that furthered that mission, Robert Blatchford's *Clarion* is the best remembered. Styled as a 'pioneer of the Journalism of the future', the paper astutely blended socialism with the techniques of the New Journalism. Launched in 1891, it attracted audiences of 30,000–60,000, and has been claimed as Britain's first mass-circulation socialist paper.[5] Blatchford's success, however, was the exception rather than the rule. In general, the 1890s saw the appearance of socialist-activist editors whose papers (often selling for a 'democratic penny' or less) found politically engaged but small audiences and normally ran at a loss.[6] In his opening editorial for the *Labour Prophet* in 1892, John Trevor captures the invidious position of such socialist editors when he states:

> we shall get nearer to God and His truth in the world in company with the few labour papers which lead such a precarious existence, coming and going like the leaves on the trees of the forest, than with all the 'religious press' of our Christian land.[7]

Such statements of principle had clear commercial costs. Deian Hopkin has observed that an ephemeral socialist press had become a significant presence by the last decade of the nineteenth century: 'Although Great Britain never developed the kind of mass circulation socialist press that emerged in Germany or the United States, there were nevertheless several hundred papers, ranging from dailies to quarterlies, published between 1890 and 1914.'[8] In its first decade, the ILP alone published over seventy papers.[9] Yet this was truly a transient literature, papers often surviving for a few years at most. Their editors faced a recurrent conundrum: while a low price was necessary to attract working-class readers, small circulations and low advertising revenue made commercial viability impossible.

A number of the socialist periodicals of the 1880s and 1890s that achieved some longevity did so through the financial support of middle-class campaigners. Despite being produced 'in the avowed interests of the working-class', communist, anarchist or socialist papers were not necessarily run by such workers themselves.[10] William Morris's Marxist *Commonweal*, the journal of the Social Democratic Federation breakaway movement the Socialist League, was launched in 1883 and kept going by donations from Morris and his supporters, with Morris himself supplying around £500 a year.[11] In the 1890s, papers as diverse as the weekly official Social Democratic Federation organ *Justice* (launched in January 1884 under H. M. Hyndman), Keir Hardie's larger-scale *Labour Leader* and John Trevor's small-scale *Labour Prophet* were still relying on subsidies from editors and readers. As manager/editor of the *Labour Leader*, Keir Hardie ploughed his own resources into the paper, even allegedly mortgaging his life-insurance.[12] John Trevor embraced similar financial risks when he launched the *Labour Prophet*. While he initially took the paper's cost as a personal liability, a circulation of 5000 made such a burden untenable by 1894.[13] His response was revealing. In March of that year, he altered the paper's title to *Prophet: A Monthly Magazine of Personal and Social Life*. By transferring some Labour Church business to Keir Hardie's now weekly *Labour Leader*, Trevor planned to produce a more commercially viable periodical. It was conceived as 'an illustrated Magazine, in which, while the quantity would be more limited, the quality should be of the best'.[14]

Trevor's editorial change of direction and the controversy that ensued might be seen to reveal in microcosm the contradictory impulses at work in the socialist press of the 1890s, torn by the demands of political doctrine and the necessities of the marketplace. The paper's fiercely dedicated band of readers demanded the return of the original periodical, Trevor reporting that 'friends write to me as though they had suffered some sudden bereavement'. In a newly restored edition of the *Labour Prophet*, Trevor was obliged to state that the paper was 'still faithful', adding that 'the omission of "that blessed word" LABOUR from the title, produced an effect quite beyond my expectations'. The active engagement of readers concerning issues of both form and political content gave such small-scale socialist papers a distinctive intimacy, and audiences were able to exercise considerable agency over the editorial process. Bowing to this pressure, Trevor agreed to return to the old format, but under new conditions:

> I will still give to the LABOUR PROPHET the time needed for its production, but I can no longer bear the loss upon it out of my own pocket. That loss I must impose upon the CENTRAL FUND [...]
>
> At the beginning of the year I had reasonable hopes of being able to meet the loss myself for another year. These hopes have been frustrated.

[...] For more than two years now I have walked, as it were, at the edge of a precipice. The strain has exhausted my nervous energy.[15]

The rebellion of Trevor's readers demonstrates their awareness of his contradictory aims for the *Prophet*. Appropriating the money-making strategies of popular journalism could appear to herald a weakening of the oppositional status of papers which, in the words of Hopkin, claimed that 'the existence of the commercial press and its propensity to distort the truth and manipulate opinion constituted their own *raison d'être*'.[16] In 1892 Trevor proclaimed that

> The publication of a paper in connection with the Labour Church movement has been undertaken, not only to meet the demand for a propagandist organ for the furtherance of our own mission, but also more generally to represent the religious life which inspires the labour movement.[17]

The *Labour Prophet* was a way to link regional churches and a campaigning organ; it was not, as H. C. Rowe reminded readers, 'a commercial venture'.[18] Yet in July 1897, when it was reported that Trevor was to retire permanently from the editorship due to ill-health, new editor R. A. Beckett used terminology that acknowledged the *Labour Prophet*'s previous partial embrace of the commercial tactics of popular journalism. Announcing that the paper had only been saved through monetary help from 'friends of the treasurer', and that the only way to stay in production would be to slash each issue to eight pages, Beckett announced:

> No one regrets this necessity more than I do. In the past we have not been content to run a propagandist organ; we have tried to give the general reader a good pennyworth for its money. This attempt has only led to disaster.[19]

This 'good pennyworth' had previously included an illustrated children's supplement – a feature that could no longer be afforded by the newly contracted paper. Trevor's original periodical had clearly been influenced by a socialist paper that had managed to balance the demands of commerce and propaganda, and for which the concept of a 'good pennyworth' had delivered a resounding success: Blatchford's *Clarion*. While the origins of the New Journalism remain contested, the term is most often applied to a series of changes in form, content and ownership that became widespread in British journalism in the period between 1880 and 1914. As Joel Wiener notes, these included a movement away from unbroken, dense type towards illustrations and photography, from parliamentary news towards a 'human interest' content and away from small editor-proprietor journals towards extensive capitalisation.[20] As Hopkin and others have shown, the *Clarion* embraced many of these changes: it featured illustrations, cartoons and innovative typography, and its snippets of news and comment were closer in style and layout to mass-circulation papers such as *Titbits* than to the dense columns of *Justice*. While popularising political tracts such as Blatchford's *Merrie England*, the *Clarion* also published fiction (including Blatchford's pseudonymous melodramatic novels), sporting columns and theatre reviews, mixing politics and levity with skill. Unlike most writers for the socialist press, Blatchford was a professional Fleet Street journalist, who had set up his new venture with other seasoned former *Morning Chronicle* regulars: A. M. Thompson ('Dangle') and E. F. Fay ('The Bounder'). In an advertisement for the *Clarion* published within Blatchford's fiction collection *Fantasias*, the paper was vaunted as 'the advance-guard of the New Journalism':

> THE CLARION
>
> Combines all the freshness of the newspaper with the literary graces of the magazine. It is more amusing than a comic paper, more elegant than a magazine, more profound than a review. It is twenty years ahead of contemporary ideas, and is the pioneer of the Journalism of the future.[21]

Blatchford was not the only editor who sought to mould political cant to the demands of mass entertainment. Though both the *Labour Leader* and the *Labour Prophet* began to engage with New Journalistic strategies, the *Leader*, claiming a circulation of 50,000 by 1895, did so more wholeheartedly. Despite limited finances and journalistic expertise, Hardie's paper adopted an eclectic formula, publishing a women's column, Ben Tillett's 'Cycling Notes', a children's column and adult fiction. However, socialist periodicals' embrace of fiction in general, and the fairy tale and children's fiction in particular, was inspired by a more complex combination of ideological and commercial motivations.

The ideological contexts of reading

Promoting the 'thrilling and telling episodes' in 'The Blood Stone' by 'Elihu (the late Samuel Washington)', a *Labour Leader* advertisement from 1896 goes on to describe 'The Gods Athirst' by H. C. Rowe:

> It is a prophetic interpretation of the Labour Movement [...] Mr. Rowe's strength as a writer is well known to readers of the *Leader*, and his new tale will place him in the front rank of writers of descriptive literature. We promise our readers a treat of no mean order in 'The Gods Athirst'.[22]

Hardie, Blatchford, Trevor and Morris assumed that fiction could function as both a commercial gambit and as a propaganda tool. *Commonweal* is best remembered for serialising Morris's *The Pilgrims of Hope* (Apr. 1885 to June 1896), *A Dream of John Ball* (Nov. 1886 to Jan. 1897) and his futuristic socialist romance *News from Nowhere* (Jan. 1890 to Oct. 1890). If Morris's romances were unusual in finding readers after serialisation, his experimentation with eclectic genres was not. A defining feature of the labour press was the small group of activists who not only contributed to a range of socialist movements, but wrote widely both within and across periodicals. Although Blatchford later distanced himself from the movement, he was seminal (along with Trevor) in founding the Manchester ILP; there was a significant degree of intertextuality between their papers.[23] Blatchford publicised 'Cinderella' philanthropic work in the *Clarion*, while the *Labour Prophet* subsequently published a *Cinderella Supplement*, for which Blatchford produced a series of articles for children. The wide range of papers to which Blatchford contributed was apparent in the comments of *Labour Prophet* writer 'Socius' in May 1894. While Blatchford's articles in the *Sunday Chronicle* had 'caused a kind of new birth' in the writer, he went on to 'read all the articles of Nunquam' in the *Workman's Times* and the *Clarion*, becoming in the process 'a Socialist and a Clarionette'.[24]

Hardie famously wrote most of the *Labour Leader* himself; in addition to political commentary, fairy tales and children's columns, there has been a debate as to whether he had some input into the women's page (written under the pseudonym 'Lily Bell').[25] Hardie occasionally provided articles for the *Labour Prophet*, while his own paper provided a weekly column for Labour Church news from 1894. Fred Brocklehurst, who was Labour Church General Secretary, was also on the *Leader* staff, and is likely to have been the 'Uncle Fred' who took over Hardie's children's column when the editor undertook an American tour in 1895. H. C. Rowe was not only active within the ILP, but was correspondence secretary for the Labour Church, and contributed extensively to the *Labour Prophet*. His submissions included non-fictional articles, adult fiction and fairy-tale translations for its children's pages.

Rowe also produced a cover article for the *Labour Prophet* in June 1895, entitled 'Socialism in Fiction', which provides an insight into the propaganda function of imaginative prose within the left-wing press in this period. Rowe's comments suggest that the aims of socialist-realist fiction were seen to be very similar to those of political reportage. Reviewing Emma Brooke's *Transition*, he refers to the attraction of the novelistic form for the author who is a defender of the cause of the 'New Woman':

> She knows that the unregenerate woman reads nothing else; that she can be reached neither through the spiritual faculty nor through her intellect, and for these reasons she puts her message into the form of a sensational, psychological novel, which is usually neither psychological nor a novel, but does the work it was meant to do.

While ostensibly defending the aims of feminism, Rowe's assumption that a significant number of Brooke's readers will be politically 'unregenerate' suggests an ambivalence about wholesale female participation in the labour movement. Emma Brooke's use of feminist-socialist propaganda, however, is not disparaged. In fact, Rowe proclaims that 'Socialists of all varieties ought to be well pleased to think that Miss Brooke's fascinating and clever variation on the Fabian Tract is gone abroad in the land'.[26]

John Trevor was happy to suggest in the *Labour Prophet* that '[m]uch of the best moral teaching is to be got nowadays from novels'.[27] Jack Mitchell, exploring the narrative fiction of the London-based socialist press of the 1880s and 1890s, suggests that strong didactic motives informed the fiction of the SDF papers *Justice* and the *Social Democrat* (the latter launched in 1897). These papers regularly published fiction based on contemporary working-class life, much of it focused on the labour movement and written anonymously by *Justice*'s editor Harry Quelch. For Mitchell, such fictions are stronger on ideological rectitude than literary merit; he is unequivocal that 'as far as imaginative prose from within the SDF was concerned, the situation at the turn of the century looked anything but promising'.[28] Mitchell's claim that the Northern-based socialist press on balance produced more engaging, less two-dimensional fiction than their Southern-based counterparts might be contested, but it does deserve some attention. The largest pockets of socialist activity in the 1890s were found in Lancashire and the West Riding, and it was in Bradford, not in London, that the first ILP conference took place. Blatchford's *Clarion* was based in Manchester, where the Labour Church movement was founded and the *Labour Prophet* published until 1896. Hardie's *Labour Leader* began in Glasgow and continued to have a wide readership base in the North, including Scotland, Newcastle and Yorkshire, when it became a weekly. These papers had strong affiliations to an ethical socialist movement, and a broad base of working-class activists, a situation that did not always apply for a London left-wing press more reliant on middle-class support.

In his analysis of late nineteenth-century socialist novels, H. Gustav Klaus asserts this literature's 'radical otherness' compared to Victorian mainstream fiction. In addition to ideological differences shaped by class-based allegiances, he locates this characteristic separateness in

> the reworking of many structural elements of the novel in the process of its critical appropriation by socialist practitioners. This difference extends to the channels of distribution [...] and often involves modes of reception quite different from the isolated act of reading.[29]

While Klaus refers to realist literature, his comments remain suggestive for fairy tales in the *Labour Prophet* and *Leader*. While an understanding of socialist strategies of revision and appropriation is vital, fairy-tale meanings were also shaped by their distinctive mode of reception – by the intimate and interactive periodical cultures of which they formed a part.

While it should not be assumed that socialist periodicals had a universally working-class readership, there is evidence to suggest that a substantial number of the *Labour Prophet*'s and *Labour Leader*'s readers were activists from a fairly low income-bracket.[30] In an appeal for increased revenue in 1895, Hardie is revealing about advertisers' assumptions of readers' incomes:

> The ordinary advertiser will scarcely look at a Labour paper. His idea of the reader of such a paper is the poor, underpaid, 16s-a-week labourer. The notion is, of course, erroneous. For a general all-round class of readers, drawn from all ranks of people, the *Leader* will hold its own against any paper going.[31]

While the paper did have a following among middle-class socialists, Hardie seems a little disingenuous in his lament to advertisers, for elsewhere he clearly targets just such underpaid readers in his ploys to raise circulation. In 1896, the prize of Thomas Carlyle's complete works, offered to the reader who could bring in the largest number of new subscribers, is pitched at a class-specific audience rather than the aforementioned 'general all-round class of readers':

> Many and intense are the struggles of the worker seeking after knowledge to obtain possession of a good book. What pinching and scraping to get together the few shillings necessary for the purchase. And what joy when the treasure has at length been secured.
> The Labour leader now places within the reach of every reader the chance to obtain, absolutely free of cost, not merely one book, but
> A COMPLETE LIBRARY.[32]

That 'pinching and scraping' was doubly poignant, for the books were from Hardie's own hard-won library, sacrificed to raise the *Leader's* circulation.[33] While Hardie neatly marries New Journalistic gimmicks with insight into the difficulties of the working-class autodidact, all workers were not assumed to be adult males: there were differents set of books offered as prizes to women and young readers respectively.[34] Hardie specifically targeted female readers with 'Lily Bell''s women's column, and the *Labour Prophet* frequently encouraged women to submit articles on female participation in the Labour movement. These persistent attempts to bring women within the papers' political discourse, however, reveal rather than disguise the continuing dominance of a male readership. The negligible number of politically active female readers was seen as a cause for concern, a fact apparent in the *Labour Prophet*'s persistent laments about lack of female participation in the paper's correspondence classes.[35]

Launched in 1894, the classes were essentially a support network to foster self-education. Tutors would mark the answers to questions submitted on a range of recommended texts, providing a course of study that traversed politics, science and literature. Published responses are particularly revealing about the most active and dedicated subsection of readers. In general, they create a picture of the very same male working-class autodidact who was Hardie's primary target in his advertising promotion. In 1894, the *Labour Prophet* announced the commencement of *Merrie England* classes, offering a prize of ten shillings to the individual who provided the best responses to questions on Blatchford's best-selling treatise on socialism. The first prize in this competition was awarded to G. Goodenough, whose accompanying letter was printed in April 1894:

> I had intended joining your Missionary Class; but, being only a poor miner, I had not Clodd's book, and was not in a position to get one; so, having 'Merrie England' by me, I thought I would have a try.[36]

Goodenough refers to Edward Clodd's *Childhood of Religions*, a recommended, but expensive, correspondence text. In contrast, Blatchford's *Merrie England* was available in a celebrated penny edition. While an adult scholarly library was impossible to assemble for many working-class readers, fairy-tale texts for their children remained more affordable. For if the days of the chapbook were long over, fairy tales were still available in new penny editions. The class-differentiated circulation of fairy-tale books is clearly illustrated in Blatchford's *Clarion* article 'On Toys':

> I presented my elder daughter with an eight-shilling copy of Caldecott's nursery tales. Her maiden aunt gave unto her a penny Red Riding Hood. The Caldecott resembles a dirty book-back and the memory of a dream, the Red Riding Hood is the favourite companion of her childhood's happy hour.[37]

An assumed knowledge of fairy tales characterised socialist papers' mode of address to both child and adult readers: if few had Blatchford's purchasing power, it was taken for granted that the penny Red Riding Hood, like the penny *Merrie England*, was widely obtainable. This assumed familiarity is clearly demonstrated by the *Leader*'s visual appropriations of the fairy tale within adult satire. In May 1895, 'An Empty Feast', a front-page cartoon by resident artist 'Jordie', creates an extended parallel between the recent Liberal budget and the tale of an invisible banquet that is recounted in the *Arabian Nights* (Figure 4.1), echoing Dickens's use of this satirical device in 'The Thousand and One Humbugs'. In the *Arabian Nights'* 'Tale of Shakálik, the Barber's Sixth Brother', a hungry man, tired of the non-existent fare, finally feigns drunkenness from invisible wine and assaults his host. In the

Figure 4.1 Jordie, 'An Empty Feast', *Labour Leader*, 18 May 1895. © The British Library Board. All Rights Reserved. NPL LON 420

Labour Leader's pictorial revision, Keir Hardie as 'Labour', trading his cloth cap for Eastern dress, looks disgruntled with his Liberal benefactor Lord Rosebery's proffered dishes of empty promises. This cartoon is interesting in its attempt to retell the tale in both visual and verbal forms:

> A certain eastern potentate (as related in the 'Arabian Nights') once invited a hungry man to dine with him. 'Eat, drink and be merry', he said. 'Taste of this delicious Home Rule Soup; do you not like it?' And at the same time presented to the hungry man an empty plate. 'And here,'

he said, 'is some fine Local Veto sauce [...] you must wash down this excellent dinner with our own particular Broken Promises wine'.[38]

The cartoon draws explicitly on a further array of promises: while Prime Minister Lord Rosebery is the potentate, Chancellor Sir William Harcourt serves up the dish of empty 'Local Veto', and further empty plates are inscribed with unfulfilled demands.

Such allegories, however, did not always rely on verbal text, and could be far simpler than the previous conceit. Following the 1895 election, in which Labour's disastrous performance culminated in the loss of Hardie's West Ham seat, the *Labour Leader*'s front page depicts Joseph Chamberlain, Radical Liberal member for Birmingham, as an ineffectual Red Riding Hood, attempting to protect the jam of his own public office from the jaws of the slavering wolf 'hunger', the spectre of Britain under a Tory majority. The wolf is set to devour the reforms of Chamberlain's 'Brum' in a mouthful (Figure 4.2). In the editorial snippets on the same page, Hardie attributes the loss of his seat partly to 'the abstention of a number of Liberals who preferred a Tory to an Independent Labour representative'; the weakness of the Liberal Red Riding Hood is depicted as just as foolish as the Tories' opportunist harnessing of this 'wolf' is dangerous.[39] Revealing potential qualifications in the paper's faith in democracy, this cartoon also seems to invoke fears about the malleability of an underclass. While the wolf 'hunger' is violent and unpredictable, it will wear the colours of whoever is in office.[40]

While such front-page cartoons were also designed to attract new readers, regular purchasers were expected to sacrifice more than a few moments of leisure. In 1896, the *Labour Prophet*'s correspondence secretary, Mary G. Burnett, states that she recognises

> the fact that those who are now engaged in active work, and those whose power of exact study is limited by long hours of labour, and by having no private room to read and study in, may yet greatly improve themselves, and their usefulness to the Cause, by a systematic course of reading.[41]

For the most dedicated subscribers to such periodicals, reading was a truly interactive experience; the consumption of both fictional and non-fictional texts had a clear social dimension, as a form of training for political activism rather than an isolated leisure activity. Burnett notes in 1895 that 'it seems as if the greater part of our students have been occupied with local elections in their different parishes, which is, of course, the right thing as being the practical outcome of their studies; and several of them were standing as candidates'.[42] Self-improvement led to social change; an assumed symbiotic relationship between the two was a tenet of ILP socialism, and was also valorised in one of the Labour Church's five principles. If 'the development of Personal Character and the improvement of Social Conditions' were 'both

Figure 4.2 Jordie, 'Little Red Riding Hood', *Labour Leader*, 10 Aug. 1895. © The British Library Board. All Rights Reserved. NPL LON 420

essential to man's emancipation from moral and social bondage', an engaged approach to literature – including fiction – was an integral part of this doctrine.[43]

Trevor perceived the labour movement to be inherently religious, with individuals undergoing conversion to its doctrines and becoming 'pioneers' for its cause. Members fully expected a socialist society in the (near) future; this was seen as an evolutionary process, and the Churches lent their staunch support to trade unionism, the ILP and the SDF, political movements that were seen as signposts on this inevitable road of progress. Yet the ultimate goal of the movement was to go beyond the materialist concerns of socialist economics and to move towards enlightened personal development. Such aspirations were embodied not only in the tenets of secular self-improvement that characterised the correspondence classes, but in wider exhortations to spiritual growth: specifically, in the non-denominational concept of religion advocated by the Labour Church.

The Church's third principle stated that 'The Religion of the Labour movement is not Sectarian or Dogmatic, but Free Religion, leaving each man free to develop his own relations with the Power that brought him into being'. While this position has traditionally been interpreted by labour historians as anachronistic (at best, a transitional stage on route from a religious society to a fully developed class politics; at worst, a cynical ploy to draw the religious working classes into a secular labour movement), recent critics have suggested that such views may tend towards oversimplification.[44] Trevor was no cynic, and placed a consistent and emphatic focus on an immanent God in his writings for the *Labour Prophet*. Frequently publishing the transcendentalist poetry of Walt Whitman as a source of spiritual inspiration for readers, Trevor's position was also heavily influenced by the pantheistic theologies of Emerson and Thoreau. The celebration of the presence of God in the world (and particularly in Nature) imbued the *Labour Prophet* with a distinctive literary and cultural identity. This was not a religious prelude to secular activism: in Labour Church theology, the two were inextricable.

A similar conception of the Divine (including the belief in socialism as the visible embodiment of both moral and social evolution) characterised Keir Hardie's own type of ethical socialism. While the *Labour Leader* used an extract from Tennyson's *In Memoriam* as a mast-head, concluding with the line 'ring in the Christ that is to be', Hardie also proclaimed in the *British Weekly*: 'I claim for Socialism that it is the embodiment of Christianity in our industrial system.'[45] The *Labour Prophet* was perceived to be an organ of both practical socialism and prognostication, Trevor asserting in his first editorial 'GOD IS IN THE LABOUR MOVEMENT. This is the word of our prophecy – the message of the Labour Church and of the *Labour Prophet*'.[46] In the same paper, Robert Blatchford announced that

> If you want socialism to be a religion, you must widen your definition of socialism. You must draw out all the ethical and spiritual implications of these desires and efforts for a juster social order [...] A new conception of life is taking shape, to which it is affectation, if not folly, to refuse the name of Religion.[47]

Blatchford, of course, considerably widens the definition of religion too. That the paper championed a humanist who was to declare in *God and my Neighbour* that 'Christianity is not true' is revealing about the range of theological positions accommodated within the Labour Church's 'free religion'.[48] Nevertheless (and despite their significant differences), the contemporary phrase 'Religion of Socialism' does remain particularly apposite to describe the socialism of Blatchford as well as Hardie and Trevor. For those assumptions of intimate connections between spiritual and secular and between individual and social change have interesting repercussions for socialist children's literature. While spiritual (particularly pantheistic) impulses can be seen to infuse both the *Labour Prophet*'s and the *Labour Leader*'s writings for children, both the former's *Cinderella Supplement* and the latter's children's columns came to advocate a doctrine of self-improvement, and to reflect distinctly political aims, as the labour movement's search for converts became more active.

Cinderella and socialism

> "Cinderella" is a stroke of genius:
> NUNQUAM BE PRAISED FOR IT.
> I wish we could get as pretty a name for the Labour Church – it seems such a hunk of a thing by the side of "Cinderella."[49]

If the *Labour Prophet*'s small scale of operation made its contents necessarily less varied than the *Labour Leader*, in one respect this much smaller-circulation paper was more ambitious. While Hardie began to provide a weekly children's section of between one and three columns in 1894, the *Labour Prophet* produced, from May of the previous year, a more substantial monthly children's paper – the *Cinderella Supplement*, an addition significant enough to be incorporated into the paper's title.[50] Information concerning Labour Church business appeared on *Cinderella* pages alongside articles for children, and the supplement was also sold separately at labour church services. In August 1893, Trevor claimed that the *Cinderella Supplement* would be 'found useful to circulate with an appeal for funds for Cinderella work, and all Cinderella children should have a copy'.[51] It therefore had a wide range of potential readerships: Labour Church activists and their children, adult philanthropists outside the movement, casual readers of the *Labour Prophet* and the 'Cinderella' children, who were the recipients of Labour activists' philanthropy through the Cinderella clubs.

Trevor made clear that the addition of an illustrated supplement was a considerable financial risk, informing readers at its inception that 'to make the enlarged paper pay expenses, the present circulation of 5,000 must be increased to 20,000'.[52] In September 1893, he explained:

> Our CINDERELLA Supplement was added to the LABOUR PROPHET, not so much to make the paper more attractive to the general reader, but as a means of extending Cinderella Work, and especially among Labour

Churches. A Labour Church which merely holds services is not a satisfactory institution [...] some organised collective effort should be made to help the individual as well as to reorganise the State.[53]

Clubs where slum children could be fed and entertained were first tentatively proposed by Robert Blatchford in 1889, while he was still a journalist for the *Sunday Chronicle*.[54] In the 'religion of socialism' phase, the fusion of such traditional philanthropy with socialist principles had its own rationale. As Stephen Yeo has noted, 'A temporary denial of the divide between structure and personal life in socialist consciousness was much more characteristic of this period'.[55] Philanthropic work was in keeping with the evolutionary ethic avowed in the *Labour Church*'s fifth principle, which maintained that socialism and individual moral development were interdependent. Trevor could therefore announce that 'The Cinderella Club and the Cinderella School will be as great a help to us as to the children whom we seek to serve' and that 'for the members themselves it will be far better and more profitable work than a deal of spouting on platforms'.[56] Cinderella work was a practical embodiment of a belief in the fellowship of man. Robert Blatchford, in his pamphlet *Altruism*, declared that 'Altruism, indeed, is more important than Socialism itself. Given universal love of man for man, and we should have something better than Socialism itself. We should have Communism of the purest and most durable kind'.[57]

By the time Trevor had established his *Cinderella* paper, this philanthropic movement was well under way. The Manchester Labour Church Cinderella Club had been running successfully for nine months, and the Church was about to embark upon a Cinderella Sunday School.[58] The establishment of these two organisations owed very little to Fabian-style state-socialism and much to Robert Blatchford's Romantic fairy-tale rhetoric. In his reply to a correspondent in the *Sunday Chronicle* in 1889, who had suggested that poor children should be sent to night school to learn science and religion, Blatchford was disparaging: 'Are there not foul smells enough in the slums but we must teach the babies to dabble in evil acids and diabolical gases?' However, he also countered, 'if anyone will take a cartload of dolls round the slums [...] or if anyone will open a play room, or if anyone will offer to read fairy tales, or show magic lanterns [...] I don't mind taking a hand in the fun'. He went on to describe 'the delight that might be afforded to the ragged robins of the slums by a good reader's reading of a few chapters of Andersen or Grimm'.[59]

Blatchford's rejection of scientific 'fact' for the wonder of fancy echoed the introduction to Taylor's Grimm, and was also reminiscent of the Dickensian nostalgia for 'fancy'. In fact, the main reading of such children, as reported in the *Labour Prophet Cinderella Supplement*, was not those books of fairy tales but the products of the New Journalism: *Comic Cuts*, the *Wonder* and *Titbits*.[60] John Trevor, however, also echoed Blatchford's whimsy when he suggested in the first *Cinderella Supplement*:

> Our first effort will be to help the helpers – Cinderella's godmothers, if we may call them so. Would that we could provide them with the fairy wand which would enable them to change the dull and dreary lot of the children to a bright and joyous one, and cause them, in true fairy style, to 'live happily ever after'.[61]

Blatchford's choice of name for the clubs may have been 'a stroke of genius', but its sentimental construction of the poor now seems rather less progressive, uneasily echoing Kingsley's 'ash-brother' Tom and *Chambers's* 'Cinderella Downstairs'. Yet there was something quite different about this Cinderella too. There was a conviction, particularly among activists in the early 1890s, that the coming socialist society would provide a conclusive solution to social problems. This combination of rational and millenarian beliefs pointed, like Morris's futuristic 'News from Nowhere', to a true 'happy-ever-after'. This is exemplified by the fairy-tale wish-fulfilment of the 1903 *Cinderella Annual*, a national report of Cinderella philanthropic work that is introduced by the heroine herself:

> I cannot feel happy, even in this beautiful Fairyland, when I think of all the sad things I have been told. I long to bring all the little children out of the misery and wickedness they live in, and keep them here until they have learned to love only what is good and beautiful, and to loathe all evil. What wonderful deeds they would be able to do! Soon would they make another Fairyland, where ugly sisters and selfish brothers would be seen no more.[62]

Cinderella children were recognised by *Clarion* and *Labour Prophet* readers as the very poorest of society, a category generally distinct (if only relatively) from activists' own children. Fairy-tale metaphors were in keeping with Cinderella clubs that, despite their socialist origins, largely replicated the structure of conventional middle-class philanthropy, the better-off working-class reader switching roles to become 'godmother' rather than recipient.[63] It is likely, however, that the name's adoption was also rather more shrewd: fundraising campaigns were partly designed to elicit money from middle-class philanthropists outside the labour movement. For this audience, 'Cinderella' celebrates individual benefaction without making the Clubs' political affiliations too overt.[64]

In his *Clarion* column of December 1891, Blatchford reviews Olive Schreiner's book *Dreams*, and refers to her fantastic tale in which a child is endowed with the gift that 'the Ideal shall be the Real'. This causes him to muse that

A greater boon is the power to turn the Real into the Ideal. *That* is the true fairy wand, and magic ring, and philosopher's stone, and rosy spectacle. To turn the denizens of the mine and the mill, the market and the forge, the ball-room and the canteen into Silas Marners, and Hetty Sorrels, and Bully Bottoms, and Becky Sharps, and Sancho Panzas, and Corporal Trims! To go out into the slums and brickfields, the rag-fairs and the railway stations, and, standing amidst the mire and the murk, and the jabber of trade and the roar of traffic, wave once the enchanter's wand and turn the whole sordid scene into – Dreamland![65]

If the realist novel is cast as an enchanting fairy tale, capable of turning the real into 'the ideal', Blatchford's journalism combines realism, fairy tale and fantasy, attempting to make non-fiction as seductive as the novel. Blatchford sentimentalises as well idealises 'the real' (including the 'denizens of the mine and the mill'). In his article for children on the founding of the Cinderella clubs, which appeared in the *Cinderella Supplement* in June 1893, he suggests mischievously:

> If I were as cock-sure about things as other big boys are, I should say that the Cinderella Clubs were started by – Who do you think?
> BY CINDERELLA!
> Yes my dears, by Cinderella herself.
> Mind; I don't mean the Cinderella of the story book, who got to be a princess because she had small feet. No; I mean a real Cinderella, a Manchester Cinderella; a poor little girl, who had neither small feet, nor a fairy godmother, and so had to sell matches in the street.[66]

Blatchford's revision of the *Cinderella* tale is particularly striking when read against the previous month's *Cinderella Supplement*, which includes the translation 'Cinderella; Or the Little Fur Slipper (From the French of Charles Perrault)'.[67] Trevor's translation remains faithful to the aristocratic milieu of Perrault's text. Cinderella is never seen by the prince without splendid dress; she ultimately marries her sisters to nobles at court. This translation of a tale of courtly manners, in which Cinderella *does* appear to be rewarded for her beauty and small feet, seems incongruous when set against both the socialist values of the *Labour Prophet* and the other contents of the first supplement, which include reports on the work of Cinderella clubs and plans for a Cinderella School for destitute children.

In Blatchford's narrative, a real Manchester child who tried to sell him matches in the street becomes the true heroine worthy of sympathy. Yet in rejecting the class and gender codes of Perrault's texts, he encourages parallels with another fairy-tale model: Andersen's 'The Little Match-Girl'.

While Blatchford questions the worthiness of small feet, he never rejects the fairy-tale promise of simple transformation. Reminiscing about the prizes offered for the cleanest children at the Manchester Cinderella Club, he exclaims: 'the week after the prizes were offered there was such a change that we almost believed there had been fairy god-mothers about, with soap instead of pumpkins, and combs and towels instead of lizards and mice'.

Such championing of cleanliness and obedience might contradict Blatchford's assertion in the article that the first club is started 'to amuse and please the children. We did not want to *teach* them anything'.[68] Nevertheless, Blatchford's article is in keeping with the ethos of the early supplement. In 1895, the *Labour Prophet* states that play is the 'School of Action', and 'the great aid to play story – Bible stories, historical stories, fairy stories &c'.[69] Many Cinderella club organisers endorsed this belief in the regenerative value of play afforded by fairy-tale literature.[70] Yet the fascination with the fairy tale also had more complex origins – for fairy tales were related to the utopian ideologies that permeated the Labour Church and ethical socialism. They were linked, not only to Romantic constructions of childhood, but to an evolutionary eschatology that equated juvenile innocence with a stage of simpler human relations, and with the fellowship ideal of a forever lost pre-industrial society.

Evolutionary frameworks: Childhood, the fairy tale and rural utopianism

In the fifth issue of the *Cinderella Supplement*, when translations of 'Cinderella' and the Grimms' tales 'The Ragamuffins' and 'Rumpelstiltskin' had already been published, Trevor used his 'Cinderella Letter' to inform child readers:

> Of all the work I do, I like none so well as translating those fairy tales for you. They do me good [...] They were made up when the world was much younger than it is now, and when grown up folk had children's hearts and children's understandings. [...] They make me feel sure that life is a sweet and noble thing, when we have learnt how to live it. And they teach me that, all the world over, man's heart is the same, with the same hopes and the same fears, the same joys and the same sorrows. For all the world over these stories are found, wherever there are men and women and little children.[71]

For Trevor, fairy tales reinforce a cherished fellowship ideal. Like the socialist movement, they are international in dimension, and like ethical socialism they foster a sense of brotherhood and empathy, revealing that 'all the world over man's heart is the same'. Yet they are also revered for their connection to a cultural past that is comparable to a state of youthful innocence: a time when 'grown-up folks had children's hearts and children's understandings'. This invocation of the recapitulation thesis was reinforced by two books that feature in the *Labour Prophet* Missionary Class, *The Childhood of Religions* (1875) and *The Childhood of the World* (1873), written by Edward Clodd. Answering correspondent J. H.'s query on Clodd's *The Childhood of Religions* in 1894, Trevor once again employs this evolutionary metaphor as conventional wisdom, remarking: 'do not let those legends of the world's childhood perplex you. They are the folk-lore of the earliest peoples – children in knowledge and intellect'.[72]

In another of his books *Tom Tit Tot: An Essay on Savage Philosophy in Folk-Tale* Clodd stated:

> The healthy-natured child, who in many things represents the savage stage of thinking, listens without question to the stories of the Giant who hid his heart in a duck's egg on an island out of harm's way, as he vainly hoped; and of Beauty and the Beast, where the princess's curiosity led to the retransformation of the enchanted prince to the shape of loathly monster.

Clodd continued to argue in terms of this psychological confluence, claiming that 'Strabo says that "in the childhood of the world men, like children, had to be taught by tales"'.[73] Heavily influenced by E. B. Tylor, Clodd assumed an anthropological framework in which the child's progression from youth to adulthood mirrors the evolutionary ladder up which all races are assumed to climb. The progressivism of Clodd's developmental model held a different appeal for some socialist activists. Trevor and Hardie adhered to an evolutionary model in which personal and social development were moving progressively (and inevitably) towards the perfection of a socialist society, a process which could be helped or hindered by individual endeavour. In a *Labour Prophet* correspondence class column of 1894, it is stated that the books by Clodd are recommended 'because they give the reader who knows nothing of Evolution (or unfolding) a very simple and clear conception of that wonderful principle as it applies to religious and social development'.[74] In Labour Church theology, the Darwinian model of evolution – branching, random and without moral direction – was rarely superimposed on a social context: it was sidelined in favour of the certainty of progressive change. In an interview with David Summers, Labour Church activist A. J. Waldegrave stated that 'Trevor accepted Evolutionary theory à *la Spencer*, and applied it to Religion –i.e. Godward evolution now revealing itself in Labour'.[75]

Yet while social, political and religious evolution was perceived to be moving ever nearer to that socialist society, it was anathema to Blatchford, Trevor and Hardie to embrace industrialism as a symbol of that progression. For many ethical socialists, the child was also linked to the nostalgia for a more recent pre-industrial moment, and was constructed, not as Clodd's savage, but as a Romantic primitive.[76] The texts sacred to ethical socialism hint at such conflicted ways of conceiving progress. In the *Clarion* pamphlet *The New Religion* (1897), Robert Blatchford declared that northern Socialism was no mere economic determinism, and owed little to the 'State-Socialism of Karl Marx': 'the new religion, which is Socialism, and something more than Socialism', he proclaimed, 'is more largely the result of the labours of Darwin, Carlyle, Ruskin, Dickens, Thoreau, and Walt Whitman'.[77] While Darwin was left out, similar influences were cited by a *Labour Prophet* correspondent:

> Since my first knowledge of the CLARION [...] my mind has been rushing at express speed through a country the chief landmarks of which are the writings of Ruskin, Carlyle, Tolstoi [sic], Thoreau, Mazzini, Clodd, Max Muller's *Sacred Books of the East*, Cobbett, Richard Jefferies.[78]

These landmark texts are telling. Thoreau's mystic nature writings and Whitman's poetic expression of an immanent, democratic religion, with nature as a window on a personal Divine, were key inspirations for the Labour Church's conception of free religion. In June 1892, Trevor invoked another transcendentalist in a reply to a correspondent. 'The Labour Church', he proclaimed, 'is an attempt to answer the question with which Emerson opens his essay on "Nature." [...] Emerson states, like religious ancestors, "Why should not we also enjoy an original relation with the Universe?"'[79] Tolstoy, Ruskin and Carlyle linked a return to nature with a rediscovery of spiritual truths; the naturalist Jefferies, well known in this period for his treatise on the agricultural labourer, *Hodge and His Masters*, was also revered by many socialists for his futuristic fiction *After London* (1885), a tale in which travelling forward is also travelling back, as British industrial society evolves into agrarianism. This work famously delighted William Morris, and it undoubtedly influenced the construction of the futuristic rural utopias of Morris's *News from Nowhere* and Blatchford's *The Sorcery Shop*.[80] In Müller's writings in particular, it is possible to see how an exploration of myth led to the spiritual beliefs of the past, and could rekindle utopian socialist desires for a post-industrial future.[81] The seemingly eclectic texts cited by this *Labour Prophet* correspondent were in fact intimately woven threads in the theology of ethical socialism, feeding a combination of impulses that were as much Romantic as revolutionary. Within this context, fairy tales, associated with both childhood and 'the folk', became talismanic. They were emblems of a relation with nature that belonged to the childhood of the world: a world whose magic had to be restored rather than lamented as lost.

Many ethical socialists saw the child and the fairy tale as epitomising these past social relations: as uncorrupted by the sophistication of culture and still connected to the spirituality of 'Nature'. Julia Dawson, in her article 'Chat for Chatterboxes' in the *Cinderella* pages of November 1896, claims that 'Children are natural; and we bigger folks are unnatural when we try to stifle their natural instincts by keeping them quiet and in order'.[82] The perception that children, less culturally contaminated than adults, shared the mindset of an earlier historical people was seen to coalesce in their 'natural' approach to fiction: their belief in the literal truth of fairy tales.

A fascinating advocate of such beliefs was Labour Church and ILP activist Allen Clarke.[83] In his 'A Talk About Fairies' (1896) for the 'Chats with Lads and Lasses' column of the *Labour Leader*, Clarke claims:

> Once upon a time – that's the way all the good old fairy tales begin – many, many hundreds of years ago, before ever a book was written or printed, our long-dead forefathers used to sit round their log-fires of a winter evening and tell tales and sing songs to one another. [...] From these long-dead ancestors we get all the fairy tales, for they believed in fairies.[84]

Yet it is not merely the pre-literate dweller of 'once upon a time', but the contemporary rural dweller in close proximity to nature who is believed to have an instinctive connection to this culture of belief. In the second part of his 'A Talk About Fairies', Clarke mentions contemporary folk beliefs of the Isle of Man and Lancashire, claiming that 'In country places you will come across old folks who yet believe that fairies visit their houses during the night'.[85] Trevor, in his autobiography *My Quest for God* (1897), describes a trip made to the Isle of Man at the age of 14:

> This was a wider opening into the world of Nature than I had yet experienced. [...] It was my first introduction, too, to the haunts of legend and myth. There were no railways on the island then. Even a boy could understand that he was in the midst of a simpler and more primitive folk; and could feel the charm of contact with a younger world. Stories of devils and monsters and mermaids seemed almost credible there.[86]

Belief in folklore and folktale becomes a signifier for an intimacy with Nature that has been lost by the urban dwelling adult, for a 'primitivism' that is not barbarous, but culturally rich. While the numbers of rural dwellers were diminishing, hopes for such continued links with the natural world were increasingly focused on children. When Clarke discussed children's belief in fairies, it emblematised something more than superstition: it was a sacred state of mind extant in both the past and the present. His tense shifts are revealing: 'Fairyland, which was (and yet is) the unseen part of our common world, was the loveliest place that ever was'; 'Fairyland is, indeed, a land of dreams; and I think the fairies lead good little children there when they are asleep.'[87] Clarke was not merely humouring his child readers: an advocate of spiritualism as well as socialism, in his writings about fairies he found, like Yeats, a way of questioning the values of industrial modernity, and of articulating his own sense of dislocation and loss.[88]

The desire to make children believe in fairies is always revealing about adult wish-fulfilment, and few wished children to believe more than Keir Hardie himself. Adopting the persona of 'Daddy Time' in his children's columns for the *Labour Leader*, Hardie told child readers that fairies set the agenda of his columns: he lived in a cave by the sea, with only fairies for company, and knew only of the issues that they dictated.[89] Hardie anticipated older readers would be sceptical, but was nevertheless insistent that children should maintain the charm of belief. While he incorporated questioning implied readers ('"Nonsense! There are no fairies," some of his young Crusaders say'), he was eager to counter 'But there are where Daddy Time is living', echoing the tensions of Kingsley's *Water-Babies*.[90]

Hardie's suggestion that fairies remain accessible for children clearly invokes the same contradictory framework as Clarke: like Clarke, Hardie had previously denied that fairies could exist at all in industrial capitalism. In an earlier children's column, Hardie claimed that friends of the fairies had told him that

> a very long time ago – long before the giant Capitalist had made slaves of the workers – that men and women, and even boys and girls, especially those who lived in the country, and loved each other, and loved the trees and fields and buttercups and daisies, and all the beautiful things that grow around us, were at times able to see the wee fairies and hear what they said.[91]

While insisting on the survival of that 'unseen world' in the dreams of children, Clarke also lamented:

> I do not think anyone sees fairies nowadays. I do not believe that anyone has seen a fairy for hundreds of years. The days when fairies haunted the forests and groves, and danced under the moon, all came and went long ago, before people knew what cotton factories and railway trains were. In the fairy-days there were no steam engines, or school boards or general elections, or cheap trips; indeed, as soon as men and women began to print books and make machinery, the fairies all vanished from the world as if by magic.[92]

While this was indeed a familiar claim, Clarke's advocacy of primitivism also exposes his equivocal attitude to democracy. For it is not merely the exploitative facets of industrialism but its potentially democratising products (mass literacy, universal schooling, general elections, cheap trips) that have killed the wonders of fairyland. Clarke expressed his desire for a practical return to the land by creating a co-operative community, known as the 'Daisy Colony Scheme'; the nostalgia that fuelled such an enterprise was clear in his joyous description of a visit to a village 'not yet chained in the convict march of steam-made progress'. At this old-fashioned village fair, Clarke perceived that time and 'steam-made progress' had arrested; he was able to sample 'those merrie Middle Ages that William Morris loves and those pleasant days *Nunquam* would like to see back again'.[93] In Clarke's 1895 retelling of 'Little Red Riding Hood' for the children's column of the *Labour Leader*, the fairy tale's 'once upon a time' has a symbolic relation to Morris's future in *News from Nowhere*. In both, historical time has come to an end, and culture and nature are one. Little Red Riding Hood, Clarke is sure,

> never went to school; there were no schools 'once upon a time'; and Red Riding Hood could not spell 'Con-stan-ti-no-ple' [...], nor pick out the nouns and verbs in a sentence [...] nor do anything of that board-school sort of thing. But though she had never passed the first standard, she could tell the name of every flower she saw.[94]

This sentiment was shared by Keir Hardie in his 'Chats with Lads and Lasses' column of May 1895, when he told his readers that 'An afternoon ramble in a glen or wood will teach you more about natural history than you will learn in ten years' book teaching at school'.[95] Yet while the fictional Red Riding Hood is placed closer to nature by her fortuitous existence in once-upon-a-time, contemporary manual labourers are also assumed to have escaped the false civilisation of the board school, and so preserved a charmed relationship with the natural world. Clarke makes an explicit parallel, telling his young readers:

> The navvy and the bricklayer and the labourer know how to do their work, even if they can't tell you the date of the Magna Charta, and there are many folks who can neither read nor write, yet know how to manage their business excellently. There are many sorts of useful knowledge that never get into the school books; indeed, what you learn at school is but a trifle; and you must never despise those who don't know anything about grammar and arithmetic, for, if they don't know that, they probably know something better, as was the case with Red Riding Hood.[96]

One wonder how many of the working-class autodidacts diligently reading the books on the *Labour Prophet*'s correspondence course would have shared Trevor's view that the 'charm of childhood [...] lingers longest among the People – the poor toilers'. The 'People and the Children', Trevor claimed, were 'the hope of the Reformer, because of their primary instincts, unspoiled by the self-consciousness of culture. These the Labour Churches are bringing together'.[97] This message was reinforced in F. J. Gould's fairy tale

'The Man Without a Heart' which appeared in the *Labour Prophet Cinderella* pages in October 1893. In this text, the protagonist visits a wise man, and agrees to take on a number of social roles in the hope of obtaining a heart. He becomes a king (and charges high taxes), a scholar and an artist (and is cut off from the people) and a rich philanthropist (when he can afford to be generous) but still remains unsuccessful. Finally he becomes a woodcutter, and begins to feel a meaningful relation to his work, family and community. Here, echoing the beliefs of Ruskin and Morris, the rural labourer is depicted as the true king, artist and scholar combined.[98]

The fact that it is the largely obsolete rural woodcutter rather than the urban navvy or bricklayer who is ultimately valorised by Gould is telling; the *Labour Leader*, *Labour Prophet* and *Clarion* all expressed beliefs that an industrial urban environment was ending fulfilling manual labour, disrupting the traditional intimacy between the individual and nature. Children's columns also fought tirelessly to inculcate rural lore, using botanical study and trips to the countryside to restore this supposedly organic link. Cinderella club outings into the country were seen to effect a spiritual change in slum children that was often described in metaphors of magical transformation. A. M. Thompson in the *Cinderella Annual* suggested that all fears for the behaviour of the 'London gutter child' were dispelled once they reached their rural destination: 'the bowers of the fairy realm had swallowed them up in its leafy enchantment'. This process of spiritual cleansing was sometimes seen to transmogrify the children themselves into supernatural beings; for Robert Blatchford children were naturally 'the pretty, dainty, unstained mortal fairies'; for the *Labour Leader*'s 'Uncle Fred', rural dwelling readers became the 'fairies of Hirst Wood'.[99]

A pantheistic programme of re-education was unequivocally advocated by Mary G. Burnett, the correspondence secretary, in the *Cinderella* pages for April 1895. In her article '"The Father's Sunday Out" is the children's Happiness', she suggests that country rambles are the most productive form of child education. Despite having been 'for a great many years a Sunday-school teacher', Burnett suggests that the whole system:

> has seemed to me artificial and unlovely, a worthy counterpart to the general ugliness and severance from natural joys engendered by our present commercial and competitive system. [...] I groan in spirit when I think of the thousands of children who might so easily be made happy in the same simple and natural way, but instead who are walled into stuffy rooms, and hear of the good God out of books, instead of direct from those things which he has created to make us happy and joyful.[100]

Fairy motifs, operating simultaneously as adult metaphors for rural and juvenile innocence and as a shrewd literary device to win over child readers, were given a key role in inculcating 'natural joys' through botanical study.

This is clearly demonstrated by the *Labour Prophet*'s publication of the adapted tale 'The Princesses' in March 1895:

> You children who live in the North of England, do you think you really know what grass is like? You have your moors, with the purple heather under the free and open sky; but I think you can hardly know how beautiful the grass meadows can be where there are no tall chimneys anywhere near to shed the black smoke upon them, and where there are heaps and heaps of flowers growing up and blossoming, and changing the green into gold.
>
> In that sort of grass there live little princesses, in tiny, tiny castles, [...] It is possible that there may be just such princesses, in just such tiny castles, hidden somewhere under the purple heather. I would advise you children to look and see.[101]

In August 1895, the *Labour Leader* published the article 'Country Rambles for Children of All Ages', by 'Father Fernie', which is strikingly close to the *Leader*'s 'The Princesses' in sentiment and intention. Although this article also attempts to lure children to botany through the seductive promise of fairies, this supernatural motif was (as in the *Labour Prophet* article) more than a literary ploy: it had symbolic value, standing as a metaphoric counterpoint to the despoliation of the environment by industrialism. Picturing a babbling brook, the writer describes its meandering course:

> past fairyland, into the town from which you have come. And the brook is sorry to have to pass through the town, and becomes ill and foul, and the ferns and moss and flowers forsake it, and the fairies are not there, the birds visit it not, and even the fish cannot live in it, for the ugly town has poured its unpleasantness into it. But there I've been tempted to stay in fairyland too long. Fairies another time. Flowers now.[102]

It is significant that the writer identifies an audience of town children; this reverence for the natural world was largely a product of an urban socialist consciousness. *Clarion* Field Clubs, which organised botanical rambles among socialists, did so for the dwellers of urban centres such as Manchester and Leeds; the group of Whitmanites who engaged in celebrations of nature were based in industrial Bolton.[103] The city dwelling socialists' lack of real knowledge of the rural environment they romanticised was partially conceded in an article by Joseph Clayton on the same page of the *Labour Leader* as Father Fernie's 'Country Rambles'. Clayton admitted that midsummer was seen by most ILP members through the 'foul mist of chimney smoke', or with only a day-tripper's familiarity of the country. Nevertheless, he was sure that the cry of 'Back to the land' would swell 'to a chorus, the echoes of which will be heard even at Westminster'.[104]

Peter C. Gould, writing on the back to nature movement within late nineteenth-century socialism, has noted that '[m]any lovers of Nature held utilitarianism responsible for severe damage done to the social fabric, cultural vitality, and the natural environment – the working classes, art, and nature had to be defended'.[105] In Hardie's fairy tale 'Jack Clearhead', the crusading Jack is given a tri-coloured rosette, symbolising the holy triumvirate of socialism, purity and nature.[106] Yet the concept of childhood innocence and naiveté so frequently celebrated by Blatchford, Trevor and Hardie was perpetually at risk of being undermined by another key tenet of the movement – the injunction to 'make socialists'.

Making socialists

'I go to few places where I am not met with the remark, "It was NUNQUAM converted me to Socialism" [...] Their eyes shine with the gladness of a new birth'.[107] Trevor's claim in the *Labour Prophet* in 1893 reveals that the embrace of socialism was conceptualised as a spiritual transformation, an event with the power and profundity of religious conversion. That missionary spirit had a profound impact on child socialisation. Mark Bevir has drawn attention to the way in which Labour Church theology caused an inexorable movement towards both child and adult education:

> Immanentist theology suggested that the social transformation had to come from within, but that once people learned to listen to the divine within, the social transformation would follow automatically [...] In this view a social revolution was assured provided one made socialists.[108]

The social transformation envisaged by the Labour Church was not merely dependent on individual self-realisation, but on a wider evolutionary unfolding; yet individual conversion remained seminal in accelerating the arrival of the ideal society. Juvenile education was perceived as vital in precipitating this process. In 1897, Bolton Labour Church reported in the *Labour Prophet* that it was forming a Sunday school, asserting 'we believe it to be one of the most permanent methods of propaganda'.[109] Keir Hardie's 'Daddy Time' noted in a *Leader* 'Chats with Lads and Lasses' column of 1895:

> If the parents would interest themselves more in their children's instruction we would soon have a race of Socialists who would be more than a match for all comers. We are going to have that in any case, but it would come all the sooner if the elders would look better after the teaching of the children.[110]

The *Labour Prophet*'s *Cinderella Supplement* was partly a result of the Labour Church's move towards practical child education, as Trevor made clear in May 1893:

> In Manchester and Salford friends have forced my hand. They are determined to go ahead at once with Cinderella Schools on the Sunday, and appeal to me for suggestions as to their conduct and management. At very short notice I have decided, therefore, to commence *Cinderella* at once as a supplement of the *Labour Prophet*.[111]

While Cinderella schools for children of the slums were initially at the forefront of the Labour Church agenda, it appears that such organisations aimed only at destitute children never became widespread. By the mid-1890s, attention had shifted to Labour Church Sunday Schools, which were more specifically directed towards the children of Labour Church members. In September 1894, H. C. Rowe proclaimed: 'We want a Sunday School in connection with every Labour Church, I.L.P., Social Democratic Federation, and Fabian branch in the country. It is, however, a matter specially for the Labour Church, where one exists.'[112] In response to this escalating child education movement, the balance of the *Cinderella* columns began to perceptibly shift away from entertainment to a more overt programme of political and moral education.

Symptomatic of this shift was the change of epigraph. While the supplement had originally been launched with a quotation from Elizabeth Barrett Browning's 'The Cry of the Children', which conjoined notions of a philanthropic crusade with an idyll of city children's return to innocence (extolling them to 'pluck your handfuls of the meadow cowslips pretty'), in January 1894 this was replaced by a poem with a very different emphasis.[113] A. Mary F. Robinson's verse instead intones portentously that training children 'makes' the future:

> We shall pass, but not our thought
> While in every one
> Lives the lesson that we taught.[114]

With this training obviously at the forefront of his mind, H. C. Rowe specifically directed Labour Church Sunday School organisers towards the children's columns of socialist periodicals, noting that 'A large collection of stories for children has been published in this paper. Others will be found in the *Labour Leader* and various other papers'.[115] Amy Payne reiterated Rowe's advice, suggesting that Labour Church Sunday School organisers should read their charges 'the children's page of the LABOUR PROPHET'.[116]

'I trust that in time the *Labour Prophet* will become far more an educational paper', Trevor had stated in 1893.[117] The fact that the children's pages were responding to this new function became increasingly apparent in

1895, when the *Labour Prophet* began to publish 'Our Cinderella Letter from the Fairy'. Introducing herself in March 1895, the Fairy is in no doubt about her socialising role:

> MY DEAR YOUNG PEOPLE,
>
> I am sure you will all understand me when I say that a very great power lies in the hands of you children. [...] you, boys and girls, who are reading this little talk of mine with you, have a great deal to do towards deciding what kind of country England shall be in the future. You will have to decide now by your lives, by your thoughts, and by the work that you do, what manner of men and women England shall possess. I think you will be able to gather, from what I say to you in an occasional chat with you, and from the stories and poems I shall give you to read, what sort of men and women we elder folks would like to see growing up around us.

The Fairy goes on to inform her readers that 'The story I am going to tell you now has a moral', a statement that would prove prophetic for her future contributions.[118] In this new context, fairies are no longer symbols of wistful loss, or gentle guides in rural lore, but a cunning imaginative coating to the pill of instruction. This Fairy has the unmistakable air of the schoolmarm: she is styled, not as a pre-industrial innocent, but a political agent, informing children in August 1895: 'Like a great many other people you know, I have been very busy electioneering.'[119]

New tales from old: Context and meaning

In May 1895, the Fairy tells her child readers, 'you, dear children, must not forget that in your hands lies the power of lessening the world's cares and troubles. We elder Socialists look to the boys and girls around us to help forward with all their might the great cause for which we are working'. Somewhat surprisingly, the Fairy falls back on a tale amenable to middle-class educators to illustrate her case:

> Now, here's a story for you, written by a good man called Hans Andersen, who loved children, and wanted to help them to lead happy, useful, self-reliant lives, and who, when he wanted to give them some good advice, wrapped it up in a beautiful story, and this time the moral is wrapped up in a story called 'There was a difference'.

The tale of an apple branch (which has a high opinion of its own value) and a humble dandelion concludes with an artist valuing both equally, for 'both are children of the kingdom of beauty'.[120] This tale, which can be persuasively read as a conservative celebration of God-given differentials, arguably activated different meanings in this context. The moral wrapped up in the story, however, is far from clear; while it might lead working-class children to challenge middle-class perceptions of their inferiority, its celebration of humility and contentment with the status quo hardly seems to encourage political action. The next month, the Fairy again entreats her readers to engage in the political battle, stating that she wants to help them grow up 'strong, healthy, happy, honest, intelligent citizens, fighting the big battle for freedom and justice with all the strength of which you are capable. We older Socialists know from sad experience what a terribly hard fight lies before you'. Yet in the appended tale, 'the Harebell's Sermon', the Harebell trots out a moral more appropriate to a Church of England hymn book:

> We are, all of us, of some use in the world, and we should never give up trying. Our heavenly Father has given each of us a place, and whether it be one of humble or high degree, we should do our very best in it […] Strive to do good – you in your small corner, and I in mine.[121]

This conservative idea of God-given place is conjoined with a conscious impetus to dispel class inequalities, a contradiction that appears perplexing. In August 1895, Andersen is presented as a type of working-class hero, a claim that ignores his rags to riches story. 'Now, here is a story which was told first of all by a dear old man called Hans Andersen. He lived more than a hundred years ago, in another land, and was poor all his life; but his happy heart was full of stories, which he told to the children who came after him.'[122] Directly following the Fairy's comments is Andersen's tale 'The Darning Needle' (in which a piece of broken glass and a blackened darning needle exhibit social snobbery). Another fairy tale is included in this month's *Cinderella* pages, a translation of a text by eighteenth-century satirist and folklorist Musäus. In 'Rubezaal; or The Wizard of the Mountains', a wizard in rural Germany, at 'one with the winds and the storms' rewards an act of philanthropy.[123] With the election fast approaching, these tales were admittedly hastily put together. While they are very different in style, neither seems particularly socialist in tone: the Andersen text warns against pride, and the Musäus tale combines a pantheistic spirituality with a conventional moral framework. However, when these tales are contextualised against Labour Church doctrines, they appear less anomalous, for it becomes apparent that the Fairy's question 'Well, and what have you young folk been doing for Socialism this month, eh?' is more compatible with traditional Christian charity than it at first seems.[124] Acts which are seen to contribute to socialism for the Fairy include reading a book to a sick friend as a way of showing 'comradeship', a philanthropic effort that would have been praised even within the pages of *Aunt Judy's Magazine*. Yet the Labour

Church's immanentist theology did not make this a problematic stance. In the *Labour Church Record* of April 1899, A. J. Waldegrave writes:

> The Labour Churches *are* Socialist bodies. But it is not in any narrow, or merely economic, sense that they use the word 'Socialism' to denote their creed and standard of conduct. With them it means justice, love, brotherhood.[125]

This broad interpretation of socialism meant children could still be educated by traditional fairy tales that valorised these non-controversial doctrines. It also meant that there was less ideological compulsion to instruct children in specific socialist tenets: the secretary of the Manchester and Salford Cinderella Club, speaking on the establishment of the first Cinderella School in May 1893, suggested that 'Our idea of the school […] is that it should be a place where the children can be trained to think, and not merely to become Socialists or Labour Church members'.[126] In fact, despite the many similarities, there were key differences between the *Labour Leader*'s and *Labour Prophet*'s methods of child socialisation.[127] The *Labour Prophet* was far more likely to use classical texts allusively, leaving children to deduce meanings that appeared to encourage the broad values of fellowship and brotherhood, in contrast to Hardie's championing of ILP socialism.

From July 1896 to April 1897, Thomas Robinson wrote a series of tales based on the Norse mythology of Odin for the *Cinderella* pages.[128] Robinson's description of Odin's lordship over Alfheim (or Elfhome), the homestead of the elves, was tied to Labour Church ideologies in a number of ways. Odin's spiritual rulership (his presence as 'all-father', a life-giving force), conjoined to his role as god of agriculture, can be seen to evoke parallels with the Labour Church's idea of free religion, with God as a pantheistic spiritual presence. The Labour Church did not invest the bible with a truth above other texts; pagan myths could be used to illustrate its theology as effectively as Christian iconography. It was the context of publication that gave these old tales new meanings. The first text, 'Odin and His One Eye', which describes Odin's sacrifice of an eye to Mimer ('memory or experience') to gain wisdom, can be read as a parable for the sacrifices to others that are necessary to become a true socialist. The tale 'The Elves and Fairies', published in October 1896, informed juvenile readers that the activities of the elves that looked after the flowers and animals in Alfheim were similar to those of children: 'But we can often do more than the elves, for goodhearted, cheerful children can go into places that are not beautiful and make them beautiful'. In the tale 'Elfhome: Charlie's Garden', children were encouraged to grow plants to create their own piece of fairyland.[129] Robinson adapted and embellished classical texts in a periodical context that embodied a call to both botanical activity and wider socialist endeavour. Reading these works within the *Labour Prophet* shows their contribution to the paper's wider ideologies, through an ability to conjoin myth, political and spiritual education. They were invested with meanings that had a resonance for their late nineteenth-century juvenile audience, readers whose parents were often familiar with Norse myth through the writings of Carlyle and Morris.[130]

The eclecticism of classical fantasy in the *Labour Prophet*'s *Cinderella Supplement* is again apparent in Jessie Hitch's translation of *Reynard the Fox*, which ran simultaneously with Robinson's 'Elfhome' stories from 1896 to 1897. This medieval beast fable, a satire on the contemporary clergy, achieves different satiric connotations in a late Victorian context. Reynard's false piety is apparent in Chapter 3, when he covetously eyes some chickens, but tells Grim the Badger that 'I was only delaying a minute, that I might say a Paternoster for the benefit of the souls of the many chickens and geese which I once stole from the good sisters'. The next week's instalment shows Reynard forgiven for his brutal transgressions due to his connections at court.[131] Religious hypocrisy was a key preoccupation of the Labour Church; the movement itself was partly born from a dawning realisation that both Anglicanism and Nonconformism were hampered by their established connections to Conservative and Liberal political interests. Through juxtaposition, this medieval satire becomes far more contemporary: it can be read as a commentary on the independence of the Labour Church, in contrast to institutionalised Christianity's continuing affiliation to wealth and power.

The most obvious example of the creation of political significance through context is the fairy-tale translation 'The Four Friends', which appeared in the *Labour Prophet* in December 1894.[132] In this tale, co-operation brings rewards. Pigeons trapped beneath a net realise they can free themselves if they all fly together, aided by their friend the mouse who chews through the ropes. The morality with which the tale concludes, 'UNITY IS STRENGTH', is very similar to the motto appended to Aesop's fable 'The Bundle of Sticks'; yet it would have had a significance for late nineteenth-century socialist readers unknown to Aesop's earlier audiences. A banner motto for the Cabinet Makers' Union, it had come to achieve a wider iconic resonance by the 1890s, exemplifying the power and promise of New Unionism.[133] This was a movement with which the *Labour Prophet* was closely connected. The Labour Church gave its collection money to strikers in Bromsgrove and Hull, and Tom Mann and Ben Tillett, both prominent union leaders, were regular contributors to the periodical. Published on the same page as a hymn to the 'Brave Sons of Labour', through juxtaposition the clichéd morality of 'The Four Friends' is transformed into an emotionally charged call for working-class solidarity.

'Joining the crusade against the giants': Keir Hardie, child readers and interactive fairy tales

If the *Labour Prophet*'s children's pages became more overtly didactic with the introduction of the Fairy, they were also more dialogic – suddenly active in the solicitation of input from readers. In her first letter, the Fairy encouraged an open-ended response from juveniles, suggesting, 'if any of you dear boys and girls like to write to me and tell me about yourselves and also about anything else you like, I shall be delighted to hear from you'. Although the Fairy offered to print the best contribution at the end of the next children's page, and hoped for 'a whole budget of letters', she was to be disappointed.[134] In April 1895, Ellie Brown from Hanley wrote in appreciation of two adapted fairy tales that had been published in the previous month's *Cinderella Supplement*, stating that she and her mother had 'liked them very much, and would like some more'. In May 1895, two child readers sent short essays on the seasons (one of which shows a literary sophistication suggestive of an editorial plant) and a photograph appeared of two female readers of around seven years old.[135] Interaction then abruptly terminated, although it is unclear why: the *Labour Prophet*'s relatively small circulation and the Fairy's tiresomely didactic tone may have been contributory factors. What is apparent, however, is the significant intertextual connections between socialist papers, for there appears to have been a definite cross-pollination of ideas between the *Labour Prophet* and *Labour Leader*. While the *Labour Prophet*'s *Cinderella Supplement* had utilised fairy-tale literature from its launch in 1893, it was 1895 before it sought a directly interactive formula. Hardie's role as 'Daddy Time' in the *Labour Leader* was surely influential: his children's columns of the previous year had been stunningly successful in creating an engaged and politicised child audience, and had done so through an astute recognition of the appeal of textual response.

In April 1894, Hardie used his children's column to establish the 'Labour Crusaders', a club for those under 16 who were willing to fight for social equality by furthering the cause of socialism. Hardie's rhetoric clearly draws on religious tactics absorbed during his earlier affiliation to the Evangelical Union and organisational strategies mastered through his role in the Temperance movement the 'Good Templars'.[136] Yet the club's name is revealing about another ideology close to Hardie's heart, for it combines signifiers associated with a religious war with a nostalgia for the perceived organic relations of pre-industrial society. Hardie establishes the role and rationale of the Crusaders through a fascinating reworking of Jack the Giant-Killer. Using the device of an excitable child reader, Hardie assumes both that child readers have prior knowledge of the classic tale and that they are unable to resist its inspirational power. Engaging children's impulse for imaginative adventure, Hardie asks rhetorically:

> First, let me ask, have you read the true story of Jack the Giant-Killer? Of course you have! Well, I thought you had, so you needn't make so much noise about it, for I have read it too. Some day I may tell you when I read it, and what I did after reading it. When you were reading the story did you not all wish that you had been with Jack to help him to kill the big giants? Well, now, isn't it strange, But I just felt like that also.[137]

Hardie's description of Jack the Giant-Killer as a 'true' story raises the intriguing issue of the interfusion of fact and fiction in the *Labour Leader*. As Anne Humpherys, analysing the blending of melodramatic and political codes in the pages of *Reynolds's Weekly Newspaper* has pointed out, 'we do not just begin with "facts"' and then make meaning of them through narrative models. It is equally the case that the stories that we use to 'explain' events may have actually shaped what we perceive to be the original 'facts'.[138] In his 'Chats with Lads and Lasses' column, Hardie demonstrates this point, claiming that his own early understanding of political injustice had been explicitly shaped through the reading of a fairy tale. He goes on to incite his readers:

> Well, now, I know where there is a whole castle full of big, ugly, dirty giants. Some of them have three heads, and some have a dozen. [...] But how would you like to begin to fight these giants? Eh! they might eat you! Well, so they might. But before going out to fight them lets [sic] form an army and I think I can give each one of you a sword of sharpness (which won't break), and a cloak of darkness, and shoes of swiftness. Now, hands up all those willing to fight the giants! Oh, my! what a crowd![139]

In Hardie's shrewd journalistic transformation of capitalist reality into fairyland, he goes a step further than Blatchford's transmutation of the 'real' into the 'ideal'. In Hardie's spirited prose, the implied reader is not merely rhetorically conscripted, but becomes the protagonist of the text. In narrative strategy, Hardie echoes his 1893 story, 'The History of a Giant'. Subtitled 'A Study in Politics for Very Young Boys', this early tale is a thinly veiled polemic which fuses the fairy tale with Bunyanesque allegory, and concerns the enslavement of the giant 'Labour' through the wiles of 'King' and 'Capitalist'. This work also seamlessly transforms fiction into fact, while the textual consumer is seemingly just as effortlessly metamorphosed into a juvenile political activist. It concludes with the grizzled giant Labour gathering forces to fight his abusers: he 'built a huge tent, the centre pole of which was set in Bradford, a village amidst the hills, and inhabited by the kindliest and trustiest of Labour's children'. Labour's children are indeed given a fundamental role, for the end of the story does not signify the end of readers' involvement, but the beginning of their role in the political struggle. Child readers are informed that 'Some day you will read for yourselves the result of the battle. But you too will be called to take part in it. On which side will you be?'[140]

Hardie's prose is certainly manipulative, but, like the *Labour Prophet* correspondence classes, his stance also demands an active, participatory response from readers. 'The History of a Giant' was published when the *Labour Leader* was still monthly: the change to weekly status in 1894 allowed Hardie to forge more regular links with his juvenile readers. At the launch of the Labour Crusaders in April 1894, the pledge of political commitment that

Hardie attempted to secure was not relegated to the future, but was practically and immediately effected through his weekly columns.

After capturing juvenile imaginations with his Jack the Giant-Killer analogies, Hardie asks children to send their names and addresses for his 'big book', 'Then, when a thousand names have been sent in, I will make you into an army, and we will go and fight the giants'. Several months later, Hardie reported the success of this literary gambit; children were actively collecting names, and the movement was gathering momentum through the weekly publication in Hardie's column of the names of each new member. Hardie suggests that adult readers have also realised the power of this strategy, claiming: 'Daddy is delighted to hear from many readers of the Labour Leader that his fairy stories and poems are very highly appreciated by the mothers and fathers of the Crusaders, as well as by the young people themselves'.[141]

The reader who corroborates this fact is almost certainly in the parental category, if not the ventriloquist voice of Hardie himself. Demonstrating that visual as well as verbal works involving fairies could be read as political allegory, Hardie recommends that readers make a visit to the National Gallery to see Sir Noel Paton's *A Midsummer Night's Dream*, printing the interpretation of (supposed) correspondent James A. Grieve, who reads the painting as a symbolic depiction of the prostitution endemic in contemporary capitalism:

> Dear Daddy Time, – Your column is my delight, and specially so since your fairy stories. Two results have flowed from them: I have liked your column better ever since, and I have gone with, if possible, more zest to study two of the finest creations in our National Gallery – I mean "A Midsummer Night's Dream" by Sir Noel Paton. Are you familiar with these pictures, Daddy? [...] In the right hand Corner, on 'The Quarrel' subject, sits a grim old knave courting a lovely woman who sits pensive, elbow on right knee, chin resting on her hand. While he solicits her, he points with his left hand to an imp who pours the glittering gold coin at her feet from a bag on his shoulder. I see this scene often on our Princes Street, the haggard old spectre of want or lust driving our sisters to part with the virtue that is our and their glory. Sir Noel also must have seen this, and often too, for in a footnote to his great creation, he asks us *to think*. – Yours affectionately,
>
> JAMES A GRIEVE.[142]

Operating as a rhetorical set piece, the insertion of the symbolic name 'A Grieve' reveals that Hardie or the adult sender of this piece made little attempt to produce a convincing child correspondent. However, despite the adult tone and subject matter of this suspiciously articulate writer, there is evidence to suggest that Hardie's reports of readerly appreciation for his fairy tales was not entirely manufactured. Children's written commitment to

Crusader membership appeared to validate the assumption that had always informed Hardie's editorship – that the interpretative pleasures of fiction could engender social activism. The expanding list of names (which included ages and addresses) testified to the success of the fairy tale in energising young readers. Hardie was energised in turn by this unequivocally positive response. His own reply was to expand the 'Jack the Giant-Killer' analogy into an extended serialised fiction. 'Jack Clearhead: A Fairy Tale for Crusaders' first appeared in a *Labour Leader* children's column on 8 September 1894, six months after the initial launch of the Crusaders, and ran until 22 October that year. This allegorical tale was far more skilful than Hardie's earlier 'History of a Giant' in marrying political satire with fairy-tale machinery. It begins in the satiric mode of his earlier tale, in an only vaguely disguised Britain: readers are told that 'Once upon a time two tribes of people inhabited an island in the western ocean'.[143] These are explained as the Sharpheads (capitalists) and the Dullards (workers). What follows is a rather unimaginative political sermon. Every year the Dullards carry the Plumduffs (Liberals) or the Piecrusts (Tories) into the Pow-Wow (Parliament), but as both groups are Sharpheads, the Dullards remain enslaved.

While this is unsubtle allegory, relying on a linguistic playfulness derivative of Lewis Carroll for its interest, in the second instalment of the tale, Hardie is far more self-referential, and begins to appropriate and revise the plot devices of the familiar fairy tale. Young Jack Sharphead gives bread to an old woman at a well; she transpires to be the fairy 'Common Sense', who rewards him with a sword of sharpness. In keeping with ethical socialism's marriage of personal and social change, Hardie unites the unique valour of the fairy-tale hero with a wider social movement, linking individual action to a contemporary political crusade. Jack is told by the fairy that the sword will help him to victory in the many battles that await him as long as he remains 'on the side of honesty and truth'. And as long as he repeats the following rhyme:

> "Sword, sword fight for me,
> I belong to the I.L.P."[144]

Hardie's sword of sharpness becomes a tool of political indoctrination: it identifies one branch of late nineteenth-century socialism as the emissary of the fairy-tale absolutes 'honesty and truth'. Further alignments of good and evil are no less polarised: Jack's confrontation with cannibalistic giants in the original tale becomes Jack's run-in with Giants owned by the Sharpheads: 'Mon-o-Poly' and his son 'Com-pe-Tition'. The narrator informs his readers that 'Cruel monsters they were, who devoured men and women and great numbers of little children every year'. Mon-o-Poly is 'a dirty, gluttonous monster' while Com-pe-Tition has 'claws like a bird of prey, with which to tear his victims in pieces'.[145] While the older reader would recognise the satire, the establishment of a black-and-white moral framework also explicitly encourages much less sophisticated readers to affiliate to the cause. Readers in their roles as Crusaders are once again rhetorically incorporated into the tale: 'Each Dame and Knight agree / To fight big ghouls like thee'.[146] Yet as readers join the socialist struggle, they also have the agency to insert themselves into the text. Published at the end of Hardie's fairy-tale instalments are the names of real readers who pledged allegiance to Jack's cause.

While in some chapbook versions of the tale Jack rescues a Duke's daughter from the dungeon of a cannibalistic giant's lair, in Hardie's tale Jack rescues the maiden 'Social-Ism' from the clutches of Giants 'Ig-no-Ramus' and 'Super-Stition'. Jack swiftly falls in love, playing on a metaphoric connection between socialism and sexual attraction. The personification of socialism as an alluringly beautiful woman was a familiar piece of verbal and visual iconography within the movement: William Morris famously described the emotional propulsion behind his political marriage to socialism as a 'delight in the life of the world; intense and overweening love of the very skin and surface of the earth on which man dwells such as a lover has in the fair flesh of the woman he loves'.[147] Hardie's adoption of the metaphor for a child audience at first seems strange; Jack appears to instantly metamorphose from child adventurer to adult hero. Yet Hardie manages to downplay the sexual implications of adult desire, containing them in the chivalric codes of fairy-tale romance. The fairy tale could be used to simplify and sanitise the most complex of political and emotional allegiances.

Truth and fiction, the mythic and the journalistic and the erotic and the innocent are indeed conflated here in intriguing ways. Hardie explicitly uses Jack's exploits to explicate contemporary events, using discussion of the fight against Mon-o-Poly and Com-pe-Tition in Chapter 4 to discuss something far less likely to catch the childish imagination: the planned meeting of the ILP National Administrative Council in Glasgow. And unlike the *Labour Prophet*'s translations of Grimm and Perrault, there is a good deal of editorial commentary from Hardie's alter ego 'Daddy Time' to deduce its relevance. Readers are told that 'The instalment of the fairy tale which the editor has sent us this week, is of special interest, and Daddy hopes that his young friends will take to heart the wise counsels which underlie the incidents of the story'.[148]

Published letters from children eager to join the Crusaders show that Daddy Time's 'young friends' did indeed take these counsels to heart – in fact, it is intriguing how persuasive the Jack the Giant-Killer analogy became for Hardie and his child correspondents, who still used the metaphor over two years later. Around the time of the July 1895 General Election, the image was particularly suggestive. On 20 July, W. Wilson, Florrie Wilson and Annie Wilson write that 'father has been at Fulham every night last week helping to slay the giants', while the next week, after Hardie had lost his West Ham seat in the election, correspondent James Frazer offers his condolences, and provides more names of children 'who are anxious to join our little army and to assist us to fight "and conquer" those big giants, the cruel tyrants, who now oppress the poor workman'.[149] In September 1896, correspondent R. Meats is envisaging his own position in the industrial workforce via recourse to such fairy-tale imagery:

> Since I became a Crusader I have started working for one of the giants, who until recently was one of our law makers. But I am, on the whole, well treated compared with some, though, as my father says, when Socialism comes, we shall have more righteousness than we have now.[150]

Meats is not the only older juvenile whose class consciousness has been shaped by Hardie's fairy tales. in October 1894, just before the sixth chapter of Jack Clearhead, a letter appears from G. N. Bunn from Walworth:

> I am fourteen next Birthday, and am working in the painters' shop of the London Tramway Company. I read the fairy tales by Mr. Keir Hardie with great pleasure. I am also one of four brothers who are all Socialists, and we endorse all the opinions of the Independent Labour Party.[151]

These letters, by turns portentous and childlike in sentiment, are in many ways representative of *Labour Leader*'s juvenile correspondence. Like most of the children who wrote to the paper, Meats was a working-class child already influenced by actively socialist parents (his sister Enid, whom he added to the list of Crusaders names, had been named after 'our Enid' – the activist Enid Stacy). While child contributions were regular, a fairly small number of names recur. Like Meats and Bunn, their contributions are often shaped by familial influence, and younger children often echo the sonorous phrases of parental dogma. Yet commitment to the Crusaders had an interesting consequence that Hardie did not perhaps anticipate: children's collective visibility became a bargaining tool to secure their interests as readers. On 27 July 1895, the number of Crusaders exceeded Hardie's target of one thousand. In September of that year, 'Uncle Fred', who had taken charge of Hardie's children's column during the editor's American tour, railed against the paper's assistant editor, suggesting to child readers that their mass presence should be used to assert their interests as literary consumers:

> Hang that fellow Davie Lowe! Just as I thought. Last week he chopped out all I wrote about the Earl's Court Exhibition to make room for a whole page report on that bally Trades Congress [...] We are now over one thousand strong, and we will not submit to having our corner 'pinched' in that fashion. So let him beware![152]

While decidedly playful in tone, 'Uncle Fred' makes a valid point: the column's space on the back page was indeed often 'pinched' to make way for adult news. From 1894 to 1896, it varied in size according to the contingencies of each issue, from less than a column to almost a full broadsheet page. Hardie returned as 'Daddy Time' in early 1896, but in July of that year, the section disappeared altogether, reappearing suddenly two months later 'after many weeks of silence'. In the newly restored column, Hardie publishes a letter from Kathleen Connell that he claims has 'frightened the editor':

> DEAR DADDY TIME, – I really cannot wait any longer. If you do not restore to the Crusaders the column you have stolen from them, I will call for a strike against you. That will soon bring you to your senses [...] If you do not stop this at once and treat us fairly, we will take the big book out of your hands, and place it in charge of the Bounder, who we understand loves little children better than anything on earth.[153]

Kathleen Connell is revealed to 'live with Uncle Fred'; her sophisticated tone suggests that she is an older reader, if not a mask for an adult joke penned by 'Uncle Fred' himself. While she threatens a strike, her real bargaining tool is the ability of young readers to forsake the *Labour Leader* for Robert Blatchford's *Clarion*: E. F. Fay ('the Bounder') was a *Clarion* journalist who had undertaken pioneering work with the Cinderella clubs. Despite the somewhat arch tone of this letter, it was possibly no idle threat, for children's letters revealed that many young readers of the *Leader* also read (and sold) the *Clarion*. On the same page as Connell's assertions appears a more simple letter from Sarah Ellen Allen of Dewsbury, who is proud to have received her Crusaders' membership card, but also demands 'I want to see our Daddy Time in the *Labour Leader* again, and I want all our Crusaders to send letters until they poke you up a bit'. Interestingly, this was also the column that published the letter from R. Meats. If joining the crusade against the giants helped Meats to question the power relations inherent in his position as child worker, it seems to have done something similar for Allen in her role as textual consumer.

It would be misleading, however, to suggest that it was always teenaged readers who subscribed to Crusader membership, or featured in *Labour Leader* correspondence. There was genuine childish engagement, as a letter from John William Roberts of Leeds, from 1895, demonstrates:

> I wish to join in the Crusade against the giant. I attend the Sunday School of the Leeds Labour Church along with my brother and two sisters, we have learnt to sing 'England Arise' and 'O come, come away, beneath our Labour banner'. I am nine years old.[154]

The considerable number of child readers who express affiliation to the Labour Church within these columns is an interesting revelation about the intimacy of the movement's links with ILP socialism. In 1895, 'Knight John

Duncan' from Leeds reports the establishment of a new Labour Church Sunday School, while in June of the same year, James Allen from Scotland mentions attending outdoor Labour Church services with his parents. In July, Alice Chadwick from Hyde tells Daddy Time that she attends the Labour Church 'almost every Sunday', while Joseph Arthur Boot writes regularly about the Newcastle Labour Church, from which he enthusiastically recruits Crusader membership.[155]

The identification of many child readers with Labour Churches makes it reasonable to assume that there would have been some familiarity with the children's pages of the *Labour Prophet*. Hardie, whose own paper provided a column for Labour Church news, would certainly have been familiar with its content. Intertextuality again becomes a distinct possibility here, for it is quite likely that Hardie's use of Jack the Giant-Killer was influenced by Trevor's strikingly similar use of the metaphor in his 'Cinderella Letter' to child readers in the September 1893 *Labour Prophet*. In the letter, Trevor, like Hardie, presumes that his readers are already familiar with the tale: 'You know that Jack the Giant-Killer found a golden trumpet hung by a silver chain on the gate of a giant's castle.' Trevor reminds readers that because Jack was brave enough to blow the trumpet, the spell was broken, 'and Jack killed the giant; and all his prisoners, who had been transformed into all kinds of shapes, were changed back into men and women, and set free'. While Trevor is not so doctrinaire as to substitute Hardie's ILP sword of sharpness for Jack's magic trumpet, a similar process of transmogrification is perceived to lie in the hands of child readers:

> My dear children, there are giant wrongs to be slain to-day, and people everywhere to be set free from their strange spells. And brave men and women are needed to blow the trumpet at the gates of their strongholds that they may tremble and fall, and the giants be slain, and strong men and fair women and tender children be restored to their proper forms, and made into the beautiful human creatures God means them to be.
> But only really brave people can blow these horns.[156]

The warped social relations of capitalism become the enchanted forms at the giant's castle; their release under socialism into economic, moral and spiritual enlightenment is a true form of fairy-tale metamorphosis. As with Hardie's text, the child is not merely the reader, but the protagonist of the tale. Trevor promises that, in the socialist crusade, every child can be a fairy-tale hero.

While Trevor's polemic was followed by no published interventions from readers, less than a year later the same rhetoric was used, with indubitable success, to launch Hardie's Labour Crusaders. The award of a Crusaders' membership card might seem a rather anti-climactic response to the thousand readers that Hardie had promised to make into an army. Yet juvenile readers appeared to distinguish the subtleties of Hardie's metaphor: with interesting overlaps with movements such as the Good Templars or the Salvation Army, Crusaders seemed aware that fighting the giants involved significant elements of display. In February 1895, reader Michael Rae mentions Glasgow Crusaders' plans to turn out for Unemployment Day, while in April of that year, two hundred Crusaders attended the ILP conference in Newcastle. In September 1896, Hardie reports that 'Archie M'Carthur [sic] of Glasgow is full of all sorts of plans for the winter. There is the Sunday School, and now he proposes a Socialist Band of Hope, a Social Guild for young people and I do not know what else besides'.[157] In fact, in 1897 McArthur was also to take over Hardie's children's column. As Socialist Sunday Schools flourished (across Scotland particularly), the children's section became a forum to link these localised movements.[158] Hardie's fight against the giants had engaged the practical commitment of the activist through the imaginative and textual pleasures of the reader, but McArthur was much less interested in fiction, and readers' use of fairy-tale metaphors gradually slipped away.

The *Labour Prophet* and *Labour Leader* testify to the power of fairy tales to undergo endless reinvention: to continually create new meanings for new editors, writers and audiences. Yet the extent to which Trevor's and Hardie's appropriation of the fairy tale was empowering or restricting for juvenile readers remains an elusive question. It may have helped teenaged readers and workers (such as Meats and Bunn) to theorise their own positions in the labour force: to use Hardie's metaphor as a conceptual tool that led to practical attempts to bring about change. It undoubtedly provided a counterpoint to the unquestioning deference to middle-class authority implicit in many contemporary children's texts. If an actively socialist upbringing made such children a potentially alienated minority, the printed Crusaders' names forged a community of interest, and made visible their collective power as readers. Interestingly (and unlike the rest of the paper), the Crusaders also succeeded in attracting a significant number of female participants. Yet the simplifications inherent in fairy-tale ascriptions of good and evil also limited dialogue. The socialism professed by young *Labour Leader* readers was uniform rather than heterodox; while many of the letters appear to be genuine, they generally converged ideologically with 'Daddy Time', the ventriloquist voice of the editor.

The directive thrust of socialist writing for children became inevitable when hopes for 'a kingdom of heaven upon earth' depended on the next generation.[159] In 1894, John Trevor pronounced that 'All roads nowadays lead to Socialism, and the road of Education is no exception'.[160] Fairy tales occupied a unique place on this educational journey. Perceived as sacred relics of the pre-industrial past, and augers of a post-industrial future, they also became political tools in forging a new generation of socialists. 'What does your child ask you for by the fire of an evening?' wrote Blatchford, 'Not

Figure 4.3 Alexis, 'Sleeping Beauty', *Labour Leader*, 25 Dec. 1897. © The British Library Board. All Rights Reserved. NPL LON 1000

an explanation of the telephone or a lesson in vulgar fractions, but for a song – or a fairy story'. Yet, as Blatchford realised, the appeal of fairy tales to adult socialists was equally irresistible. For the 'grown-up child', such artistic forms articulated something beyond materialism – for art, like ethical socialism, was 'always the outward and visible form of the inward and spiritual hunger for something *better than life* – for a world more perfect and beautiful than this world in which we live'.[161]

A front-page *Labour Leader* cartoon from 1897 reprises such sentiments: a working man cuts through the briars that have sprung from the bushes of 'Capitalism' and 'Feudalism', and ascends the palace steps to claim the radiant maiden 'Socialism' (Figure 4.3).[162] While this Sleeping Beauty allegory might tell us something about troubled attitudes to feminism in the *Labour Leader* (and indeed echoes Jack's sexual prize in 'Jack Clearhead'), it also articulates a longing that is more potent than sexual desire: the need to see the socialist struggle as a quest narrative with a pre-determined happy ending. While labour periodicals were caught in the political upheavals of the present, the fairy tale could be aligned with the millenarian tendencies of the 'religion of socialism': both relied on a predictable trajectory of events, and an ultimately joyous conclusion. William Morris owed more to Marx than either Hardie or Trevor, assuming that the joyous moment would come only after revolutionary violence and brutal class conflict. Yet he also suggested that the fairy tale would characterise that future epoch at rest. In the Hall of Bloomsbury Market, *News From Nowhere*'s time-travelling William Guest finds, in the next millennium, images of 'queer old-world myths' decorating the walls:

> I smiled, and said: 'Well, I scarcely expected to find record of the Seven Swans and the King of the Golden Mountain and Faithful Henry, and such curious pleasant imaginations as Jacob Grimm got together from the childhood of the world, barely lingering even in his time': I should have thought you would have forgotten such childishness by this time.[163]

Old Hammond rejoices in that second childhood that has restored supposedly timeless art: Clara is more ambivalent about the fate of culture in an epoch when class conflict (and therefore history) is over. If there are mild hints of unease in the text itself, the stasis of Morris's *Nowhere* was a clear target of H. G. Wells in his Fabian stage. In *A Modern Utopia* of 1905, Wells's narrator (the ponderous 'Owner of the Voice') notes pointedly:

> The utopias of a modern dreamer must needs differ in one fundamental aspect from the Nowheres and Utopias men planned before Darwin quickened the thought of the world. Those were all perfect and static states, a balance of happiness won forever against the forces of unrest and disorder that inhere in things.[164]

In Robert Blatchford's 1892 *Clarion* fairy tale 'Elevenpence to the Shilling', he suggests that Darwinian evolution is more wonderful than the tales in the *Arabian Nights*, but also that it entails a profound sense of loss:

> Fairies were right outside the pale of Darwinism; fairies had no 'origin,' no 'skeleton,' no species and no period. The mastodon had left his bones in the rock [...] but the fairies had left nothing anywhere, except a kind of wistful regret in the minds of ignorant poets and children.[165]

In the socialist press's preoccupation with fairy tale and folklore that wistfulness is often evident, revealing attempts to hold on to dreams of a future that can transcend political as well as biological unrest and disorder. For when ethical socialism looked back to 'the childhood of the world', it was also predicting the future – creating the longed-for happy-ever-after through a union of political science and 'impossible romance'.

5
'All art is at once surface and symbol': Fairy Tales and *fin-de-siècle* Little Magazines

> There is no such thing as a moral or an immoral book.[1]
>
> The true end and object of a fairy tale – if that can be said to be an object which moves by instinct to its goal – is the expression of the joy of living. There begins and ends the morality of the fairy tale: its value consists in its optimism.[2]

Referring to his second collection of fairy tales, Oscar Wilde famously claimed that 'in building this *House of Pomegranates* I had about as much intention of pleasing the British child as I had of pleasing the British public'.[3] Wilde's comment is arch, but is also commercially shrewd, a knowing attempt to capitalise on a lucrative niche market. Expensive, sexually explicit fairy-tale editions, including Sir Richard Burton's *The Book of the Thousand Nights and a Night*, had already circulated among connoisseurs of erotica. In the wake of Wilde's collections, Aubrey Beardsley was inspired by Cinderella in the *Yellow Book*, while fairy tales were written by his fellow contributors Evelyn Sharp, Vernon Lee and Max Beerbohm.[4]

Why were fairy tales so revered among these coterie writers and audiences? This chapter offers some answers to that question, contextualising this genre's forgotten role in the avant-garde debates of the 1890s. Both the fairy tales discussed here and the little magazines that published them were implicated in a range of *fin-de-siècle* movements, from Arts and Crafts and the Celtic Revival to Symbolism and decadence. Here, I explore the ingenious ways that these artistic communities reclaimed the fairy tale: for folk culture and for the avant-garde, in defence of both decadent and anti-decadent sensibilities, and in service of national identity and emergent gay culture.

The work of Laurence Housman marks an obvious point of convergence between the fairy tale, the periodical and such experimental movements. A writer, illustrator and frequent little magazine contributor, Housman's virtuosity makes him particularly a rich focus for analysis: he was involved in both literary and graphic modes of fairy-tale production, popular and avant-garde ventures.[5] As an illustrator and book designer, Housman worked on the production of both folktale collections and adult poetic works (including a well-known edition of Christina Rossetti's *Goblin Market*). As a creator of the 'total' book, he was writer and illustrator of four original fairy-tale collections.[6] He was also a promoter of 'classic' fairy tales, providing an introduction to Taylor and Cruikshank's *Gammer Grethel's Fairy Tales* (1905) and retelling the *Arabian Nights* in two stylish adult-orientated collaborations with Edmund Dulac (1907 and 1913).

Housman's contributions to minority periodical culture included drawings, poems, short stories and fairy tales in many of the key little magazines of the *fin de siècle*, from the *Yellow Book* and the *Dome* to the *Pageant* and the *Butterfly*. He also embarked with W. Somerset Maugham on his own small press periodical production, the *Venture* (1903/5).[7] A minor figure in the avant-garde circles that gathered around the Café Royal in the 1890s, influenced stylistically and personally by the decadent illustrator Charles Ricketts and by Oscar Wilde, Housman juggled a number of professional and political identities (including writer, illustrator and book designer; feminist, socialist and homosexual). This chapter uses Housman's original fairy tales in the little magazines in the 1890s as a starting point from which to explore this subgenre's wider appropriation for (and by) both artistic and sexual minority audiences.

'Too highbrow to be popular': Little magazines, elitism and commerce

Sumptuous and stylish, with pretensions beyond the ephemeral format, the little magazine is one of the most distinctive markers of *fin-de-siècle* experimentalism. For early twentieth-century critics such as Holbrook Jackson, such periodicals encapsulate 'the unique qualities in the literature and art of the decade'; for Ian Fletcher, writing in the 1970s, the little magazine stands as 'perhaps the most forceful emblem of decadent anxiety'.[8] Yet one of the most striking features of this influential literary form is its heterogeneity. Jackson's list includes periodicals that vary widely in terms of price, frequency and type of publisher.[9] Definition is slippery.

If these periodicals evade easy classification, it is possible to note some shared experimental strategies. They frequently tested the short story as an emerging literary form; they generally engaged with the graphic arts as well as literature. This inter-generic content, which included the showcasing of Oriental-, Symbolist- and Pre-Raphaelite-influenced visual works, was accompanied by self-conscious innovation in format, typography and style. For critics such as Linda Dowling, it is this new relationship between the visual and the verbal, articulated through a more complex approach to the combined arts, that is one of the defining characteristics of the 'literary' periodicals of the 1890s.[10] The new process engraving was used to startling effect in Beardsley's art nouveau *Yellow Book* productions, while the *Pageant*, an expensive art annual, edited by book designer and illustrator Charles Shannon and art critic Gleeson White, reproduced late Pre-Raphaelite images and Symbolist works by Puvis de Chavannes, Gustave Moreau and Charles Ricketts.[11] One periodical sub-group, while including fiction, was explicitly linked to particular schools of art. The *Quest*, the *Quarto* and the *Beam* showcased work by affiliates of the Birmingham School of Art, the Slade and the National Art Training School respectively.[12]

Speaking in retrospect of his own literary/art periodical the *Venture*, Laurence Housman suggested that 'the whole thing was, of course, too highbrow to be popular'; it should, he believed, have been priced much higher.[13] Housman foregrounds the fact that price and taste were frequently conflated by little magazine producers and consumers, yet such magazines existed across a broad price continuum. The *Dial*, at seven shillings and sixpence, the product of Shannon and Ricketts' art press the Vale, was a notably more elite product than the later shilling *Dome*.[14] Categorisation by price also ignores anomalies: the monthly *Butterfly* was placed in Jackson's list of more popular periodicals, presumably due to its cheap price of sixpence.[15] Launched in 1893, and rather incongruously subtitled *A Humorous and Artistic Monthly*, the *Butterfly* might initially appear to be a half-way house between a wholly experimental and an overtly commercial periodical. It folded in 1894 and restarted in 1899, clearly influenced in its second phase by titles such as the *Yellow Book*, but from the beginning the periodical bore the marks of the typographical and artistic innovations of Whistler (from whose signature its title probably derives), exhibited a fascination with Japanese art and showcased then little-known decadent writers such as John Gray.

While the periodical was comparatively cheap and (unlike most of the periodicals under discussion) included some commercial advertising, it was also marked by the minority tastes of a coterie magazine, introducing works by former students from the Lambeth School of Art. At its initial termination in 1894, co-editor Arnold Golsworthy noted the haphazard nature of production: put together by 'a handful of artists and writers' with the aim of having 'a magazine of their own', their intentions were to be remunerated 'so far as to enable us ultimately to give our whole time to its preparation and production'.[16] Like the *Quarto*, the *Butterfly* had been produced in time 'snatched with difficulty' from other jobs. The modest hopes of the *Butterfly*'s editors had been frustrated by net profits of 'exactly 0', causing the periodical's five-year suspension.[17]

As the *Butterfly*'s editorial valediction suggests, one way of categorising these publications was in terms of their precarious position in the literary marketplace: such titles often conspicuously targeted select audiences. At the most private end of the market, titles such as the *Dial* and the *Quest*, like their influential predecessor the *Century Guild Hobby Horse*, averaged a circulation of less than three hundred per issue.[18] While in 1884 Arthur

Heygate Mackmurdo notes that an editorial preface is only necessary in the unlikely contingency that 'our "Hobby Horse" rides out, unknown to us, into circles beyond those compassing personal friends', the *Quarto* states in 1896 that 'we cater for none'. In 1893, William Sharp, in the forward of the *Pagan Review*, a single-authored, single-issue periodical that took private production to its most schizophrenic extremes, announces superbly that 'We aim at thorough-going unpopularity: and there is every reason to believe that, with the blessed who expect little, we shall not be disappointed'.[19]

The *Butterfly* asserts 'we have no Mission'; the *Quarto* makes clear that the periodical 'proclaims nothing, boasts nothing, and at least we are saved from failing to come up to high-flown expectations'.[20] While appearing to reject commerce, these arch-editorials establish their own niche market position: for, as Pierre Bourdieu has noted, the avant-garde commonly defines itself in just such a 'quasi negative way, as the sum of the refusals of all socially recognized tastes'.[21] In their assertions of 'Art for Art's sake', little magazines often styled themselves as the antithesis to the mass media, a counterpoint to the huge circulation papers and periodicals that courted an ever expanding reading public through the techniques of the New Journalism. In a marketplace in which the *Daily Mail* sold close to a million copies, and monthlies such as the *Strand* fed a mass appetite for illustrated subgenre fiction, little magazines pointed wryly to the associations between literature and commerce: to the supposedly lower middle class, middle-brow values that had become synonymous with the popular. In the *Dome* for Michelmas 1897, the writer of 'Four Notes' sneered:

> Some person who is quite good enough for *The Daily Mail* has been reading the twelve lines by Mr. W. B. Yeats which appeared in our last number. This 'Sonnet,' as he intelligently calls it, had the effect of sending him 'careering back to commonplaces with a sigh of relief.' All humane men and women will feel glad that the *Daily Mail* person returned to his own place so safe and sound, and nice and early, after his venturesome little excursion in foreign parts.[22]

If little magazines were ideologically attuned to the minority, they could also enjoy, like the socialist press, a more shrewd relationship with the popular literary marketplace than the *Dome*'s rhetoric-led critics to believe. *The Yellow Book* was the most successful example of a magazine that maintained a prudent balance between artistic and commercial aspiration. By the time of the magazine's launch in 1894, John Lane was already well known as a publisher of attractively packaged literary works that appealed to the aesthete collector. While Beardsley's cover designs and drawings could be intentionally provocative, literature editor Henry Harland combined decadent work by Beardsley and Symons with less controversial short stories and visual material. Indeed, the *Yellow Book*'s love–hate relationship with middle-class and popular tastes (a commercial agenda that famously led to Beardsley's removal after the Wilde trials) has been fruitfully explored elsewhere.[23] The *Dome*'s embrace of a similar recipe of mockery and circumspection reveals its own commercial as well as artistic interests. At a shilling, the *Dome* expected to sell not a few hundred, but seven-and-a-half thousand copies of its first edition: a strategy closer to the shrewd niche marketing of the *Yellow Book* than the more esoteric pitch of the *Century Guild Hobby Horse*, or of occasional concerns such as the *Dial* or the *Venture*.

Self-referentially aware of New Journalistic cliché, *The Yellow Book* and the *Dome* disguised the ambiguity of their aims by mocking their own dealings in the commercial marketplace. A (vaguely) pseudonymous fictional satire by the editor and proprietor Ernest J. Oldmeadow, which appeared in the *Dome* in November 1898, is particularly revealing about the periodical's self-promotional techniques.[24] This slight tale focuses on the editor of a magazine named the 'The Jonquil', which has an obvious resemblance to the *Strand*. The class snobbery of the piece is explicit, equating such material with working- or lower-middle-class audiences: it is the editor's office boy who most enthusiastically reads the *Jonquil*'s melodramatic romances and sensation fictions, speaking excitedly of 'Dorrerthy's Love-Story, or my Fice is My Fortune'.[25] This heavy-handed parody is reminiscent of the *Yellow Book*'s references to the class who 'read the works of Mr. All Kine'.[26] In the *Dome* satire, such popular fiction brings on a brain fever in its editor, whose recovery is marked by his ability to eschew detective stories in favour of Dante Gabriel Rossetti and Elizabeth Barrett Browning. If such a fiction is self-referential and tongue-in-cheek, it is also shrewd enough to both mock the New Journalism and to use its techniques to delineate its audience by flattery.

However, if detective fiction and the romantic novel were subject to the *Dome*'s mockery, why did the fairy tale, another genre that the *Strand* took up enthusiastically, find room in the *Dome*'s own pages as high art? The periodical published two literary fairy tales by Laurence Housman, 'A Capful of Moonshine' and 'How Little Duke Jarl Saved the Castle', in addition to the Byam Shaw drawing 'Beauty and the Beast', and a range of folklore-inspired Symbolist poetry and prose by W. B. Yeats. The *Dome* was not, in fact, exceptional in according the fairy tale an elevated position in this hierarchy of taste.

Beauty and use: Arts and Crafts and the fairy tale

In the first number of the *Quest*, the periodical of the Birmingham Guild of Handicraft, Laurence Housman's fairy-tale collection 'A Farm in Fairyland' receives a mixed reception: it is criticised for its failure to achieve total visual/verbal harmony, the reviewer suggesting that the best of his drawings 'would be seen to more advantage if taken out of the book'.

The fact that such criticisms target the adult collector of fine art books rather than the child reader is amply illustrated by the comments on *More Celtic Fairy Tales*, edited and selected by Joseph Jacobs and illustrated by John D. Batten:

> Mr. Batten's line is often poor, and the spacing of his black and white is sometimes blotchy and shows want of thought and care. The book is not well printed, and the Initial letters are commonplace and mostly ugly – but these are faults which its young readers will readily forgive.

This title was published by David Nutt, who had 'made a speciality of publishing works relating to Celtic Myth, Legend, and Romance', as a full-page advertisement at the back of this edition of the *Quest* reminds readers. In this promotional material, Nutt's fairy-tale titles are pitched at 'lovers of Black and White Art'. Collectability through scarcity is demonstrated by Nutt's promotion of the first edition of Oscar Wilde's *The Happy Prince and other Tales*: 'a few copies' are described as still available at over twice the price of the second edition, a book which boasts not just Wilde's aesthetic prose, but illustrations by Walter Crane.[27]

Housman's fairy-tale collections were clearly bought for adult as well as child readers. The *Dome*'s reviewer, like the *Quest*'s, is lukewarm about Housman's prose, but insists that even if the fairy tales in *The Field of Clover* were worse, 'the illustrations, with which in this notice we are mainly concerned, would make it worth having'.[28] Interestingly, Housman noted in his autobiography that a Kegan Paul bookseller had encountered the opposite response; the book illustrations were so unpopular that the bookseller had 'not merely failed to find a market for them, but was met with derision when he offered them'. Housman's joke to the salesman – that he should tell his customers that his drawings were currently 'the thing', produced by the publisher to meet 'a depraved taste' – casts a knowing wink at the distinctions between these consumers: child and adult, provincial and metropolitan, philistine and connoisseur.[29]

The *Quest*'s advertisement for the *Happy Prince* suggests that it may be Crane, not Wilde, who will sell this book to the *Quest*'s Arts and Crafts-affiliated readership. While Cruikshank's illustrations to Grimms' *German Popular Stories* had achieved the status of honoured classic by mid-century, Walter Crane's artistic interpretations of the same tales were equally legendary arbiters of taste in the minority magazines as the century drew to a close. In his 'Lecture on Art' in the *Century Guild Hobby Horse* (1884), Selwyn Image had drawn attention to the wider definition of 'art' set in train by the Arts and Crafts movement. It was now common to 'set that accomplished artist Mr. Walter Crane to illustrate our children's nursery rhymes – and that vigorous but most delicate poet Mr. William Morris to design our wallpapers and hearth-rugs'.[30]

In the *Quarto* of 1898, Arthur H. J. Gaskin's illustrations for *Stories & Fairy Tales from Hans Andersen* are evaluated in terms of this illustrious predecessor: 'though scarcely on a level with the now classic volume of Grimm's [sic] Stories, illustrated by Mr. Walter Crane, Mr. Gaskin has put some of his best work into these drawings'.[31] Gaskin was one of the 'Birmingham School' of artists with Guild and socialist affiliations, and regularly displayed work with the Arts and Crafts Exhibition Society. The *Quest*'s advertisements for fairy-tale works mention, not just Gaskin, but a number of other artists affiliated to the Birmingham School of Art, foregrounding a recurring interest in such subjects among this group.[32] The major book commission of Joseph Southall, socialist, Arts and Crafts exhibitor and close friend of Gaskin, was an illustrated edition of Perrault's *The Story of Bluebeard*. These artists' fascination with the fairy tale, like Crane's joint role as Symbolist painter and children's illustrator, questioned the status distinctions between book illustration and high art.[33]

'Rapunzel', by the Birmingham School artist Sidney Meteyard, is the frontispiece to the *Quest* for July 1896, and invokes a chain of literary references familiar to this coterie readership (Figure 5.1). While Meteyard clearly references the well-known Grimms' folktale, he also alludes to William Morris's poem of the same name. Meteyard's ideological and aesthetic affiliations with Morris are unmistakable, as are the profound influences of Pre-Raphaelite romance on both.[34] In Morris's poetic interplay of voices, his sequestered heroine, the golden-haired Guendolen, asserts that it is the witch, who is a 'black hair'd woman, tall and bold', who is actually named Rapunzel. This adds an extra element of ambiguity to the visual interpretation of Meteyard's Jane Morris-like, raven-haired beauty: while decorative lettering to the left and right of the image names both 'Rapunzel' and 'Guendoline', Meteyard's female figure could be read as a conflation of Morris's passive imprisoned female and his malevolent sorceress. Meteyard's image encourages the prefabrication of alternative cultural histories, reclaiming a tale familiar from a nineteenth-century German collection for a British medieval past.[35]

The works of Gaskin, Meteyard and Morris (the last of whom was a one-off contributor to the *Quest*) can be seen to integrate ideologically with the wider aims of the periodical. Morris's desire to combat the purely commercial basis of contemporary book manufacture ('the utilitarian production of makeshifts') is echoed in the aims of the Birmingham Guild of Handicraft, as advertised in the *Quest*: 'It is the aim of the Guild to supply hand-made articles superior in beauty of design and soundness of workmanship to those made by machinery; and to make only such as shall give just pleasure both to the craftsman and to the buyer of them.'[36] Morris clearly articulated the role of literary production in this communal ideal:

> If I were asked to say what is at once the most important production of Art and the thing most to be longed for, I should answer, A beautiful

Figure 5.1 Sidney Meteyard, 'Rapunzel', *Quest*, 1896. Used by permission of the University of London Library.

House; and if I were further asked to name the production next in importance [...] I should answer, A beautiful Book.

Morris's 'Ideal Book' was 'not limited by commercial exigencies of price: we can do what we like with it, according to what its nature, as a book, demands of Art'.[37] Yet, as in the case of the Kelmscott Press, such books became a different kind of consumer product, fetishised by an elite audience as a rare collector's item. That the periodical as well as the book could achieve this status is demonstrated by the fact that the *Butterfly*, the *Pageant*, the *Dome* and the *Quarto* were manufactured as two different products that targeted two different audiences: on the one hand the aesthete book collector who sought an expensive limited edition and on the other a broader readership who paid the standard retail price.[38]

However, while children's book illustration neatly dovetailed with the desires of Arts and Crafts-affiliated artists to integrate both use and beauty, their fascination with the fairy tale appears to have more complex origins. For William Morris, both the prose romance and the fairy tale had an emblematic value as communal art forms that were the antithesis of reified capitalist modes of production. This attempt to return to the literature of a more culturally integrated past is everywhere apparent in the *Quest*.

The neo-medievalism of John Ruskin, and his conception of the fairy tale as the literature of a more culturally rich, pre-industrial past, provide an obvious line of influence to Morris and the Birmingham Guild of Handicraft. More surprising, perhaps, is the direct Ruskinian influence on Laurence Housman, a writer with affiliations to both decadence and Symbolism. Housman's 1905 preface to *Gammer Grethel's Fairy Tales* quotes significant parts of Ruskin's introduction to *German Popular Stories* verbatim:

> Many years ago Ruskin, in an introduction to Edgar Taylor's translation from Grimm, and Cruikshank's illustrations, drew the distinction between old and new which no literary art can disguise. 'In the best stories recently written for the young there is,' he declares, 'a taint which is not easy to define, but inevitably follows from the author addressing himself to children bred in school-rooms and drawing-rooms instead of fields and woods – children whose favourite amusements are premature imitations of the vanities of elder people, and whose conceptions of beauty are dependent partly on costliness of dress'.[39]

Housman uncritically echoes Ruskin's complaint against the loss of innocence in the modern child, an indictment of an industrial capitalism that is perceived to pervert the child's harmonious relationship with the natural world. Yet Housman's own tales, often highly stylised and densely symbolic, were expensive art productions, often marketed to adults or middle-class juveniles, certainly not to the child of the 'fields and woods'. If Housman's references seem disingenuous, an even greater irony is apparent in Evelyn Sharp's pamphlet *Fairy Tales: As They Are, as They Were, as They Should Be* (1889), in which she states:

> there are some who think that at all costs we must move with the times, that Andersen is old-fashioned, Grimm positively archaic, and that far preferable to these two familiar friends of our childhood are the so-called fairy tales of the present day, published in magazines or tastily bound volumes, and profusely illustrated by our most advanced artists with pre-Raphaelite goblins, and peacock-blue princesses.[40]

Sharp, remembered for her arch and brittle short stories for the *Yellow Book*, produced the very type of self-consciously 'modern' fairy tales that she castigates. Illustrated by one of the most innovative and 'advanced' artists of the 1890s, Mabel Dearmer, Sharp's books *Wymps and Other Tales* (1897) and *All the Way to Fairy Land* (1898) were certainly 'tastily bound' and designed volumes, published and promoted by that shrewd purveyor of *belles lettres* John Lane. So far did such books seem from 'old-fashioned' fairy tales that Lane felt obliged to point out in his advertisement that they were 'suitable for children'.[41]

Innocents and epicures: Decadence, Symbolism and the child

Both Housman and Sharp invoke a rural child who is not their own target reader, but a symbolic innocent for adult consumption. Sharp laments the 'want of imagination' in the 'clumsy and slow' lower classes, yet suggests they might be celebrated for their primitivism: 'It would be no difficult matter to make them believe in the existence of fairies; for the character of village children is, in the matter of simplicity and credulity, as true as it is proverbial.'[42] As we saw in Chapter 4, utopian socialists frequently used the child to symbolise hopes for post-capitalist (and post-industrial) cultural integration. Yet children's supposed freedom from social convention could also allow them to be categorised in a rather different way: as decadent emblems of individualism. These two positions were not as incompatible as one might think: while Sharp and Housman showed affiliations to both socialism and decadence, Oscar Wilde, blending socialism with Paterian notions of subjectivity, found the child could become a metaphor for an enlightened society that freed the individual. In 'The Soul of Man under Socialism', published in the *Fortnightly Review* in February 1891, Wilde claimed that the free, tolerant personality of the future would be 'as wonderful as the personality of a child'. In both this essay and the fairy tale 'The Selfish Giant', Wilde used the child as an icon of humanity uncorrupted by social convention, a signifier of untrammelled individuality and Christ-like innocence.[43] Quoting from Whitman, the *Beam* used just such a symbol in its 'Introduction' of January 1896: the periodical's aim was to set sail for the Great City 'where children are taught to be laws to themselves'.[44]

This conception of the pre-socialised child as 'naturally' wiser, more selfless, and more responsive than adults infiltrated many little magazines, even those that appeared to condone moral relativism. John Lane advertised a range of texts that valorised the child for adult consumption: K. Douglas King's *The Child Who Will Never Grow Old* (anticipating Barrie's 'Peter Pan') promised to capture a state both fleeting and ever-present: to illustrate, in stories 'drawn from life', the 'humour and wisdom, the dauntless mirth, the infinite self-sacrifice of childhood'.[45] The child as icon of happiness, goodness and self-sacrifice appeared to promise a corrective to both the corruption of industrial capitalism and the more solipsistic excesses of Art for Art's sake.

Vernon Lee's short story 'Prince Alberic and the Snake Lady', in the *Yellow Book* of July 1896, uses both the notion of the child primitive and fairy-tale typology as a frame around which to weave a distinctly decadent fantasy. This dream-like narrative, set within the elaborate ducal opulence of late sixteenth century Italy, focuses on the child Prince Alberic and his obsession with a serpent-tailed woman on a tapestry of 'old and Gothic taste'. She is revealed in folk belief to be the enchanted fairy Oriana, who has beguiled Alberic's ancestors in a bid to return to human form. Lee's narrative exhibits a number of symbolic themes shared by other decadent texts, particularly with Wilde's *The Picture of Dorian Gray* and his fairy tale 'The Fisherman and his Soul': the worship of strange, pagan objects, whose beauty lies in their perversity; overblown descriptions of precious, artificial parodies of nature; the fascination with dream-like mental states and with the sexuality of an unnatural, hybrid female figure.

Lee's sinuous prose, while borrowing from Gothic fiction, makes obvious allusions to a fairy-tale heritage. Taught about the tapestry by a peasant nurse, Alberic learns of the snake lady's mythology from an old man who 'united in his tattered person the trades of mending crockery and reciting fairy tales'. Alberic is exiled to the 'Castle of the Sparkling Waters' to live among peasants, and his cultural regression is pictured not only as a merging of fantasy and reality, but, like the Arts and Crafts production, a literal travelling back in time through Art: he has a 'growing sense that he was in the tapestry, but that the tapestry had become the whole world'.[46] While Lee draws on the Mélusine myth, her anonymously published preface to 'Tuscan Fairy Tales' reveals a direct line of influence from her role as fairy-tale translator to her later *Yellow Book* short story. In the former, she informs readers that there exist memories of 'a well-nigh extinct belief in fairies, magicians, elves and mermaids' among the Tuscan people: of 'the fairies (*fate*) who were lovely women six days of the week, and turned into snakes on the seventh'.[47] Alberic's belief in the snake lady links him to a primal innocence: an innocence that not only contrasts with the decayed aestheticism of his grandfather, but is a counterbalance to Lee's own passages of decadent excess.

Lee was an acknowledged disciple of Pater; for both, beauty was the central criterion by which to evaluate an art object. Lee's narrative suggests that the fairy tale is valued, not for its moral lessons, but for its ability to replicate a childlike responsiveness and freshness of perception. In Gleeson White's *Dome* appreciation of Botticelli (1897), he speaks of Botticelli's 'reawakening in Pagan lore' and makes analogies with both Ruskin and the fairy tale:

> The classic legends Botticelli received 'as a child in later years recovers the forgotten dearness of a nursery tale' – a sentence for which one forgives Mr. Ruskin more than needs forgiveness. [...] He caught the legend of spring as it appealed to the classic world, and re-pictured it in the garb of the Florentines. True that the secret of re-capturing the eternal youth of Art is not his alone; the well-beloved Lucca della Robbia in his Majolica, or the equally well-beloved Robert Louis Stevenson in his *Child's Garden of Verses*, go to prove that at all times an artist with the soul of a little child can re-state the legends of the past, or of his own infancy, with all their native freshness. It is not that Botticelli painted children and angels as children, or that Lucca della Robbia caught the grace of babyhood; it is the simple frankness of the innocence of all ages that infuses their work with limpid sweetness.[48]

While for White innocence is associated with both childhood and the past, it is not confined to these forever lost states: the older child can become young again by recovering the fairy tale, just as the true artist can achieve 'the soul of a little child', telescoping personal and historical time to create myth anew. White stresses that such artists capture not the mere appearance of childhood, but innocence as a transhistorical, primal truth. For Housman, like White, it is not the child, but the artist who has attained child-like characteristics who can articulate such truths. George Cruikshank's drawings for Grimms' fairy tales were 'so honestly and unaffectedly at one with the spirit which brought fairy tales to life' because he was able to approach them 'with that tireless mind of adventurous innocence which does not know better – because it does not know worse'.[49]

In the *Fortnightly Review* in 1874, Pater had expressed a fascination with Wordsworth's consciousness. In Wordsworth's writing, earlier historical epochs could be glimpsed through recollection of the child's mind, while the growth of the individual mind echoed the trajectory of cultural development. Pater described Wordsworth's :

> oft-reiterated regrets for a half-ideal childhood, when the relics of Paradise still clung about the soul – a childhood, as it seemed, full of the fruits of old age, lost for all, in a degree, in the passing away of the youth

of the world, lost for each one, over again, in the passing away of actual youth.[50]

This variant of the recapitulation thesis, although expressed in characteristic Paterian prose, is nevertheless familiar, invoked by the juvenile magazines of the 1860s as well as by the 1890s socialist press. However, as Sally Shuttleworth, Carolyn Steedman and Jenny Taylor have shown, in the late nineteenth century the child was an object of renewed scientific fascination as part of an attempt to trace the development of human consciousness.[51] When Victorian folkloric scholarship engaged with these debates, its constructions of the mind of childhood were far from consistent. In his article 'Folk-Lore in Relation to Psychology and Education' in the first *Folk-Lore Journal* of 1883, John Fenton argued that the study of folktales offered insights into both the individual development of the child's mind and into cultural and racial origins:

> Not only have we considerable scientific support for the conjecture that children to-day reflect in their mental growth the stages of the mental growth of their race, but we have the direct testimony of competent observers to the childlike character of many of the lower races, so that we may reasonably expect to have some light thrown upon the psychological state of the lower races by an examination of the psychology of our own children.

When debating the relative significance of philological and anthropological approaches, the dispute, as Fenton had realised, was more than a mere question of the significance of 'vocabularies and roots': it was an argument over 'our notion of what is reasonable or unreasonable in savage thought [...] in one word, of our theory of the psychology of early man'. The question was also how the mysterious riddle posed by Fenton, 'what is a child?' could be answered when this dispute over psychology remained unresolved.[52] As Henry James was to reveal in the 'Turn of the Screw', these contradictory constructions of early man – as spiritual and innocent or as amoral, brutal and savage – could both be projected onto the mind of the child, to deeply unsettling effect. Such contradictions were articulated in intriguing ways in little magazines. In his *Dome* fairy tale 'How Little Duke Jarl Saved the Castle' (1899), Laurence Housman presents the child as a Romantic archetype, a self-sacrificing saviour of a close-knit ancient warrior community. Yet in his short story 'The Defence of Farvingdon', published in the magazine in the same year, Housman echoes James in constructing an inscrutable, disturbing, uncanny child, potentially capable of bizarre and savage violence.[53]

Interestingly, in Housman's fairy tales 'A Capful of Moonshine' and 'A Gander and his Geese', published in the *Dome* and the *Butterfly* respectively, the true innocent is not the child but the unsocialised adult. While Pater's article on Wordsworth suggested that the youth of the world had long passed away into industrialism, and personal youth into adulthood, Housman's two fairy tales represent the desire to rediscover both in a single moment: to create pre-industrial adults with simple minds, who appear to never grow up. In 'A Capful of Moonshine' in the *Dome* of October 1898, Old Toonie is told by a faggot-maker that to see the fairies requires 'a handful of courage, a mouthful of silence, and a capful of moonshine'. In three successive attempts, he is tricked into relinquishing these and becomes the fairies' bondsmen. Soon afterwards a child is born to his wife, after whom people despair: 'for as he grew older it became apparent that his tongue was tied, seeing that he remained quite dumb in spite of all that was done to teach him; and his head was full of moonshine, so that he could understand nothing clearly by day'. Despite being rejected and sold to a farmer by his mother, it is this mysterious son, 'Little Toonie', who unwittingly gains access to the fairies and is able to rescue his father. Silent and carrying moonshine in his head, his handful of courage comes naturally after years of the farmer's beatings.

Even in this pre-industrial world of fairy tale, true morality lies not with the cohesive community, but the outsider who has retained the pre-social attributes of the child. Toonie's wits gather at night, and the moonshine that he carries is emblematic of a more primal value system. While the fairies offer Little Toonie beauty, youth or gold, 'because the moonbeams were laying their white hands on his hair, he chose the weak, shrivelled old man'. The tale concludes with the inversion of familiar definitions of both mad and sane and wise and foolish, with old Toonie stating that 'wisdom is justified in her children'.[54]

In 'The Soul of Man Under Socialism', Oscar Wilde states that 'one of the results of the extraordinary tyranny of authority is that words are absolutely distorted from their proper and simple meaning, and are used to express the obverse of their right signification'.[55] While in tales such as Wilde's 'The Selfish Giant' it is the child who still enshrines such 'proper and simple' meanings, in Housman's tales they are accessible to the 'simple' adult, untouched by social convention. Such symbolic themes are repeated in Housman's 'A Gander and his Geese', published in the *Butterfly* in 1900. In this tale, the geese have delayed too long in flying south for the winter; they are warned by the gander to distrust 'all but the very simplest' human, for 'if there were any so simple as to do us a good turn for nothing, he would be so out of the ways of other men that he himself would be starving'.[56] The geese are taken in by Peter Simple, who is indeed starving and ostracised. When a neighbour gives Peter the idea of selling them, his loss of simplicity through engagement with commerce is depicted as an intrinsic loss of decency. In these tales (with clear Ruskinian and Wildean overtones), Housman destabilises social ascriptions of intelligence or wisdom, so that the truly compassionate become mad in the eyes of contemporary society. Yet while both tales reveal the influence of Arts and Crafts ideologies, they do not champion a Ruskinian organic realm of pre-industrial social harmony.

Both Simple and Little Toonie are ultimately individuals, lost in private, solipsistic worlds of their own making.

This tension between the social and the individual, between public morality and private consciousness, is articulated in fascinating ways in these little magazine fairy tales. While for Morris art had an explicitly moral and social value, decadent rejections of an objective morality in favour of a personal experience of beauty led to the individual search for intense, subjective impressions; to the pursuit of Pater's question 'what is this song or picture, this engaging personality presented in life or in a book, to *me*?'[57] Periodicals such as the *Dome*, the product of a range of artists, could be ideologically heterodox enough to articulate both positions. In 'Neo-Ruskinism: A Protest' (1899), John Runciman asserted, 'We shall get on very well without moral lessons, provided we always make for the beautiful: that is, for what we think to be beautiful'.[58]

Housman's fairy tale in the *Dome* should be read not only in the context of the periodical's wider Arts and Crafts' ideologies, but its embrace of the poetry and fiction of W. B. Yeats and Fiona Macleod (William Sharp), and their own attempts to marry the communal, the personal and the mystical: to link peasant folklore to a symbolic language with its own mysterious access to spiritual truths. In the same issue as 'A Capful of Moonshine', the periodical published Yeats's 'Song of Mongan', a poem voiced by the wizard king of Celtic poetry; 'The Last Night of Artan the Culdee' and 'The Monody of Isla the Singer' by Fiona Macleod; and 'A Snowdrop Song', a lyric poem by the Irish Celticist Nora Hopper. Significantly, this number also includes Arthur Symons's reflections on Symbolism: showing obvious parallels with the Celtic fixation with the folk, Symons focuses on the relationship between this ideal language and popular 'democratic' art forms.[59]

In the *Dome*, Celtic Symbolists appropriated folktale mythology to express a visionary consciousness. Communal folkloric forms also became conduits for a super-sensory realm of beauty. Less than a year after the publication of 'A Capful of Moonshine', the *Dome* published 'Dust Hath Closed Helen's Eye', Yeats's prose meditation on researching folklore in Baile-laoi in County Galway which would later form part of *The Celtic Twilight*. Speaking of Mary Hynes who had died there 60 years previously, and the blind poet Raftery who sang about her, Yeats implies that their myths will undergo a mystical transformation that will transcend local folkloric significance:

> It may be that in a few years Fable, who changes mortalities to immortalities in her cauldron, will have changed Mary Hynes and Raftery to perfect symbols of the sorrow of beauty and of the magnificence and penury of dreams.[60]

These symbols remain fresh and 'perfect' through their evolution from a literature that appears to escape modernity, one that preserves the communal mindset of pre-industrial culture, capturing the spiritual purity of youth.[61] This hope of regeneration through a literature that remains ever young had earlier been articulated by Arthur Galton in the *Century Guild Hobby Horse*. Reviewing Lady Wilde's *Ancient Legends of Ireland*, Galton proclaimed: '[h]e will be the most winning artist, especially will he be the most winning poet, who can learn how to fascinate our over-taught, thought-wearied generation with the young-eyed freshness, the entrancing rapture of Celtic Naturalism'.[62]

The irony that this peasant 'freshness' was a desired commodity sought by the educated, English avant-garde writer was not always lost on the commercially astute *Dome*. In a curiously self-referential tale by J. T. Kingsley Tarpey, 'The Merrow', the *Dome* places the Celtic Revival in the context of an audience of cultured English consumers with obvious parallels to its own. Using the classic distancing techniques of the Gothic novel, the story is told through a series of letters, supposedly received by the narrator, who claims: 'I make no comment, leaving it to the individual reader to separate for himself fact from visionary imaginings, and reason from superstition.' The letters are written by a cultured landowner who returns to Ireland after 25 years, and nevertheless makes claim to an inheritance of primitivism. Describing himself as 'three parts English' of 'the dull Philistine, aristocratic class' and one part Irish, he claims at the breast of his foster-mother 'Mammy Cleary' to have become 'half-peasant':

> I cannot doubt that whatever of poet I may be I owe to this kindly influence in my childhood. You critics, who obscure your impressions by ticketing them with phrases, have nicknamed me a 'mystic.' [...] Here the 'Good People' still dwell with us. [...] Those poems of mine, written in Germany, which you all found so fantastic, would be received as plain common sense here.

Paralleling the appropriation of folklore by mystic and Symbolist Irish writers such as Yeats and AE, the narrator of the letters distinguishes himself from the English literati by stating his own connection to 'the folk' and their beliefs. Yet his work, like the *Dome* itself, is clearly sold to that connoisseur metropolitan audience. Through his letters, the educated landowner tells an ambiguous narrative that appropriates a familiar folktale motif; readers can choose to believe or doubt that his wife was the 'merrow' or water spirit that the local peasantry believed her to be. When the narrator describes England as a 'rank growth of cities spreading out like a disease' he invokes a return to nature as a counter to urban decadence, and echoes the Scottish little magazine the *Evergreen*, which saw itself as a manifesto for the Celtic Revival.[63]

The writers of 'Proem' in the Spring 1895 issue of the *Evergreen* use the very same metaphor of social pathology. Many of the sons of Edinburgh are seen to be 'of service in carrying on the wasting business of that metropolitan life which resembles so much the proliferation of a cancer'. In the *Evergreen*, the folktale-influenced works of Fiona Macleod were also prominent, although serving a more consistent agenda: the periodical invoked fairy tale and myth to reforge links with the rhythm of the seasons, in a conscious attempt to counter literary and biological degeneration. For the periodical's motive force, the Edinburgh town-planner and biologist Patrick Geddes, as for other *Evergreen* contributors, the connections between biological and literary degeneration were more than casually metaphoric. In 1895, W. Macdonald and J. Arthur Thomson claim of decadence:

> For while at one social level, all the land over, it fills the gaze with a vision of slums and the hearing with outcries of coarseness and cretinous insanity – at another it is trumpeted as a boast and worn as a badge and studied as the ultimate syllable of this world's wisdom. So many clever writers emulously working in a rotten vineyard, so many healthy young men eager for the distinction of decay! And yet, out of each other's sight as those two worlds lie, there is but a step between and their kinship is unmistakable.

For the *Evergreen*, hope is offered to counter biological and urban decadence in the cyclical renewal of nature, and in the genetic renewal of each new generation. The fairy tale has a double significance; it is connected with the optimistic promise of childhood, but it is also linked to nature myths that auger seasonal renewal. Both the child and spring symbolise 'Renascence'. While the authors of 'Proem' believe that 'to all simple peoples in history, as to the young in every age, the seasons have meant much', they are also assured that 'the eternal newness of every Child is an undying promise for the Race'.[64]

If decadent literature could be allied with biological degeneration, the fairy tale is presented here as its antidote, read interchangeably in literary and biological terms. This conflation of science and myth is most intriguingly developed by the authors of 'The Moral Evolution of Sex' in the Summer 1896 edition of the *Evergreen*. Using a motif from romance, Patrick Geddes and J. Arthur Thomson suggest that 'Every age of chivalry follows a period of decadence, of moral decline, and is the protest of the new order – is the expression of the new young life, breaking into the very citadel of evil, slaying its mightiest giants, its most infernal dragons'. They go on to develop even more explicit connections between social and biological health, and the fairy tale:

> The giant-killer, the dragon-slayer, is the son of a god very often – very often too the son of nobody in particular; which, as already noted, may amount to the same thing. He is Jack, Tom Thumb, Dummling, Gareth

the scullion-knave, and so on. And the heroine, who is she? Very possibly the giant's own daughter, the heiress of the rascally or the sleeping king of the story; the Cinderella of the household, the beggar-maid of Cophetua; rarely has she the good pure pedigree of the peasant maid of Domrémy.

This, of course, should lead into an examination of the biological realities of pedigree, which like everything else has to be looked at along the lines of organic reality, and shows us pure blood and cur blood in palace and hovel alike. [...] Are men curs and swine as some tell us? Shall we believe these decadent novelists, bemired half way between old ideals and new?

This optimistic view of heredity is explicitly linked to the linguistic vitality of folk literature.[65] Yet if the *Evergreen* used both the child and the fairy tale as the ultimate symbols of counter-decadence, such appropriations of myth could also embrace a more controversial notion of 'chivalry', which implicitly questioned the *Evergreen*'s claim that 'the love of women is the way of life'.[66] In his second article on 'The Myth of Demeter and Persephone' (1876), Pater drew, like the *Evergreen*, on Müller's solar theory of mythological development, and celebrated the survival of the 'primitive, popular legend' among 'children, and unchanging childlike people'. Yet Pater's essay also embraced homoerotic language, and explored decadent constructions of nature.[67] In fact, the *Evergreen*'s own appropriations of myth sometimes incorporated, rather than challenged, the very decadent traits that myth and fairy tale ostensibly opposed: the homoerotic visual contributions by John Duncan are the most notable examples.[68]

In other contexts, too, nature mythology and the child could be used to celebrate the very literary tendencies that the *Evergreen* railed against. Annihilating time and personality into disconnected moments of sensory experience, Pater used the conclusion to *The Renaissance* to call for a quickened individual responsiveness which cast off habit and stereotyped ways of seeing.[69] While the social innocent and the dandy appear to be polar opposites, the *fin-de-siècle* aesthete could indeed see in the pre-socialised child just such Paterian freshness and intensity of perception: an individuality that the socialised adult could never fully reclaim. Paradoxically, innocence becomes the consummate Epicurean experience: the spectre of the aesthete who wishes to collect 'sensations' but remains forever young, is, like Dorian Gray, a decadent parody of youth, an inverted child who will not grow up. Little magazines were often fascinated by the dandy's anachronism. When the *Pageant* published an article by Edmund Gosse on Jules Barbey d'Aurevilly, he was presented in the self-delusion of old age as both pathetic and admirable, unaware of the travesty of youth he had become.[70]

Jan B. Gordon has suggested that it is the conflation of two conflicting conceptions of child growth, marrying ideas of a child's natural development with a belief in growth through 'socialization and engagement' that engendered this desire for such paradoxical states in the decadent artist; for 'the eternal flower of perpetual childhood, and the gregarious socialization of the dandy'. For Gordon, the growth in children's literature and the 'overly stylised aesthetic responses of the effete and the experienced' are both aspects of this contradictory stance.[71] However, the obsession with childhood in the last years of the nineteenth century might also be seen as an acknowledgement by decadent writers of the circularity of their own strategies. In 1899, Arthur Symons described decadence as 'half a mock-interlude'. Claiming that 'Nothing, not even conventional virtue, is so provincial as conventional vice', he declared that 'the desire to "bewilder the middle-classes" is itself middle-class'.[72] Housman, in his *Quarto* article 'The Zeit-Geist' of 1898, acknowledged something very similar:

> As the majority had found a ventilation to its wrath, the care of the minority was clearly to provide fuel for the flames. And a very industrious little minority ran 'decadence' for all (and more than) it was worth.
> Yet it would seem now that we are much where we were before.[73]

Max Beerbohm showed a witty awareness of the decadent paradox in his article 'Be It Cosiness', published in the *Pageant* in 1896. Parodying Pater's aestheticism, he mentions his attempts in the first year of Oxford to 'avoid "sensations," "pulsations," and "exquisite moments" that were not purely intellectual'. Beerbohm realised that the decadent's desire to anger the bourgeois moralist was merely an oppositional stance that led to the continual supersession of one strategy of artistic confrontation by another: 'Once, in the delusion that Art, loving the recluse, would make his life happy, I wrote a little for a yellow quarterly [...] I shall write no more. Already I feel myself to be a trifle outmoded. I belong to the Beardsley period.' Ironically suggesting that he has become passé in his early twenties, Beerbohm announces that he will retire to the suburbs: having exhausted all avant-garde tactics, opposition and bourgeois convention indeed become one and the same. In this world of collapsed oppositions, it is the innocent child rather than the debauched aesthete (who now appears 'almost ascetic') who is able to experience the most profound sensations and pulsations: 'It is only mystery – such mystery as besets the eyes of children – that makes things superb.'[74]

The child as the ultimate cipher of individualism and receiver of sensory experience is captured perfectly in the article 'Of Purple Jars', a tour de force which appeared in the *Pageant* in 1897. Heavily influenced by Pater, Edward Purcell's construction of the child is similar to Wilde's: 'Wisdom is bound up in the heart of a child together with foolishness. The free, fearless mind of his fathers he inherits: their prejudices he has to be taught.' While the child's logic is undeveloped,

> he often swoops right down into the very heart of the truth, and that chiefly because such truth as he has espied is one which lies quite bare

and on the surface, but which mature sapience has long ago decreed to be invisible. For this he is invariably reproved.

The child, before he is entrapped by the 'cage' of social convention, exists in a state of extreme responsivity. Purcell's wry rewriting of Maria Edgeworth's 'Purple Jars' (a moral fable in which a child chooses a beautiful jar in a chemist's window, which later transpires to be clear glass, above a new pair of shoes) transforms a moral praising usefulness into a soliloquy about Art for Art's sake:

> dear, dull, English matron! [...] what your child sees is no mere paltry chemist's bottle but the divine illusions of Art and Beauty; that eager, quivering voice is more than childish petulance, – it is the faint birth-cry of the very spirit of the archangels, of Michael and of Raphael.

Purcell's praise for 'the child's barbaric, untrained, yet holy admiration of beauty such as he sees it; [...] his choice – sadly wrong no doubt, but for all that truly heroic – of the Beautiful before the Useful', anticipates the preoccupations of the dandy as collector of beautiful objects. 'The whole domain of child-land is swayed by this beneficent lust of the eye, this exquisite delight of the young stranger in a world so full of beautiful surprises', claims Purcell, directly echoing Pater's arguments that in early life the child sees with 'unstinted delight'.

In fact, Purcell's narrator expresses a direct conflation of interests between child innocent and aesthete collector. He imagines the story's heroine coming to tea where he will regale her with wonders more exotic than the *Arabian Nights*, holding:

> high banquet on sweet forbidden dainties from dishes which have each a history, and Rosamund shall marvel for the hundredth time at my pots and pans and graven images many and outlandish, and shall even handle my chiefest treasure, which no mortal housemaid may touch and live, the vase of old emerald crackle smothered with gouts and tears of foaming enamel.

The narrator closely resembles the archetypal decadent hero (or antihero) of J.-K. Huysman's *À Rebours* (1884), Des Esseintes, who devotes his life entirely to the accumulation of beautiful, useless and arcane objects. This analogy is explicitly encouraged by the periodical's editors (one of whom was the distinctly dandyish Charles Shannon) who chose to place a portrait of Huysmans by William Rothenstein between the pages of the text. Another pictorial/text juxtaposition is also telling: interleaved between the pages of this article is 'the Genius of Greek poetry' by George Frederick Watts, a drawing which suggests parallels between Greek vase painting and the vigour and youth of cultural childhood. For Purcell, the fairy tale is a point where nature and culture meet. He promises the tale's heroine that they will go beyond suburbia, collecting flowers to transform the disappointing jar into 'the selfsame Crystal Vase that eternally droops its sprays over the couch of the Sleeping Beauty. And thou, dear child, to whom all fairyland and its wonders are familiar, wilt know it again at once'. The narrator asserts that the child will be allowed to weave 'her wildest, silliest fancies', 'because we both believe in all goodness and fairyland'. Echoing Pater's claim that the child sees 'inwardly', belief in the fairy tale is seen as a training in the appreciation of beauty. Such imaginative identification is the first step towards the truly artistic sensibility.[75]

By mischievously finding in Edgeworth's tale the very opposite moral to that the author intended, Purcell takes the position of Wilde's critic as artist, highlighting the ultimate subjectivity of the reading process.[76] Such an approach in effect denies the possibility of the transparent moral tale. Wilde, who proclaims in the preface to *The Picture of Dorian Gray* that there is 'no such thing as a moral or an immoral book', also asserts archly in his fairy tale 'The Devoted Friend' that to tell a story with a moral 'is always a very dangerous thing to do'.[77] Housman's fairy tale 'Blind Love' in the *Pageant* echoes the morally subjective stance of the same issue's 'Of Purple Jars', and the two texts in fact produce complementary meanings when read against each other, for Housman's tale not only explores the possibility of moral relativism, but uses the adult who has escaped the cage of convention to question the social norms upon which sexual morality is based.

Housman, who edited and introduced a selection from Blake's poetry in 1893, was clearly influenced by *Songs of Innocence* (1789) and *Songs of Experience* (1794), and his *Pageant* tale retains strong thematic similarities with Blake's poem from the latter, 'A Little Girl Lost'. This short story moves away from the simple folktale style of 'A Capful of Moonshine'. In keeping with the arch and sophisticated tone of the *Pageant*, the narrator who tells the tale of Princess Innygreth is more polished, echoing a medieval romance tradition: 'How shall I tell this gentle story so that they who read may not weep too much for the sorrows that are told therein; for, indeed, none must grieve too greatly, seeing that all comes to a good ending.' Rather than creating the Wordsworthian adult primitives of 'A Capful of Moonshine' and 'A Gander and his Geese', Housman resorts to a more fantastic plot twist to ensure the preservation of his protagonist's innocence – invisibility. King Agwisaunce refuses the sexual advances of a beautiful fairy, and her revenge is to ensure that his wife will bear a child who 'from the hour of her birth [...] shall be invisible, and so shall she remain till she also play the wanton'. This invisible daughter's very innocence is the result of unfettered experience, for Innygreth

> being so sheltered by her birthright, at once from the assaults and the safeguards men make on womanly innocence, whether to foul or to

foster it, had great knowledge of many things that are shuttered from the eyes of most maidens. Therefore she was honest without confusion, and had modesty without fear; and having had no shame for her own body since the day of her birth, had no shame of it in others.

Innygreth's freedom causes fear in both her father and potential suitors: 'the King began thinking that to have her roaming free, fluttering the downy wings of her unguarded virginity, was a tempting of God's providence'. While the king is willing to allow Innygreth to obtain visibility the night before her wedding with a suitor of his choice, so that both can monitor her movements, she escapes and becomes visible in the presence of her love Sir Percyn. Innygreth's loss of virginity is described as the opposite of wanton: 'free from the bonds that hold others' she visits Percyn in his prison chamber, where he beholds her 'modesty without fear and a trust that dreaded no shame'. Housman wryly reverses the expected conclusion of the tale:

Therefore is an end come to my story.
  Now, had the King been as other men, and let the fairy's will be in the first place, none of these sorrows had come about, nor need any have been wise concerning that thing, nor this have been written. Wherefore ye who like this tale be glad that the King erred not in faith to his wife; and ye that like it not, be grieved.

While readers appear to be given a moral choice, the narrator places them in a paradoxical position: to castigate Innygreth as a 'wanton' is to castigate the king's own faithfulness to his wife. The metaphor of invisibility highlights the sexual hypocrisy of such moral codes; transgression only counts as such when it is seen. Like Blake's lovers in 'A Little Girl Lost' who 'Naked in the sunny beams delight', Housman questions the meanings of 'innocent' and 'wanton'. In its exploration of female chastity as a commodity, this tale anticipates both Housman's active involvement with the feminist Women's Social and Political Union (he was to circulate a petition for women's suffrage in 1909) and his campaigning activities for the open discussion of sexual issues. In keeping with the periodical's frequent forays into Symbolism, it also demonstrates a move towards more mystical levels of representation. The tale involves a clear conflation of spiritual and sexual meanings. On climbing down the trellis to escape into her lover's cell, Innygreth suffers thorn wounds in her hands and feet; the jailer brings Percyn bread and wine as a last meal, and Innygreth enters and kisses him 'as one kisses the shrine of saints'. On route to her condemned beloved, Innygreth encounters another symbol made flesh: the white 'hound of death'.[78]

  In his article 'A Symbolic Artist and the Coming of Symbolic Art' (1898) in the *Dome*, Yeats suggests that such preoccupations are central to a wider Symbolist movement: 'The only two powers that trouble the deeps are religion and love, the others make a little trouble upon the surface.' Yeats's suggestion that the Irish mystic AE is 'the most subtle and spiritual poet of his generation, and a visionary who may find room besides Swedenborg and Blake', is significant; it is no coincidence that the *Pageant*, *Dome* and the *Savoy*, like the *Century Guild Hobby Horse* before them, made Blake a hero as artist and visionary.[79] Blake's mysticism and his development of his own spiritual iconography was often invoked in defence of these periodicals' drift towards Symbolism. In his introduction to Blake's poetry, Housman articulates a further connection between this poet and the imaginative power of the child:

> He gave expression to the unreasoning dreams and fabulous delights that perish for most of us in our childhood, and gave us also, on the grounds of Berkeley's philosophy, a reason for being reverent as well as glad in retaining them. He maintained that the evidence of the senses could not be the outside limit of argument.[80]

Blake becomes a visionary, who, like the child, is perceived to see 'inwardly': to grasp spiritual truths beyond normal sensory perception. For Berkeley, the world was inseparable from its mental perception, the mind of man linked to the mind of God. Berkeley and Blake are both re-appropriated by Housman in the service of a Symbolist aesthetic, in which the child gains privileged access to a realm of ideals. Yet such powers, Housman suggests, need not be lost to the adult: the fairy tale can itself operate as a form of training in such visionary perception. As he argued in the preface to *Gammer Grethel's Fairy Tales*:

> That is the true value of the fairy-tale: it has, for a time at least, in the lives of most of us, put foolish fact in its proper perspective, persuasively voicing the scientific truth, which the routine of experience inclines us to forget, that existence is merely thought. And if the fairy-tale can go on doing that, its value increases rather than diminishes alongside of the harsh and obscuring effects of modern civilisation.[81]

In this analysis, the fairy tale challenges modern society not with a return to pre-industrial values, but with the retreat into a mystic realm. Yet this is not entirely solipsistic, for reality itself is grounded within that mental perception: Berkeley's *esse est percipi* ('to be is to be perceived'). In the *Symbolist Movement in Literature*, dedicated to Yeats as the perfect sympathetic reader, Arthur Symons claimed that Symbolist literature was that in which 'the visible world is no longer a reality, and the unseen world no longer a dream'[82]. If the child was associated, through innocence and imaginative power, with the truths of this unseen world, so was the fairy tale: it too could articulate the mysteries of religion, love and death. Mabel Cox, writing on Housman's book illustrations in the *Artist* in 1898, also alludes to the symbolic function of fairyland as a projection of this unseen realm:

> It is from a visionary world that Housman speaks, through ideal and symbolic art, to the imagination. He would not have us feel that his figures can step out of their frames into everyday life [...] he wishes them to appear and remain improbable to those who cannot see into fairyland with their mind's eye. Thus to many people his work is and will be a dead letter. Not so to children; they, with the profound wisdom of their open minds, follow him one and all delightedly. [...] Any one who will take the trouble to follow him may gain entry into that world of ideals.[83]

Children's supposed ability to retreat into fairyland is proof of their access to more profound mental states: their entry into a spiritual world of ideals which can indeed counter 'the harsh and obscuring effects of modern civilisation'. This movement away from decadence and towards Symbolism was articulated by Symons in 1899, who claimed that decadence had

> diverted the attention of the critics while something more serious was in preparation. That something more serious has crystallised, for the time, under the form of Symbolism, in which art returns to the one pathway, leading through beautiful things to the eternal beauty.[84]

There were, of course, no clear definitions of these concepts in a British context; as G. L. L. Morris's article in the *Beam* of 1896 reminded readers, Symons had earlier described Symbolism, in a *Harper's* article of 1893, not as the successor to decadence, but as one of its manifestations. Symons had stated that decadence, as a 'new and beautiful and interesting disease', could be

> divided into two main branches, impressionism and symbolism. The impressionist flashes upon you an exact image of what you have just seen, and the symbolist would also flash upon you the soul of that which can be apprehended by the soul.[85]

The 'apprehension of a soul' had been explored by the second generation of a movement that was perhaps Symbolism's most direct British antecedent – Pre-Raphaelitism. Housman's conflation of sexual and spiritual typography in his fairy tale 'Blind Love' echoed a classic strategy of Dante Gabriel Rossetti, and is significantly situated in a broader periodical context in which visual material is heavily weighted towards late Pre-Raphaelite productions (Rossetti and Burne-Jones) as well as continental Symbolists. Pre-Raphaelitism remained a key influence on many little magazines. Dante Gabriel Rossetti's short story 'Hand and Soul', first published in the *Germ* in 1849, was also republished in the *Dome* 50 years later. In this short story, the thirteenth-century painter Chiaro dell' Erma, haunted by an 'extreme longing after a visible embodiment of his thoughts' receives a vision of his own soul, which he paints to create the consummate masterpiece.[86] Chiaro's painting no longer expresses externals, but the inner recesses of his self. This story prefigures the way in which Rossetti himself artistically turned inward and conflated depictions of his own spirituality with portrayals of sensual (and sexual) desire. Like the abstracted ciphers with the face of Jane Morris in Rossetti's later paintings, Chiaro's soul appears in female form.

Housman's fairy tale 'The Helping Hands', published in the *Butterfly* in July 1899, invokes Symbolist strategies that use the part to represent the whole, and the physical to emblematise the spiritual, melding Pre-Raphaelite and fairy-tale typography. In a variation of the Snow White tale, a princess is lured to a castle by her stepmother's henchman to be killed. Unlike the Grimms' text, in which the henchman saves her life, the Princess is startled by her assailant while praying; he misses her body and cuts off her hands, a clear allusion to the father's actions in the Grimms' tale 'The Girl without Hands'.[87] While the Princess dies and is buried, the hands remain to haunt the castle; when discovered by a prince, they become an emblem for the purity of the woman they will later reanimate. The Prince kisses the disembodied hands as if they were 'the Princess herself'; he carries them close to his breast, gives them his signet ring, and 'love grew up in his heart like a green tree bearing golden fruit'.

The Prince's wish to ask the King for 'the hand of your daughter in marriage' is more than a macabre joke; the physical and the spiritual have no clear point of separation.[88] While Chiaro's hands in 'Hand and Soul' can make his soul appear (sexualised) flesh, in Housman's tale the flesh literally becomes the soul: the Prince has nothing but the disembodied hands through which to perceive the spiritual essence of the Princess. In his essay on Rossetti, Pater stated that spirit and matter had generally been opposed with a 'false contrast or antagonism by schoolmen, whose artificial creation those abstractions really are. In our actual concrete experience, the two trains of phenomena which the words *matter* and *spirit* do but roughly distinguish, play inextricably into each other'.[89] Writing on the late Pre-Raphaelite artist Simeon Solomon's prose-poem *A Vision of Love Revealed in Sleep* in the aesthetic Oxford University magazine the *Dark Blue* in July 1871, Swinburne argued that Solomon's synaesthetic mode of artistic production embodied just such a conflation:

> The subtle interfusion of art with art, of sound with form, of vocal words with silent colours, is as perceptible to the sense and as explicable to the understanding of such men as the interfusion of spirit with flesh is to all men in common; and in fact when perceived of no less significance than this, but rather a part and complement of the same truth.

Claiming that Solomon's visual studies of 'complex or it may be perverse nature' appeal to the student of 'strange beauty and abnormal refinement', Swinburne added that 'there is a mixture of utmost delicacy with a fine cruelty in some of these faces of fair feminine youth'.[90] Solomon's productions of abstracted, androgynous heads could be invested with subjective readings both sacred and profane: Arthur Symons suggested of Solomon's paintings that 'The same face, varied a little in mood, scarcely in feature, serves for Christ and the two Marys, for Sleep and for Lust. The lips are scarcely roughened to indicate a man, the throats scarcely lengthened to indicate a woman'.[91] Solomon (who caused a scandal when he was arrested for sex with another man in a public toilet in 1873) was frequently airbrushed from Pre-Raphaelite memoirs, but his work achieved a cult following among 1890s aesthetes. The *Century Guild Hobby Horse* published Solomon drawings, and Wilde owned one of his more openly homoerotic productions.[92] As Richard Dellamora notes, Solomon's work could activate different meanings for different subcultural audiences: Oxford undergraduate displays of Solomon's 'Love among the Schoolboys' in many cases served 'in order to indicate its owner's fashionableness; a drawing by Solomon, however, might also signal a sexual interest recognizable to those in the know'.[93].

Wilde's use of such coded symbols went beyond his ownership of Solomon's works. As Ian Small, writing on Wilde's short fiction, has suggested:

> On the one hand, the stories fulfil the demands of their respective genres by being accessible to a very wide audience; but the contexts they use invariably work in a coded way, and are to be recognised only by a coterie audience. This dual function makes for the stories' paradoxical qualities – their simplicity and complexity, their heterodoxy and orthodoxy, their appeals to adults and children.[94]

The fairy tale was particularly open to such strategies: as Mabel Cox suggests, writing of Housman's illustrations in 1898, 'in the everyday world, symbols, like miracles, are not; but in the fairy world we expect them'.[95] In fact, as verbal and visual symbols became more recondite, the fairy tale became the specific target of a more covert subcultural appropriation.

Alternative masculinities: The fairy tale and coded gay discourse

The connections between the fairy tale, the east and the erotic were known to late Victorian audiences through the controversy generated by a notorious publication: Richard Burton's *A Thousand Nights and a Night* (1885). Available by private subscription, and published under the false imprint of the 'Kama Shastra Society' of Benares to avoid prosecution, Burton's translation was also reissued in the 1890s by the rather less exotic Leonard Smithers of Stoke Newington.[96] In a 'Terminal Essay' which was overloaded with scholarly reference, Section D, 'Pederasty', went beyond literary allusion in the text itself to claim the existence of a 'Sotadic Zone', encompassing Asia, Italy, Greece, the coast of Africa, and Indo-China, where sexual relations between men and boys were commonplace.[97] While there has been recent interest in resituating Burton's edition in the context of the periodical debate that followed in its wake, its shaping influence on Orientalist discourse, and its role in Victorian theorisations of obscenity, the evidence for the appropriation of fairy tales by a subculture of homosexual readers has not been widely explored.[98] Housman certainly wished to signal his own familiarity with Burton. In the preface to his 1907 *Arabian Nights* collaboration with Edmund Dulac, aimed at an adult audience, Housman directs his readers towards this edition in somewhat evasive terms, noting that Scheherazadè, as a romance device, makes 'even those deeper indiscretions, which Burton has so faithfully recorded, seem then but a wise adaptation of vile means to a noble end'.[99] As we shall see, when Housman's fairy tale 'The Blue Moon' was published in the *Butterfly* in May 1899, the writer's choice of a dream-like eastern location not only made links with fairy-tale predecessors, but implicated Housman's narrative in a more complex web of *fin-de-siècle* debates – anthropological, aesthetic and sexual.[100]

Appropriated by 'New Women' as well as male writers to explore sexual fantasies, fascination with the vaguely defined region which Francesca Vanke terms the 'Islamic Orient' became a familiar trope within decadent constructions of the erotic.[101] The exotic prose of Wilde's 'The Fisherman and his Soul' clearly echoes the *Nights* explorations of forbidden sensual and sexual desire, but the alternative sexualities projected onto North Africa and the Middle East were female as well as male. Texts such as Flaubert's *Salammbô* (1862), reprising the myth of the mysterious and impassive Eastern seductress, and mythological archetypes such as Salome and the Sphinx not only informed Wilde's *Salome*, but realist short stories such as Victoria Cross's 'Theodora: A Fragment' in the *Yellow Book* (1895) and fantasies such as Clo Graves' 'Apamé' in the *Butterfly* (1893).[102] An early periodical text which played wryly with such expectations was John Gray's 'The Great Worm', a fairy tale which draws heavily on Countess d'Aulnoy's 'Green Serpent' and which appeared in the first *Dial* (1889), accompanied by a coloured lithograph and illustrations by Charles Ricketts. This tale's luxurious prose evokes a dream-like Orient: Gray's narrative, seemingly both a parody of and a homage to Wilde, tells the self-referential tale of a white and gold 'worm' (a Chinese Dragon) of enormous size from a mountain range 'somewhere [...] in Central Asia, with a name as ragged as its silhouette'. The worm, entering a neighbouring city, is recruited into the Prince's army. Its fearful presence allows the Prince to conquer many lands until, reaching a city of gold, silver and amber, the worm is presented with a lily by a mysterious white figure who is eroticised in decadent prose: 'Her body had the undulations of a pod, ripe and swollen to bursting; her breasts were like mounds under moonlit snow. Her hair, gold as corn at noon, was prodigal as a waterfall; and her eyes were like pansies.' The symbolic value of this figure is ambiguous: while she is clearly sexualised, she is also referred to as 'the white child'.[103] The worm dies of love, and the lily, nurtured by the blood of the worm's heart, blooms on its chest; there are obvious echoes of some of the symbolic motifs of Wilde's fairy tale 'The Nightingale and the Rose'.[104]

As Gray's central emblem of 'the great worm' suggests, it was not only stereotypes associated with the Islamic Orient that informed the erotic fairy-tale dreamscapes of coterie writers and readers. Japanese culture was a central preoccupation for the little magazines of the 1890s, as epitomised by the *Dome*'s published appreciations of Hokusai, Hirosage and Utamaro, accompanied by both black and white and coloured collectors' prints. Such works were recognised as key influences on contemporary Western art; as C. J. Holmes notes in his article on Hirosage, 'To have a share with Velasquez in the making of Mr. Whistler's style is no slight honour'.[105] Holmes's claim in his article on Utamaro, that he is 'an artist with one absorbing passion – the love of woman', refers rather decorously to Utamaro's widely-known status as an erotic artist.[106] Beardsley is known to have decorated his bedroom with Utamaro's prints, and Wilde's Tite Street house in the 1880s was furnished in lavish Japanese style.[107] If Japan was perceived as a mythical realm of sexual exoticism for many late nineteenth-century writers, another stereotype associated with the art works of Japan, based on the comparative method and its ethnocentric notions of national progress, had obvious parallels with fascinations with the folktale. Both were revered as productions from a state of cultural childhood. In 1893, Percival Lowell claimed that the Japanese were 'still in that childish state of development before self-consciousness has spoiled the sweet simplicity of nature' and suggested that their artistic perceptions were based on 'instinct' and intuition.[108]

The Japanese influence emerges in an intriguing form in Byam Shaw's drawing 'Beauty and the Beast' in the *Dome* (Figure 5.2).[109] Employing a decorative scrolled border, Shaw combines verbal and visual iconography. A familiar citation from the text has been medievalised, while the typographical style, with its elaborate capitals, is reminiscent of Kelmscott editions. The presence of a dark-haired Pre-Raphaelite beauty also creates parallels with Morris and Sidney Meteyard's 'Rapunzel'. Yet Byam Shaw's drawing also explicitly embraces the wider interfusion of movements of the 1890s that distinguishes his host periodical from the *Quest*. Shaw chooses to symbolically interpret the beast as a Chinese dragon, complementing the *Dome*'s wider contributions that explore Oriental art and culture. In addition to the obvious Arts and Crafts influences, Shaw uses the East as a decadent signifier: for the exotic, the erotic and the perverse.

Figure 5.2 [John] Byam [Liston] Shaw, 'Beauty and the Beast', *Dome*, 1898. Used by permission of the University of London Library

Of all the periodicals under discussion, the *Butterfly* was perhaps the most enthusiastic exponent of Japanese art, publishing classic prints and short stories exploring national customs. It was stylistically defined by the frequent contributions from contemporary artist Edgar Wilson, whose head and tailpieces depicting fish or peacocks paid obvious tribute to Japanese graphic styles.[110] In its first publication in the *Butterfly*, it is the periodical's general fascination with Japan which allows 'The Blue Moon' to create intertextual meanings. The text manipulates the east's contemporary associations with both a revered cultural primitivism and a realm of alternative sexual possibilities. Inventively conflating the exotica of the *Nights* with the folktale motifs of the Grimms, Housman's choice of names for his lovers ('Nilly-Will' and 'Hands-Pansy') produces some curious gender reversals. Hands-Pansy, the peasant male protagonist, while suggesting the 'Hans' of the archetypal Grimms' peasant hero, also evokes Wildean aestheticism: connections between homosexual men and flowers (Wilde's lilies, sunflowers and green carnation are the most obvious examples) were well established in the public consciousness after the Wilde trials.[111] Such flower imagery in Housman's tale is explicitly linked to a socially forbidden love: Nilly-Will, taken from her peasant childhood with Hands-Pansy to be brought up as a princess, finds 'all she could do for love was to fill her garden with dark-eyed pansies'.[112] While Gray's eroticised 'white child' has 'eyes like pansies', Housman's gender reversal makes a male figure the object of desire. The correlation between men and flowers as sexual objects also echoes 'The Rooted Lover', a tale in Housman's first fairy-tale collection, in which a ploughboy is turned into a poppy to win the love of a princess.[113]

Housman self-consciously appropriates the Grimms' folktale cadences, speaking of the 'real princess hiding her birthright in the home of a poor peasant'; 'the most honest and good heart ever sprung out of poverty and humble parentage', and Hands' walk of 'five thousand miles' in wooden clogs to reach his love. Yet their forbidden love cannot be reconciled happily-ever-after on earth, but only in an alternative realm and a different linguistic register. Told that a princess can only love a peasant 'once in a Blue Moon', the changes wrought by the Blue Moon's appearance also signals a shift towards decadent prose.[114] Havelock Ellis, in 'A Note on Paul Bourget' in the *Pioneer* of October 1889, suggested that

> A style of decadence is one in which the unity of the book is decomposed to give place to the independence of the page, in which the page is decomposed to give place to the independence of the phrase, and the phrase to give place to the independence of the word.[115]

This breaking down of narrative unity, the privileging of subjective impression rather than transparent expression, is in marked contrast to the fairy tale's expected emphasis on simple plot development. In both Wilde's and

Housman's tales, simple descriptions compete with the 'jewelled and seductive prose' which Regenia Gagnier suggests Wilde uses to target 'a select audience of artful young men'.[116] The over-scrutinising of emotion characteristic of decadence leads to the artistic creation of mood rather narrative; building on the exotic language of the *Nights*, Wilde turns fairy-tale landscapes into landscapes of the mind. Similar experiments with language are demonstrated by Laurence Housman in 'The Blue Moon':

> All the world seemed carven out of blue stone; trees with stems dark-veined as marble rose up to give rest to boughs which drooped the altered hues of their foliage like the feathers of peacocks at roost. Jewel within jewel burned through every shade from blue to onyx. The white blossoms of a cherry-tree had become changed into turquoise, and the tossing spray of a fountain as it drifted and swung was like a column of blue fire. Where a long inlet of sea reached in and touched the feet of the hanging gardens, the stars showed like glow-worms, emerald in a floor of amethyst.
>
> There was no motion abroad, nor sound: even the voice of the nightingale was stilled because the passion of her desire had become visible before her eyes.[117]

The homage to Wilde is self-conscious – a reader in the know would recognise in this description of peacocks and fountains Charles Ricketts's cover illustration to *A House of Pomegranates*. While Housman alludes to the moon in 'A Capful of Moonshine' as a realm of alternative social values, it conjures another sexual realm in Housman's 'Blind Love': Innygreth calls her forbidden love 'thou moon of madness'. In the same edition of the *Pageant*, Max Beerbohm's fairy tale 'Yai and the Moon' manipulates both an Oriental setting and notions of transgressive desire. Bequeathed by her father to a passionless scholar, Yai longs for the moon to be her lover, and is found drowned after attempting to embrace its reflection.[118] This link between the moon and alternative sexualities is familiar in the decadent literature of the 1890s, one of the best known examples being the English edition of Oscar Wilde's *Salome* (1894). As Lorraine Kooistra Janzen has noted, Aubrey Beardsley's satiric illustration of 'The Woman in the Moon' in Wilde's play enacts its own gender inversion. It displays not the woman promised by both the caption and the text, but an obvious caricature of Wilde, whose eyes are lasciviously directed towards a naked and effeminate male.[119] To a reader familiar with these texts, the appearance of Housman's 'Moon Fairy' would have invoked a suggestive train of references:

> Before them, facing the sea, stood two great reindeer, their high horns reaching to the overhead boughs; and behind them lay a sledge, long and

with deep sides like the sides of a ship. All blue they seemed in that strange light.

There, too, but nearer to hand, was the moon-fairy himself waiting – a great figure of lofty stature, clad in furs of blue fox-skin, and with herons' wings fastened above the flaps of his hood; and these lifted themselves and clapped as Hands and the princess drew near.

'Are you coming to the blue moon?' called the fairy, and his voice whistled and shrewed to them like the voice of a wind.[120]

Housman's fur-clad figure, emerging on a reindeer-driven sleigh from a landscape of snow, clearly references Hans Christian Andersen's 'Snow Queen'; yet he is an image of love rather than emotional frigidity. There are obvious parallels with Eros, the Greek god of love; the presence of the sea and the winged fairy's description are also reminiscent of the figure of a boyish Eros in Simeon Solomon's painting *Love in Autumn*. In Solomon's prose-poem *A Vision of Love Revealed in Sleep*, there is an homoerotic dynamic to the portrayal of Eros as an androgynously beautiful winged youth, a double meaning explored more explicitly in Solomon's privately circulated drawing *The Bride, The Bridegroom and Sad Love*.[121] In 'The Work of Laurence Housman' in the *Book-Lover's Magazine* of 1908, Charles Kains-Jackson allies Housman's verbal and visual evocations of fairyland with praise for his affinities with the Greek in his poem 'Puss in Winter':

> The makers of myth are not dead. The Greeks before Homer who listened to how Orpheus fell in love with Calaïs, the beautiful Wind, and how the winged youth returned his love, would have made the 'Snow-White Cat' a living legend of the hilly lands and little hill towns of Thrace.[122]

In Housman's conflation of folkloric and classical allusion in 'The Blue Moon', the moon fairy, whose voice shrews 'like the wind', produces associations with both Eros and the 'winged youth' Calaïs, 'beautiful Wind' and lover of Orpheus. Kains-Jackson's authorship of this article is significant, for the myth of Orpheus embodied a subsumed level of cultural reference for a select group of readers. In Burton's 'Terminal Essay' to the tenth volume of *The Thousand Nights and a Night*, he notes that the ancient Greeks 'attributed the formal apostolate of Sotadism to Orpheus', and provides supporting passages from Ovid. After failing to rescue Eurydice from Hades, Orpheus is torn to pieces by Maeniads for refusing them. The potential significance of this myth for a late nineteenth-century homosexual subculture becomes apparent when Burton's lines are translated: 'And Orpheus had shunned all love for women [...] He set the example for the Thracians by giving his love to young boys, and enjoying the springtime and first flower of their youth.'

Burton was aware that his erudite scholarly register provided a coded way to discuss the unmentionable. He mocked the hypocrisy of the censor of morals (and particularly the mainstream periodical critic) who would happily read of such behaviour 'veiled in the decent obscurity of a learned language'.[123] Yet this learned classical discourse, as Linda Dowling has elaborated, could not only, like Burton's text, bring alternative sexual mores into focus, but could also provide a respectable literary conduit for the expression of love between males.[124] Reading the classics (including the *Symposium*) at Oxford enabled John Addington Symonds to articulate a Platonic ideal of spiritual bonds between men, which resonated powerfully in contemporary male culture. Symonds claimed that while the lover who was creative in body 'begets children', 'if the soul be the chief creative principle in the lover's nature, then he turns to young men of "fair and noble and well-nurtured spirit", and in them begets the immortal progeny of high thoughts and generous emotions'.[125] Crucially, in Greek culture, such sentimental unions were associated with valour rather than effeminacy. Both Symonds and Burton refer to the battle of Chæronea of 338 BC, in which a 'Sacred band of Thebans', valiant but doomed, were defeated and killed by Philip of Macedonia. These soldiers stand as emblems of male honour and bravery; yet this remains in keeping with their presentation by Burton as a 'Holy Regiment composed of mutual lovers, testifying to the majesty of Eros'.[126]

Burton's rather prurient and condemnatory explorations of 'Sotadic' sexuality are very different from Symonds celebration of spiritual bonds between men, and it is important to acknowledge the contested ways in which classical scholarship was used to explore sexual and social relationships between men in this period.[127] There is, however, no doubt that Platonic discourse focusing on the elevated male beloved, like the paintings of Solomon, had sexual as well as spiritual connotations for some reading communities prior to the Wilde trials. Symonds notes that the Greeks 'worshipped Eros, as they worshipped Aphrodite, under the twofold titles of Ouranios (celestial) and Pandemos (vulgar, or *volvivaga*)'; and while Symonds takes pains to praise the spiritual and disparage the physical, his readers are made aware that the god could embody both meanings.[128] The existence of 'Uranian' or homosexual subcultural expression in the minority periodical press prior to the Wilde trials has been explored by Ian Fletcher, Timothy d'Arch Smith, and more recently, Laurel Brake, who engages with the *Artist and Journal of Home Culture* under Charles Kains-Jackson as a key site in which 'gay discourse' was both articulated and censored.[129]

Housman's own position within these pre- and post-trial subcultural groups is intriguing. As Jeffrey Weeks has noted, the diaries of George Cecil Ives reveal Housman to have been a prominent member of a secret homosexual society which ran from the 1890s well into the twentieth century. Taking its name from the martial ideal of Greek love cited by both Symonds and Burton ('the Order of Chæronea'), members included Charles Kains-Jackson, C. R. Ashbee (a leading member of the Arts and Crafts movement) and a number of minor poets. Weeks notes that the organisation, international in scope, bound members to each other 'not only by their sense of solidarity in secrecy but also by the ritual of initiation ceremonies and by common symbols'.[130] Fairy-tale texts and illustrations appear to have been a shared interest among a number of this group. While Kains-Jackson wrote appreciatively of Housman's fairy-tale productions, Ashbee would have been aware that his father had introduced Leonard Smithers to a number of erotic fairy tales, including *Fairy Tales by the Abbé Voisenon*. Smithers used false imprints to publish a range of sexually explicit fairy-tale material (such as *Harlequin: A Romance* and *Aglae, an Erotic Fairy Tale*). Readers were alerted through advertisements at the back of such editions to the availability of explicitly homosexual texts, including *Teleny*.[131]

There were clear links between little magazines and the circulation of Smithers' more outré texts: Aubrey Beardsley's Wagnerian fantasy *Under the Hill* famously appeared in heavily censored form in the *Savoy*, as well as enjoying unexpurgated covert circulation.[132] If Beardsley's erotic imagination utilised both text and illustration, the same seems to be true in the appropriations of the fairy tale by members of Housman's circle. Leaving his own possible familiarity with Smithers' erotic lists aside, there seems to be an iconic link among homoerotic explorations of 'Greek love', the moon fairy in 'The Blue Moon' and Housman's fairy-tale illustrative work, connecting an early book commission, his own fairy-tale editions and his periodical the *Venture*. Kains-Jackson, commenting on the cover of the *Venture*, stated: 'It is a handsome quarto and bears on its cover a vigorous drawing: a terminal or caryatid figure of Love the Archer. The type is extremely manly and the drawing shows a strong line.'[133] Kains-Jackson's comments initially appear curious, for this figure, which appears in a range of texts, seems far from 'manly' according to dominant archetypes of the 1890s. The frontispiece of *The Field of Clover* features a tortured, etiolated figure with the statue of an androgynously beautiful Eros; the frontispiece of *A Farm in Fairyland* displays a similar Eros figure along with some Beardsleyesque females, while the cover of the *House of Joy* shows two such caryatids (one picked out in gold) supporting a carriage of Pre-Raphaelite women. These statues had earlier appeared repeatedly in illustrations to Jane Barlow's *The End of Elfin-Town*, one of Housman's earliest illustrative commissions (Figure 5.3).

While this icon can be read as a conventional cipher of heterosexual love, Kains-Jackson's comments are also potentially suggestive of the male relationships enshrined by the Greek chivalric ideal; an ideal which forced a reappraisal of what it meant to be 'manly'. Gleeson White, the most enthusiastic champion of Housman's art, spoke in the *Studio* in 1894 of the androgynous winged male emblems in *The End of Elfin-Town* as the embodiment of a perfect physical ideal: 'A long search would fail to discover a more refined and faultless beauty of face and hands.'[134] White, like Kains-Jackson, was at the centre of a circle of 'Uranian' poets; like Kains-Jackson, he used his editorship of an art periodical to foster a coded discourse that explored the

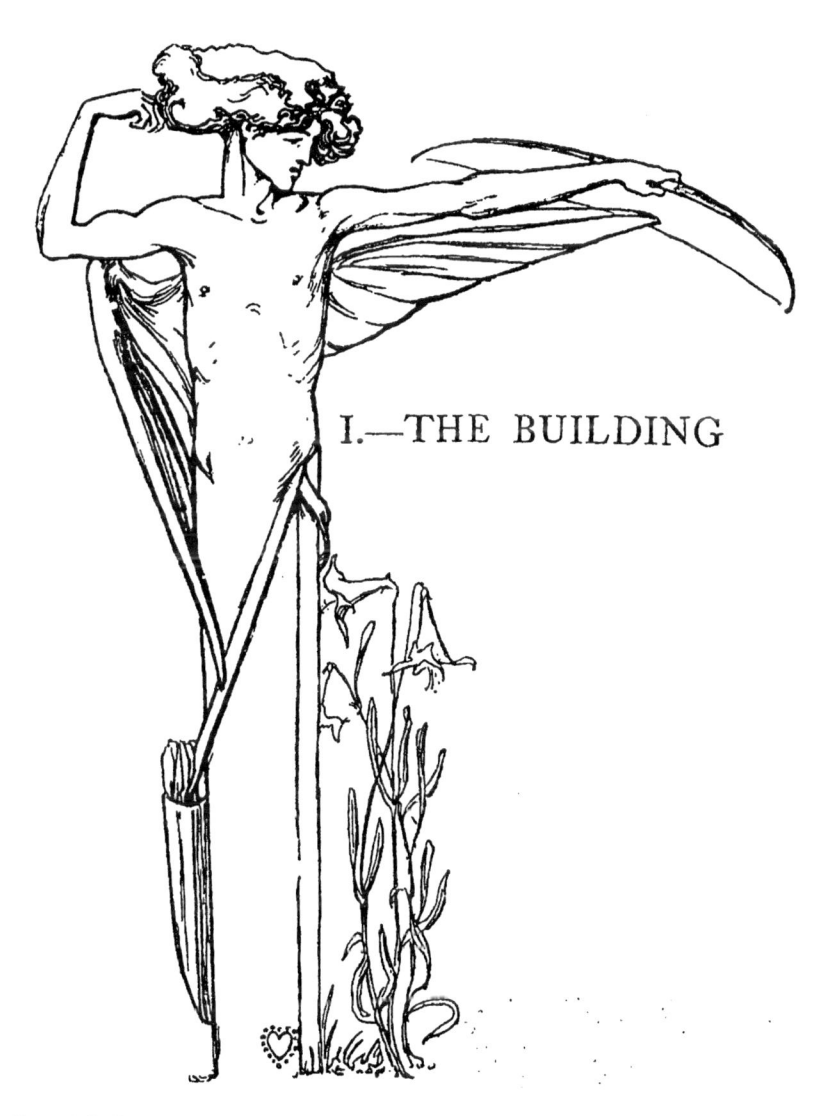

Figure 5.3 Laurence Housman, illustration to Jane Barlow, *The End of Elfin-Town*, 1894. © The British Library Board. All Rights Reserved. KTC.35.a.4. Used by permission of the Random House Group Ltd.

expression of love between men.[135] Yeats suggested that love was one of the two preoccupations at the heart of Symbolic art. Those iconographic systems were also available to those whose love could not openly speak its name.

The fact that Housman's male icon of love is a fairy also has specific significance in relation to popular and scientific explorations of homosexuality and cross-dressing. Housman, who in the early twentieth century was chairman of the British Society for the Study of Sex Psychology (BSSP), had been interested in medical and psychological investigations of homosexuality from a much earlier date, as his correspondence with Havelock Ellis testifies.[136] One of the earliest recorded medical uses of the word 'fairy' appears in a discussion in the *American Journal of Psychology* in 1895. Speaking of 'the peculiar societies of inverts', the writer claims that

> Coffee-clatches, where the members dress themselves with aprons, etc., and knit, gossip and crochet; balls, where men adopt the ladies' evening dress, are well known in Europe. 'The Fairies' of New York are said to be a similar secret organisation.[137]

As George Chauncey has shown, the term was also widely used in New York popular culture of the 1890s to describe the effeminate and cross-dressing men who were a familiar sight in the Bowery area of the city. He cites a contemporary who 'identified several "low class fairies" in a Bowery salon, wearing their "hair a la mode de Oscar Wilde"'.[138] While such usages of the term equate homosexuality with effeminacy, Housman's fairy tale enacts some cross-dressing of its own: in using folkloric and classical models to manipulate the gender identities of its characters, Housman destabilises expected constructions of masculine and feminine. It is certainly possible to read Housman's literary inversions in the context of his wider awareness of medical and cultural theories concerning homosexuality in the late 1890s. In 1897, an English edition of Havelock Ellis's *Sexual Inversion* was published, a collaboration with John Addington Symonds that theorised homosexuality in scientific terms, as a biological merging of sexual traits. Ellis and Symonds drew on the work of Karl Ulrichs, whose complex classificatory system suggested that 'Urnings' or 'Uranians' combined the physical form of one sex with the soul of another. Ulrichs's terminology (with its mythical rather than pathological associations) was adopted – or adapted – by many practising homosexuals.[139] Such theories were to culminate in Edward Carpenter's defence of a homosexual 'intermediate sex' in the early years of the new century: 'sometimes it seems possible that a new sex is on the make'.[140]

As Ghislaine Wood and Paul Greenhalgh note, the 'apparently contrary forces of rational science and mysticism' were fused in intriguing ways in the late nineteenth century. While the androgyne was the subject of new sciences such as sexology, it was also a figure in mystical and alchemical symbolism, and was a recurring subject for the Rose + Croix school of Symbolists in France. Its founder, Sâr Joséphin Péladan, was heavily influenced by the

Pre-Raphaelites, and the influence of scientific, sexual, mystic and artistic explorations of the androgyne mingled in unexpected ways in British little magazines.[141] Housman was not the only writer in such periodicals who allied explorations of androgynous sexuality with fairy or folktale forms. There was some suggestion of gender inversion in Baron Corvo's 'Stories Toto Told Me', the last of which, like Housman's tale, was also published in the *Butterfly*.[142] Readers of the *Yellow Book* would already be familiar with Corvo's literary conceit, in which the Italian peasant 'Toto' tells folkloric tales which draw on Catholic mythology. In both the *Yellow Book* sequence and the *Butterfly* text, the tales are framed by the dialogues between Toto and an aristocratic first person narrator, whose master–servant relationship is sexually ambiguous. In the *Yellow Book*'s 'About Beata Beatrice and the Mamma of San Pietro', a sexually charged description of Toto is followed by the introduction of his lover; a peasant girl dressed in male clothes, who 'would pass anywhere for a very pretty boy'.[143] A month before Corvo's final story in the *Butterfly*, S. H. Sime published a drawing of Sarah Bernhardt as a strikingly masculine (and Wildean) Hamlet.[144]

Reading intertextually between little magazines, readers would have been presented with a range of literary and artistic explorations of sexual ambiguity. Some of these images and texts certainly seem to tap into the subcultural knowledge of the initiated reader. The *Century Guild Hobby Horse* used Simeon Solomon's androgynous Baccus as a frontispiece in July 1891, a painting which had already been subject to the coded appreciation of Walter Pater.[145] The passive androgyne became a blank canvas on which the observer could register the uniqueness of their own subjective impression. Like Pater's praise of the 'fittingly inexpressive expression' of Myron's *Discobolus*, for Symons Solomon's faces are erotically charged through the very fact that they are 'without sex; they have brooded among ghosts of passions till they have become the ghosts of themselves; the energy of virtue or sin has gone out of them, and they hang in space, dry, rattling, the husks of desire'.[146] As Ian Fletcher has noted, the *Dome*'s artistic policy was heavily influenced by that of Charles Shannon at the *Pageant*. These periodicals reproduced a number of paintings by Rossetti and Burne-Jones (and in the *Pageant*'s case, Ricketts, Shannon and Moreau) that explore androgynous or hybrid sexual states.[147]

Frederick Wedmore's criticism in the *Academy* of Housman's *Yellow Book* drawing 'The Reflected Faun' as too much 'the sexless Pre-Raphaelite' must be read in the context of such debates: a context in which the adjective 'sexless' expresses a dangerous vacuum susceptible to the sexual proclivities of the viewer.[148] In fact, Housman's illustrations display a number of strategies previously utilised by Solomon – the conflation of the sexual within the propriety of the religious, the use of mythological typography and the sublimation of the erotic in an androgynous, mystical ideal – which also reveal a debt to the writings of Pater. Housman's 'Reflected Faun', with its narcissus-like male hybrid figure (Figure 5.4), was rejected by Lane as a frontispiece for Francis

Figure 5.4 Laurence Housman, 'The Reflected Faun', *Yellow Book*, 1894. Used by permission of the University of London Library and the Random House Group Ltd.

Thompson's poems. While Housman provided a detailed typographical key for John Lane to interpret a further illustration, 'Barren Life', Lane remained uncomfortable with Housman's fusion of nudity and religious symbolism, turning down the drawing in its intended role as a frontispiece for another collection by the same poet.[149]

Significantly, both drawings were accepted for the *Yellow Book*. Appearing in fairly close proximity in the 1897 *Pageant* to Burne-Jones's *The Sea Nymph* and *Perseus and Medusa*, Housman's drawing *Death and the Bather* reveals his engagement with a Symbolist iconography that embraces both the sexual and the mystic aspects of androgyny. In this drawing, a number of naked male figures provide a background to a full-frontal male nude adorned with flowers, a figure which can function simultaneously as a spiritual symbol for the mysteries of the afterlife and an erotic focus for homosexual or heterosexual desire.

If Housman's manipulation of androgyny could be read in different ways by different audiences, Housman's fairy tales also maintains a chain of references that make links to other little magazines and to a select band of readers. 'Tales of a Woodcutter', which appeared in the *Butterfly* in February 1900, consists of two short tales which draw on religious and folkloric iconography, Housman's own poetry, a contribution by Richard Le Gallienne in the *Yellow Book* and the fairy tales of Oscar Wilde. This text also exhibits a more obvious debt to the Grimms' – the peasant narrator as a linking frame recalls the connecting voice of 'Gammer Grethel' in the edition of the Grimms' tales later edited by Housman. Yet, like Wilde's tale 'The Devoted Friend', the story is filtered through a number of interpreters; the unidentified narrator recalls stories told to him by the woodcutter, who himself interprets the words of the trees. In the first tale, 'The Old Yew Tree', the woodcutter relates to the narrator the yew's story of his unwilling entrapment of two fairy lovers, again invoking the motif of socially prohibited love: 'they were lovers, it seems, clandestinely. She was an Erl-king's daughter, and he a mere nobody; but they loved, so the old yew told me, like two lobes of quicksilver. It seemed to be a real tearing of themselves in two to break out of each other's arms'. When the erotic transgression of Housman's lovers is discovered they are pursued by the other fairies; finding a crack in the tree, the persecuted fairies enter to hide. Torrential rain puts off the pursuers, but swells the rind of the tree, so that the fairy lovers are entrapped until death. '"My heart is hollow," said the old yew tree; "yet night and day I think of my two lovers and their sad story, who died because I held them, and could not let go"'.[150]

Openly subverting the fairy tale's expected happy ending, Housman's meditation on social and physical imprisonment draws on early pagan and Christian mythology, and on a number of little magazine predecessors. Housman's tree as a narrator of doomed love has parallels with T. H. Prichard's poem 'The Elm Recounts', published in the *Dome* in 1898, which may even have inspired Housman's narrative:

> An elm tree told this story to the copse;
> Deep sighed his friends, and shook their leafy tops.
> "Two lovers came to-day into the wood;
> Those lovers cannot come to any good".[151]

Housman's tree as symbolic icon of both love and death also finds a precursor in his own poem 'The Poison Tree' in the *Dome*, in which the tree of death stays barren because of its love for the tree of life.[152] The 'Tree of Life' would be a familiar symbol to readers of Yeats's Celtic mythology and prose, published across the little magazines, while the 'Dry Tree', a symbol of death overcome by Christ's sacrifice, was also an emblem still familiar from medieval typology.[153] A number of these myths were manipulated by Richard le Gallienne's poem 'Tree-Worship', published in the first volume of the *Yellow Book*.[154] The tree with 'So hard a rind' which shields 'so soft a heart' (l. 17) is home to the enthralling dryad who 'sways within thine arms and sings a fairy tune'(l. 26). Yet it is also the tree that crucified Christ: 'I picture thee some bloodstained Holyrood' (l. 37). It also has more recent associations with the outlaw:

> Then, maybe, dangling from thy gloomy gallows boughs,
> A human corpse swings, mournful, rattling bones and chains –
>
> (ll. 45–46)

Both associations are present in the second part of Housman's text 'The Whitethorn's Story', in which the tree becomes an unwilling gallows for an outlaw who has taken refuge in the forest. While there are obvious associations with the crucifixion, the tale's equation of love and martyrdom also alludes to forbidden desire:

> 'There is one thing,' said the Woodcutter, 'that men would be surprised to know, and that is the strong love that all trees have in their hearts. [...] The greatest cause of sorrow where trees are concerned is love – not for one another, but for things higher than themselves; for to love higher than one's self ennobles, but does not bring happiness'.

The idealisation of the spiritually elevated beloved had been notably defended by Wilde at his first trial: the 'Love that dare not speak its name', which 'Plato made the very basis of his philosophy', is 'that deep, spiritual affection that is as pure as it is perfect [...] it repeatedly exists between an elder and a younger man'.[155] Housman's invocation of the tree as a lover which 'kills the thing he loves' may intentionally echo Wilde's own downfall, a parallel strengthened by the intriguing typological overlaps with Wilde's fairy tale 'The Selfish Giant'.[156] In Wilde's text, the child who teaches the giant the meaning of selflessness becomes a Christ-like icon who causes a tree to break into blossom. In Housman's tale, the white blossom is an equally central symbol, but of martyrdom rather than redemption. Housman depicts the thorn tree's developing love for the outlaw: loving first contentedly, then wistfully, 'the tree's heart softened towards him, and its whole life became a sense of his coming and going'. Yet in May when the tree is in blossom, men and hounds ride through the woods: when they leave, the outlaw has been hung from its boughs.[157] The reference to a month invokes a specific biographical resonance with Wilde: the twenty-fifth of May 1895 marked the close of Wilde's last trial, and was the day on which he was sentenced to two years of hard labour.[158]

While such parallels may appear merely coincidental, there were reasons why Wilde would have been at the forefront of Housman's mind at the time of this text's publication. Five months earlier he had visited Wilde in exile in France, delivering financial assistance from the artistic circle that frequented the Café Royal. The meeting had a profound effect on Housman, and inspired the semi-fictional account of the event, *Echo de Paris*, which was published more than 20 years later. Housman's extended footnote to this text provided an articulate plea for homosexuality to be recognised as a biological and congenital rather than a cultural (and criminal) state, drawing in support on Housman's own campaigns for sexual reform.[159] In Housman's account, Wilde is depicted as a raconteur who told spontaneous fairy tales of impossible longing and loss. Something of Wilde's fairy-tale conflation of the spiritual and the physical, and his evocation of the doomed nature of socially prohibited love is caught in 'The Whitethorn's Story'. In Housman's text, the grieving tree asks a fairy to look into the dead man's eyes: the outlaw, whose own head 'was white as a tree in full blossom' reflects in his vacant eyes only the tree's blossom and the spring weather. Housman's fairy-tale anthropomorphism is poignant, erotic and lyrical:

> 'Do not look any longer!' it cried. 'Oh, do not look, lest I grow jealous! For all in his eyes is mine, and I am his. Because his hands never took hold of them, because he loved me, he has gathered my blossoms with his eyes, and is holding them there in the dim twilight. Come away, good one, and do not look!'
>
> And the little fairy came down and left that strange bridal, and the dead man's eyes covered softly over with the shadow of blossoms and leaves.[160]

'That strange bridal', in which love is truly in the eye of the beholder, is surprising in more ways than one. As Ian Fletcher has noted, a subculturally recognised strategy in 'Uranian' writing in little magazines was to ensure that the narrator's gender was linguistically ambiguous, constructing an objectified male lover who was the potential focus of either male or female desire.[161] Lord Alfred Douglas's poem 'Prince Charming', which appeared in the *Artist and Journal of Home Culture* (and was suggestively juxtaposed with Kains-Jackson's 'The New Chivalry'), had previously used just such a strategy.[162]

In fact, wider subcultural appropriations of fairy-tale motifs are apparent in the persistent literary engagements with a subject Timothy d'Arch Smith terms 'the Uranians' myth-making of the "Pauper" into the "Prince", the myth indeed of the boy who, thanks to a man's intervention in his life, overrides and supersedes his lower-class birthright and becomes a boy of great beauty and intellect'. D'Arch Smith's claim that this strategy was used to articulate 'the extraordinary longing for an attachment to a boy either of a far higher or, more often, of a far lower social rank', a 'well-nigh universally used idea' in Uranian verse, might add a more complex contextual frame through which to read Housman's persistent return in his fairy tales to a love that transgresses class hierarchies.[163]

Within the codes of the fairy tale, where magic and fantasy are expected, we look, as Mabel Cox suggested, for symbols: the attraction of such texts for sexual minority audiences may have resided in part in this wilful ambiguity. Housman's sorrowing whitethorn tree is an unrequited lover which pointedly remains an 'it' throughout the narrative, open to the reader's own imposition of gender. Like Housman's illustration to his fairy tale 'Blind Love' in the *Pageant*, 'The Invisible Princess', in which a prince grasps at an invisible lover amid medieval battlements (Figure 5.5), the reader can insert their own gendered beloved and create their own fantasies.[164] In fact, focusing on Housman's visual and verbal fairy-tale productions offers a rather different perspective on homoerotic expression after the Wilde trials than the more familiar narrative of wholesale censorship and sexual repression. Rather than the termination of coded gay expression, it is possible to see significant pre- and post-trial continuities: to see, in the use of myth and fairy tale by members of the Order of Chæronea, the reutilisation of strategies formerly used by Solomon, Pater and Wilde.

While Wilde celebrated the critic as artist, Burton also placed significant emphasis on the interpretative role of the reader, pointedly prefacing his edition of the *Nights* with the claim '[t]o the pure, all things are pure'. Yet if the fairy tale could be used to foreground the subjective nature of interpretation, it could also offer the illusion of escape from a solipsistic relativism into a realm of moral certitude. While many artists turned to Catholicism as an escape from the cul-de-sac of decadence, by 1908 Charles Kains-Jackson was suggesting that Housman's fairy-tale illustrations symbolised not 'the morrow of Epicurean asceticism, but the after-morrow of Catholicism'. In Jackson's schema, the fairy tale has almost become a replacement for religion – a solution to the decadent refutation of moral certainty. Quoting,

Figure 5.5 Laurence Housman, 'Blind Love', *Pageant*, 1897. Used by permission of the University of London Library and the Random House Group Ltd.

via Housman, the reassuring moral certitudes about the 'old-fashioned' fairy tale delineated by Ruskin in his introduction to Taylor's Grimm, the argument about fairy tales as repositories for an instinctive and unconscious morality appears, post-decadence, to have come full circle. Kains-Jackson makes an analogy between the agnostic and Ruskin's ideal child reader of the fairy tale:

> It will not be the embroidered copes which will attract him, as the millinery and satin slippers were thought by Ruskin to attract the modern child to the modern Märchen. But it will be the Mystery which the cope is worn to honour, even as the children of pre-Reformation England were chiefly attracted, as again says the Sage of Coniston, by the enchantments that the fairies worked. And if anything in the future will entice the really wise to leave the authentic garden of Epicurus (which is the garden of unexhausting pleasures, the pleasures of the soul), that temptation will be Mr. Housman's, luring the world to Old Religion by way of a walk through Fairyland.

Kains-Jackson, however, not only reprises Ruskinian arguments, but also self-consciously links Housman to a range of 'Epicurean' homosexual artists, including Lord Alfred Douglas and Count Stenbock. This article would have created entirely different meanings within the underground sexual subculture to which both Housman and Kains-Jackson pledged allegiance.[165] Creating coded homosexual expression through ingenious double meanings, the article also reprises a sleight of hand employed in many *fin-de-siècle* constructions of childhood. The child and the fairy become deeply ambiguous ciphers: both emblems of, and safeguards against, epicurean pleasure; both icons of absolute morality, and icons of sensory individualism. In the experimental literary culture of the *fin de siècle*, then, fairy tales performed many symbolic roles. Participating in debates over degeneration, aesthetics and sexuality, they were also appropriated to acknowledge the end of decadence: to console for the limitations of the shock of the new.

Conclusion: Myth in the Marketplace

> the art of storytelling is coming to an end. [...] One reason for this phenomenon is obvious: experience has fallen in value. And it looks as if it is continuing to fall into bottomlessness. Every glance at a newspaper demonstrates that it has reached a new low, that our picture, not only of the external world but of the moral world as well, overnight has undergone changes that were never thought possible.[1]

> 'And they lived happily ever after,' says the fairy tale. The fairy tale, which to this day is the first tutor of children because it was once the first tutor of mankind, secretly lives on in the story. The first true storyteller is, and will continue to be, the teller of fairy tales.[2]

My epigraphs may already seem familiar. The fairy tale is the truest form of storytelling: not just because it is the first literature of childhood, but because it is a vital form that recapitulates the childhood of mankind. Among storytelling's destroyers is the newspaper, the agent of a distorted information age that has killed folk culture, cheapened experience and engendered a loss of moral value. This is not W. B. Yeats, writing in the 1890s, but Walter Benjamin, writing of the transfigured mental landscape after the Great War in his 1936 article 'The Storyteller'. While fairy tales speak in distinctive ways to each political moment, nineteenth-century constructions of the genre have left their mark: not only in the twentieth century, but also in our own.

Benjamin's hope that a utopian spirit of storytelling might live on against the odds is, of course, familiar too. For Dickens, the fairy tale existed in a realm beyond the strictures of utilitarianism, and beyond politics itself. For Yeats, it offered a connection to both an Irish folk mind and the mystical truths of which 'the folk' were only dimly aware. For Benjamin, while the 'full control of the middle class' was perpetuated by the press, 'one of the most important instruments in fully developed capitalism', the spirit of the fairy tale was still (just) surviving outside that realm: enduring in defiance of the newspaper, the novel and the rise of the 'solitary individual'.[3]

More recently, Jack Zipes has argued that 'What belonged to archaic societies, what belonged to pagan tribes and communities was passed down by word of mouth as a good only to be hardened in script, Christian and patriarchal [...] all the tools of modern industrial society (the printing press, the radio, the camera, the film, the record, the videocassette) have made their mark on the fairy tale to make it classical ultimately in the name of the bourgeoisie'. For Zipes, Benjamin's totalising view of the mass media co-exists with an equally powerful conviction that 'liberating' and 'utopian' fairy tales can somehow survive.[4] Yet to focus on fairy tales in the press, one of the most important 'tools of modern industrial society', is also to think critically about that socialisation process. For the very classification of Victorian fairy tales (as liberating or controlling, radical or conservative) does not depend wholly on authorial intention: it depends on who does the reading, and the contexts in which they read. As we have seen, Keir Hardie's fairy tales could function as both political propaganda and as texts that encouraged child workers to imaginatively rethink their own lives: their utopian or coercive possibilities were not the same for all readers. Laurence Housman's fairy tales were different texts in the hands of different subcultures. For the group of homosexual men who used the fairy tale as a way of signalling a shared, covert identity, it was not just writing but inventive ways of reading that allowed the exploration of new sexual possibilities.

In truth, the fairy tale's backward-looking gaze was rarely simply 'escapist': the search for origins was inseparable from the critical scrutiny of the present. If the fairy tale's supposed links with the 'childhood of the race' fostered a sense of imaginative time-travel, giving readers the illusion of access to a moment before history began, it was also appropriated to conceptualise very different futures, from the expansion of the Empire to the end of industrial capitalism. From Kingsley's child sweep and Thackeray Ritchie's articles on servants to the philanthropists of *Aunt Judy's Magazine* and the socialist Cinderella clubs, the fairy tale also became a familiar tool in the visualisation of class relations. If 'fancy' and 'romance' could be used to expose social problems in ways impossible within domestic realism – to gesture towards the fantastic foundations that underpinned middle-class reality – the motivating spirit was not always reforming. In some contexts, to conceive of life as Andersen's 'wonderful fairy tale' was also to see social hierarchies as natural and God-given. Fantasy could also deny the possibility of significant change and could be used to console for a failure of political imagination.

If this book has argued that periodical culture helped to reinvent the fairy tale, it is also mindful of the myths of authenticity that the press helped to perpetuate. For if magazines both celebrated and sought to displace the chapbook, they were also convinced that the fairy tale's origin was ancient, communal and oral: cheap print could also venerate a pure 'spirit of the folk', always just beyond the reach of literacy and print culture. Nevertheless, newspapers and magazines also reveal that the nineteenth-century fascination with the fairy tale was no simple attempt to find an imaginative counterpoint to rationalism, to protest against the 'dark experiments' of science. In her article on 'The Origin of Language', published in *Macmillan's* in 1862, Julia Wedgwood argued that the most significant aspect of Max Müller's lectures was not their content but their status: when Müller spoke before the Royal Institution, he demonstrated that a discipline which had previously been a branch of literature had proved itself fit to be crowned a science. Yet in the process philology had lost none of its poetic significance: in the same way that geology had destroyed 'a barrier in Time', Wedgwood told her readers that the study of language was 'destined to achieve an analogous triumph over the weakness of our imaginations'.[5] If the *Origin* ushered in 'Darwinian romance', it evolved alongside that developing strand of philological romance; registers that shaped non-fiction as well as fairy tale and fantasy.[6] Victorian permutations of the Romantic child (from Kingsley's spiritually responsive idealists to Hardie's nature-loving socialist activists and the mini-aesthetes of little magazines) were also the offspring of science. They owed much to biological theories of recapitulation, as well as to the philological researches which Müller placed at the heart of 'The Science of Man'.

Yet the emergence of anthropological thought also led to a very different history of myth and folktale: the possibility that the 'childhood of fiction' did not originate with Müller's spiritual primitives, but had sprung instead from a long 'savage and blood-stained past'. While this was a 'dreary' prospect for writers such as Wedgwood, the assumption of 'savage survivals' in memory could also be invigorating – linked to its own form of anthropological romance.[7] For Andrew Lang, indefatigable populariser for the anthropological school, the fairy tale could still inhabit that utopian space outside modernity; linked not only to a savage past, but also to the seductive fantasy of a bookless future. In *The Red Fairy Book* (1890), Lang claimed:

> Stories like these will live, or will revive, when, in the changes of human fortunes, science has been lost, when electricity, and steam, and chemistry are buried with their engines and crucibles beneath the ruins of the world [...] They are our oldest legacy, they will be our last bequest, flitting from mouth to mouth when the printing press is in ruins and the alphabet has to be re-invented.[8]

In his much loved fairy-tale series, Lang fantasised about the destruction of his own texts, as well as the end of science and civilisation: the rebirth of the 'true' fairy tale after the death of print.[9] Yet Lang's primitivist dream of the destruction of science was made possible by the comparative science that created the savage. His fantasy about the destruction of print joined his staggering body of printed matter: not just his series of fairy books, but a remarkable number of articles in newspapers and magazines. Perhaps we are not too far from where we began, with Yeats and the newspaper. In fact, Yeats owed a significant debt to Lang's constructions of myth and ritual: as Sinéad Garrigan Mattar has persuasively argued, the savage of comparative science shaped the Modernist strain within the Irish Revival. If we need to be more attentive to the place of the fairy tale in those debates and those transitions between Victorian and Modernist writing, we also need to acknowledge that its history was forged in the interplay between literature and science.[10] In 1853, the *Athenæum* pronounced that 'Coincident with the world of Fact, in nearly all ages and among all nations, and lying by the side of that world like a fantastic shadow, has been the world of fairy Fiction'.[11] Yet science and the fairy tale were more than merely 'coincident'; they could be mutually transformative. The fairy tale was never simply fact's fantastic shadow.

Susan Stewart has claimed that 'The emergence of commercial publishing, of a writing destined for strangers, effects a compensation in the form of an encapsulated sense of "community" implied in the reproduction of folkloric forms'.[12] The press's appropriation of the fairy tale might be seen as particularly apt for Stewart's argument: the print form most associated with industrial, urban modernity casting itself as guardian of the rural, folk past. Periodicals could indeed use fairy tales to evoke tradition in the age of speed, news and mass literacy, but there was not always an inevitable sense of loss. 'Imagined' communities forged by print did not always need to compensate for the physical communities they were often accused of displacing.[13] In his autobiography, the nineteenth-century Finnish writer Pietari Päivärinta reminisced about his youth, recalling a storytelling session which occurred in western Finland in the 1830s:

> 'I told you beggar boys are good at telling stories,' someone chipped in, as if to boast at his correct prediction. 'But it wasn't a tale,' said another, 'where did you hear that story?' he then asked me. 'I read it,' I replied. 'Read it? Where?' came many a wondering, questioning voice. 'My master, Esa Kivioja, had a long book where nothing was continued to the end; before the long bits ended, there were shorter ones in between, and whenever one broke off, it said "more later"', I replied. [...] "It's a newspaper," said another.[14]

Whether the newspaper is depicted as a wonderful discovery that reinvigorates storytelling or the agent that has helped to bring about its demise, such writings have much to tell us about the nineteenth-century's contested ways of seeing mass culture, mass literacy and progress.[15] For to accept that cheap print had reached the distant places where the 'timeless' spirit of the fairy tale was supposed to have survived was also to acknowledge that there was no place from which it could return. It was to expose Lang's future 'when the printing press is in ruins' as the ultimate fantasy of a literate modernity.

Abbreviations Used in Notes

Manuscript sources

Add. MSS	Macmillan Papers, British Library
H.A.S.	Papers of the Hunter Archaeological Society, Sheffield Archives

Periodicals

AYR	*All the Year Round*
AJM	*Aunt Judy's Magazine for Young People*
Artist	*The Artist and Journal of Home Culture* and successor, *The Artist: An Illustrated Monthly Record of Arts Crafts and Industries*
Blackwood's	*Blackwood's Edinburgh Magazine*
Boys of England	*Boys of England: A Journal of Sport, Sensation, Fun and Instruction*
Bentley's	*Bentley's Miscellany*
Chambers's	*Chambers's Edinburgh Journal* and successor, *Chambers's Journal of Popular Literature, Science and Arts*
CM	*Cornhill Magazine*
Dome	*The Dome: A Quarterly Containing Examples of All the Arts*
Fraser's	*Fraser's Magazine for Town and Country*
GT	*Good Things for the Young/Boys and Girls of all Ages*
GWY	*Good Words for the Young*
Howitt's	*Howitt's Journal of Literature and Popular Progress*
HW	*Household Words*
LL	*Labour Leader*
LP	*Labour Prophet: The Organ of the Labour Church*
MM	*Macmillan's Magazine*
MP	*Monthly Packet: Readings for Younger Members of the English Church*
NMM	*New Monthly Magazine*
Quarto	*Quarto: An Artistic, Literary and Musical Quarterly*
VPR	*Victorian Periodicals Review*
VS	*Victorian Studies*
YB	*The Yellow Book: An Illustrated Quarterly*

Notes

Introduction

1. 'How we get our Newspapers', *AYR*, 25 Dec. 1875, 305–09 (305). This article also refers to weekly magazines under the general title 'papers'. My own use of the term 'press' includes all those serials contemporaneously classed as the 'periodical press' – magazines that appeared weekly, monthly, and quarterly, erratic little magazine issues, and daily and weekly newspapers.
2. *HW*, 4 Feb. 1854, 540–46. The article to which the Magician refers is Sala's 'A Case of Real Distress', *HW*, 14 Jan. 1854, 457–60.
3. Anon., 'Ingleborough Within', *Chambers's*, 29 May 1858, 341–44 (342).
4. Cuthbert Bede, 'Story-hunting in the Western Highlands', *Belgravia*, 31 (Jan. 1877), 275–81 (275).
5. Anon., 'Fairyland and Fairies', *Chambers's*, 15 July 1882, 454–56 (455).
6. David Vincent's claim that the folklore collectors were 'united in their conviction that merely by writing about superstitions they stood on the other side of a divide from those who still accepted them' is not always supported by writings on folklore in the press. See Vincent, *Literacy and Popular Culture* (Cambridge: Cambridge University Press, 1989), 157.
7. As far as I am aware, there is no major study of this issue in British or international contexts. The few English magazines that have received attention have featured mainly in author-centred discussions of gender. U. C. Knoepflmacher engages with *Aunt Judy's Magazine* in *Ventures into Childland: Victorians, Fairy Tales, and Femininity* (Chicago, IL: University of Chicago Press, 1998), while Claudia Nelson includes some fairy tales from the *Strand Magazine* in 'Fantasies de Siècle: Sex and Sexuality in the Late-Victorian Fairy Tale', in *Transforming Genres: New Approaches to British Fiction in the 1890s*, ed. Nikki Lee Manos and Meri-Jane Rochelson (Basingstoke: Macmillan, 1994), 87–107. Research on the fairy tale in Dickens's periodicals (which has often sought to illuminate Dickens's writing rather than broader press contexts) is referenced in Chapter 1.
8. *HW*, 1 Oct. 1853, 97–100 (97).
9. 'Bouncing Boys', *AYR*, 5 Aug. 1865, 37–40 (38).
10. Quotations from *Fairy and Folk Tales of the Irish Peasantry*, Edited and Selected by W. B. Yeats (London: Scott, 1888), x and Yeats, 'The Symbolism of Poetry', in *Ideas of Good and Evil* (London: Macmillan, 1903), 237–56 (238–39). Yeats acknowledges these magazine sources for articles and tales by Patrick Kennedy and Letitia Maclintock in *Fairy and Folk Tales*, xviii.
11. Preface, *English Fairy Tales*, collected by Joseph Jacobs (London: Nutt, 1890), viii. One of Jacobs's tales is extremely close to the Grimms' 'The Juniper Tree'.
12. See Jennifer Schacker, *National Dreams: The Remaking of Fairy Tales in Nineteenth-Century England* (Philadelphia, PA: University of Pennsylvania Press, 2003). The term 'communications circuit' (used by Schacker) is Robert Darnton's: see *The Kiss of Lamourette: Studies in Cultural History* (London: Faber and Faber 1990). For an important attempt to link folk forms to reading and publishing history in an earlier context, see Roger Chartier, *The Cultural Uses of Print in Early Modern France*,

trans. Lydia G. Cochrane (Princeton, NJ: Princeton University Press, 1987), 240–336.
13. The term 'folks-story' is Andrew Lang's: see 'Mythology and Fairy Tales', *Fortnightly Review*, n.s. 13 (May 1873), 618–31.
14. Canepa and Ansani, Introduction, *Out of the Woods: The Origins of the Literary Fairy Tale in Italy and France*, ed. Nancy L. Canepa (Detroit, MI: Wayne State University Press, 1997), 9–33 (10). On much earlier innovation in the genre in response to changing contexts and audiences, see Ruth B. Bottigheimer, *Fairy Godfather: Straparola, Venice, and the Fairy Tale Tradition* (Philadelphia, PA: University of Pennsylvania Press, 2002).
15. On poetry and fairy painting, see Nicola Bown, *Fairies in Nineteenth-Century Art and Literature* (Cambridge: Cambridge University Press, 2001), and Carole G. Silver, *Strange and Secret Peoples: Fairies and Victorian Consciousness* (New York: Oxford University Press, 1999). See also *Victorian Fairy Painting*, ed. Jane Martineau (London: Merrell Holberton, 1997). Pantomime and fairy ballet are beyond the scope of this study, but Peter Stoneley has offered a valuable discussion of the latter in *A Queer History of the Ballet* (London: Routledge, 2006), 22–45. Diane Purkiss offers a brief engagement with fairy pantomime in *Troublesome Things: A History of Fairies and Fairy Stories* (London: Penguin, 2000), 225–38.
16. The repeal of the paper tax in 1861 was also influential. For a brief account of the technological changes in printing and paper-making, see David Reed, *The Popular Magazine in Britain and the United States 1880–1960* (London: British Library, 1997), 27–28.
17. Routledge and Nelson also set up juvenile departments in the 1860s: see Peter Hunt, *An Introduction to Children's Literature* (Oxford: Oxford University Press, 1994), 59–61.
18. Zipes, ed., *Victorian Fairy Tales: The Revolt of the Fairies and the Elves* (New York: Methuen, 1987; repr. New York: Routledge, 1991), xix.
19. Letter, 24 June 1847, in *Hans Christian Andersen's Visits to Charles Dickens as Described in his Letters*, comp. Ejnar Munksgaard (Copenhagen: Levin & Munksgaard, 1970), 13–14.
20. [Mary Howitt], 'Memoir of Hans Christian Andersen', *Howitt's Journal*, 26 June 1847, 352–55. See also 'A Danish Story-book', *Chambers's*, 10 Oct. 1846, 239 (which included 'The Daisy'); 'The Red Shoes' (trans. Mary Howitt), in *Howitt's Journal*, 11 Sept. 1847, 171–73; and 'The Little Ugly Duck', *London Journal*, 6 (Nov. 1847), 148.
21. Andersen regularly sent such papers to the Collin family in Denmark. See in particular the letters to Edvard Collin dated 27 June and 21 July 1847: in the latter Andersen hopes a glowing review in the English *Literary Gazette* will be extracted in Danish newspapers (Munksgaard, *Hans Christian*, 14 and 17). Andersen's reception in the British press is also discussed in Jackie Wullschlager's *Hans Christian Andersen: The Life of a Storyteller* (London: Penguin, 2001), 286–313.
22. The three translators were Mary Howitt (*Wonderful Stories for Children*), Charles Boner (*A Danish Story Book*) and Caroline Peachey (*Danish Fairy Legends and Tales*).
23. The text was published as 'The Mermaid' (trans. Lady Duff Gordon), *Bentley's*, 19 (Apr. 1846), 377–90.
24. *Fraser's*, 35 (Jan. 1847), 111–26 (125); *Athenæum*, 25 July 1846, 759.
25. On serial time, see the 'Critical Theory Special Issue' of *VPR*, 12 (1989), ed. Laurel Brake and Anne Humpherys; Linda K Hughes and Michael Lund, *The Victorian Serial* (Charlottesville: Virginia University Press), 1991; and Mark W. Turner, 'Time, Periodicals, and Literary Studies', *VPR*, 39 (2006), 309–16. On the periodical's

'open and closed' traits, see Margaret Beetham, 'Towards a Theory of the Periodical as a Publishing Genre', in *Investigating Victorian Journalism*, ed. Laurel Brake, Aled Jones and Lionel Madden (Basingstoke: Macmillan, 1990), 19–32. On reading communities and spaces more generally, see Stephen Colclough, *Consuming Texts: Readers and Reading Communities 1695–1870* (Basingstoke: Palgrave Macmillan, 2007). Accounts of magazine and newspaper reading are also recorded in the *Reading Experience Database* at http://www.open.ac.uk/Arts/reading/.
26. De Certeau, *The Practice of Everyday Life*, trans. Stephen Rendall (Berkeley, University of California Press, 1984), 165–76; Schenda, 'Telling Tales – Spreading Tales: Change in the Communicative Forms of a Popular Genre', in *Fairy Tales and Society: Illusion, Allusion and Paradigm*, ed. Ruth B. Bottigheimer (Philadelphia, PA: University of Pennsylvania Press, 1986), 75–94.
27. Rose, *The Intellectual Life of the British Working Classes* (New Haven, CT: Yale University Press, 2001), 371.
28. While the implied reader, extrapolated from the text, and historical readers are clearly very different, I stress the need for dialogue between these approaches. For an advocate of such a combined method, see Darnton, *Lamourette*, 154–87.
29. Zipes, ed., *Victorian Fairy Tales*; Auerbach and Knoepflmacher, eds, *Forbidden Journeys: Fairy Tales and Fantasies by Victorian Women Writers* (Chicago, IL: University of Chicago Press, 1992); Hearn, ed., *The Victorian Fairy Tale Book* (New York: Pantheon, 1988).
30. Bennett, 'Text, Readers, Reading Formations', *Literature and History*, 9 (1983), 214–27 (225). Other well known attempts to situate texts in wider networks of production and reception are D. F. McKenzie's *Bibliography and the Sociology of Texts* (London: British Library, 1986) and Jerome McGann's *The Beauty of Inflections* (Oxford: Clarendon Press, 1985).
31. The phrase 'progress and pause' is Hughes and Lund's: see *Victorian Serial*, 63. While Auerbach and Knoepflmacher acknowledge the importance of children's periodicals for a number of the writers that they discuss in *Forbidden Journeys*, Christina Rossetti's 'Nick' and Anne Thackeray Ritchie's 'Beauty and the Beast' and 'The Sleeping Beauty in the Wood' are dated and discussed as contributions to books, with no mention of their earlier appearances in magazines for adults. The same is true of Thackeray Ritchie's 'Cinderella' (published under the name Anne Isabella Ritchie) in Zipes's *Victorian Fairy Tales*. Zipes does, however, reference magazine sources for works by Dickens and J. H. Ewing.
32. The authors in question include Jean Ingelow, Anne Thackeray Ritchie, Christina Rossetti and Mrs Molesworth. See Zipes, *Victorian Fairy Tales*, xxiii and Auerbach and Knoepflmacher, *Forbidden Journeys*, 1–10.
33. *Athenæum*, 22 Aug. 1846, 862–63.
34. Dorson, *American Folklore* (Chicago, IL: University of Chicago Press, 1959), 278.
35. The phrase 'the Fairies' Farewell' was used by Richard Corbett in the subtitle of a ballad in 1591. On print in general as a supposed destroyer of folklore prior to the nineteenth century, see Schacker, *National Dreams*, 5–8.
36. On these tropes in nineteenth-century literature and art, See Bown, *Fairies*, 163–97, and Silver, *Strange*, 185–212.
37. Garrigan Mattar, *Primitivism, Science, and the Irish Revival* (Oxford: Oxford University Press, 2004); Silver, *Strange*, 117–47. See also Julia Reid, *Robert Louis Stevenson, Science and the Fin de Siècle* (Basingstoke: Palgrave Macmillan, 2006), which analyses of the role of folklore and comparative science in shaping Stevenson's literary practice.

38. Zipes, *Victorian Fairy Tales*, xxiv. On Carroll's interest in maximising profit for *Alice's Adventures in Wonderland*, see his letters to Alexander Macmillan in *The Selected Letters of Lewis Carroll*, ed. Morton N. Cohen (London: Macmillan, 1979), 31–32. Oscar Wilde was the editor of *Woman's World* from 1887–1889; MacDonald and Ewing's editorships of juvenile magazines are discussed in Chapter 2.
39. Quote from Zipes, *Fairy Tales and the Art of Subversion* (New York: Routledge, 1983), 102.
40. Quotes from Clodd, *Fairy Tales from Hans Andersen* (London: Wells Gardner, Darton, 1901), vii; and Anon., *Church Quarterly Review*, 3 (Jan. 1877), 380–93 (384).

1 An Alternative History of the Fairy Tale

1. Mew, 'The Arabian Nights', *CM*, 32 (Dec. 1875), 711–32 (717).
2. Letter to Gaskell (1851), cited in Winfred Gérin, *Elizabeth Gaskell: A Biography* (Oxford: Clarendon, 1976), 123.
3. For details of these serialisations, see Robert D. Mayo's invaluable *The English Novel in the Magazines, 1740–1815* (Evanston: Northwestern University Press, 1962), 59. On the *Nights* nineteenth-century reinventions and serialisations, see Muhsin Jassim Ali, *Scheherazade in England: A Study of Nineteenth-Century English Criticism of the Arabian Nights* (Washington, DC: Three Continents Press, 1981), 11–14; and Robert Irwin, *The Arabian Nights: A Companion* (London: Allen Lane, 1994), 237–92.
4. Lang, ed., *The Blue Fairy Book* (London: Longmans Green, 1889), xix.
5. *Universal Spectator*, 786–88 (29 Oct. to 12 Nov. 1743); Mayo, 616.
6. Quotation from *Examiner*, 4 July 1846, 419. Mayo's catalogue of 'Magazine Novels and Novelettes' (431–620) excludes texts under 5000 words, so may overlook a considerable number of fairy tales, but offers a useful indication of the range of fantastic genres that were popular. 'Novels of circulation' have been discussed under a variety of names, including 'it-narratives', 'object tales' and 'spy novels': see *The Secret Life of Things*, ed. Mark Blackwell (Lewisburg: Bucknell University Press, 2007), 10.
7. On some of the earliest English translations, see Ali, *Scheherazade*; Irwin, *Arabian Nights*; and Iona and Peter Opie, *The Classic Fairy Tales* (London: Paladin, 1984). Fairy tales in other languages, from Basile and Straparola to the writers of the French court, were also familiar to some middle-class readers. Single-authored and published in two volumes, the *Young Misses Magazine* is closer in form to a book than a periodical as subsequently conceived.
8. See Bottigheimer, 'The Ultimate Fairy Tale: Oral Transmission in a Literature World', in *A Companion to the Fairy Tale*, ed. Hilda Ellis Davidson and Anna Chaudhri (Cambridge: Boydell and Brewer, 2003), 57–70.
9. Hunter, *Before Novels: The Cultural Contexts of Eighteenth Century English Fiction* (New York: Norton, 1990), 142.
10. Harries, *Twice Upon a Time: Women Writers and the History of the Fairy Tale* (Princeton: Princeton University Press, 2001), 73–98; Burke, *Popular Culture in Early Modern Europe*, rev. edn (Aldershot: Ashgate, 1999), 8, 21. On the Grimms' editorial revisions, the influence of print and the questionable nature of some of their 'folk' sources, see John M. Ellis, *One Fairy Story Too Many: The Brothers*

Grimm and Their Tales (Chicago, IL: University of Chicago Press, 1985); Jack Zipes, *When Dreams Came True: Classical Fairy Tales and Their Tradition* (Routledge: New York, 1999), 61–79; Maria Tatar, *The Hard Facts of the Grimms' Fairy Tales* (Princeton, NJ: Princeton University Press, 1987).

11. On challenges to that Romantic legacy, see *The Invention of Tradition*, ed. Eric Hobsbawm and Terence Ranger (Cambridge: Cambridge University Press, 1983); Regina Bendix, 'The Uses of Disciplinary History', *Radical History Review*, 84 (2002), 110–14; Dave Harker, *Fakesong: The Manufacture of British 'Folk Song', 1700 to the Present* (Milton Keynes: Open University Press, 1985).
12. See *Hibernian* (Dec. 1873, 646–48, June 1874, 312–14), and Mayo, 455.
13. On *The Lilliputian Magazine; or Children's Repository*, which possibly appeared in 1773–74, see M. O. Grenby, 'Tame Fairies Make Good Teachers: The Popularity of Early British Fairy Tales', *The Lion and the Unicorn*, 30 (2006), 1–24 (10).
14. Richardson, *Literature, Education and Romanticism: Reading as Social Practice, 1780–1832* (Cambridge: Cambridge University Press, 1994), 118. This is Mitzi Myers's term. For further evidence of the use made of the fairy tale by didactic writers in the early nineteenth century, see Grenby, 'Tame Fairies'.
15. This has been noted by both Richardson, *Literature* (49) and by Grenby in his introduction to the reissue of the *Guardian of Education*, 5 vols (Bristol: Thoemmes, 2002), i–xxxiv.
16. Quotations from *Guardian of Education*, 1 (1 June 1802), 61–66 [italics in original].
17. *Guardian of Education*, 1 (Nov. 1802), 425.
18. Quotations from *Guardian of Education*, 1 (June 1802), 15 [italics in original].
19. Richardson, *Literature*, 45. Richardson cites the stamp duty statistics, which show a leap in circulation from just under seven-and-a-half million to over fifteen million in these years.
20. Stewart, *Crimes of Writing: Problems of Representation and Containment* (Oxford: Oxford University Press, 1991), 75, 105.
21. *Quarterly Review*, 21 (Jan. 1819), 91–112 (91).
22. See Mayo, *English Novel*, 368 and 456.
23. In fact, in the 1820s–1830s, fairy and folkloric material (including tales from Thomas Crofton Croker's *Fairy Legends and Traditions*) was also republished in cheap Gothic anthologies: see the appendix to Franz J. Potter, *The History of Gothic Publishing 1800–1835* (Basingstoke: Palgrave Macmillan, 2005), 179–89.
24. *Quarterly Review*, 21 (Jan. 1819), 92.
25. Richardson, *Literature*, 222.
26. The two-penny version of Cobbett's *Political Register* had a particularly high circulation in 1816 – Richard D. Altick estimates between 40,000 and 70,000 – and led both to the emergence of a significant unstamped press, and its repression through the 'six acts' in the year in which Cohen was writing. The circulation of stamped papers was around thirty million by 1830. See *The English Common Reader: A Social History of the Mass Reading Public*, 2nd edn (Columbus, OH: Ohio State University Press, 1998), 324–30.
27. *Quarterly Review*, 21 (Jan. 1819), 11, 92 and 100. For a discussion of Taylor's Grimm in the context of Teutonism and Englishness, see Schacker, *National Dreams*, 20–21.
28. Taylor, *German Popular Stories, Translated from the Kinder und Haus Märchen, Collected by M. M. Grimm, From Oral Tradition*, 2 vols (London: C. Baldwyn, 1823–26), I, v.
29. Quotations from 'German Popular and Traditionary Literature No. 1V', *NMM*, 4 (Apr. 1822), 289–96, 292.

30. [G. B. Depping], 'The Smith Velant', *NMM*, 4 (June 1822), 527–33 (533).
31. 'German Popular and Traditionary Literature No. 1', *NMM*, 2 (Aug. 1821), 146–52.
32. *The Five-Book Prelude*, ed. Duncan Wu (Oxford: Blackwell, 1997), Book Four, ll. 422, 403, 413, 447–52.
33. *NMM*, 2 (Aug. 1821) 146–47.
34. Selling for 3s. 6d. in the 1820s, the *New Monthly Magazine* was at the most expensive end of the monthly periodical market.
35. In *Fraser's*, see 'Dorf Juystein', 5 (May 1832), 489–92; 'The Mountain-Dew Men by the Ettrick Shepherd', 6 (Sept. 1832), 161–70; 'Dissent in the Church in Wales: Conditions of the Welsh Peasantry', 6 (Sept. 1832), 170–83; 'The Tale', 6 (Oct. 1832), 257–78. While Hogg was prized for his proximity to the folk, *Fraser's* also used a review of Hogg's *Altive Tales* (May 1832, 482–89) to mock, as *Blackwood's* had done before them, Hogg's attendance at a debating society attended by 'young grocers', ridiculing his intellectual presumption. Hogg's *Confessions of a Justified Sinner* (1824) – in which the writer enters his own novel as both dialect-speaking sheep farmer and through one of his own polished *Blackwood's* contributions on folklore – reveals a self-reflexivity about his uncomfortable status within higher periodical culture.
36. [James Roscoe], 'My After-Dinner Adventures with Peter Schlemihl', *Blackwood's*, 45 (Apr. 1839), 467–80; 'Pietro D'Abano; A Tale of Enchantment, from the German of Tieck' [trans. James Ferrier], *Blackwood's*, 46 (Aug. 1839), 228–55.
37. Trans. Burke, *Popular*, 5. As Burke notes, while the term *Volksmärchen* was used in the late eighteenth century, *Volksbuch* became popular in the early nineteenth after the publication of an essay by Joseph Görres, and 'its nearest English equivalent is the traditional term 'chap-book' (3).
38. Sarah Austin, cited in the review of her *Fragments from German Prose Writers*, *Athenæum*, 29 May 1841, 424.
39. *Athenæum*, 22 Aug. 1846, 862–63; also reprinted in *The Study of Folklore*, ed. Alan Dundes (Eagelwood Cliffs, NJ: Prentice Hall, 1965), 4–6.
40. See, for example, *Gammer Gurton's Famous Histories of Sir Guy of Warwick, Sir Bevis of Hampton, Tom Hickathrift, Friar Bacon, Robin Hood, and the King and the Cobbler*. Newly Revised and Amended by Amb Mei (London: Joseph Cundall, 1846). The full series of books were produced between 1841 and 1849.
41. *Little Red Riding Hood. An Entirely New Edition. With New Pictures by an Eminent Artist*. Edited by Felix Summerly (London: Joseph Cundall, 1843), 5–6 (6). On the *Felix Summerly* series, see Dennis Butts, 'The Beginnings of Victorianism 1820–1850', in *Children's Literature: An Illustrated History*, ed. Peter Hunt (Oxford: Oxford University Press, 1995), 77–101. The two series were bound together when Sampson Low issued the *Home Treasury of Old Story Books* in 1859.
42. Clodd, *Fairy Tales from Hans Andersen*, xii.
43. *Fairy and Folk Tales*, xvi. These texts were not always penny chapbooks: *Royal Hibernian Tales* circulated as a sixpenny novelette in the 1820s.
44. Yeats, *Fairy and Folk Tales*, 326; Yeats, *Letters*, cited in Garrigan Mattar, *Primitivism*, 45. In *Irish Fairy Tales* (London: Unwin, 1892), Yeats would add his own contributions to *The Scots Observer* and the *National Observer* to this list (236).
45. Earls, 'Supernatural Legends in Nineteenth-Century Irish Writing', *Béaloideas*, 60–61 (1992–1993), 93–144.
46. 'Superstitions of the Irish Peasantry – No V – The Luprechaun', *Dublin and London Magazine* (July 1825), 193–97 (193).

47. 'The Hermit in Ireland No V: Doings at Carlow', *Dublin and London Magazine* (July 1825), 205–8 (207). This article uses the spelling 'Leprachaun' throughout, and discusses the variant spellings in a footnote (206). The magazine ran from 1825 to 1828 under the editorship of M. J. Whitty.
48. Quotations from 'Sketches from the Country no II: Bringing a Wife to Reason', *Irish Penny Magazine*, 14 Dec. 1833, 397–400.
49. Earls, 'Supernatural', 98.
50. 'Chambers's Edinburgh Journal', *Chambers's*, 2 Feb. 1833, 1–2; Louis James, *Fiction for the Working Man, 1830–50* (London: Penguin, 1974), 12.
51. Quotations from Webb, *The British Working-Class Reader 1790–1848: Literacy and Social Tension* (London: Unwin, 1955), 30.
52. On circulations, see 'Chambers's Edinburgh Journal', *Chambers's*, 27 Jan. 1838, 8, and 2 Feb. 1833, 1–2.
53. 'Chambers's Edinburgh Journal', *Chambers's*, 12 Oct. 1833, 296; 'Chap-Book Literature', 7 July 1855, 1–2; 'Chap-Books', 1 Feb. 1862, 72–74; 'Some Humorous Chapbooks', 15 Oct. 1881, 657–60.
54. 'Newspapers', *Chambers's*, 9 Nov. 1844, 296.
55. Earls, 'Supernatural', 97; *Dublin and London Magazine* (July 1825), 205–8.
56. On links between folklore, the Gothic and debates over nationalism, see Siobhán Kilfeather, 'Ireland and Europe in 1825: situating the Banims', in *Ireland and Europe in the Nineteenth Century*, ed. Leon Litvack and Colin Graham (Dublin: Four Courts, 2006), 29–50.
57. Yeats, 'Irish Fairies', *Leisure Hour*, Oct. 1890, in Yeats, *Uncollected Prose*, ed. John Frayne and Colton Johnson, 2 vols (Basingstoke: Macmillan, 1970–75), I, 175–82. A very similar passage appears in Yeats's *Irish Fairy Tales* where 'the daily papers' is replaced by 'the hum of the printing presses' (1).
58. Yeats, *The Celtic Twilight* (London: Bullen, 1902), 69–70. I am grateful to David Dwan for this reference. Although, as Warwick Gould and Deidre Toomey note, the *Irish Times* is significant here for its Unionist and conservative politics, the newspaper also carries a symbolic weight beyond its political affiliation. See Yeats, *Mythologies*, ed. Gould and Toomey (Basingstoke: Palgrave Macmillan, 2005), 27 and 238.
59. See Paddy Lyons, 'Mass Literacy in Nineteenth-Century Ireland, Britain and Europe', in *Ireland and Europe*, ed. Litvack and Graham, 89–100. Other print sources (including children's school books) also shaped oral tale-telling in Irish as well as English. On children reading Douglas Hyde's *Leabhar Sgeulauigheachta* to men in the fields in County Kerry, see Earls, 'Supernatural'.
60. 'Author's Preface' to 2nd volume, repr. in Croker, *Fairy Legends and Traditions of the South of Ireland*, a new and complete edition ed. T. Wright (London: Tegg, 1870), xxx.
61. See Angela Bourke, *The Burning of Bridget Cleary: A True Story* (London: Pimlico, 1999), 114–53.
62. Quotations from Yeats, *Fairy and Folk Tales*, xv; Garrigan Mattar, *Primitivism*, 48–49.
63. On Croker's self-referentiality about print and oral relationships, see *Fairy Legends*, 91 and Schacker, *National Dreams*, 55.
64. Ashton, *Chapbooks in the Eighteenth Century* (London: Chatto and Windus, 1882), v–xii.
65. Satu Apo, *The Narrative World of Finnish Fairy Tales* (Helsinki: Swedish Academy of Science and Letters, 1995), 41.

66. See Niklaus R. Schweizer, 'Kahaunani: "Snowwhite" in Hawaiian: A Study in Acculturation' in *East Meets West – Homage to Edgar C. Knowlton, Jnr*, ed. Roger L. Hadlich and J. D. Ellsworth (Hawaii: University of Hawaii, 1988), 283–89; and Christina Bacchilega and Noelani Arista, The *Arabian Nights* in a Nineteenth-Century Hawaiian Newspaper: Reflections on the Politics of Translation', *Fabula*, 45 (2004), 189–206.
67. *Folk-Lore Journal*, 1 (1878), 235–45 (244).
68. 'The Philosophy of Rumpelstiltskin', *Folk-Lore Journal*, 7 (1889), 135–63.
69. 'Nurse's Stories', *AYR*, 8 Sept. 1860, 517–19.
70. Forster, *The Life of Charles Dickens*, ed. J. W. T. Ley (London: Palmer, 1928), 43–44.
71. 'The String of Pearls' was serialised in *People's Periodical*, Nov. 1846 to Mar. 1847; 'The Twelfth-Cake Goblin' appeared 26 Dec. 1846, 185–8. In 1840, a gruesome tale of cannibalism, bearing a close relationships to the Grimms' 'The Juniper Tree' also found its way on to the front pages of Lloyd's *Penny Sunday Times*: see Rosalind Crone, 'Violent Crime Reporting', in 'Violence and Entertainment in Nineteenth-century London' (unpublished doctoral thesis: University of Cambridge, 2006). On the phenomenal circulation of Lloyd's publications, see Ian Haywood, *The Revolution in Popular Literature: Print, Politics and the People, 1790–1860* (Cambridge: Cambridge University Press, 2004), and Raymond Williams, *The Long Revolution*. (London: Penguin, 1965), 213.
72. See *Grimm's Goblins: Fairy Books for Boys and Girls* (London: Vickers, 1861).
73. *HW*, 21 Aug. 1858, 217–22.
74. *HW*, 30 Mar. 1850, 1.
75. *HW*, 29 Apr. 1854, 237–42 (239). The serialisation ran from April to August.
76. *HW*, 17 June 1854, 405–9 (409).
77. Quotations from Morley, 'Little Red Working-Coat', *HW*, 27 Dec. 1851, 324–25.
78. Morley's 'Ground in the Mill', a shocking indictment of factory deaths, was commissioned to appear on 22 Apr. 1854, 224–27, when *Hard Times* was in serialisation. The magazine also offered rousing calls to working-class self-help in the context of poor housing in 'To Working Men', 7 Oct. 1854, 169–70. Slackbridge in *Hard Times*, however, is a damning caricature of the union man (June 10, 380–86); here, Dickens chooses to exaggerate the influence of the 'cunning' orator (a comparator to the 'professional speaker' Gruffshaw in Dickens's non-fictional article 'On Strike', 11 Feb. 1854, 553–59) above the agency of the operatives themselves.
79. *HW*, 1 Oct. 1853, 97–100 (97).
80. *HW*, 21 Apr. 1855, 255–57 and 28 Apr. 1855, 289–92.
81. Kotzin, *Dickens and the Fairy Tale* (Bowling Green, OH: Bowling Green University Popular Press, 37). See also Harry Stone, *Dickens and the Invisible World: Fairy Tales, Fantasy and Novel-Making* (Bloomington, IN: Indiana University Press, 1979).
82. Dickens, *HW*, 1 Oct. 1853, 97–100; Dickens, *Nonesuch Letters*, II, cited in Kotzin, 38.
83. Roscoe, 'Children's Fairy Tales, and George Cruikshank', *Inquirer*, 1854, repr. in *A Peculiar Gift – Nineteenth-Century Writing on Books for Children*, ed. Lance Salway (Harmondsworth: Penguin, 1976), 119–26 (123); Hutton, 'Miss Muloch's [sic] Fairy Book', *Spectator*, 9 May 1863, 1985–86.
84. 'Children's Literature of the Last Century II: Didactic Fiction', *MM*, 20 (Aug. 1869), 302–10 (306).

85. Ruskin, Introduction, *German Popular Stories, with Illustrations after the Original Designs by George Cruikshank* (London: John Camden Hotten, 1868), x.
86. Ruskin, *German Popular Stories*, xiv.
87. *Fraser's*, 33 (Apr. 1846), 495–502 (497).
88. 'Memoir for Laura', cited by Winifred Gérin in *Anne Thackeray Ritchie: A Biography* (Oxford: Oxford University Press, 1983), 21.
89. As James Milroy has noted, Müller's lecture series at the Royal Institution in 1861 and 1863 were attended by 'the social elité of London'. See *The Language of Gerard Manley Hopkins* (London: André Deutsch, 1977), 50. See also The Wellesley Index to Victorian Periodicals 1824–1900 at http://wellesley.chadwyck.co.uk.
90. *The Red Fairy Book*, ed. Andrew Lang (London: Longman's Green, 1890), xi.
91. Quotes from Lang, 'Mythology and Fairy Tales', *Fortnightly Review*, n.s. 13 (May 1873), 618–31. See also Lang, introduction, *Grimms' Household Tales*, trans. Margaret Hunt, 2 vols (London: Bell and Sons, 1884), I, x–lxxi. For the Jacobs and Dorson citations, see *Peasant Customs and Savage Myths: Selections from the British Folklorists*, ed. Richard M. Dorson, 2 vols (Chicago, IL: University of Chicago Press; London: Routledge & Kegan Paul, 1968), 192–93.
92. Gilbert, *Sources for Victorian Fairy Tales: A Series of Researches* (Bristol: Thoemmes, 2002). As Harries notes, there are a few scattered references before the OED citation in a book title in 1750, including in Sarah Fielding's *The Governess* (London: the Author, 1749) of the previous year (*Twice*, 6).
93. Lang, *Illustrated London News*, 3 Dec. 1892, 714; Yeats, *Fairy Tales and Folk Tales*, xvi.
94. Harries has argued that the exclusion from the current fairy-tale canon of many of the complex, self-reflexive literary tales by the female aristocratic French taletellers of the 1690s (L'Héritier, Marie-Catherine d'Aulnoy and Comtesse de Marat) is in part due to the preference among writers such as the Grimms for authored tales that seemed closer to the supposed simplicity of the folk (*Twice*, 152). Through writers such as Yeats and Lang, that prejudice can be seen to shape canon formation in English and Irish contexts.
95. *The Science of Fairy Tales: An Inquiry into Fairy Mythology* (London: Walter Scott, 1891), 4; 'Children's Literature of the Last Century III: Class Literature of the Last Thirty Years', *MM*, 20 (Sept. 1869), 448–56 (452).
96. MacDonald, 'The Fantastic Imagination' in *A Dish of Orts: Chiefly Papers on the Imagination, and on Shakespeare* (London: Sampson Low, 1893), 313–22 (313).
97. *MM*, 20 (Aug. 1869), 306.
98. *HW*, 1 Oct. 1853, 97.
99. *MM*, 20 (Aug. 1869), 306–7.
100. On circulation, see Sally Wood, *W. T. Stead and his Books for the Bairns* (Edinburgh: Salvia, 1987), 13. Quotations from Stead, preface, *Cinderella, and Other Fairy-Tales. Books for the Bairns 7* (London:"Review of Reviews" Office [Sept. 1896]), 3 and Stead, preface, *The Water-Babies. A Fairy Tale for a Land-Baby. Books for the Bairns 111* (London: Office of *Books for the Bairns* [May 1905]), 2.
101. While levels of literacy are notoriously difficult to calculate, the registrar general's figures present a steady increase in male literacy from 67 to 97 per cent between 1841 and 1900; female literacy by 1900 had reached similar levels, from an 1840 figure of around 50 per cent. As Altick notes, the significant leaps occurred from the 1850s onwards, not just after Forster's education bill (*Common Reader*, 171).

102. *MM*, 20 (Aug. 1869), 306; *HW*, 1 Oct. 1853, 97.
103. See *The Frog Prince and Other Stories from Grimm's* [sic] *Fairy Tales. Books for the Bairns 13* (London: Review of Review's Office [Mar. 1897]). In his preface, Stead claims that 'when all Europe was full of the trampling of war-horses and the roaring of canon', the brothers 'thought it was much better work to gather up these fairy stories than to go a-soldiering' (2).
104. Quotation from *George Cruikshank's Fairy Library* (London: Routledge & Sons, 1854), 34.

2 Myths of Origin: Magazines for Children

1. Anon., 'The Progress of the British Boy – Past and Present', *Boys of England*, 24 Nov. 1866, 4–5 (4).
2. Dinah Mulock Craik, 'The Last News of the Fairies', *GWY*, 2 (Mar. 1870), 256–60 (256).
3. 'The Progress of the British Boy', *Boys of England*, 24 Nov. 1866, 4–5.
4. Emerson described language as 'Fossil Poetry' in his 1844 essay 'The Poet': see *Essays, First and Second Series* (New York: Vintage Library of America, 1990), 227. It was equally well known from its appropriation by the philologist Richard Chenevix Trench in his 1851 lectures: see *The Stuff of Words. Five Lectures*, 8th edn (London: Parker, 1858), 68–69.
5. Egoff, *Children's Periodicals in the Nineteenth Century. A Survey and Bibliography* (London: Library Association, 1951), 28–43. *The Cambridge Bibliography of English Literature*, ed. Joanne Shattock (Cambridge: Cambridge University Press: 1999), IV, 3rd edn, cols 1903–1920, provides another useful list of children's magazine titles. See also Diana Dixon, 'Magazines for Children', in *Victorian Periodicals: A Guide to Research*, ed. J. Don Vann and Rosemary VanArsdel, 2 vols (New York: Modern Language Association, 1978–1989), II (1989), 91–98.
6. For a discussion of these long-lived religious titles, see Kirsten Drotner, *English Children and Their Magazines 1751–1945* (New Haven, CT: Yale University Press, 1988), 49–60. Some commercial monthlies pre-dated the sixties boom; Samuel Beeton's *Boys Own Magazine*, launched in 1855, targeted a broad middle-class readership, achieving an impressive circulation of 40,000 by 1863. See *Penny Dreadfuls and Comics: English Periodicals for Children from Victorian Times to the Present Day* (London: Victoria & Albert Museum, 1983), 45.
7. Turner, *Trollope and the Magazines: Gendered Issues in Mid-Victorian Britain* (Basingstoke: Macmillan 2000), 48 and 67–70. Turner notes that the periodical began as the *Christian Guest*, a halfpenny weekly, in February 1859.
8. 'Editor's Address', *GWY*, 1 (Oct. 1869), 590. MacDonald left the editorship of *Good Words for the Young* at the end of 1872 (when the periodical became *Good Things for the Young of all Ages*).
9. See Margaret Gatty, 'Introduction', *AJM*, 1 (May 1866), 1–2 (1).
10. The *Parables from Nature*, written under the name of Mrs. Alfred Gatty and published by Bell & Sons, appeared in five series from 1855 to 1871, and ran through a number of editions. The editors of *Good Words for the Young* were both ordained: 'Norman Macleod, DD' was identified in the periodical as 'One of her Majesty's Chaplains for Scotland', while MacDonald was a former Congregationalist minister.
11. *AJM*, 8 (Jan. 1870), 189, emphasis in original.

12. 'Hints on Reading', *MP*, n.s. 23 (Jan. 1877), 95.
13. See, for example, *AJM*, 14 (Aug. 1876), 638. While readers generally used pseudonyms, the full names supplied by older correspondents setting up reading societies and drawing clubs were almost universally female.
14. *MP*, 1 (Jan. 1851), i–iv and *MP*, n.s. 1 (Jan. 1866), inside cover. Although the first editor's address also makes cursory mention of the magazine's suitability for boys and the servants' hall, these audiences rarely feature as implied readers.
15. On the complexities of the family and Sunday reading markets in this period, see Turner, *Trollope*, 48–68.
16. 'Magazine Literature', *Church Quarterly Review*, 3 (Jan. 1877), 380–93 (388), and Drotner, *English*, 118. See also *MP*, n.s. 1 (Apr. 1866), 379–83; and *MP*, n.s. 1 (May 1866), 478–79. A number of printed letters, such as *MP*, 1 (Jan. 1866), 91–93, seem to be editorial plants.
17. Sometimes a review of an *AJM* text in Yonge's periodical was itself discussed in the pages of the first magazine. See *AJM*, 4 (Nov. 1867), 63.
18. 'Introduction', *AJM*, 1 (May 1866), 1–2 (2).
19. 'Editor's Address', *GWY*, 1 (Oct. 1869), 590.
20. *AJM*, 4 (Nov. 1867), 1–3 (1). Contributors were paid 10s. a page for original work, and 5s. for translation – considerably better rates than those paid by the *Monthly Packet*. However, Margaret Gatty's editorial terms – £10 a month for the first year's sales up to 15,000 – were much poorer than MacDonald's. See Christobel Maxwell, *Mrs Gatty and Mrs Ewing* (London: Constable, 1949), 148.
21. [Charles Stevens], 'The Editor's Address', *Boys of England*, 24 Nov. 1866, 16. The issue of whether these publications offered some liberation to their lower-class readers through their rebellious boy heroes remains contentious. Louis James finds 'strong middle-class aspirations' in *Boys of England*; see 'Tom Brown's Imperialist Sons', *VS*, 17 (1973), 89–99 (90). Jonathan Rose provides an interesting discussion of working class readers' experiences of the penny dreadful in *Intellectual Life*, 367–71, although his assumption that 'only canonical literature could produce epiphanies in common readers' could certainly be challenged (371).
22. See Reed, *Popular*, 84 and James, 'Tom Brown', 92. The latter notes that by the early 1870s *Boys of England* was selling an estimated 250,000 copies per week.
23. See, for example, in the annual vol. of *Chatterbox* for 1883, 'Jane's Apology', 343, and 'The Independent Boy (Founded on Fact)', 62–63.
24. *Boys of England*, 13 July 1867, 128.
25. *MP*, 23 (Jan. 1877 to June 1877), 95.
26. *MP*, n.s. 3 (Mar. 1867), 282–87 (287). Signed 'W.'
27. 'Bad Literature for the Young', *Contemporary Review*, 26 (Nov. 1875), 981–91 (983 and 986). Strahan provides his own readers with a considerable number of salacious extracts from these 'vile' publications.
28. Letter, 4 May 1881, MS, Bell's Publishing Company, cited by Marjory Lang in 'Childhood's Champions: Mid-Victorian Children's Periodicals and the Critics', *VPR*, 13 (1980), 17–31 (24). *Aunt Judy's Magazine* was published by Bell & Daldy from May 1866 to Oct. 1881. Its continuing lack of financial viability is demonstrated by the fact that it went through three further publishers (Allen, Bemrose and Hatchards) before its termination in 1885.
29. *AJM*, 4 (Nov. 1867), 1–3 (1). One of the magazine's most ardent admirers was John Ruskin, who in 1881 pledged £100 to prevent the price from rising to a shilling: see Maxwell, *Gatty*, 232. These acknowledged difficulties make U. C. Knoepflmacher's claim that by 1869 *Aunt Judy's Magazine* no longer required 'translations of Hans Christian Andersen or a story by Lewis Carroll ("Bruno's

Revenge") to attract a wider audience of middle-class juveniles' questionable: see *Ventures*, 388.
30. Cited in William Raeper, *George MacDonald* (Tring: Lion Publishing, 1987), 269.
31. *GWY*, 3 (Apr. 1871), 329–33.
32. *GWY*, 2 (Mar. 1870), 256–60 (256); Charles C. Smith, 'Fairies at Ilkley Well', *Folk-Lore Record*, 1 (1878), 229–231.
33. 'Bruno's Revenge', *AJM*, 4 (Dec. 1867), 65–78; 'Cat "Folk-Lore" and a "Post-Amble"', *AJM*, 4 (Mar. 1868), 278–82 (282).
34. *Chambers's*, 25 June 1887, 401.
35. There are, of course, many different 'Romantic' constructions of the child, taking different inflections in the work of Wordsworth, Coleridge and others. It is impossible to do their complexities justice here, but they have been usefully discussed in Judith Plotz, *Romanticism and the Vocation of Childhood* (Basingstoke: Palgrave Macmillan, 2001), in *Romanticism and Children's Literature*, ed. James Holt McGavran Jr. (Athens: University of Georgia Press, 1991) and by Richardson in *Literature*.
36. 'The Children's Books of a Hundred Years Ago' (Lecture given to the Royal Institution, 1895), repr. in Salway, *A Peculiar Gift*, 74. Emphasis in original.
37. 'The Balancing of Child and Adult: An Approach to Victorian Fantasies for Children', *Nineteenth Century Fiction*, 37 (1983), 497–530 (500).
38. *GWY*, 2 (Mar. 1870), 281–87 (287). The text was serialised from Nov. 1869 to Oct. 1870.
39. *GWY*, 1 (Jan. 1869), back cover. In 'The Fantastic Imagination' in *A Dish of Orts*, MacDonald gave his own endorsement of the adult's Romantic retreat into the fairy tale, stating 'he who will be a man, and will not be a child, must – he cannot help himself – become a little man, that is, a dwarf' (322).
40. Gould, *Ontogeny and Phylogeny* (London: Harvard University Press, 1977), 485. Gould has claimed 'as an import from evolutionary theory into other fields [the recapitulation thesis] was exceeded only by natural selection during the nineteenth century'; see *The Mismeasure of Man*, rev. edn (Harmondsworth: Penguin, 1997), 115. On child psychology and recapitulation, see Ernst Haeckel, *The Evolution of Man: A Popular Scientific Study*, trans. Joseph McCabe, 5th edn (London: Watts, 1906), 7–8, 355.
41. 'A Lump of Coal', *GWY*, 1 (Dec. 1868), 102–05 (102).
42. Müller, *MM*, 7 (Mar. 1863) 337–349 (337), and Farrar, *MM*, 7 (Mar. 1863), 252–57 (254). On philological and geological parallels, see Megan Perigoe Stitt, *Metaphors of Change in the Language of Nineteenth-Century Fiction* (Oxford: Clarendon, 1998), 41–83.
43. Quotations from Macmillan, *GWY*, 1 (Dec. 1868), 105; and Kingsley, 'Madam How and Lady Why, No. VI – "The True Fairy Tale"', *GWY*, 1 (Apr. 1869), 257–62 (261–62).
44. Kingsley appears to echo Coleridge's claims that fairy tales can play an essential role in habituating the childish mind 'to the Vast'; see Coleridge, *Collected Letters*, ed. Earl Leslie Griggs, 6 vols (Oxford: Clarendon Press, 1956–71), I, 354. On Victorian engagements with this permutation of the Romantic child, see James R. Kincaid, *Child-Loving: The Erotic Child and Victorian Culture* (New York: Routledge, 1992), 74. 'Child of feeling' is Kincaid's term.
45. *MP*, 30 (Oct. 1865), 408–26 (409).
46. *MP*, 25 (Jan. 1878), 80–94.
47. On the new philology, see Hans Aarsleff, *The Study of Language in England, 1760–1860* (Princeton, NJ: Princeton University Press, 1967), 165–67; and George W. Stocking Jr, *Victorian Anthropology* (Macmillan: New York, 1987), 21–22.

48. *AJM*, 23 (Nov. 1885), 20–32 (24).
49. *MP*, 25 (Jan. 1878), 80–94 (93).
50. Martin Maw has also stressed the significance of Müller's inheritance from Romanticism: 'The Romantic intelligence grasped language as a key to identity. Its impulse seemed to spring from the Absolute [...] It was in this spirit that Müller worked'. See *Visions of India: Fulfilment Theology, the Aryan Race Theory and the Work of British Protestant Missionaries in Victorian India* (Frankfurt: Peter Lang, 1990), 28.
51. 'Comparative Mythology', in *Chips from a German Workshop*, 4 vols (London: Longmans, Green, 1867–75), II (1867) 1–143 (67–68).
52. For a broader discussion of this aspect of Müller's thesis, see Dorson, 'The Eclipse of Solar Mythology', in *The Study of Folklore*, ed. Dundes, 57–83 (64).
53. *Printer's Register*, 6 Feb. 1868, referenced by Müller in 'Comparative Mythology', *Chips*, rev. edn, 4 vols (New York: Scribner, Armstrong), 1871–76, II (1872). Repr. in Dorson, ed., *Peasant Customs* I, 67–119 (69–70n).
54. 'At the Back of the North Wind', *GWY*, 2 (Sept. 1870), 584–90 (588–89). The Wordsworthian influence on MacDonald is also elaborated by Roderick McGillis in 'Childhood and Growth: George MacDonald and William Wordsworth', in McGavran, ed., *Romanticism*, 150–67. See also J. P. Ward, '"Came from yon fountain": Wordsworth's influence on Victorian Educators', *VS*, 29 (1986), 405–36.
55. Originally appearing in the single stanza poem beginning 'My heart leaps up when I behold' (1804), Wordsworth later added the line as a preface to 'Ode: Intimations of Immortality from Recollections of Early Childhood' (1815). See *The Poetical Works of William Wordsworth*, new edn, 6 vols (London: Moxon, 1849–50), I (147) and V (149).
56. John Pennington has also made a detailed case for MacDonald's references to Müller and the solar mythology thesis in a short fairy tale interpolated within *North Wind*: see 'Solar Mythology in George MacDonald's "Little Daylight" and "The Day Boy and the Night Girl"', *Journal of the Fantastic in the Arts*, 10 (1999), 308–20.
57. *MP*, 25 (Jan. 1878), 80–94 (80).
58. *GWY*, 2 (Mar. 1870), 257.
59. Introduction, *German Popular Stories* (1868 edn), vi.
60. *The King of the Golden River, or the Black Brothers* (London: J Wiley, 1851). Ruskin was not only a close friend of George MacDonald, but was a great admirer of J. H. Ewing's writing. As her commonplace book reveals, Ewing was equally impressed by Ruskin's work; see H.A.S. 78.
61. Correspondence with Margaret Gatty, Letter 73, 31 Jan. 1869, in *Canada Home: Juliana Horatia Ewing's Fredericton Letters 1867–1869*, ed. Margaret Howard Blom and Thomas E. Blom (Vancouver: University of British Columbia Press, 1983), 256–7. See also Ewing's 1869 Diary, H.A.S. 41. Ewing's assertions contradict U. C. Knoepflmacher's claim that as a woman writer she was 'sceptical of the deformation of traditional fairy tales' by the Grimms: see *Ventures*, 5. The first 8 stories appeared from Nov. 1869 to Sept. 1870, and all but the 4th were anonymous in monthly issue. When the periodical was bound, however, they were grouped under the title 'Old-fashioned Fairy Tales by Juliana Horatia Ewing'. The 20 tales were published in *AJM* from 1869 to 1876; 19 were republished in *Old-Fashioned Fairy Tales* (London: S.P.C.K., 1882).
62. See letter to C. T. Gatty, 13 Mar. 1874, in Horatia K. F. Eden, *Juliana Horatia Ewing: Her Books and Letters* (London: S.P.C.K., 1896),194–96 (195).

63. *Popular Tales from the Norse*, new edn (Edinburgh: Douglas, 1903), xix.
64. Dasent, *Popular*, xxi; Müller citing Emerson, 'Comparative Mythology' (1867 edn), 52.
65. 'I: "Wonderful Horns"', *MP*, 29 (Feb. 1865), 156–61 (157). Atkinson, the incumbent of Danby in Cleveland, was a folklorist of the antiquarian school, who also wrote for scholarly audiences.
66. 'VI: Hobs', *MP*, 30 (Sept. 1865), 316–22 (322).
67. Thomas Keightley's *Tales and Popular Fictions* (London: Whittaker, 1834) was one of the earliest sustained folkloric investigations to compare common fairy-tale plots across disparate cultures and regions. *The Fairy Mythology* (1828), a treatise on rural folklore, was reprinted, revised and widely read throughout the Victorian period: see Dorson, *Peasant Customs*, I, 36.
68. Quotations from *MP*, 30 (Dec. 1865), 658–701 (680 and 696). Ewing's extended domestic tale *Lob-Lie-by-the-Fire* (1871) also drew on a similar folkloric character (the 'Lob' or Brownie). In Ewing's tale, John Broom, a mysterious gypsy child, is adopted by middle-class spinsters; after running away and encountering various military adventures, John returns to work in secret for his adoptive family in the manner of the children in Ewing's *Monthly Packet* tale. See *Lob Lie-by-the-Fire and other Tales* (London: S.P.C.K., 1882), 11–105.
69. See Maxwell, *Gatty*, 145–46.
70. In her address to readers, *MP*, n.s. 1 (Jan. 1866), inside cover, Yonge drew attention to the fact that the magazine's first series had consisted almost entirely of extended serials.
71. See letter to Margaret Gatty, 23 Feb. 1870, in Eden, ed., *Juliana Horatia Ewing*, 185.
72. See 'The Hillman and the Housewife', *AJM*, 8 (May 1870), 432–34; 'Under the Sun', *AJM*, 8 (July 1870), 570–73; and Atkinson, 'Trolls', *MP*, n.s. 1 (Mar. 1866), 248–58 (255).
73. *AJM*, 14 (Nov. 1875), 37–41 (36).
74. *Old-Fashioned Fairy Tales*, v.
75. *AJM*, 9 (Apr. 1871), 375–80; and *AJM*, 10 (Feb. 1872), 210–16.
76. On Ewing's reading of George MacDonald's Scottish dialect novels, see her letter to Eleanor Lloyd, 14 Dec. 1868, H.A.S. 65/34; on her reading of Spanish folktales, see Ewing, Letter 73, *Canada Home*, 257. See also H. K. F. Gatty, 'Juliana Horatia Ewing – In Memoriam', *AJM*, 23 (July 1885) 534–52 (537), in which Gatty describes Ewing's childhood love of the tales of the Grimms, Andersen and Bechstein.
77. Goldney, *AJM*, 23 (Nov. 1885), 31. Macleod, *GWY*, 3 (Dec. 1870), 116–19 (119).
78. Macleod, *GWY*, 3 (Dec. 1870), 116.
79. S. M. Gidley, 'Little Brown Girls', *AJM*, 14 (Sept. 1876), 693–700 (698).
80. Alexander Allardyce, 'The Bengalees at School', *GWY*, 4 (Jan. 1872), 170–74 (174).
81. *MM*, 7 (Mar. 1863), 256.
82. Macleod, *GWY*, 3 (Dec. 1870), 119. Macleod's position was a familiar one: folklorist Sabine Baring Gould used a geological metaphor to describe the evolutionary status of the Khonds, claiming human sacrifice was not perpetrated by Aryan Hindus, but 'the Dravidian races underlying them'; see *A Book of Folk-Lore* (London: Collins, [n.d.]), 103.
83. See Tylor, *Primitive Culture: Researches into the Development of Mythology, Philosophy, Language, Religion, Art and Custom*, 2nd edn, 2 vols (London: John Murray, 1873); and Lang, 'Mythology and Fairy Tales', 618–31. See also Dorson, *The British Folklorists: A History* (London: Routledge & Kegan Paul, 1968),

187–220. On the comparative method, see Adam Kuper, *The Invention of Primitive Society: Transformations of an Illusion* (London: Routledge, 1988), 78–82.
84. For a summary of the thesis of folkloric survivals in civilisation, see Andrew Lang's preface to *Grimms' Household Tales*, trans. Margaret Hunt, I, x–lxxi.
85. 'My Ogre', *AJM*, 3 (July 1867), 143–46 (143).
86. *GWY*, 1 (Apr. 1869), 257–62 (258–60).
87. Atkinson, 'Trolls', 250n. See also Taylor, *NMM*, 2 (Oct. 1821), 329–36 (33–34). For an exploration of the influence of folkloric race myths on Victorian literature more generally, see Silver, *Strange*, 117-47.
88. *GWY*, 3 (Nov. 1870), 1–6 (2).
89. *GWY*, 3 (Jan. 1871), 129–36 (132).
90. However, as Stephen Prickett has noted, Curdie is later revealed to be of Royal blood, suggesting tensions in attitudes towards class within the text itself: See *Victorian Fantasy* (Sussex: Harvester, 1979), 184–87.
91. *GWY*, 3 (July 1871), 465–67(466).
92. 'The Princess and Curdie', *GT* (Apr. 1877), 193–200 (198). The text was serialised from Jan. 1877 to June 1877.
93. 'The Seven-Leagued Boots', *GWY*, 2 (Dec. 1869), 71–78; 'Mrs. Blundebore's Trials', *GWY*, 2 (Jan. 1870), 127–32.
94. On responses to the hot air balloon and the steam train in fairy painting, see Bown, *Fairies*, 39–97.
95. 'Sinbad in England, III: "Kordicus the Demon"', *GT*, 1 (Dec. 1872), 80–88; and V: 'Of a Sail Above the Clouds', *GT*, 1 (Mar. 1873), 250–57.
96. Thackeray's article was published in *Fraser's*, 17 (Mar. 1838), 279–90.
97. Stocking uses as an example J. F. McLennan's 1869 article 'The Early History of Man' in the North British Review, 50 (1869), 272–90, in which savage survivals include 'predatory bands' in contemporary London 'leading the life of the lowest nomads': see Stocking, Victorian, 219.
98. *Chatterbox*, annual vol. 1883, 55, 182, 208 and 357.
99. *GWY*, 2 (July 1870), 474–76 (476).
100. *AJM*, 14 (Nov. 1876), 1–11 (1).
101. On Andersen's contradictory conceptions of his own place in the Danish class structure, see Zipes, *Dreams*, 80–110.
102. *Chatterbox*, annual vol. 1883, 367.
103. *Chatterbox*, 20 Jan. 1875, 62–63 (63).
104. *Old-Fashioned Fairy Tales*, vii.
105. *AJM*, 9 (Feb. 1871), 240–45.
106. Cited in Maxwell, *Gatty*, 116.
107. *AJM*, 23 (Oct. 1885), 763–64.
108. See *AJM*, 4 (Apr. 1868), 337.
109. *You're a Brick, Angela! A New Look at Girls' Fiction from 1839 to 1975* (London: Gollancz, 1976), 22.
110. Quotations from *MP*, 25 (Feb. 1878), 164–196 (176).
111. *MP*, 25 (Feb. 1878), 3–4.
112. H.A.S. 78.
113. *AJM*, 1 (June 1866), 123.
114. Knoepflmacher, *Ventures*, 409; 'Timothy's Shoes', *AJM*, 9 (Nov. 1870), 3–12 and (Dec. 1870), 81–87; (Jan. 1871), 153–60. Andersen's Karen wears frivolous shoes to her confirmation and is forced to dance until her feet are cut off; the eponymous heroine of *Goody Two-Shoes*, a text first published by John Newbery in

1765 (and possibly by Oliver Goldsmith) was a familiar symbol of childish propriety to Victorian readers.
115. Cited in Maxwell, *Gatty*, 186.
116. In correspondence with Margaret Gatty, Ewing chose to subdivide her own output into 'real' fairy tales and texts which utilised 'fairy machinery' (or introduced fantasy into a contemporary domestic setting); see Letter 73, *Canada Home*, 256–57.
117. On the mythology of female tale-telling more generally, see Marina Warner, *From the Beast to the Blonde: On Fairy Tales and Their Tellers* (London: Vintage, 1995).
118. *AJM*, 9 (Dec. 1870), 89–101 (89).
119. *AJM*, 14 (Dec. 1875), 86–100 (88–89).
120. *AJM*, 4 (Nov. 1867), 28–37.
121. See *AJM*, 3 (Aug. 1867), back page. Margaret Gatty's possible editorial influence here is interesting: she approved of female scientific education, and had herself produced a classificatory volume on seaweeds that became a significant text in the field. She was, however, more ambivalent about women's roles as public speakers or in the professions: see Maxwell, *Gatty*, 138.
122. See diary entry for 27 Apr. 1870, H.A.S. 41.
123. *AJM* 14 (Feb. 1876), 247–51 (249).
124. *AJM*, 10 (Mar. 1872), 2 59–65 (263).
125. *AJM*, 9 (June 1871), 463–468 (463). Jack Zipes reprints this text in *Victorian Fairy Tales*, 129–33.
126. In Letter 73, *Canada Home*, 257, Ewing refers directly to the 'Popular Tales from Andalucia', which had been collected by 'Fernán Caballero' (Cecilia Böhl de Faber, a female writer and folklorist), translated by Caroline Peachey, and published in *Aunt Judy's Magazine*. In the Andalusian tale in *AJM*, 4 (Feb. 1868), 226–28, a suitor demands that his intended bride prove that she can sew, embroider and spin before he will marry her. Fairies execute the work for her in secret, but when her husband sees that the work has caused the fairies' extended forearms and poor eyesight, he decrees that his wife should never sew again.
127. *AJM*, 7 (Sept. 1869), 189.
128. *AJM*, 7 (July 1869), 189.
129. *AJM*, 9 (Dec. 1870), 127.
130. Margaret (Mrs. Alfred) Gatty's *Aunt Judy's Tales* was published in 1859, followed by *Aunt Judy's Letters* (1862), both by Bell & Sons. The extent to which the magazine depended upon both Ewing's literary contributions and her addition to the 'Aunt Judy' mythology was made apparent by the periodical's abrupt termination at her death in 1885.
131. See Maxwell, *Gatty*, 49.
132. See Gatty family magazines, H.A.S. 76. These strategies have parallels with the playful referencing of *Blackwood's* in the Brontë juvenilia. Ewing was 15 when she edited the first edition of *Anon!* Mock adverts in the 21 March 1860 edition which includes '"Weekly Whispers to Gentle Girls" edited by the Rev. E - e C - e at ½ d a number', humorously anticipated Erskine Clarke's later periodical endeavour *Chatterbox*, while the 14 Jan. 1858 edition of *Le Cache* claimed to be published by 'Dell and Baldy' of Fleet Street, a clear parody of Gatty's own publisher.
133. An entry in 'Aunt Judy's Correspondence' from "Violet", who wished to join an Essay Society whose members were girls between 14 and 21 years of age, was

fairly representative. This correspondent gave her own age as 19. See *AJM*, 14 (July 1876), 574.
134. *AJM*, 13 (Dec. 1874), 2–7 (2).
135. *AJM*, 14 (Feb. 1876), 233 and 253–54.
136. *AJM*, 9 (Jan. 1871), 253.
137. *AJM*, 3 (June 1867); *AJM*, 4 (Nov. 1867 and Jan. 1868), inside cover.
138. See Barbara Onslow, *Women and the Press in Nineteenth-Century Britain* (Basingstoke: Macmillan, 2001), 26, 165, and June Sturrock, 'Establishing Identity: Editorial Correspondence from the Early Years of *The Monthly Packet*', *VPR*, 39 (Fall 2006), 266–79.
139. See 'Editor's Address', *Boys of England*, 24 Nov. 1866, 16; Mathew Browne, 'Comptroller', 'The Letter-Box', *GT*, 1 (Dec. 1872), 105–06; and Browne's 'The Boy Who Wanted to be a Great Author', *GT*, 1 (Oct. 1873), 643–44 (643).
140. Drotner, *English*, 57.
141. Quotations from *AJM*, 7 (May 1869), 44–47.
142. *AJM*, 7 (July 1869), 189–90.
143. See Beetham, 'Towards a Theory', 28–29.

3   Fairy Tale and Fantasy in the Adult Monthly

1. Charles Kingsley, *The Water-Babies: A Fairy Tale for a Land-Baby*, *MM*, 8 (Sept. 1862), 355–62 (357). Serialised Aug. 1862 to Mar. 1863.
2. [Anne Thackeray Ritchie], 'Jack and the Beanstalk', Part I, *CM*, 18 (Sept. 1873), 311–34 (322). Anne Isabella Thackeray used a number of different titles after her marriage in 1877. These included Mrs. Richmond Ritchie, Anne Ritchie, Anne Thackeray Ritchie, and after the knighthood of her husband, Lady Ritchie. She was unmarried and writing under the name of 'Miss Thackeray' when the *Cornhill* fairy-tale series was published, but to avoid confusion I have used 'Thackeray Ritchie' throughout.
3. 'Mr Kingsley's Water-Babies', *Times*, 26 Jan. 1864, 6.
4. Letter, 20 May 1862, Add. MSS 55380 (1) 117. In fact, Kingsley negotiated offers with both periodicals but gave *Macmillan's* first refusal; see Macmillan to Kingsley, Add. MSS 55380 (1) f. 107.
5. The quotation is from the *Times*, 26 Jan.1864, 6.
6. See [Thomas Hughes, J. M. Ludlow and David Masson], 'The Colloquy of the Round Table', *MM*, 1 (Nov. 1859), 72–80; and Thackeray, 'Roundabout Papers – No. I: "On a Lazy Idle Boy"', *CM*, 1 (Jan. 1860), 124–28 (128).
7. In her retrospective article 'The First Number of "The Cornhill"', Thackeray Ritchie placed the first number's circulation at 120,000, 'something quite phenomenal'; see *CM*, n.s. 1 (July 1896), 1–16 (1). John Sutherland reveals that it was in fact 110,000, but this was still an unprecedented readership for a monthly. See '*Cornhill*'s Sales and Payments: The First Decade,' *VPR*, 19 (1986), 106–08 (106). However, as Barbara Quinn Schmidt notes, sales were in the region of 25,000 when Leslie Stephen took over the editorship in 1871, and less than half this figure at his departure. See 'Introduction – *The Cornhill Magazine*: Celebrating Success', *VPR*, 32 (1999), 202–08 (206).
8. Alexander Macmillan revealed that he was satisfied with selling out of the first month's issue, which had less than a tenth of the circulation of the *Cornhill's* opening number: see Add. MSS 55837 (fol. 150), and Add. MSS 55838 (fols 206–10). In the second letter, dated 25 July 1860, Macmillan noted 'We have risen

from an actual [...] sale of between 8,000 and 9,000 to 13,000'. As is well known, the *Cornhill's* policy of providing literature suitable for family reading clashed with the personal views of both W. M. Thackeray (in the editorial chair from Jan. 1860 to May 1862) and Leslie Stephen (from Apr. 1871 to Dec. 1882). See E. T. Cook, 'The Jubilee of the "Cornhill"', *CM*, n.s. 28 (Jan. 1910), 8–27; W. E. Norris, 'Leslie Stephen, Editor', *CM*, n.s. 28 (Jan. 1910), 46–50; and Laurel Brake, *Subjugated Knowledges: Journalism, Gender and Literature in the Nineteenth Century* (Basingstoke: Macmillan, 1994), 9–11.

9. 'Children's Literature of the Last Century III', *MM*, 20 (Sept. 1869), 448–56 (452).
10. MacNiece, *Varieties of Parable* (Cambridge: Cambridge University Press, 1965), 83; Cunningham, 'Soiled Fairy: *The Water-Babies* in its Time', *Essays in Criticism*, 35 (Apr. 1985), 121–48 (121–22).
11. Kingsley knew Alexander Macmillan, David Masson (editor until 1868) and many of the magazine's contributors through a shared involvement in the Christian Socialist movement in the 1840s. Macmillan had delayed founding the magazine in 1858 when he found Kingsley 'only half-hearted in the enterprise': see George J. Worth, *Macmillan's Magazine 1859–1907* (Aldershot: Ashgate, 2003), 8. Kingsley (as well as his brother Henry) became a significant contributor to *Macmillan's* and sometimes attended the Thursday night meetings of contributors when in London: see Add. MSS 55838 (fols 206–10).
12. Both quotations from *CM*, 5 (Jan. 1862), 36–42. On Kant's influence on Hinton, see Bown, *Fairies*, 98–102. For other articles that use this metaphor, see Edmund Ollier, 'A Scientific Figment', *HW* (23 Dec. 1854), 453–56 and 'Soluble Silver', *Chambers's*, 6 June 1896, 367–68.
13. 'Sir Charles Lyell on the Antiquity of Man', *MM*, 7 (Apr. 1863), 476–87 (485).
14. *CM*, 19 (Jan. 1869), 30–44 (42).
15. *MM*, 3 (Jan. 1861), 213–24 (24).
16. On Prichard's influence on Franz Bopp and his significance in the establishment of Celtic Studies, see Garrigan Mattar, *Primitivism*, 23.
17. 'The Study of Celtic Literature: Part 1', *CM*, 13 (Mar. 1866), 282–96 (287–89).
18. Garrigan Mattar also acknowledges Arnold's critical engagement with Ernest Renan, whose 'La Poesie des races celtiques' played a seminal role in inaugurating the comparative study of Celtic See *Primitivism*, 24–26.
19. Quotations from 'The Study of Celtic Literature: Part IV', *CM*, 14 (July 1866), 110–28 (119); Part I, *CM*, 13 (Mar. 1866), 282–96 (287) and Part III, *CM*, 13 (May 1866), 538–55 (544). Part II appeared in *CM*, 13 (Apr. 1866), 469–83.
20. Quotations from Masson, *MM*, 3 (Jan. 1861), 213–24. If Müller later became uneasy about the equation of linguistic and racial groups, in his article 'Introductory Lecture on the Science of Language' in *Macmillan's* he did collapse those distinctions: 'at a very remote, but a very real period in the history of the world, the ancestors of the Homeric poets and the poets of the Veda must have lived together as members of one and the same race, as speakers of one and the same language': see *MM*, 7 (Mar. 1863) 337–49 (340).
21. *MM*, 6 (Oct. 1862), 433–44 (442).
22. *MM*, 3 (Jan. 1861), 213–24 (220).
23. Kingsley, *The Roman and the Teuton* (Cambridge and London: Macmillan, 1864), 2–9 and 207. Müller introduced the 1092 Macmillan edition of this text after Kingsley's death, but also suggested in the preface that he would 'gladly have altered or struck out whole lines' in the 'ethnological passages'.
24. *MM*, 7 (Jan. 1863) 209–18 (215–16).
25. *MM*, 7 (Dec. 1862), 95–105 (97–98).

26. *MM*, 6 (Oct. 1862), 433–44 (434). See also Kingsley's letter to Professor Rolleston, in which he states 'the soul of each living being down to the lowest secretes the body thereof [...] the body is nothing more than the expression in terms of matter, of the stage of development to which the being has arrived. [...] I wish you would *envisager* the gorilla brain in that way, and the baboon brain also under the fancy of their being *degraded* forms'. In *Charles Kingsley: His Letters and Memories of His Life*, ed. Frances Kingsley, 2 vols (London: King, 1977), II, 44. On Kingsley and monogenesis, see Stitt, *Metaphors*, 84.
27. *MM*, 6 (Oct. 1862), 433–44 (434); *MM*, 7 (Jan. 1863), 215. Writing to the naturalist W. Bates, Kingsley claimed God's 'greatness, wisdom, and perpetual care, I never understood as I have since I became a convert to Darwin's views'. Kingsley, *Letters* I, 154–55.
28. *MM*, 6 (Aug. 1862), 273–83 (279–83).
29. On the influence of Darwin on theories of racial extinction, see Patrick Brantlinger, *Dark Vanishings: Discourse on the Extinction of Primitive Races, 188–1930* (Ithaca, NY: Cornell University Press, 2003).
30. Kingsley, *Letters*, 107.
31. See, for instance, E.D. Dicey's 'The New England States', *MM*, 6 (Aug. 1862), 284–97 which directly follows the first chapter of *The Water-Babies*. On *Macmillan's* responses to the war, see Worth, *Macmillan's Magazine*, 29–32 and Worth, '*Macmillan's Magazine* and the American Civil War: A Reconsideration', *VPR*, 26 (1993), 193–98.
32. Kingsley, *Letters*, 134.
33. Uffelman and Scott have argued that Kingsley's pro-Southern as well as anti-American position is evident in a number of references removed in the subsequent book revision: see 'Kingsley's Serial Novels, II: The Water-Babies', *VPR*, 19 (1986), 122–30. In an unpublished letter to Thomas Hughes, Kingsley argued, 'I could not help finding out, when I came to read up, that the Northerners have exaggerated the case against the South infamously', but his support as expressed to the pro-Northerner Hughes was guarded: 'I, on the whole, respect the South one-millionth of a grain more than I do the North'. Cited in John O. Waller, 'Charles Kingsley and the American Civil War', *Studies in Philology* 60 (July 1963), 554–68 (560n). As Waller also notes, in *The Roman and the Teuton*, Kingsley had argued that Southern gentleman was 'at least a Teuton not a Roman' (Kingsley, 20n), and suggested that slavery would die a natural death.
34. *MM*, 7 (Nov. 1862), 3–13 (3).
35. *MM*, 7 (Jan. 1863), 209–18 (217).
36. Add. MSS 55840 fol. 18. The significance of Huxley and Du Chaillu in these debates have been widely discussed elsewhere: see, for example, Peter Raby, *Bright Paradise: Victorian Scientific Travellers* (London: Chatto and Windus, 1996) and Hodgson, 'Defining the Species: Apes, Savages and Humans in Scientific and Literary Writing of the 1890s', *Journal of Victorian Culture*, 4 (Autumn 1999), 228–51, (231–35).
37. Hodgson, 231–35; *Punch*, 43 (Oct. 18, 1862), 165.
38. *Darwin's Plots: Evolutionary Narrative in Darwin, George Eliot and Nineteenth-Century Fiction* (London: Routledge, 1983), 139.
39. *MM*, 7 (Apr. 1863), 476–87 (478).
40. 'Mr Max Müller on the Origin of Language', *MM*, 7 (Nov. 1862), 54–60. Wedgwood argues against Müller's dismissal of the role of onomatopoeia in the origin of language.

41. Müller, *MM*, 7 (Mar. 1863) 337–349 (337). Müller originally made this point in his first series of 'Lectures on the Science of Language': 'the one great barrier between the brute and man is *Language* [...] no process of natural selection will ever distill significant words out of the notes of birds or the cries of beasts'. See *Lectures on the Science of Language* (London: Longman, 1861), 340.
42. On Kingsley's letter to Darwin – part of which is cited in a revised edition of *The Origin of Species*, see *Charles Darwin: His Life Told in an Autobiographical Chapter, and in a Selected Series of his Published Letters*, ed. Francis Darwin (London: Murray, 1892), 228–29.
43. Darwin read both Huxley and Wedgwood's reviews of *The Origin* in *Macmillan's* and praised them both. He told Wedgwood that she understood his book 'perfectly' although he also confessed that he was unable to fully follow (or perhaps endorse?) her 'metaphysical trains of thought'. See *Charles Darwin: His Life*, 62.
44. On Tylor's reference to *The Water-Babies* in *Primitive Culture*, see Beer, *Darwin's Plots*, 257; and J. A. V. Chapple, *Science and Literature in the Nineteenth Century* (Basingstoke, Macmillan, 1986), 140.
45. 'The Boundaries of Science – A Dialogue I', *MM*, 2 (June 1860), 134–38 and II *MM*, 4 (July 1861), 237–47 (247).
46. *MM*, 1 (Mar. 1860), 402–06.
47. *MM*, 2 (Aug. 1860), 285–92 (285–88).
48. See *Fraser's*, 78 (Sept. 1868), 353–62. In this later article, Greg discusses the possibility of a republic in which the poor are forbidden to reproduce. On Greg's relationship to Darwinism, see Greta Jones, *Social Darwinism and English Thought: The Interaction between Biological and Social Theory* (Sussex: Harvester, 1980), 35–36.
49. Collins, Beggars, *MM*, 5 (Jan. 1862), 210–18 (210).
50. See Darwin, *The Origin of Species*, ed. John Burrow (London: Penguin 1985), 179, for the passage to which Howman refers.
51. Quotations from Howman, *MM*, 5 (Jan. 1862), 225–29 (225–26).
52. *CM*, 1 (Feb. 1860), 199–207.
53. *MM*, 6 (Aug. 1862), 273–83 (280).
54. *MM*, 5 (Jan. 1862), 225–29 (228).
55. *CM*, 5 (Mar. 1862), 311–18 (318). In suggesting that the Creator endowed 'one primordial form' with life, Dixon, like Kingsley, attempts to reconcile natural selection and God, although his moral prognosis is darker. Jennifer Phegley offers a rather unconvincing feminist reading of this text in 'Clearing Away "The Briars and Brambles": The Education and Professionalization of the *Cornhill Magazine*'s Women Readers, 1860–65', *VPR*, 33 (2000), 22–43 (36).
56. All quotations from *CM*, 36 (Sept. 1877), 325–32. The phrase is Dickens's.
57. Add. MSS 55837 (fol. 156).
58. *MM*, 2 (June 1860), 134–38 (138).
59. *MM*, 6 (July 1862), 192–202 (196–97).
60. *MM*, 6 (Aug. 1862), 273–83 (278).
61. *MM*, 7 (Feb. 1863), 316–27 (325).
62. Introduction, *The Water-Babies*, ed. Brian Alderson (Oxford: World's Classics 1995), xv. Parents did, however, read the text out to their children, Alexander Macmillan among them: see Add. MSS 55380 (1) fol. 162.
63. Quotation from Alexander Macmillan, Add. MSS 55380 (2) fols 617–18.
64. Beer, *Darwin's Plots*, 125.
65. *MM*, 6 (Sept. 1862), 353–63 (362). For a detailed analysis of differences between the serial and the book revision, see Uffelman and Scott. 'Kingsley's Serial Novels'.

66. Cunningham, 'Soiled', 125.
67. *Chambers's*, July 1882, 423.
68. *CM*, 13 (June 1866), 721–42 (733–34).
69. Quotations from *CM*, 30 (Sept. 1874), 281–96 and *CM*, 15 (June 1867), 676–709.
70. Quotations from *MM*, 7 (May 1863), 32. Mary Arseneau's reading of the 'Prince's Progress' as spiritual allegory of the soul's journey towards God is convincing, and reveals the longer poem's debt to Spencer, Dante, Bunyon, and the Song of Solomon. She makes no mention, however, of its *Macmillan's Magazine* predecessor. See *Recovering Christina Rossetti: Female Community and Incarnational Poetics* (Basingstoke: Palgrave Macmillan, 2004), 136–62.
71. 'Sit Down in the Lowest Room', which was published in the magazine in March the following year, creates an interesting dialogue with this text, and reveals Rossetti's complex attitude to female self-assertion. As Rossetti sought to establish her reputation, she experimented with fairy-tale motifs in a range of genres. She published prose fairy tales in the *National Magazine* ('Nick', 1857), the *Argosy* ('Hero', 1865) and later wrote the children's volume *Speaking Likenesses* (1874), a fantasy that owed a considerable debt to *Alice's Adventures in Wonderland*. All three are republished in Christina Rossetti, *Poems and Prose*, ed. Jan Marsh (London: Everyman, 1994), 286–304 and 325–53.
72. For the full list of titles and dates, see George J. Worth, *Macmillan's Magazine*, 45. Rossetti's wider contributions to *Macmillan's* are discussed briefly by Alexis Easley in *First Person Anonymous*: *Women Writers and Victorian Print Media* (Aldershot: Ashgate, 2004), 168–67.
73. Quotations from Ruskin and Dante Gabriel Rossetti in *The Rossetti Macmillan Letters*, ed. Lona Mosk Packer (London: Cambridge University Press, 1963), 5–6.
74. Macmillan to Dante Gabriel Rossetti, 28 Oct. 1861, Add. MSS 55481, fol. 4.
75. All quotations from Caroline Norton, 'The Angel in the House' and 'The Goblin Market', *MM*, 8 (Sept. 1863), (398–404), 401–03. For Norton, as readers would have been aware, the lesson of marriage had not read 'like a romance'. After separating from her husband in the 1830s, Norton had published a pamphlet detailing her fight for custody of her children, and became notorious in the British press: see Easley, *First Person Anonymous*, 58n.
76. Rossetti's twentieth-century appropriation in *Playboy* is discussed by Lorraine Kooistra Janzen in *Christina Rossetti and Illustration* (Athens: Ohio University Press), 240–47.
77. See *Macmillan's* 'Colloquy of the Round Table', *MM*, 1 (Nov. 1859) 72–80. On debates over women's rights in the magazine more generally, see Andrea Broomfield, 'Towards a More Tolerant Society: *Macmillan's Magazine* and the Women's Suffrage Question', *VPR* 23 (1990), 120–26; Rosemary T. VanArsdel, '*Macmillan's Magazine* and the Fair Sex 1859–1874, Part I', *VPR*, 33 (2000), 374–96 and 'Part II', *VPR*, 34 (2001), 2–15 and Worth, *Macmillan's Magazine*, 74–97.
78. [Martineau], 'Middle-Class Education in England – Girls', *CM*, 10 (Nov. 1864), 549–68 (567).
79. Phegley, 'Clearing', 33.
80. All quotations from *CM*, 13 (May 1866), 556–66. I develop this argument in relation to other short stories in this series in 'Extending the Parameters of the Text: Anne Thackeray's Fairy Tales in the *Cornhill Magazine*', *VPR*, 33:1 (Spring 2000), 65–80 and in 'The Spinster Tale-teller in the Victorian Marketplace', *New Comparison*, 27/28 (Spring–Autumn 1999), 83–97.
81. All quotations from 'A Dull Life', *MM*, 16 (May 1867), 47–53.

82. *CM*, 3 (Mar. 1861), 318–31. On Thackeray Ritchie's later support for women's suffrage, see Lillian F. Shankman, *Anne Thackeray Ritchie: Journals and Letters*, ed. Abigail Burnham Bloom and John Maynard (Columbus, OH: Ohio State University Press, 1994), 168.
83. *MM*, 20 (Oct. 1869), 552–61
84. Arseneau, *Recovering*, 36.
85. 'Blackstick Papers: No. V: "Egeria in Brighton"', *CM*, n.s. 10 (June 1901), 722–29 (727).
86. Jack Zipes, for example, categorises Thackeray Ritchie with writers who have 'rarely a hint of social criticism' in their fiction, while Lillian F. Shankman claims that her fairy tales are heavily moralistic and lack her father's 'light touch and irony'; see *Victorian Fairy Tales*, xxiii; and *Anne Thackeray Ritchie: Journals and Letters*, 166. Auerbach and Knoepflmacher, in contrast, see a strong feminist agenda in Thackeray Ritchie's tales: see *Forbidden Journeys*, 11–20.
87. Like Gaskell's work, Thackeray Ritchie's tales are semi-autonomous parts that appeared intermittently. Nine of these fairy-tale inspired short stories were published in the *Cornhill* between 1866 and 1874. They were republished in revised form in two book editions by Smith, Elder, *Five Old Friends and a Young Prince* (London: 1868); and *Bluebeard's Keys and Other Stories* (London: 1874). 'Miss Williamson' was the narrator for many of Thackeray Ritchie's novels and fictions in the *Cornhill*, a metafictional device that also helped her to negotiate the periodical's policy of anonymity.
88. Beer, *Darwin's Plots*, 114.
89. *MM*, 1 (Nov. 1859) 72–80; Darwin, letter to W. D. Fox, *Charles Darwin: His Life*, I, 160–62.
90. The assumption that Christian socialism was analogous with a call for either state intervention or later forms of socialism is misleading: see K. S. Inglis, *The Churches and the Working Classes in Victorian England* (London: Routledge & Kegan Paul, 1963), 262–71.

4 The Politics of the Fairy Tale in the Labour Press

1. [Charles] Allen Clarke, 'A Talk about Fairies', *LL*, 6 June 1896, 196.
2. [James] Keir Hardie, 'Jack Clearhead, A Fairy Tale for Crusaders', *LL*, 29 Sept. 1894, 11.
3. The origins of this title are somewhat confusing. Keir Hardie briefly changed the name of the *Miner* to the *Labour Leader* before its termination in 1899; there was also a *Labor Leader* edited by socialist Fred Henderson (1891). In 1893, Hardie's *Labour Leader* was launched as a Glasgow-based monthly; it became a London-based ILP weekly in 1894, running under this title until Sept. 1922. *The Labour Prophet: The Organ of the Labour Church*, ed. John Trevor, ran from Jan. 1892 to Sept. 1898, with the subheading 'with our *Cinderella Supplement*' from May 1893 to June 1897. Published by the Labour Church in London and Manchester, it was entitled *Labour Prophet and Labour Church Record* from Sept. 1895 to Sept. 1898, after which it was replaced with the free quarterly *Labour Church Record*, edited by Allan Clarke, which ran until 1901.
4. See Yeo, 'A NEW LIFE: The Religion of Socialism in Britain, 1883–1896', *History Workshop*, 4 (1977), 5–56. For an astute attempt to refine Yeo's terms, see Mark Bevir, 'The Labour Church Movement, 1891–1902', *Journal of British Studies*, 38 (Apr. 1999), 217–45.

5. Advertisement in the cover of Robert Blatchford's *Fantasias* (Manchester and London: John Heywood, 1892). On the *Clarion*'s popularity, see Deian Hopkin, 'The Left-Wing Press and the New Journalism', in *Papers for the Millions: The New Journalism in Britain, 1850s to 1914*, ed. Joel H. Wiener (London and New York: Greenwood, 1988), 225–41 (227). On circulation, see Peter Broks, *Media Science before the Great War* (Basingstoke: Macmillan, 1996), 26.
6. The phrase 'democratic penny' was used in an advertisement for the *Labour Leader* on the inside cover of the *ILP. Songbook* (Manchester: Labour Press and Clarion Office, 1897).
7. *LP*, 1 (Jan. 1892), 4. John Trevor, formerly a Unitarian minister, was the motive force behind the Labour Church, and inaugurated its first service in Manchester in October 1891. See David Summers, 'The Labour Church and Affiliated Movements' (unpublished doctoral thesis, University of Edinburgh, 1958), 311.
8. Hopkin, 'The Left-Wing Press', 226.
9. See Hopkin, 'The Labour Party Press', in *The First Labour Party 1906–14*, ed. K. D. Brown (Beckenham: Croom Helm, 1985), 105–28 (107–08).
10. *The Warwick Guide to British Labour Periodicals 1790–1970*, comp. by Royden Harrison, Gillian B. Woolven and Robert Duncan (Sussex: Harvester, 1977), xiii–xiv.
11. See Stanley Harrison, *Poor Men's Guardians: A Record of the Struggles for a Democratic Newspaper Press, 1763–1973* (London: Lawrence and Wishart, 1974), 162–63, and E. P. Thompson, *The Struggle for a Free Press* (London: People's Press, 1952), 15.
12. The change from Scottish monthly to national weekly issue became possible when Hardie amassed sufficient share capital. The first weekly *Leader* appeared on 31 March 1894. Hardie owned his own presses and had unusual control over the production process. See Kenneth O. Morgan, *Keir Hardie: Radical and Socialist* (London: Weidenfeld and Nicolson, 1975), 66–68 and 84–85. On Hardie's financial input into the paper, see Harrison, *Poor*, 169.
13. On the paper's circulation, see *LP*, 1 (Feb. 1892), 16; *LP*, 2 (May 1893), 38, and Inglis, *Churches*, 222.
14. Trevor, 'Our Altered Form', *Prophet*, 1 (Mar. 1894), 1.
15. Previous three quotations from *LP*, 3 (Mar./Apr. 1894), 40.
16. Hopkin, 'The Left-wing Press', 225.
17. *LP*, 1 (Jan. 1892), 4.
18. 'Ways and Means', *LP*, 2 (May 1894), 62.
19. 'Our New Programme', *LP*, 6 (July 1897), 101.
20. See Joel Wiener, 'How New was the New Journalism?', *Papers for the Millions*, 47–71 and Harrison, *Poor*, 179. Coined by Mathew Arnold in 1887, the conflicting contemporaneous meanings of this term have been discussed by Brake in *Subjugated Knowledges*, 83–103, and by Beetham in *A Magazine of her Own? Desire and Domesticity in the Woman's Magazine, 1800–1914* (London and New York: Routledge, 1996), 119–25.
21. *Fantasias*, inside cover.
22. *LL*, 4 Jan. 1896, 12.
23. Blatchford spoke at the 2nd Labour Church Service, in Oct. 1891, to record crowds, while Hardie was a Labour Church speaker in March 1892. See *LP*, 1 (Jan. 1892), 7–8; and *LP*, 1 (Mar. 1892), 24.
24. *LP*, 3 (May 1894), 53. The *Workman's Times* (Aug. 1890 to Mar. 1894) was a Northern-based socialist paper, edited by Joseph Burgess. Burgess was present at a meeting to discuss the setting up of a Labour Church in London in 1892 and

his paper played a key role in canvassing support for an Independent Labour Party. See David Kynaston, *King Labour: The British Working Class 1850–1914* (London: Unwin, 1976), 133. Blatchford left the *Sunday Chronicle* to set up the *Clarion* in 1891. As a member of both the ILP and S.D.F., Blatchford encouraged *Clarion* readers to join both organisations.
25. Morgan, *Keir Hardie*, 66, claims Hardie's input into the women's columns, although others have questioned this.
26. Previous two quotations from *LP*, 4 (June 1895), 81–83 (82–83).
27. *LP*, 3 (Oct. 1894), 139. In this month, fictional texts were added to the works of suggested study in the *Labour Prophet* correspondence class, and this comment was made in relation to George Eliot's *Silas Marner*. Jack Mitchell has noted that many late nineteenth-century socialist periodicals did not reject the bourgeois tradition, and Dickens, Eliot and Defoe were among the recommended texts in Morris's *Commonweal*. See 'Tendencies in Narrative Fiction in the London-based Socialist Press of the 1880s and 1890s', in *The Rise of Socialist Fiction 1880–1914*, ed. H. Gustav Klaus (Sussex: Harvester, 1987), 49–72 (50). Familiar texts by middle-class authors regularly made the *Labour Prophet*'s reading lists, although its own fiction was normally of an overtly socialist nature. For a comprehensive survey of fiction serialised in the socialist press, see Deborah Mutch, *English Socialist Periodicals 1880–1900: A Reference Source* (Aldershot: Ashgate 2005).
28. Mitchell, 'Tendencies in Narrative Fiction', 71.
29. Klaus, *The Rise of Socialist Fiction*, 2.
30. On the social complexities of Labour Church membership, see *Spectator*, 21 Apr. 1894, 533–35; and Stanley Pierson, 'John Trevor and the Labour Church Movement in England, 1891–1900', *Church History*, 29 (Dec. 1960), 463–76 (468–69).
31. *LL*, 3 Aug. 1895, 2.
32. *LL*, 7 Mar. 1896, 84.
33. Caroline Benn, *Keir Hardie: A Biography* (London: Metro, 1997), 119.
34. Interestingly, one of the women's prizes was suffragist Florence Dixie's futursitic fiction *Gloriana; or, The Coming Revolution* (1890). In this text, an aristocratic woman disguised as a man is ultimately elected prime minister, passing a bill for female suffrage in 1900. In an attempted coup, her position is defended by a military corps of upper-class females and the male working classes – an interesting example of how the interests of the *Leader*'s working-class women were frequently sidelined in both feminist and socialist debates.
35. See 52, 55 and the report of Tom Mann's address on 'The Future of Trade Unionism', *LP*, 1 (Feb. 1892), 16, where it was reported that 'The one drawback was the absence of women, as usual.'
36. *LP*, 3 (Apr. 1894), 48. *Merrie England* classes were first proposed in the *Labour Prophet* in Jan. 1894, and included 10s. prizes for both classes and corresponding individuals. The 'Missionary Class' incorporated a wider programme of textual study, and included instruction on subjects ranging from elocution to evolution. From autumn 1894 the 'Missionary Class' and 'Pioneer Class' were subsumed by the 'Correspondence Class', which was specifically entrusted with the extension of adult education work. See Summers, 'Labour Church', 139 and 150–53.
37. *Clarion*, 9 July 1892, 7. The article was written under the pseudonym 'M'Ginnis', used by Blatchford in his more frivolous literary roles.
38. *LL*, 18 May 1895, 1. See *The Thousand and One Nights, Commonly Called, in England, The Arabian Nights Entertainments: A New Translation from the Arabic*

    with Copious Notes, trans. Edward W. Lane, 3 vols (London: Charles Knight, 1839–41), I (1839), 410–15.
39. *LL*, 10 Aug. 1895, 1.
40. On *LL* and attitudes to democracy, see Logie Barrow and Ian Bullock, *Democratic Ideas and the British Labour Movement, 1880–1914* (Cambridge: Cambridge University Press, 1996), 75–87.
41. *LP*, 5 (Nov. 1896), 183.
42. *LP*, 4 (Jan. 1895), 15.
43. The Labour Church principles were first published in *LP*, 1 (Feb. 1892), 16, and were republished every month.
44. The first viewpoint is adopted by Inglis, and to some extent by Henry Pelling, in *The Origins of the Labour Party 1880–1900*, 2nd edn (Oxford: Oxford University Press, 1965). Pelling interprets the Labour Church as 'a symptom of religious decline' (142). For more revisionary approaches, see Yeo, 'New Life', and Bevir, 'Labour Church'.
45. See *In Memoriam and Other Poems* (London: Dent, 1994), 75–153 (137), CVI, and Hardie, *British Weekly*, 18 Jan. 1894, cited by Pelling, *Origins*, 140.
46. *LP*, 1 (Jan. 1892), 4. While the sentiments are similar, Hardie and Trevor used different terminology. Trevor always avoided the term 'Christian' as a description of his own faith or that of the Labour Church movement.
47. *LP*, 6 (Apr. 1897), cited by Yeo, 'New Life', 5–6.
48. Blachford, *God and My Neighbour* (London: Clarion Press, 1903), 7. Italics in original.
49. Trevor, *LP*, 2 (May 1893), 41.
50. Although the *Labour Prophet* was subtitled 'with our *Cinderella Supplement*', the children's paper itself was headed '*Cinderella: A Paper Devoted to the Service of Cinderella Children*', and from Jan. 1894, *Cinderella: A Paper for the Children*.
51. *LP*, 2 (Aug. 1893), 77.
52. *LP*, 2 (May 1893), 38.
53. *LP*, 1 (Sept. 1893), 86.
54. Accounts of the movement's inception are given in Blatchford's own article 'Our Cinderella', *LP*, 2 (June 1893), 54–55, and by A. M. Thompson in 'Of the Birth of Cinderella', in the *Cinderella Annual – The Book of the National Cinderella Society*, ed. Lizzie MacDonald (London: Lizzie MacDonald [n.d.]), 13–19.
55. Yeo, 'New Life', 14.
56. *LP*, 2 (Sept. 1893), 86; and *LP*, 2 (May 1893), 43.
57. Blatchford, *Altruism: Christ's Glorious Gospel of Love Against Man's Dismal Science of Greed* (London: Clarion Newspaper Company, 1902), 6.
58. The setting up of the Manchester Cinderella Club is discussed in *LP*, 1 (Nov. 1892), 88. Cinderella work was publicised in the *Clarion*, and club organisers included members of a range of socialist groups (most frequently ILP, and later Clarion Cyclists and Fellowship members).
59. Cited in Thompson, 'The Birth of Cinderella', in MacDonald, ed., *Cinderella Annual*, 13–15.
60. *LP*, 2 (May 1893), 44. *Comic Cuts* (1890) and the *Wonder* (1892) were both Harmsworth comics.
61. *LP*, 2 (May 1893), 42.
62. Anon., 'Of Cinderella the First. Her Greeting', in *Cinderella Annual*, 9–11.
63. In *LP*, 5 (Oct. 1896), 54, Trevor wrote of Cinderella's helpers, 'These people live amongst those they are trying to help, but one step above them in the scale of poverty'. Although it was only 'one step', a distinction was made nevertheless.

64. The movement's ultimate inability to avoid colonisation by middle- and upper-class philanthropists is revealed in the article 'Our Cinderella Club and What Became of It' (*Clarion*, 20 Feb. 1892, 6). As Chris Waters notes, by 1913, the Earl and Countess of Derby, the Lord Mayors of Manchester and Salford, and four Members of Parliament were patrons of the Manchester Cinderella Club. See *British Socialists and the Politics of Popular Culture, 1884–1914* (Manchester: Manchester University Press, 1990), 88.
65. Quotations from 'Nunquam', 'As I Lay a Thynkynge', *Clarion*, 19 Dec. 1891, 2.
66. 'Our Cinderella', *LP*, 2 (June 1893), 54–55.
67. *LP*, 2 (May 1893), 42–43.
68. 'Our Cinderella', 54.
69. E. M. M., 'The Garden of Children', *LP*, 4 (Jan. 1895), 5. The writer praises Froebel's Kindergarten system as a valuable form of child socialisation.
70. The Birmingham Cinderella Club's report on its weekly Cinderella meetings noted that the children were entertained with 'games, music, and a fairy tale'; a *Labour Prophet* correspondent suggested in 1893 that children in Cinderella clubs should be rewarded for winning games with 'a fairy story book given to them by Nunquam'. The Tottenham Cinderella Club reported on its first meeting in 1897: 'We sang old choruses, we told old nursery tales'. *LP*, 3 (Jan. 1894), 14; *LP*, 2 (Aug. 1893), 80, and *LP*, 6 (Feb. 1897), 30.
71. *LP*, 2 (Oct. 1893), 101.
72. *LP*, 3 (Mar./Apr. 1894), 48.
73. Quotations from *Tom Tit Tot: An Essay on Savage Philosophy in Folk-Tale* (London: Duckworth, 1898), 2–3 and 30–31.
74. *LP*, 3 (Aug. 1894), 111. The Labour Church subscribed to a notion of evolutionary progress without jettisoning the idea of a religious directive, as exemplified in the Church's fourth principle, 'That the emancipation of Labour can only be realised so far as men learn both the Economic and Moral Laws of God, and heartily endeavour to obey them'. Answering correspondent W.H.A. in Feb. 1894, Trevor summarised this idea of human action working with an evolutionary power succinctly: 'I should describe the religion of the Labour movement as working with God for the progress of Humanity'; see *LP*, 3 (Feb. 1894), 31.
75. Summers, 'Labour Church', 226. This application of Spencerian theory was reinforced by the new *Labour Prophet* editor Reginald A. Beckett in 1897, who stated that 'even our materialist philosophers tell us that there is a force in human affairs, which they name Evolution, by the irresistible operation of whose laws beneficent social changes are being inevitably brought about [..] we fight with Evolution and not against it'. See *LP*, 6 (Aug. 1897), 106. A text entitled *The Religion of Evolution* was also recommended in the correspondence class; see *LP*, 5 (Nov. 1896), 183.
76. Clodd's assertion that there was once a unity between 'nature' and 'super-nature' perhaps left him open to this reappropriation: see *Tom Tit Tot*, 2.
77. *The New Religion: Clarion Pamphlet 20* (London: Clarion Newspaper, 1897), 3.
78. *LP*, 4 (1895), 94.
79. *LP*, 1 (June 1892), 40.
80. Morris read aloud from *After London* to a meeting of Sheffield socialists in 1885. See Peter C. Gould, *Early Green Politics: Back to Nature, Back to the Land and Socialism in Britain 1880–1900* (Sussex: Harvester, 1988), 25 and 169n. *The Sorcery Shop*, subtitled 'an impossible romance', and serialised in the *Clarion* in 1907,

depicts a post-industrial Manchester. See Waters, *British Socialists*, 50–51, and 57–59.
81. See Müller, 'Comparative Mythology', in *Chips* (1867 edn), 1–143.
82. *LP*, 5 (Nov. 1896), 179.
83. Clarke edited a number of papers (*Teddy Ashton's Northern Weekly*, the *Cotton Factory Times* and *Liverpool Weekly Post*) all of which featured regional fictions by working-class writers. These are re-evaluated by Paul Salveson in 'Allen Clarke and the Lancashire School of Working-class Novelists', in Klaus, ed., *Rise of Socialist Fiction*, 172–202.
84. *LL*, 6 June 1896, 196. There were occasional changes in the column's title. For a period in 1895 it became 'Our Crusaders' before reverting to the former name.
85. *LL*, 20 June 1896, 214.
86. *My Quest for God* (London: Labour Prophet Office, 1897), 27 [italics in original].
87. 'A Talk About Fairies', *LL*, 20 June 1896, 214.
88. For an account of Clarke's role within the spiritualist movement, see Logie Barrow, *Independent Spirits: Spiritualism and English Plebeians, 1850–1900* (London: Routledge & Kegan Paul, 1986), 118–19.
89. Morgan has suggested that despite its anonymity, 'The children's column by "Daddy Time", with its sentimental references to pit ponies and to the countryside ("Mother Earth in her spring dress") was signed in every line' (*Keir Hardie*, 66). While such sensibilities were not restricted to Hardie alone, Morgan appears to be right, for the columns refer to Scottish childhood of 'Daddy Time', and the columns were passed over to 'Uncle Fred' for the duration of Hardie's American tour after the 1895 general election.
90. *LL*, 21 July 1894, 11.
91. *LL*, 14 July 1894, 11.
92. 'A Talk about Fairies', *LL*, 6 June 1896, 196.
93. Clarke in the *Clarion*, cited by Gould, *Early*, 38. On Clarke's co-operative community, see Paul Salveson, 'Getting Back to the Land. The Daisy Colony Experiment', *North West Labour History*, 10 (1984), 31–36.
94. *LL*, 26 Oct. 1895, 12.
95. *LL*, 18 May 1895, 12.
96. *LL*, 26 Oct. 1895, 12.
97. *LP*, 5 (Oct. 1896), 154.
98. *LP*, 1 (Oct. 1893), 101–02.
99. Thompson, 'Of the Birth of Cinderella' and Blatchford, 'Of the Children', in *The Cinderella Annual*, ed. MacDonald, 13–19 (16) and 24–28 (24); and *LL*, 28 Sept. 1895, 12.
100. *LP*, 4 (Apr. 1895), 63.
101. Anon., *LP*, 3 (Mar. 1895), 44. I expand this discussion of socialist attitudes to science in 'Making Socialists, or Murdering to Dissect? Natural History and Child Socialisation in the *Labour Prophet* and *Labour Leader*', in *Culture and Science in the Nineteenth-Century Media*, ed. Louise Henson et al. (Aldershot: Ashgate, 2004), 29–42.
102. *LL*, 31 Aug. 1895, 5.
103. Peter C. Gould notes that the Whitmanite club met for 25 years, singing songs, decorating boughs, and passing 'loving cups of comradeship' (*Early*, 32).
104. 'The Darkness of Midsummer', *LL*, 31 Aug. 1895, 5.
105. Peter C. Gould, *Early*, 15.
106. *LL*, 6 Oct. 1894, 11.

107. *LP*, 2 (Dec. 1893), 124. The text, first serialised in the *Clarion*, was available in book form in Nov. 1893.
108. Bevir, 'Labour Church', 240.
109. *LP*, 6 (May 1897), 77. This comment followed articles for children on the *Cinderella* pages.
110. *LL*, 22 June 1895, 12.
111. *LP*, 2 (May 1893), 38.
112. 'Sunday Schools for the Children', *LP*, 2 (Sept. 1894), 121.
113. See *The Complete Works of Elizabeth Barrett Browning*, ed. Charlotte Porter and Helen A. Clarke, 6 vols (New York: Crowell, 1900; repr. AMS Press, 1973), III, 53–59 (55).
114. *LP*, 3 (Jan. 1894), 12.
115. *LP*, 3 (Sept. 1894), 121.
116. 'Work in Our Sunday Schools', *LP*, 3 (Dec. 1894), 175.
117. *LP*, 2 (May 1893), 41.
118. *LP*, 4 (Mar. 1895), 44. All contributions by the fairy appeared under the title 'Our Cinderella Letter'.
119. *LP*, 4 (Aug. 1895), 126.
120. Quotations from *LP*, 4 (May 1895), 75–77.
121. Quotations from *LP*, 4 (June 1895), 93.
122. *LP*, 4 (Aug. 1895), 126. The writer is obviously somewhat confused about Andersen's date of birth.
123. *LP*, 4 (Aug. 1895), 27. Johann August Musäus's *Volksmärchen der Deutschen* (German Popular Tales) appeared in 5 vols in 1782. Musäus's fairy tales were translated by Thomas Carlyle, (*German Romance*, 2 vols, 1827). The works of Carlyle featured strongly in the recommended reading in working-class socialist periodicals, and his *Translations from Musäus, Tieck and Richter* feature among the books that could be won in the *Labour Leader* advertising promotion.
124. *LP*, 4 (July 1895), 110.
125. *Labour Church Record*, 2 (Apr. 1899), 1.
126. *LP*, 2 (May 1893), 43.
127. Such distinctions became less apparent during the period 'Uncle Fred' took over Hardie's columns, when the writer emphasised pantheism rather than ILP dogma. See *LL*, 24 Aug. 1895, 12.
128. As Andrew Wawn has shown, Norse mythology had filtered into children's literature by mid-century with the Keary sisters' highly popular *The Heroes of Asgard* (1857), which was re-issued in new editions in 1883 and 1891. See *The Vikings and the Victorians: Inventing the Old North in Nineteenth-Century Britain* (Cambridge: D. S. Brewer, 2000), 197–201.
129. See *LP*, 5 (Aug. 1896), 132–33; *LP*, 5 (Oct. 1896), 165; and *LP*, 6 (Apr. 1897), 61.
130. The first lecture in Carlyle's *On Heroes and Hero-Worship* (1841) is 'The Hero as Divinity', on Odin, paganism, and Scandinavian mythology. The book was featured as a set text in *Labour Prophet* Correspondence classes: see *LP*, 5 (Nov. 1896), 183.
131. *LP*, 6 (Dec. 1897), 197; and *LP*, 7 (Jan. 1897), 12.
132. *LP*, 3 (Dec. 1894), 174.
133. The fable of 'The Bundle of Sticks' was also directly alluded to on a number of union banners; see Gwyn A. Williams, Introduction to John Gorman, *Banner Bright* (Buckhurst Hill: Scorpion, 1986), 18–35.
134. *LP*, 4 (Mar. 1895), 46.

135. *LP*, 4 (Apr. 1895), 61; and *LP*, 4 (May 1895), 75.
136. For details of Hardie's involvement in these movements, see Morgan, *Keir Hardie* 9.
137. *LL*, 2 Apr. 1894, 11.
138. Humpherys, 'Popular Narrative and Political Discourse in *Reynolds's Weekly Newspaper*', in *Investigating Victorian Journalism*, 33–47 (34).
139. *LL*, 2 Apr. 1894, 11.
140. *LL*, 8 Apr. 1893, 1–3 (3). Bradford was the site of the inaugural meeting of the ILP in Jan. 1893, at which Hardie was instituted as Chairman.
141. *LL*, 25 Aug. 1894, 11.
142. *LL*, 25 Aug. 1894, 11.
143. *LL*, 8 Sept. 1894, 11.
144. *LL*, 15 Sept. 1894, 11.
145. Quotations from *LL*, 22 Sept. 1894, 11.
146. *LL*, 29 Sept. 1894, 11.
147. Morris cited in Yeo, 'New Life', 9. Yeo notes that one of Edward Carpenter's poems in his *Towards Democracy* (1883–1905) was entitled 'As a Woman to a Man', in which the poet takes a feminine persona, and 'Democracy' is presented as a highly sexualised male, an interesting homoerotic variant of the allegory used by Morris and Hardie.
148. *LL*, 29 Sept. 1894, 11.
149. *LL*, 20 and 27 July 1895, 12.
150. *LL*, 12 Sept. 1896, 322.
151. *LL*, 6 Oct. 1894, 11.
152. *LL*, 14 Sept. 1895, 12. After losing his parliamentary seat, Hardie left Britain in September for a four-month American tour. 'Uncle Fred' took over the column from 24 Aug. 1895 until Hardie's return in Jan. 1896.
153. Quotations from *LL*, 12 Sept. 1896, 322. See also *LL*, 27 Mar. 1897, 106, when Allen wrote back to complain about the reduced size of the section, with the reminder that the Crusaders were '1, 452 strong'.
154. *LL*, 2 Mar. 1895, 12.
155. See *LL*, 9 Feb., 1 June, 13 and 27 July, and 12 Oct. 1895, 12.
156. *LP*, 2 (Oct. 1893), 101.
157. *LL*, 9 Feb. and 27 Apr. 1895, 12; and 12 Sept. 1896, 322.
158. For further information on McArthur's role, see F. Reid, 'Socialist Sunday Schools in Britain 1892–1939', *International Review of Social History*, 11 (1966), 18–47.
159. *LP*, 5 (Oct. 1896), 166.
160. *LP*, 3 (Aug. 1894), 105.
161. Blatchford, *Fantasias*, 12.
162. *LL*, 25 Dec. 1897, 425.
163. *Commonweal*, 17 May 1890.
164. Wells, *A Modern Utopia*, ed. Gregory Claeys and Patrick Parrinder (London: Penguin, 2005), 11.
165. *Clarion*, 8 Oct. 1892, 2. Subsequently repr. as *The Tramp and Bob's Fairy, Clarion Tales for the People No.1* (London: Clarion Newspaper [n.d.]).

5 Fairy Tales and *fin-de-siècle* Little Magazines

1. Oscar Wilde, Preface, *The Picture of Dorian Gray* (1891 edn), in Wilde, *Plays Prose and Poems*, ed. Anthony Fothergill (London: Everyman, 1996) 138–253 (138).

2. Laurence Housman, Introduction, *Gammer Grethel's Fairy Tales* (London: Moring, 1905), v.
3. Letter to the editor of the *Pall Mall Gazette*, Dec. 1891, in *The Letters of Oscar Wilde*, ed. Rupert Hart-Davis (London: Hart-Davis, 1962), 301–02 (302).
4. For Beardsley's decadent visual/verbal parody, see 'The Slippers of Cinderella', *Yellow Book*, 2 (July 1894), 85.
5. While Laurence Housman is remembered as a minor dramatist, his own prolific output of stories, poetry, novels and fairy tales remains largely unexplored. Lorraine Kooistra Janzen's *The Artist as Critic: Bitextuality in fin-de-siècle Illustrated Books* (Aldershot: Scolar Press, 1995) analyses a number of Housman's illustrated texts, but refers to the fairy tales only in passing. Housman's 'The White Doe' is among fairy tales discussed by Claudia Nelson in 'Fantasies', 87–107.
6. Housman illustrated R. Nisbet Bain's *Weird Tales from the Northern Seas*, translated from the Danish folktales of Jonas Lie, for Kegan Paul in 1893. He was commissioned by Macmillan to design and illustrate an edition of Christina Rossetti's *Goblin Market* in the same year, and the first edition of *The End of Elfin-Town* for the same publisher in 1894. His own fairy-tale collections are *A Farm in Fairyland* (1894), *The House of Joy* (1895), *The Field of Clover* (1898), and *The Blue Moon* (1904). Two tales have been reprinted in anthologies: 'The Rooted Lover' from *A Farm in Fairyland* by Jack Zipes in *Victorian Fairy Tales*, 319–26; and 'Rocking-Horse Land', from *The Field of Clover* by Michael Patrick Hearn in the *Victorian Fairy Tale Book*, 318–24.
7. *The Venture*, ed. Laurence Housman and W. Somerset Maugham (London: Baillie, 1903/05).
8. Jackson, *The 1890s: A Review of Art and Ideas at the Close of the Nineteenth Century*, new edn (Hassocks: Harvester Press, 1913/1976), 36. Fletcher, 'Decadence and the Little Magazines' in *Decadence and the 1890s*, ed. Ian Fletcher (London: Edward Arnold, 1979), 173–202 (202).
9. Jackson's list includes The *Dome*, ed. Ernest J. Oldmeadow (London: Unicorn Press, Mar. 1897 to July 1900), quarterly, then monthly from Oct. 1898, 1s. The *Pageant*, ed. C. Hazelwood Shannon (Art) and Gleeson White (Literature) (London: Henry, 1896/97), annual, 6s. *The Parade: A Gift-Book for Boys and Girls*, ed. Gleeson White (London: Henry, 1897), one issue.
10. Dowling, 'Letterpress and Picture in the Literary Periodicals of the 1890s', *Yearbook of English Studies*, 16 (1986), 117–31.
11. Shannon was the designer of Wilde's *House of Pomegranates*.
12. The *Quest*, (Birmingham: Cornish Brothers; Boston: Updike, 1894–96), 6 issues, 2s. 6d. The *Quarto*, ed. John Bernard Holborn (London: Virtue, 1896–98), 6 issues. The *Beam*, ed. Alfred Jones (Manchester and London: John Heywood, 1896), 9d., bi-monthly.
13. Cited in Rodney Engen by *Laurence Housman* (Stroud: Catalpa Press, 1983), 95.
14. *The Dial*, ed. and publ. C. Hazelwood Shannon and Charles Ricketts (Chelsea: Vale Press, 1889–97), 5 issues, 7s. 6d.
15. Jackson, 36. The *Butterfly*, ed. Arnold Golsworthy and Leonard Raven Hill (London: Walter Haddon/Morland Judd, May 1893 to Feb. 1894; Grant Richards/New Century Press, Mar. 1899 to Feb. 1900), monthly, 6d.
16. 'VALE!', *Butterfly*, n.s. 2 (Feb. 1894), 248–49 (248).
17. Quotations from [John Bernard Holborn], 'Preface', *Quarto*, 4 (1898), 6–7 (6), and Golsworthy, 'VALE!', 248.
18. The first number of the *Quest* (Nov. 1894) notes that each edition is limited to 300 copies; the last edition of the *Quarto* was also 'strictly limited'; see *Quarto*,

4 (1898), 6. The *Dial* produced only 260 numbered copies per issue. On the *Century Guild Hobby Horse*'s sales, see Fletcher, 'Decadence', 183.
19. Arthur H. Mackmurdo, MCG [Member of Century Guild], 'The Guild's Flag Unfurling', *Century Guild Hobby Horse*, 1 (Apr. 1884), 2–13 (2). Ed. A. H. Mackmurdo and H. Horne (Orpington and London: G. Allan Sunnyside/Kegan Paul/Chiswick Press, 1884–92). Its spin-off was the *Hobby Horse* (Elkin Mathews and John Lane, 1893–94). Other quotations from J. B. H. [John Bernard Holborn], 'Preface', *Quarto*, 1 (1896), 9–10 (9), and *Pagan Review* (Aug. 1892), 1. Sharp pseudonymously provided the 'we' of the entire content, complete with advertisements at the back for the books of his alter egos.
20. Quotations from [L. Raven Hill and Arnold Golsworthy], 'Apology', *Butterfly*, 1 (May 1893), 5–7 (6), and J. B. H. [John Bernard Holborn],'Preface', *Quarto*, 1 (1896), 9–10 (9).
21. *Distinction: A Social Critique of the Judgement of Taste*, trans. Richard Nice (London: Routledge, 1986), 294.
22. *Dome*, 3 (Michelmas 1897), 92–93 (93).
23. See in particular Brake, 'Endgames: The Politics of the *Yellow Book* or, Decadence, Gender and the New Journalism', in *The Ending of Epochs*, ed. Laurel Brake (Woodbridge: D. S. Brewer, 1995), 38–64.
24. On Oldmeadow's numerous roles (and pseudonyms) within the *Dome*, see Arthur P. Ziegler Jr, 'The *Dome* and its Editor Publisher: An Exploration', *American Book Collector*, 15 (1965), 19–21.
25. 'J. E. Woodmeald' [Ernest J. Oldmeadow], 'The Editor of "The Jonquil"– A short story à la mode', *Dome*, n.s. 1 (Nov. 1898), 167–81 (176).
26. 'The Yellow Dwarf' [Henry Harland], 'A Birthday Letter from "The Yellow Dwarf"', *Yellow Book*, 9 (Apr. 1896), 11–22 (16).
27. All quotations from *Quest*, 1 (Nov. 1894), 43–46 and iv. On the marketing of *The House of Pomegranates* for adult audiences, see Josephine M. Guy and Ian Small, *Oscar Wilde's Profession: Writing and the Culture Industry in the Late Nineteenth Century* (Oxford: Oxford University Press, 2000), 77–83.
28. 'Reviews and Notices', *Dome*, n.s. 2 (Feb. 1899), 176.
29. *The Unexpected Years* (London: Cape, 1937), 114. Housman did publish his extended fairy tale 'The Enchanted Princess' (later republished as 'The Bound Princess' in *The Field of Clover*) in a children's periodical context. However, the *Parade* was a high-concept production that clearly targeted the adult collector as well as the children's market.
30. Image, 'A Lecture on Art', *Century Guild Hobby Horse*, 1 (Apr. 1884), 34–70 (36).
31. 'Some Reviews', *Quarto*, 4 (1898), 90–94 (90). The text under discussion is *Fairy Tales from Hans Andersen* (London: George Allen, 1898).
32. *Quest*, 2 (Mar. 1895), 'Advertisements', i.
33. Southall, for instance, exhibited his watercolour *Cinderella* at the Royal Academy. See *The Last Romantics: The Romantic Tradition in British Art, Burne Jones to Stanley Spencer*, ed. John Christian (London: Lund Humphries, 1989), 104–06.
34. Sidney Meteyard, 'Rapunzel', *Quest*, 6 (July 1896), 94. Meteyard taught at the Birmingham School of Art. In keeping with the view of civic arts encouraged by the Birmingham Guild, he also contributed to the Town Hall murals (1890) and was a respected designer in stained glass. See Christian, *Last Romantics*, 109–10.
35. See 'Rapunzel', in *The Early Romances of William Morris*, 2nd edn (London: Dent, 1913), 60–71 (69). 'The Prince's Song' from 'Rapunzel' was first published as 'Hands' in *Oxford and Cambridge Magazine*, 6 (July 1856).

36. Morris, 'Some Thoughts on the Ornamented Manuscripts of the Middle Ages', in *The Ideal Book: Essays and Lectures on the Arts of the Book*, ed. William S. Peterson (Berkeley: University of California Press, 1982), 1–14 (1); *Quest*, 1 (Nov. 1894), 'Advertisements', iii.
37. Morris, *Ideal Book*, 1 and 67.
38. For advertisements for collectors' and deluxe editions, see *Quarto*, 1 (1896), inside cover; *Dome*, 1 (Spring 1897), 88; *Butterfly*, 1 (Sept. 1893), 257. The trend for collectors' editions was perhaps most cynically exploited by the *Yellow Book*, which, though reprinted, was always passed off as a first edition: see Norman Denny, 'Bibliographical Note', *The Yellow Book: A Selection* (London: Spring Books [1949]), 14.
39. Housman, *Gammer Grethel*, vi.
40. *Fairy Tales: As They Are, as They Were, as They Should Be* (Brighton: Friend, 1889), 2–3.
41. 'A List of Books for and about Children' (London: Lane, [nd]), 10. Sharp's *Round the World to Wympland* (1902) was illustrated by an equally fashionable artist, Alice B. Woodward.
42. Sharp, *Fairy Tales*, 6.
43. 'The Soul of Man Under Socialism' in Wilde, *Plays, Prose*, 32; 'The Selfish Giant', in *The Happy Prince and Other Tales* (London: David Nutt, 1888), 42–55.
44. 'Introduction', *Beam*, 1 (Jan. 1896), 1–4 (3).
45. 'A List of Books', 7. J. M. Barrie's play *Peter Pan, or the Boy Who Wouldn't Grow Up* was first performed in London in 1904.
46. All quotations from *YB*, 10 (July 1896), 289–344. See also 'The Fisherman and his Soul' in *A House of Pomegranates* (London: Osgood, McIlvaine, 1891), 63–128.
47. Preface, *Tuscan Fairy Tales: Taken down from the Mouths of the People* (London: Satchell, 1880), 6–8. In medieval French romance, Mélusine is a fairy's daughter who is transformed into a serpent on every seventh day.
48. 'Sandro Botticelli (Filipepi)', *Dome*, 1 (Spring 1897), 81–87 (83).
49. Housman, Preface, *Gammer Grethel's Fairy Tales*, vi–vii.
50. 'Wordsworth', *Fortnightly Review*, Apr. 1874, repr. in *Appreciations*, 2nd edn (London: Macmillan, 1890), 37–63 (54).
51. See Steedman, *Strange Dislocations: Childhood and the Idea of Human Interiority, 1780–1930* (London: Virago, 1995), 81–95, Shuttleworth, 'The Psychology of Childhood in Victorian Literature and Medicine', in *Literature, Science and Psychoanalysis 1830–1870 – Essays in Honour of Gillian Beer*, ed. Helen Small and Trudi Tate (Oxford: Oxford University Press, 2003) 86–101 and Taylor, Jenny Bourne, 'Between Atavism and Altruism: The Child on the Threshold in Victorian Psychology and Edwardian Children's Fiction', in *Children in Culture*, ed. Karín Lenik-Oberstein (Basingstoke: Macmillan, 1998), 88–121.
52. All quotations from Fenton, 'Folk-Lore in Relation to Psychology and Education', *Folk-Lore Journal*, 1 (Aug. 1883), 258–66.
53. 'How Little Duke Jarl Saved the Castle', *Dome*, n.s. 4 (Oct. 1899), 174–78; 'The Defence of Farvingdon', *Dome*, n.s. 2 (Jan. 1899), 2–16.
54. Quotations from *Dome*, n.s. 1 (Oct. 1898), 7–12.
55. Wilde, 'Soul of Man', 43. For a discussion of Wilde's 'inversion of established relations between concepts', see Regenia Gagnier, *Idylls of the Marketplace: Oscar Wilde and the Victorian Public* (Aldershot: Scolar Press, 1987), 10 and 31–34.
56. *Butterfly*, n.s. 2 (Jan. 1900), 228–36 (228).
57. Preface, *The Renaissance: Studies in Art and Poetry, the 1893 Text*, ed. Donald L. Hill (Berkeley: University of California Press, 1980), xix–xxv (xx).

58. *Dome*, n.s. 2 (Feb. 1899), 118–24 (124).
59. See *Dome*, n.s. 1 (Oct. 1898). In Ballet, Pantomime and Poetic Drama' (65–71), Symons's descriptions of pantomime could easily be applied to the folktale: 'it addresses itself, by the artful limitations of its craft, to universal human experience [...] And it appeals, perhaps a little too democratically, to people of all nations' (67).
60. *Dome*, n. s. 4 (Aug. 1899), 162–66 (166).
61. In his introduction to *Fairy Tales and Folk Tales* Yeats claimed that 'These folktales are full of simplicity and musical occurrences, for they are the literature of a class for whom every incident in the old rut of birth, love, pain and death has cropped up unchanged for centuries: who have steeped everything in the heart: to whom everything is a symbol' (xii).
62. 'Ancient Legends of Ireland', *Century Guild Hobby Horse*, 2 (1887), 67–74 (73).
63. All quotations from *Dome*, n.s. 3 (July 1899), 209–18 (209).
64. All quotations from 'Proem', *Evergreen* (Spring 1895), 9–15. *The Evergreen*, ed. Patrick Geddes (Edinburgh: Patrick Geddes; London: T. Fisher Unwin; America: J. B. Lippincott, 1894–96), 5s. *The New Evergreen: The Christmas Book of University Hall* appeared in 1894, then 4 issues were produced over a year-and-a-half, titled in accordance with the seasons.
65. *Evergreen* (Summer 1896), 73–85 (81). Linda Dowling has suggested that oral folk forms enjoyed a renaissance in the 1890s as a response to fears over linguistic degeneration: see *Language and Decadence in the Victorian Fin de Siècle* (Princeton, NJ: Princeton University Press, 1986), 181–83 and 244–83.
66. Quotations from Thomson, 'Germinal, Floreal, Prairial', 25, and Thomson and MacDonald, 'Proem', 15.
67. 'The Myth of Demeter and Persephone II', *Fortnightly Review*, Feb. 1876, repr. in *Greek Studies* (London: Macmillan, 1895), 114–55 (128). In his first article, Pater clearly shows the influence of Müller and the solar mythology thesis, yoking Greek mythological heroes such as Adonis, Hyacinth and Adrastus with 'the English Sleeping Beauty' as allegories for seasonal change. See 'The Myth of Demeter and Persephone I', *Fortnightly Review*, Jan. 1876., repr. in *Greek Studies*, 79–113 (109–10). For analysis of coded discourse in Pater's mythological studies, see Richard Dellamora, *Masculine Desire: The Sexual Politics of Victorian Aestheticism* (Chapel Hill, NC: University of North Carolina Press, 1990), 167–92.
68. In John Duncan's 'Apollo's School-Days', which directly followed a scientific counter-blast against decadence by Patrick Geddes, a leering Pan holds a naked Apollo. Another homoerotic drawing by Duncan, 'Out-Faring', appeared in the same edition. See *Evergreen* (Spring 1895), 40 and 54.
69. Conclusion, *The Renaissance*, 186–90 (189).
70. 'Jules Barbey D'Aurevilly', *Pageant*, 2 (1897), 18–31. See also Dion Clayton Calthrop's visual image 'Tying a Stock', *Butterfly*, n.s. 2 (Feb. 1900), 291.
71. '"Decadent Spaces": Notes for a Phenomenology of the *Fin de Siècle*', in *Decadence and the 1890s*, ed. Fletcher, 31–58 (33–34).
72. Symons, *The Symbolist Movement in Literature*, 2nd edn (London: Constable, 1908), 7.
73. *Quarto*, 4 (1898), 17–20 (19).
74. *Pageant*, 1 (1896), 230–35
75. All quotations from 'Of Purple Jars', *Pageant*, 2 (1897), 199–220 and Pater, 'The Child in the House: An Imaginary Portrait' in *Macmillan's Magazine*, Aug. 1878, repr. in *Miscellaneous Studies*, 3rd edn (London: Macmillan, 1900), 147–69 (150).

See also Huysmans, *Against Nature*, trans. Robert Baldick (Penguin: Harmondsworth, 1959).
76. See 'The Critic as Artist', in *Intentions*, 8th edn (London: Methuen, 1913), 153–217.
77. Preface, *The Picture of Dorian Gray* (138); 'The Devoted Friend', in *The Happy Prince and Other Tales* (London: David Nutt, 1888), 57–85 (85).
78. All quotations from 'Blind Love', *Pageant*, 2 (1897), 64–81. See also *Selections from the Writings of William Blake: With an Introductory Essay by Laurence Housman* (London: Kegan, Paul, Trench, Trübner, 1893), 95–96, II, 9.
79. Quotations from *Dome*, n.s. 1 (Dec. 1898), 233–37 (233).
80. *Selections from the Writings of William Blake*, xxii.
81. Housman, *Gammer Grethel*, vii.
82. Symons, *Symbolist Movement*, 8.
83. 'The Book Illustrations of Laurence Housman', *Artist*, 21 (Feb. 1898), 99–103 (102).
84. *Symbolist Movement*, 7.
85. Symons cited by G. L. L. Morris in 'Notes on Decadence,' *Beam*, 2 (Mar. 1896), 55–59 (55–56). Despite describing Symons as 'an aggressive youth', Morris is broadly in agreement with his analysis.
86. *Dome*, n.s. 5 (Nov. 1899), 67–80 (68).
87. In the Grimms' text, the devil tricks a miller into promising him his daughter, but her piety means that he can only take hold of her if her father cuts off her hands. She obediently consents, but weeps pure tears on the stumps so that she is still beyond the devil's reach. She marries a king; her trust in God means she is protected by an angel through various trials set by the devil, and eventually her hands grow back. Housman inverts the tale (it is the body, not the hands, that reappear) and infuses the daughter's obedience, piety and self-abnegation with more complex erotic implications. While 'The Girl without Hands' was not included in Edgar Taylor's edition, readers would be likely to be familiar with this text from its publication in *Grimms' Household Tales*, trans. Margaret Hunt (1884), I, 127–32.
88. All quotations from 'The Helping Hands', *Butterfly*, n.s. 1 (July 1899), 220–28.
89. Pater, 'Dante Gabriel Rossetti', in *Appreciations*, 213–27 (220–21), original emphasis. Pater presents Rossetti's fusion of the concrete and the abstract as a return to origins, drawing on the solar mythology thesis: 'With him indeed, as in some revival of the old mythopœic age, common things – dawn, noon, night – are full of human or personal expression, full of sentiment' (219).
90. 'Simeon Solomon: Notes on his "Vision of Love" and other Studies', *Dark Blue* (July 1871), 568–77 (568).
91. 'The Painting of the Nineteenth Century', in *Studies in the Seven Arts* (London: Constable, 1906), 33–68 (61).
92. The drawing owned by Wilde was 'Love amongst the Schoolboys', later auctioned at his bankruptcy. See Simon Reynolds, *The Vision of Simeon Solomon* (Stroud: Catalpa Press, 1984), 26.
93. Dellamora, *Masculine*, 46.
94. Small, Introduction, Oscar Wilde, *The Complete Short Fiction*, ed. Ian Small (London: Penguin, 1994), xxvii.
95. *Artist*, 21 (Feb. 1898), 99–103 (102).
96. Burton added the *Supplemental Nights* in 1887. The Kama Shastra Society was founded by Burton, F. F. Arbuthnot and Richard Moncton-Milnes and published a number of erotic Indian and Arab works. After Burton's death, in collaboration

with H. S. Nichols, Smithers issued a twelve-volume edition of Burton's translation (1894–97), which censored some of the 'Terminal Essay'. See Collette Colligan, '"Esoteric Pornography": Sir Richard Burton's *Arabian Nights* and the Origins of Pornography'. *Victorian Review* 28: 2 (2002), 31–64; and Colligan, *The Traffic in Obscenity from Byron to Beardsley* (Basingstoke: Palgrave Macmillan, 2006), 56–95.

97. Burton, 'Terminal Essay: Section D, "Pederasty"', *The Book of the Thousand Nights and a Night: A Plain and Literal Translation of the Arabian Nights Entertainments*, 10 vols ([n.p.] Burton Club: [1886]), X, 63–260, 179–80. Burton claimed that region had a key part to play, finding pederasty to be 'geographical and climatic, not racial' (180).

98. On the debate over pornography that this work engendered in nineteenth-century periodicals, see Ali, Colligan and Dane Kennedy, '"Captain Burton's Oriental Muck Heap": *The Book of the Thousand Nights* and the Uses of Orientalism', *Journal of British Studies*, 39 (2000), 317–39. Matt Cook offers a brief discussion of the text in *London and the Culture of Homosexuality, 1885–1914* (Cambridge: Cambridge University Press, 2003), but doesn't focus explicitly on its reception (92, 97).

99. Preface, *Stories from the Arabian Nights* (London: Hodder and Stoughton, 1907), vi–vii.

100. *Butterfly*, n.s. 1 (May 1899), 89–98.

101. See Vanke, 'Arabesques: North Africa, Arabia and Europe', in *Art Nouveau 1890–1914*, ed. Paul Greenhalgh (London: V&A Publications, 2000), 114–25.

102. In 'Theodora: A Fragment', *Yellow Book*, 4 (Jan. 1895), 156–88; Eastern artefacts become metaphors for both male and female desire and seduction. See also 'Apamé', *Butterfly*, 1 (Aug. 1893), 197–206.

103. Quotations from 'The Great Worm', *Dial*, 1 (1889), 14–18. See also 'Green-Serpent', in *The Fairy Tales of the Countess d'Aulnoy*, ed. J. R. Planché (London: Routledge, 1855), 302–31. The visual similarities between Ricketts' work on 'The Great Worm' and his head and tail pieces for *The House of Pomegranates* are striking.

104. In Wilde's tale, a nightingale pierces her heart with a thorn to turn a white rose red, so that a student may dance with his love, a professor's daughter. The rose is scorned by the lover in favour of jewels, and the nightingale dies in vain – an ironic reversal of the H. C. Andersen tale, in which nature is finally prized over artifice. See 'The Nightingale and the Rose', in *The Happy Prince and Other Tales*, 25–41.

105. 'Hirosage: An Appreciation', *Dome*, 3 (Winter 1897), 63–70 (70).

106. 'Utamaro: An Appreciation', *Dome*, n.s. 1 (Oct. 1898), 21–26 (23).

107. On Wilde, Japan and aestheticism, see Matt Cook, *London*, 97.

108. Lowell cited by Anna Jackson in 'Orient and Occident', in *Art Nouveau*, ed. Greenhalgh, 100–113 (111).

109. *Dome*, 5 (May 1898), 81. [John] Byam [Liston] Shaw trained at the Royal Academy and exhibited there from 1893. The Arts and Crafts influence can be detected in Shaw's eclecticism: as well as a painter and illustrator, he was a designer of stained glass, theatrical sets and tapestry: see Christian, *Last Romantics*, 121–22.

110. In the *Venture*, Housman alluded to a very different Oriental culture, providing a drawing of four mandarins which later became an illustration to 'A Chinese Fairy Tale', a text published in *The Blue Moon*, Housman's fourth fairy-tale collection. China was associated particularly with stereotypes of degeneracy and sexuality, including homosexuality in Burton's account; see Matt Cook, *London*, 92.

111. Eve Kosovsky Sedgwick is among the many writers who have stressed the importance of the trials in creating a publicly defined concept of homosexual identity: see *Between Men: English Literature and Male Homosocial Desire* (New York: Columbia University Press, 1985), 216–17. Alan Sinfield and Joseph Bristow have both seen the trials as the key moment at which effeminacy and homosexuality became linked in the public consciousness: see Sinfield, *The Wilde Century: Effeminacy, Oscar Wilde, and the Queer Moment* (New York: Columbia University Press, 1994) and Bristow, *Effeminate England: Homoerotic Writing After 1885* (New York: Columbia University Press, 1995).
112. 'The Blue Moon', *Butterfly*, n.s. 1 (May 1899), 89–98 (90).
113. Although the date of its first usage is unclear, the term 'pansy' for a homosexual man was extremely common in the New York of the 1920s and 1930s: see George Chauncey, *Gay New York: The Making of the Gay Male World, 1890–1940* (London: Flamingo, 1995). The earliest entry in the *OED* as slang for 'an effeminate man or homosexual' dates from 1929. See *A Farm in Fairyland*, 59–75.
114. 'The Blue Moon', 89–90.
115. Cited by R. K. R. Thornton, in '"Decadence" in Later Nineteenth-Century England', in *Decadence and the 1890s*, ed. Fletcher, 15–29 (19–20).
116. Gagnier, *Idylls*, 19.
117. 'The Blue Moon', 94.
118. 'Blind Love', *Pageant*, 2 (1897), 73; 'Yai and the Moon', 143–55.
119. See Janzen, *Bitextuality*, 156. On the moon's wider associations with female sexuality in this period, see Bram Dijkstra, *Idols of Perversity: Fantasies of Feminine Evil in fin-de-siècle Culture* (Oxford: Oxford University Press, 1986), 119–32 and 238–39.
120. 'The Blue Moon, 94 and 97.
121. *A Vision of Love Revealed in Sleep* (private publication, 1871), repr. in Reynolds, *The Vision of Simeon Solomon*, 39–79.
122. 'The Work of Laurence Housman', repr. in Engen, *Laurence Housman*, 139–47 (141). Kains-Jackson elaborates Housman's Hellenistic influences: 'The New Orpheus', *Dome*, n.s. 2 (Feb. 1899), 94–98, is also singled out for attention, while Housman's tendency to draw small heads is seen to incline 'to the Greek'. Kains-Jackson also notes that the 'female figure in Mr. Housman's drawings is perhaps less prominent than the male' (144–46).
123. Quotations from Burton, 'Terminal Essay', 183, 218. The translation from Ovid, *Metamorphoses* (book 10.1. 79–80, 83–85) is that given by Chris White in *Nineteenth-Century Writings on Homosexuality: A Sourcebook*, ed. Chris White (London: Routledge, 1999), 347n.
124. Dowling, *Hellenism and Homosexuality in Victorian Oxford* (Ithaca, NY: Cornell University Press, 1994), 67–103.
125. 'The Dantesque and Platonic Ideals of Love', in *In the Key of Blue and Other Prose Essays* (London: Elkin Mathews, 1893, repr. 1918), 55–86 (70).
126. Quotations from Symonds, 'Dantesque', 65; and Burton, 'Terminal Essay', 186.
127. My own use of the term 'homosexual' largely follows Dellamora, who uses the word in relation to pre-1890s culture only with care (*Masculine*, 167). Bristow makes a useful observation concerning the 'uneven' cultural transformation in ways of both naming and conceiving such sexualities in this period: his own range of terms include 'homophile', 'same-sex' and 'homosexual' (*Effeminate*, 3).
128. Symonds, *A Problem in Greek Ethics* (private publication, 1883), vi–xx repr. in Chris White, *Nineteenth-Century Writings*, 165–73 (165–66).
129. See Fletcher, 'Decadence', 182–88; Brake, '"Gay Discourse" and the *Artist and Journal of Home Culture*', in *Nineteenth-Century Media and the Construction of*

Identities, ed. Laurel Brake, Bill Bell and David Finkelstein (Basingstoke: Palgrave Macmillan, 2000), 271–91; and d'Arch Smith, *Love in Earnest: Some Notes on the Lives and Writings of English 'Uranian' Poets from 1889–1930* (London: Routledge & Kegan Paul, 1970). It should be noted that there are problems with d'Arch Smith's approach (he uses the term 'Uranian' to denote 'boy-love' rather than the more varied manifestations of homosexuality in this period). Kains-Jackson's article 'The New Chivalry', which used Darwinian and neo-Malthusian arguments to assert the spiritually (and by implication) sexually elevated status of male/male relationships, led to his resignation. See *Artist*, 15 (Apr. 1894), 102–04. The response to this article confirms the point made by both Brake and Bristow: that hostility to this use of classical discourse was registered before as well as after the Wilde trials.

130. *Coming Out: Homosexual Politics in Britain from the Nineteenth Century to the Present*, rev. edn (London: Quartet Books, 1990), 122–27 (122). See also Weeks, *Sex, Politics and Society: The Regulation of Sexuality since 1800* (London: Longman, 1981), 114; and John Stokes, *Oscar Wilde: Myths, Miracles and Imitations* (Cambridge: Cambridge University Press, 1996), 68. Stokes dates the beginning of the order around 1893.

131. *Fairy Tales by the Abbé Voisenon*, trans. R. B. Douglas. A hundred copies were printed, which like Burton's text, gave a false place of publication. The British Library copy retains an inserted manuscript letter from Smithers to 'My Dear Ashbee'. Henry Spencer Ashbee ['Pisanus Fraxi'] was responsible for a three-volume bibliography of historical obscenity between 1877 and 1885 (see Colligan, *Traffic*, 7). He is likely to be the same Ashbee referenced in pencil marginalia at the front of the BL copy of *The New and Gorgeous Pantomime entitled Harelquin Prince Cherrytop and the Good Fairy Fairfuck: or the Frig the Fuck and the Fairy (Theatre Royal Olymprick Private Imprint)*. On Teleny, which was completed as a collaborative text in a Soho bookshop before being revised and republished by Smithers, see Matt Cook, *London*, 104–05.

132. Beardsley's fantasy has already received significant scholarly attention: see, for example, Prickett, *Victorian Fantasy*, 107–12, and Emma Sutton, *Aubrey Beardsley and British Wagnerism* (Oxford: Oxford University Press, 2002), 143–65.

133. Kains-Jackson, 'The Work of Laurence Housman', 144.

134. Gleeson White, 'The Editor's Room', *Studio*, 4–6 (Oct. 1894 to Jan. 1896), xli.

135. See d'Arch Smith, *Love*, 62 and 66; and Brake, 'Gay Discourse', 272.

136. The BSSP, established in 1914, campaigned for sexual reform in a range of areas. Edward Carpenter was the first president, and homosexual men were always significant in its membership. See Weeks, *Coming Out*, 124 and 132; and Housman, *Echo de Paris: A Study from Life* (London: Jonathan Cape, 1923), 56–60. See also the letter from Havelock Ellis to Housman dated 31 May 1903, in the Adelman Collection, LH1, Brynmawr College Library, in which Ellis informs Housman about the new edition of *Sexual Inversion*. I am grateful to Miriam B. Spectre, Special Collections Librarian, for information about Housman holdings.

137. *OED*. Quotation from the *American Journal of Psychology*, 7 (1895), 216.

138. Chauncey, *Gay*, 54. On appropriations of fairy ballet in this context, see Stoneley, *Queer History*, 22–45.

139. Symonds remained anonymous on publication. For a detailed summary of Ulrich's theory, see Symonds, '*A Problem in Modern Ethics': Being an Enquiry into the Phenomenon of Sexual Inversion* (Davos: [n. pub] [1891?]), 64–88. As Bristow notes, Symonds also challenged the extent of Ulrich's biological determinism, and was more willing to acknowledge cultural explanations (*Effeminate*, 134).

140. *The Intermediate Sex: A Study of Some Transitional Types of Men and Women*, 2nd edn (London: S. Sonnenschein, 1909), 10.
141. 'Symbols of the Sacred and Profane', in *Art Nouveau*, ed. Greenhalgh, 78.
142. 'Stories Toto Told Me: "About What is Due to Repentance"', *Butterfly*, n.s. 1 (Aug. 1899), 267–75.
143. *Yellow Book*, 9 (Apr. 1896), 93–101 (96).
144. *Butterfly*, n.s. 1 (July 1899), 192.
145. On Pater's oblique references to Solomon, see Dellamora, *Masculine*, 177–78.
146. Symons, *Studies*, 61; Pater, 'The Age of Athletic Prizemen: A Chapter in Greek Art', in *Greek Studies*, 283–315 (304).
147. See, for example, Ricketts, 'Psyche in the House' and 'Oedipus – after a pen drawing' (*Pageant*, 1 (1896), 53 and 65); Moreau, 'Hercules and the Hydra'; Rossetti, 'La Pia' and 'Hamlet and Ophelia'; and Burne-Jones, 'Perseus and the Sea-Maidens' (*Pageant*, 2 (1897), frontispiece, 43, 57 and 99) and 'Vivien and Merlin' *Dome*, 3 (Michelmas 1897), 53.
148. Wedmore cited by Fletcher in 'Decadence', 195. See 'The Reflected Faun', *YB*, 1 (Apr. 1894), 117.
149. See Engen, *Laurence Housman*, 55–56. 'Barren Life' was published in *YB*, 10 (July 1896), 261–63.
150. Quotations from 'Tales of a Woodcutter', *Butterfly*, n.s. 2 (Feb. 1900), 249–58.
151. *Dome*, n.s. 1 (Oct. 1898), 90 (l. 1–4).
152. *Dome*, 5 (May 1898), 30.
153. Yeats provided a symbolic key to his 'Song of Mongan': 'the hazel tree was the Irish tree of Life or of Knowledge, and in Ireland it was doubtless, as elsewhere, the tree of the heavens'. See *Dome*, n.s. 1 (Oct. 1898), 36. On the 'Dry Tree', see Amanda Hodgson, *The Romances of William Morris* (Cambridge: Cambridge University Press, 1987), 174 and 193.
154. *Yellow Book*, 1 (Apr. 1894), 57–60.
155. 'Tales of a Woodcutter', 254; Richard Ellmann, *Oscar Wilde* (Harmondsworth: Penguin, 1988), 435.
156. Quotation from 'The Ballad of Reading Gaol', in *Plays Prose and Poems*, 60–74 (61), l. 37.
157. 'Tales of a Woodcutter', 257. There appear to be interesting intertextual connections between Housman's tale, A. E. Housman's *A Shropshire Lad*, and Wilde's 'The Ballad of Reading Gaol'. In 1897, Wilde wrote to Laurence Housman, mentioning reading 'your brother's lovely lyrical poems'. In the same year, Wilde replied to a letter from Laurence, noting 'I am occupied in finishing a poem, terribly realistic for me [...] I will send it to you, if you allow me, when it appears'. Housman received 'Reading Gaol' in early 1898: see *More Letters of Oscar Wilde*, ed. Rupert Hart-Davis (Oxford: Oxford University Press, 1985), 152 and 167. Ruth Robbins has highlighted the similarities between A. E. Housman's poem IX, about the prisoners in Shrewsbury jail who 'dead on air will stand', and Wilde's reference to a similar 'dance upon the air' in *The Ballad of Reading Gaol*; it is likely that Laurence's intimate knowledge of both texts influenced his use of this particular metaphor for social martyrdom. See Robbins, '"A very curious construction": Masculinity and the Poetry of A. E. Housman and Oscar Wilde', in *Cultural Politics at the Fin de Siècle*, ed. Sally Ledger and Scott McCracken (Cambridge: Cambridge University Press, 1995), 137–59 (153).
158. See Ellmann, *Oscar Wilde*, 445–49.
159. See Housman, *Echo de Paris*, 55–60.

160. 'Tales of a Woodcutter', 258.
161. Fletcher, 'Union and Beauty' (unpublished doctoral dissertation, University of Reading, 1965), 518.
162. 'Prince Charming', *Artist and Journal of Home Culture*, 15 (Apr. 1894), 102; 'The New Chivalry', 102–04.
163. D'Arch Smith, 191. He points in particular to Douglas's poems 'Perkin Warbeck' (in which the son of a weaver is elevated to the status of king) and 'Jonquil and Fleur-de-Lys', in which a prince and a shepherd reverse roles (191–95).
164. There are interesting parallels between such strategies and those utilised in the book that made Housman's name, *An Englishwoman's Love Letters* (London: John Murray, 1900). This anonymous fictional account of a woman's unrequited love for a man was widely praised in the press when its author was thought to be a woman; the book was heavily criticised when Housman's gender became apparent. See Engen, *Laurence Housman*, 110.
165. 'The Work of Laurence Housman', repr. in Engen, *Laurence Housman*, 139–47 (147.) Kains-Jackson suggests that while Housman's note in poetry 'is wholly his own', 'Lord Alfred Douglas is of the company'; one of Housman's illustrations to Clemence Housman's *The Werewolf* is seen to evoke 'something that Aubrey Beardsley never quite reached with the pencil; though Count Eric Stenbock in England and Guy de Maupassant in France (so also Apuleius in his decadent Latin) have reached it in prose' (141). Even in the decade after the Wilde trials, Douglas's name had an obvious resonance. Count Stenbock also used fairy-tale and fantasy motifs to engage with homoerotic themes. While Kains-Jackson attempts to ally Housman with decadence as an inter-generic stylistic movement, his examples clearly link sexuality and style.

Conclusion: Myth in the Marketplace

1. Benjamin, 'The Storyteller; Reflections of the Works of Nikolai Leskov', in *Illuminations*, ed. Hannah Arendt, trans. Harry Zohn (London; Fontana, 1973), 83–109 (83–84).
2. Benjamin, 'Storyteller', 102.
3. Benjamin, 'Storyteller', 87–88. On perceptions of mass print's corrosive influence, see also Benjamin, *One-Way Street & Other Writings*, trans. Edmund Jephcott and Kingsley Shorter (London: NLB, 1979), 62.
4. Zipes, *Fairy Tale as Myth Myth as Fairy Tale* (Kentucky: University Press of Kentucky, 1994), 6. Benjamin refers to the fairy tale's 'liberating magic' ('Storyteller', 102); Zipes discusses its 'liberating potential', and argues that some Victorian writers were able to recognise 'the utopian kernel in the original folktales' (*Subversion*, 100–01). Although Zipes's recent work has focused on 'memes' as ways of theorising the transmission of classic fairy tales in *Why Fairy Tales Stick* (London: Routledge, 2006), he does not disavow the political assumptions of earlier work.
5. *MM*, 7 (Nov. 1862), 54–60 (60).
6. The phrase 'Darwinian romance' is Beer's; see *Darwin's Plots*, 123.
7. See for instance, Julia Reid's exploration of 'organic memory' and evolutionary psychology in *Stevenson*, 13–29.
8. *The Red Fairy Book*, xvi.

9. The bookless future was a common trope in the 1890s: see Brantlinger, *The Reading Lesson: The Threat of Mass Literacy in Nineteenth-Century British Fiction* (Bloomington, IN: Indiana University Press, 1998).
10. Garrigan Mattar, *Primitivism*, 247.
11. 'Reviews', *Athenæum*, 26 Feb. 1853, 247–48 (247).
12. Stewart, *Crimes*, 69.
13. The best-known recent formulation of an 'imagined community' forged through the simultaneous, virtual newspaper moment is Benedict Andersons: see *Imagined Communities* (London: Verso, 1983), 39–40.
14. Autobiography of Pietari Päivärinta (1877), cited and trans. Apo, *Narrative*, 45. I am grateful to Neil Philip for this reference.
15. Although the press is very different in the 1830s and the 1890s, I have argued elsewhere that the belief that the mass media had just arrived was expressed in every decade from at least the 1830s: see Sumpter, 'The Cheap Press and the "Reading Crowd": Visualising Mass Culture and Modernity, 1838–1910', *Media History*, 12 (Autumn 2006), 233–52.

Bibliography

Archival material

Gatty family papers, Hunter Archaeological Society, Sheffield Archives.
Macmillan Papers, British Library

Other material

Aarsleff, Hans, *The Study of Language in England, 1760–1860* (Princeton, NJ: Princeton University Press, 1967).
Ali, Muhsin Jassim, *Scheherazade in England: A Study of Nineteenth-Century English Criticism of the Arabian Nights* (Washington, DC: Three Continents Press, 1981).
Altick, Richard, *The English Common Reader: A Social History of the Mass Reading Public*. 2nd edn (1957; Columbus, OH: Ohio State University Press, 1998).
Anderson, Benedict, *Imagined Communities* (London: Verso, 1983).
Andersen, Hans Christian, *Danish Fairy Legends and Tales* [trans. Caroline Peachey], (London: William Pickering, 1846).
——, *A Danish Story Book*, trans. Charles Boner (London: Joseph Cundall, 1846).
——, 'The Dying Child', trans. H. Ward, *AJM*, 4 (Apr. 1868), 337.
——, *Fairy Tales from Hans Andersen: With an Introduction by Edward Clodd* (London: Wells Gardner, Darton, 1901).
——, *Hans Christian Andersen's Visits to Charles Dickens as Described in his Letters*. Comp. Ejnar Munksgaard (Copenhagen: Levin & Munksgaard, 1970).
——, 'The Little Ugly Duck', *London Journal*, 6 (Nov. 1847), 148.
——, 'The Mermaid', trans. Lady Duff-Gordon, *Bentley's Miscellany*, 19 (Apr. 1846), 377–90.
——, 'The Red Shoes' [trans. Mary Howitt], *Howitt's Journal*, 11 Sept. 1847, 171–73.
——, 'Two Stories from Hans Christian Andersen', *GWY*, 2 (July 1870), 474–76.
——, *Wonderful Stories for Children*, trans. Mary Howitt (London: Chapman and Hall, 1846).
Anon., 'Altrive Tales: Collected among the Peasantry of Scotland' (Review), *Fraser's*, 5 (May 1832), 482–89.
——, 'The Arabian Nights Entertainments', *Chatterbox* (1883), 55.
——, Books for Children', *Athenæum*, 25 July 1846, 759.
——, 'Chap-Books', *Chambers's*, 1 Feb. 1862, 72–74.
——, 'Chap-Book Literature', *Chambers's*, 7 July 1855, 1–2.
——, 'Chambers's Edinburgh Journal', *Chambers's*, 2 Feb. 1833, 1–2; 27 Jan. 1838, 8.
——, 'Children's Literature', *London Quarterly Review*, 13 (Jan. 1860), 469–500.
——, 'Cinderella Downstairs', *Chambers' Journal* (July 1882), 423–24.
——, 'A Danish Story-book', *Chambers's*, 10 Oct. 1846, 239.
——, 'Dissent in the Church in Wales: Conditions of the Welsh Peasantry', *Fraser's*, 6 (Sept. 1832), 170–83.
——, 'Dorf Juystein', *Fraser's*, 5 (May 1832) 489–92.
——, 'Fairyland and Fairies', *Chambers's*, 15 July 1882, 454–56.
——, 'Fairy Tales', *MP*, n.s. 25 (Jan. 1878), 80–94.

——, 'The Four Friends: A Translation', *Cinderella*, *LP*, 3 (Dec. 1894), 174.
——, 'Four Notes', *Dome*, 3 (Michelmas 1897), 92–93.
——, 'Fragments from German Prose Writers', *Athenæum*, 29 May 1841, 424.
——, 'How we get our Newspapers', *AYR*, 25 Dec. 1875, 305–09.
——, 'The Hermit in Ireland No V: Doings at Carlow', *Dublin and London Magazine* (July 1825), 205–08.
——, 'Ingleborough Within', *Chambers's*, 29 May 1858, 341–44 (342).
——, 'King Arthur's Great Boar Hunt: An Ancient British Fairy Tale II', *GWY*, 3 (Apr. 1871), 329–33.
——, 'Magazine Literature', *Church Quarterly Review*, 3 (Jan. 1877), 380–93.
——, 'Marty's Escape', *AJM*, 7 (May 1869), 44–47.
——, 'Mr Kingsley's Water-Babies', *Times*, 26 Jan. 1864, 6.
——, 'Newspapers', *Chambers's*, 9 Nov. 1844, 296.
——, 'Princess Bluestocking or, the Rival Brothers', *AJM*, 9 (Dec. 1870), 89–101.
——, 'The Princesses (adapted)', *LP*, 4 (Mar. 1895), 44.
——, 'Progress of the British Boy – Past and Present', *Boys of England*, 24 Nov. 1866, 4–5.
——, 'Shoemaker, stick to your last', *Chatterbox*, 20 Jan. 1875, 62–63.
——, 'Soluble Silver', *Chambers's* (6 June 1896), 367–68.
——, 'Some Humorous Chapbooks', 15 Oct. 1881, 657–60.
——, 'Sketches from the Country no II: Bringing a Wife to Reason', *Irish Penny Magazine*, 14 Dec. 1833, 397–400.
——, 'Some Illustrated Books', *Quest*, 1 (Nov. 1894), 43–46.
——, 'Superstitions of the Irish Peasantry – No V – The Luprechaun', *Dublin and London Magazine* (July 1825), 193–97.
——, 'The Twelfth-Cake Goblin' 26 Dec. 1846, 185–8.
——, 'Workhouse Visiting', *MP*, 25 (Feb. 1878), 164–96.
——, *The New and Gorgeous Pantomime entitled Harelquin Prince Cherrytop and the Good Fairy Fairfuck: or the Frig the Fuck and the Fairy* (Theatre Royal Olymprick Private Imprint, nd).
Apo, Satu, *The Narrative World of Finnish Fairy Tales: Structure, Agency, and Evaluation in Southwestern Finnish Folktales* (Helsinki: Swedish Academy of Science and Letters, 1995).
A. R. B., 'The Independent Boy (Founded on Fact)', *Chatterbox* (1883), 62–63.
Arnold, Matthew, 'The Study of Celtic Literature: Part I', *CM*, 13 (Mar. 1866), 282–96; 'Part II', *CM*, 13 (Apr. 1866), 469–83; 'Part III', *CM*, 13 (May 1866), 538–55; 'Part IV', *CM*, 14 (July 1866), 110–28.
Arseneau, Mary, *Recovering Christina Rossetti: Female Community and Incarnational Poetics* (Basingstoke: Palgrave Macmillan, 2004).
Ashton, *Chapbooks in the Eighteenth Century* (London: Chatto and Windus, 1882).
Atkinson, J. C., 'Comparative Danish and Northumbrian Folk Lore': I, 'Wonderful Horns', *MP*, 29 (Feb. 1865), 156–61, VI, 'Hobs', *MP*, 30 (Sept. 1865), 316–22; 'Trolls', *MP*, n.s. 1 (Mar. 1866), 248–58.
Auerbach, Nina, and U. C. Knoepflmacher, eds, *Forbidden Journeys: Fairy Tales and Fantasies by Victorian Women Writers* (Chicago, IL: University of Chicago Press, 1992)
Bacchilega, Christina and Noelani Arista, The *Arabian Nights* in a Nineteenth-Century Hawaiian Newspaper: Reflections on the Politics of Translation', *Fabula*, 45 (2004) 189–206.
Barlow, Jane, *The End of Elfin-Town* (London: Macmillan, 1894).
Barrow, Logie, *Independent Spirits: Spiritualism and English Plebeians, 1850–1900* (London: Routledge & Kegan Paul, 1986).

——, and Ian Bullock, *Democratic Ideas and the British Labour Movement, 1880–1914* (Cambridge: Cambridge University Press, 1996).
Beardsley, Aubrey, 'Under the Hill: A Romantic Novel/Story', *Savoy*, 1 (Jan. 1896), 151–70; *Savoy*, 2 (Apr. 1896), 187–96.
Beckett, R. A. 'Our New Programme', *LP*, 6 (July 1897), 101.
Bede, Cuthbert, 'Story-hunting in the Western Highlands', *Belgravia*, 31 (Jan. 1877), 275–81.
Beer, Gillian, *Darwin's Plots: Evolutionary Narrative in Darwin, George Eliot and Nineteenth-Century Fiction* (London: Routledge, 1983).
Beerbohm, Max, 'Be it Cosiness', *Pageant*, 1 (1896), 230–35.
——, 'Yai and the Moon', *Pageant*, 2 (1897), 143–55.
Beetham, Margaret, 'Towards a Theory of the Periodical as a Publishing Genre', in *Investigating Victorian Journalism*, ed. Laurel Brake, Aled Jones and Lionel Madden (Basingstoke: Macmillan, 1990), 19–32.
——, *A Magazine of Her Own? Domesticity and Desire in the Woman's Magazine, 1800–1914* (London: Routledge, 1996)
Bell, Edward, 'Hans Christian Andersen', *AJM*, 14 (Nov. 1876), 1–11.
Bendix, Regina, 'The Uses of Disciplinary History', *Radical History Review*, 84 (2002), 110–14.
Benjamin, Walter. *Illuminations*, ed. Hannah Arendt, trans. Harry Zohn (London: Fontana, 1973).
——, *One-Way Street & Other Writings*, trans. Edmund Jephcott and Kingsley Shorter (London: NLB, 1979).
Benn, Caroline, *Keir Hardie: A Biography* (London: Metro, 1997), 119.
Bennett, Tony, 'Text, Readers, Reading Formations', *Literature and History*, 9 (1983), 214–27.
Bevir, Mark, 'The Labour Church Movement, 1891–1902', *Journal of British Studies*, 38 (Apr. 1999), 217–45.
Blackwell, Mark, ed., *The Secret Life of Things: Animals, Objects and It-Narratives in Eighteenth-Century England* (Lewisburg: Bucknell University Press, 2007).
Blake, William, *Selections from the Writings of William Blake: With an Introductory Essay by Laurence Housman* (London: Kegan, Paul, Trench, Trübner, 1893).
Blatchford, Robert, *Altruism: Christ's Glorious Gospel of Love against Man's Dismal Science of Greed* (London: Clarion Newspaper Company, 1902).
——, 'As I Lay a Thynkynge', *Clarion*, 19 Dec. 1891, 2.
——, 'Elevenpence to the Shilling. A Fairy Tale for Children of all Ages', *Clarion*, 8 Oct. 1892, 2.
——, *Fantasias* (Manchester: John Heywood, 1892).
——, *God and My Neighbour* (London: Clarion Press, 1903).
——, *The New Religion: Clarion Pamphlet 20* (London: Clarion Newspaper, 1897).
——, 'Our Cinderella', *LP*, 2 (June 1893), 53.
——, *The Tramp and Bob's Fairy*, Clarion Tales for the People No. 1 (London: Clarion Newspaper [n.d.]).
Bodichon, Barbara, 'A Dull Life', *MM*, 16 (May 1867), 47–53.
Bottigheimer, Ruth, *Fairy Godfather: Straparola, Venice, and the Fairy Tale Tradition* (Philadelphia, PA: University of Pennsylvania Press, 2002).
——, 'The Ultimate Fairy Tale: Oral Transmission in a Literature World', in *A Companion to the Fairy Tale*, ed. Hilda Ellis Davidson and Anna Chaudhri (Cambridge: Boydell and Brewer, 2003), 57–70.
Bourdieu, Pierre, *Distinction: A Social Critique of the Judgement of Taste*, trans. Richard Nice (London: Routledge, 1986).

Bourke, Angela, *The Burning of Bridget Cleary: A True Story* (London: Pimlico, 1999).
Bown, Nicola, *Fairies in Nineteenth-Century Art and Literature* (Cambridge: Cambridge University Press, 2001).
Brake, Laurel, 'Endgames: The Politics of the *Yellow Book* or, Decadence, Gender and the New Journalism', in *The Ending of Epochs*, ed. Laurel Brake (Woodbridge: D. S. Brewer, 1995), 38–64.
——, '"Gay Discourse" and the *Artist and Journal of Home Culture*', in *Nineteenth-Century Media and the Construction of Identities*, ed. Laurel Brake, Bill Bell and David Finkelstein (Basingstoke: Palgrave Macmillan, 2000), 271–91.
——, and Anne Humpherys, eds, 'Critical Theory Special Issue', *VPR*, 12 (1989).
——, *Subjugated Knowledges: Journalism, Gender and Literature in the Nineteenth Century* (Basingstoke: Macmillan, 1994).
Brantlinger, Patrick, *Dark Vanishings: Discourse on the Extinction of Primitive Races, 1800–1930* (Ithaca, NY: Cornell University Press, 2003).
——, *The Reading Lesson: The Threat of Mass Literacy in Nineteenth-Century British Fiction* (Bloomington, IN: Indiana University Press, 1998).
Bristow, Joseph, *Effeminate England: Homoerotic Writing after 1885* (New York: Columbia University Press, 1995).
Broks, Peter, *Media Science before the Great War* (Basingstoke: Macmillan, 1996).
Broomfield, Andrea, 'Towards a More Tolerant Society: *Macmillan's Magazine* and the Women's Suffrage Question', *VPR*, 23 (1990), 120–26.
Browne, Mathew, 'The Boy Who Wanted to be a Great Author', *GT*, 1 (Oct. 1873), 643–44.
——, 'The Letter-Box,' *GT*, 1 (Dec. 1872), 105–06.
Browning, Elizabeth Barrett, *Complete Works of Elizabeth Barrett Browning*, ed. Charlotte Porter and Helen A. Clarke, 6 vols (New York: Crowell, 1900; repr. AMS Press, 1973).
Burke, *Popular Culture in Early Modern Europe* (1897; Aldershot: Ashgate, 1999).
Burnett, Mary G., 'The "Father's Sunday Out" is the children's happiness', *LP*, 4 (Apr. 1895), 63.
Burton, Richard, *The Book of the Thousand Nights and a Night: A Plain and Literal Translation of the Arabian Nights Entertainments*, 10 vols ([n.p.]: Burton Club [1886]).
Cadogan, Mary, and Patricia Craig, *You're a Brick, Angela! A New Look at Girls' Fiction from 1839 to 1975* (London: Gollancz, 1976).
Canepa, Nancy L., and Antonella Ansani, eds, *Out of the Woods – The Origins of the Literary Fairy Tale in Italy and France* (Detroit: Wayne State University Press, 1997).
[Carlill, James Briggs], 'Comparative Mythology', *CM*, 19 (Jan. 1869), 30–44.
Carlyle, Thomas, 'The Hero as Divinity', in Sartor Resartus and Lectures on Heroes (London: Chapman and Hall, 1869).
Carpenter, Edward, *The Intermediate Sex: A Study of Some Transitional Types of Men and Women*, 2nd edn (London: S. Sonnenschein, 1909).
Carroll, Lewis [Charles Ludwidge Dodgson] Bruno's Revenge', *AJM*, 4 (Dec. 1867), 65–78.
——, *The Selected Letters of Lewis Carroll*, ed. Morton N. Cohen (London: Macmillan, 1979).
Chapple, J. A. V, *Science and Literature in the Nineteenth Century* (Basingstoke: Macmillan, 1986).
Chartier, Roger. *The Cultural Uses of Print in Early Modern France*, trans. Lydia G. Cochrane (Princeton, NJ: Princeton University Press, 1987), 240–336.
Chauncey, George, *Gay New York: The Making of the Gay Male World, 1890–1940* (London: Flamingo, 1995).

Chermside, Richard, 'Self-help', *MM*, 1 (March 1860), 402–06.
Christian, John, ed., *The Last Romantics: The Romantic Tradition in British Art* (London: Lund Humphries, 1989).
Clarke, [Charles] Alan, 'A Talk About Fairies', *LL*, 6 June 1896, 196; 20 June 1896, 214.
——, 'Little Red Riding Hood', *LL*, 26 Oct., 2 Nov. and 9 Nov. 1895, 12.
Clayton, Joseph, 'The Darkness of Midsummer', *LL*, 31 Aug. 1895, 5.
Clodd, Edward, *The Childhood of Religions* (London: Kegan Paul, Trench, 1889).
——, *Fairy Tales from Hans Andersen* (London: Wells Gardner, Darton, 1901).
——, *Tom Tit Tot: An Essay on Savage Philosophy in Folk-Tale* (London: Duckworth, 1898).
——, 'The Philosophy of Rumpelstiltskin', *Folk-Lore Journal*, 7 (1889), 135–63.
Cohen, Francis, 'Antiquities of Nursery Literature', *Quarterly Review*, 21 (Jan. 1819), 91–112.
Colclough, Stephen, *Consuming Texts: Readers and Reading Communities 1695–1870* (Basingstoke: Palgrave Macmillan, 2007).
[Cole, Henry], ed., Little Red Riding Hood. An Entirely New Edition. With New Pictures by an Eminent Artist. Edited by Felix Summerly (London: Joseph Cundall, 1843).
Coleridge, Samuel Taylor, *Collected Letters*, ed. Earl Leslie Griggs, 6 vols (Oxford: Clarendon Press, 1956–71).
Colligan, Collette, '"Esoteric Pornography": Sir Richard Burton's *Arabian Nights* and the Origins of Pornography', *Victorian Review* 28: 2 (2002), 31–64.
——, *The Traffic in Obscenity from Byron to Beardsley* (Basingstoke: Palgrave Macmillan, 2006).
Collins, Charles Alston, 'Beggars', *MM*, 5 (Jan. 1862), 210–18.
[Collins, Wilkie], 'The Unknown Public', *HW*, 21 Aug. 1858, 217–22.
Cook, E. T., 'The Jubilee of the "Cornhill"', *CM*, n.s. 28 (Jan. 1910), 8–27.
Cook, Matt, *London and the Culture of Homosexuality, 1885–1914* (Cambridge: Cambridge University Press, 2003).
Cox, Mabel, 'The Book Illustrations of Laurence Housman', *Artist*, 21 (Feb. 1898), 99–103.
Craik, Dinah Mulock, *The Fairy Book* (London: Macmillan, 1863).
——, 'The Last News of the Fairies', *GWY*, 2 (Mar. 1870), 256–60.
Croker, Thomas Crofton, *Fairy Legends and Traditions of the South of Ireland*, a new and complete edition edited by T. Wright (London: Tegg, 1870).
Crone, Rosalind, 'Violence and Entertainment in Nineteenth-century London' (unpublished doctoral thesis, University of Cambridge, 2006).
Cross, Victoria, 'Theodora: A Fragment', *YB*, 4 (Jan. 1895), 156–88.
Cruikshank, George, *George Cruikshank's Fairy Library* (London: Routledge & Sons, 1854).
Cunningham, Valentine. 'Soiled Fairy: *The Water-Babies* in its Time', *Essays in Criticism*, 35 (Apr. 1985) 121–48.
d'Arch Smith, Timothy, Love in Earnest: Some Notes on the Lives and Writings of English 'Uranian' Poets from 1889–1930 (London: Routledge and Kegan Paul, 1970).
Dark, Sidney, 'Books Worth Reading', *LL*, 5 May 1894, 3.
Darnton, Robert, *The Kiss of Lamourette: Studies in Cultural History* (London: Faber & Faber, 1990).
Darwin, Charles, *Charles Darwin: His Life Told in an Autobiographical Chapter, and in a Selected Series of His Published Letter*s, ed Francis Darwin (London: Murray, 1892), 228–29.

——, *The Origin of Species*, ed John Burrow (London: Penguin Classics, 1985).
Dasent, George, *Popular Tales from the Norse*, new edn (Edinburgh: Douglas, 1903).
d'Aulnoy, Marie-Catherine, *The Fairy Tales of the Countess d'Aulnoy*, trans. J. R. Planché, (London: Routledge, 1855).
Dawson, Julia, 'Chat for Chatterboxes', *LP*, 5 (Nov. 1896), 179–80.
D. B., 'Jane's Apology', *Chatterbox* (1883), 343.
De Certeau, Michel, *The Practice of Everyday Life*, trans. Stephen Rendall (Berkeley: University of California Press, 1984).
Dellamora, Richard, *Masculine Desire: The Sexual Politics of Victorian Aestheticism* (Chapel Hill, NC: University of North Carolina Press, 1990).
Denny, Norman, comp., *The Yellow Book: A Selection* (London: Spring Books [1949]).
[Depping, G. B.], 'The Smith Velant', *NMM*, 4 (June 1822), 527–33.
Dicey, E. D., 'The New England States', *MM*, 6 (Aug. 1862), 284–97.
[Dickens, Charles] 'Frauds on the Fairies', *HW*, 1 Oct. 1853, 97–100.
[——], *Hard Times*, *HW*, April to August 1854.
[——], 'Nurse's Stories', *AYR*, 8 Sept. 1860, 517–18.
[——], 'On Strike' *HW*, 11 Feb. 1854, 553–59.
[——] 'Preliminary Word', *HW*, 30 Mar. 1850, 1.
[——], 'A Thousand and One Humbugs', *HW*, 21 Apr. 1855, 255–57; 28 Apr. 1855, 289–92.
Dijkstra, Bram, *Idols of Perversity: Fantasies of Feminine Evil in Fin-de-Siècle Culture* (Oxford: Oxford University Press, 1986).
Dixon, E. S., 'A Vision of Animal Existences', *CM*, 5 (Mar. 1862), 311–18.
Dorson, Richard M., *American Folklore* (Chicago, IL: University of Chicago Press, 1959), 278.
——, *The British Folklorists: A History* (London: Routledge & Kegan Paul, 1968).
——, ed., *Peasant Customs and Savage Myths: Selections from the British Folklorists*, 2 vols (Chicago, IL: University of Chicago Press; London: Routledge & Kegan Paul, 1968).
Dowling, Linda, *Hellenism and Homosexuality in Victorian Oxford* (Ithaca, NY: Cornell University Press, 1994).
——, *Language and Decadence in the Victorian Fin de Siècle* (Princeton, NJ: Princeton University Press, 1986)
——, 'Letterpress and Picture in the Literary Periodicals of the 1890s', *The Yearbook of English Studies*, 16 (1986), 117–131.
Drotner, Kirsten, *English Children and Their Magazines 1751–1945* (New Haven, CT: Yale University Press, 1988).
Dundes, Alan, ed., *The Study of Folklore* (Eagelwood Cliffs, NJ: Prentice Hall, 1965).
Earls, Brian, 'Supernatural Legends in Nineteenth-Century Irish Writing', *Béaloideas*, 60–61 (1992–1993), 93–144.
Easley, Alexis, *First Person Anonymous*: *Women Writers and Victorian Print Media* (Aldershot: Ashgate, 2004), 168–67.
Eden, H. K. F. (née Gatty), *Juliana Horatia Ewing: Her Books and Letters* (London: S.P.C.K., 1896).
Egerton, George [Mary Chavelita Dunne], *Keynotes and Discords* (London: Virago 1983), 1–36.
Egoff, Sheila, *Children's Periodicals in the Nineteenth Century: A Survey and Bibliography* (London: Library Association, 1951).
Ellis, John M., *One Fairy Story Too Many: The Brothers Grimm and Their Tales* (Chicago, IL: University of Chicago Press, 1985).
Ellmann, Richard, *Oscar Wilde* (Harmondsworth: Penguin, 1988).

Emerson, Ralph Waldo, *Essays, First and Second Series* (New York: Vintage Library of America, 1990).
Engen, Rodney, *Laurence Housman* (Stroud: Catalpa Press, 1983).
Ewing, J[uliana] H[oratia], 'Amelia and the Dwarfs', *AJM*, 8 (Feb–March 1870).
——, 'The Brownies: A Fairy Story', *MP*, 30 (Dec. 1865), 658–701.
——, *Canada Home: Juliana Horatia Ewing's Fredericton Letters 1867–1869*, ed. Margaret Howard Blom and Thomas E. Blom (Vancouver: University of British Columbia Press, 1983).
——, The Kyrekegrim Turned Preacher. A Legend', *AJM*, 14 (Nov. 1875), 37–41.
——, 'In Memoriam, Margaret Gatty', *AJM*, 13 (Dec. 1874), 2–7.
——, 'Laetus Sorte Meâ, or, The Story of a Short Life', *AJM*, 20 (May–Oct. 1882).
——, *Lob Lie-by-the-Fire and other Tales* (London: S.P.C.K., 1882).
——, *Old-Fashioned Fairy Tales* (London: S.P.C.K, 1882).
——, 'The Blind Man and the Talking Dog', *AJM* 14 (Feb. 1876), 247–51.
——, 'The Hillman and the Housewife', *AJM*, 8 (May 1870), 432–34.
——, 'The Laird and the Man of Peace', *AJM*, 9 (Apr. 1871), 375–80.
——, 'The Magician's Gifts', *AJM*, 10 (Mar. 1872), 259–65.
——, 'Murdoch's Rath', *AJM*, 10 (Feb. 1872), 210–16.
——, 'The Neck', *AJM*, 8 (June 1870), 466–72.
——, 'The Nix in Mischief', *AJM*, 8 (Apr. 1870), 363–66.
——, 'The Widows and the Strangers', *AJM*, 9 (Feb. 1871), 240–45.
——, Timothy's Shoes', *AJM*, 9 (Nov. 1870), 3–12; (Dec. 1870), 81–87; (Jan. 1871), 153–60.
Fletcher, Ian, 'Union and Beauty' (unpublished doctoral dissertation, University of Reading, 1965).
——, 'Decadence and the Little Magazines', in *Decadence and the 1890s*, ed. Ian Fletcher (London: Edward Arnold, 1979), 173–202.
Forman, H. Buxton, 'King Wiseacre and the Six Professors', *AJM*, 4 (Nov. 1867), 28–37.
Forster, John, *The Life of Charles Dickens*, ed. J. W. T Ley (London: Palmer, 1928), 43–44.
Fraser, Alexander Campbell, 'The Real World of Berkeley', *MM*, 6 (July 1862), 192–202.
Frere, Mary, 'Less Inequality than We Suppose', *Chatterbox* (1883), 367.
Gagnier, Regenia, *Idylls of the Marketplace: Oscar Wilde and the Victorian Public* (Aldershot: Scholar Press, 1987).
Gale, Norman, 'To Thee', *Butterfly*, n.s. 1 (May 1899), 98.
Galton, Arthur, 'Ancient Legends of Ireland by Lady Wilde', *Century Guild Hobby Horse*, 2 (1887), 67–74.
Gaskell, Elizabeth, 'Cranford', *Household Words*, 13 Dec. 1851 to 1 May 1853.
Gatty, Alfred Scott, '"Rumpelstiltskin": An Extravaganza adapted from one of the Grimm's [sic] Household Stories', *AJM*, 18 (Jan. 1880), 98–113.
Gatty, H. K. F., 'Farewell Address', *AJM*, 23 (Oct. 1885), 763–64.
——, 'Juliana Horatia Ewing – In Memoriam', I, *AJM*, 23 (July 1885) 534–52; II (Aug. 1885), 577–95.
Gatty, Mrs Alfred [Margaret], *Aunt Judy's Tales* (London: Bell & Sons, 1859).
——, *Aunt Judy's Letters* (London: Bell & Sons, 1862).
——, 'Cat "Folk-Lore" and a "Post-Amble"', *AJM*, 4 (Mar. 1868), 278–82.
——, 'Editor's Address', *AJM*, 4 (Nov. 1867), 1–3.
——, 'Introduction', *AJM*, 1 (May 1866), 1–2.
——, *The Fairy Godmothers and Other Tales* (London: George Bell, 1851).
Gatty, S. H., 'The Galoshes of Happiness', *AJM*, 14 (Dec. 1875), 86–100.

[Geddes, Patrick and J. Arthur Thomson], 'The Moral Evolution of Sex', *Evergreen* (Summer 1896), 73–85.
Gérin, Winifred, *Anne Thackeray Ritchie: A Biography* (Oxford: Oxford University Press, 1983).
——, *Elizabeth Gaskell: A Biography* (Oxford: Clarendon, 1976).
Gidley, S. M., 'Little Brown Girls', *AJM*, 14 (Sept. 1876), 693–700.
Gilbert, R. A., *Sources for Victorian Fairy Tales: A Series of Researches* (Bristol: Thoemmes, 2002).
Gilbert, William, 'Mrs. Blundebore's Trials', *GWY*, 2 (Jan. 1870), 127–32.
——, 'The Seven-Leagued Boots', *GWY*, 2 (Dec. 1869), 71–78.
——, 'Sinbad in England', *GT*, 1 (Nov. 1872 to Oct. 1873).
Goethe, Johann Wolfgang, 'The Tale', 6 (Oct. 1832), 257–78.
Goldney, S., 'Fables and Fairy Tales', *AJM*, 23 (Nov. 1885), 20–32.
[Golsworthy, Arnold], 'VALE!', *Butterfly*, n.s. 2 (Feb. 1894), 248–49.
Gordon, Jan B., '"Decadent Spaces": Notes for a Phenomenology of the *fin de siècle*', in *Decadence and the 1890s*, ed. Ian Fletcher (London: Edward Arnold, 1979), 31–58.
Gorman, John, *Banner Bright* (Buckhurst Hill: Scorpion, 1986).
Gosse, Edmund, 'Jules Barbey D'Aurevilly', *Pageant*, 2 (1897), 18–31.
Gould, F. J., 'The Man Without a Heart', *Cinderella*, *LP*, 1 (Oct. 1893), 101–02.
Gould, Sabine Baring, *A Book of Folk-Lore* (Collins: London and Glasgow, [n.d.]).
Gould, Stephen Jay, *The Mismeasure of Man*, rev. edn (Harmondsworth: Penguin, 1997).
——, *Ontogeny and Phylogeny* (London: Harvard University Press, 1977).
Graves, Clo[tilde], 'Apamé', *Butterfly*, 1 (Aug. 1893), 200–06.
Gray, John, 'The Great Worm', *Dial*, 1 (1889), 14–18.
——, 'Fiorenzo of Maggiolo', *Butterfly*, 1 (June 1893), 69–78.
Greenhalgh, Paul, ed., *Art Nouveau 1890–1914* (London: V&A Publications, 2000).
Greg, Percy, 'The Artisan's Saturday Night', *MM*, 2 (Aug. 1860), 285–92.
——, 'On the Failure of "Natural Selection" in the Case of Man', *Fraser's*, 78 (Sept. 1868), 353–62.
Grenby, M.O., 'Tame Fairies Make Good Teachers: The Popularity of Early British Fairy Tales', *The Lion and the Unicorn*, 30 (2006), 1–24.
Grimm, Jacob, *Teutonic Mythology*, trans. from the 4th edn by James Steven Stallybrass, 4 vols (London: Bell & Sons, 1882-88), I (1882).
Grimm, Jacob and Wilhelm, *German Popular Stories, Translated from the Kinder und Haus Märchen, Collected by M.M. Grimm, From Oral Tradition*, trans. Edgar Taylor (London: C. Baldwyn, 1823).
——, *German Popular Stories, with Illustrations after the Original Designs by George Cruikshank*, trans. Edgar Taylor, with Introduction by John Ruskin (London: John Camden Hotten, 1868).
——, *Gammer Grethel's Fairy Tales*, trans. Edgar Taylor, with Introduction by Laurence Housman (London: Alexander Moring, 1905).
——, *Grimms' Household Tales*, trans. Margaret Hunt, 2 vols (London: Bell and Sons, 1884).
——, *Grimm's Goblins: Fairy Books for Boys and Girls* (London: Vickers, 1861).
Guizot de Witt, Madame, 'The Two Hunchbacks. A Breton Legend', *GWY*, 2 (May 1870).
——, 'The Lost Child. A Legend of Brittany', *GWY*, 2 (Sept. 1870), 563–65.
Guy, Josephine M., and Small, Ian, *Oscar Wilde's Profession: Writing and the Culture Industry in the Late Nineteenth Century* (Oxford: Oxford University Press, 2000).

Haeckel, Ernst, *The Evolution of Man: A Popular Scientific Study*, trans. Joseph McCabe, 5th edn (London: Watts, 1906).
[Halliday, Andrew], 'Bouncing Boys', *AYR*, 5 Aug. 1865, 37–40.
Hardie, [James] Keir, 'The History of a Giant. Being a study in Politics for very Young Boys', *LL*, 8 Apr. 1893, 1–3.
——, 'Jack Clearhead. A Fairy Tale for Crusaders', *LL*, 8 Sept. 1894 to 22 Oct. 1894, 11.
Harker, Dave, *Fakesong: The Manufacture of British 'Folk Song', 1700 to the Present* (Milton Keynes: Open University Press, 1985).
[Harland, Henry], 'The Yellow Dwarf', 'A Birthday Letter from "The Yellow Dwarf', *YB*, 9 (Apr. 1896), 11–22.
[——], 'The Yellow Dwarf', 'A Letter to the Editor and an Offer of a Prize', *YB*, 7 (Oct. 1895), 125–43.
Harries, Elizabeth Wanning, *Twice Upon a Tale: Women Writers and the History of the Fairy Tale* (Princeton, NJ: Princeton University Press, 2001).
Harrison, Royden, Gillian B. Woolven and Robert Duncan, comp., *Warwick Guide to British Labour Periodicals 1790–1970* (Sussex: Harvester, 1977).
Harrison, Stanley, *Poor Men's Guardians: A Record of the Struggles for a Democratic Newspaper Press, 1763–1973* (London: Lawrence and Wishart, 1974).
Hartland, Edwin Sidney, *The Science of Fairy Tales: An Inquiry into Fairy Mythology* (London: Walter Scott, 1891).
Haywood, Ian, *The Revolution in Popular Literature: Print, Politics and the People, 1790–1860* (Cambridge: Cambridge University Press, 2004).
Hearn, Michael Patrick, ed., *The Victorian Fairy Tale Book* (New York: Pantheon, 1988).
Hincks, J. G., 'Andalusian Folk Lore', *MP*, 30 (Oct. 1865), 408–26.
Hines, George, *Co-operative Fairy Tales* (London: Co-operative Printing Society, 1888).
[Hinton, James] 'The Fairy Land of Science', *CM*, 5 (Jan. 1862), 36–42.
Hitch, Jessie, 'Reynard the Fox', *LP*, 6 (Dec. 1897), 197; *LP*, 7 (Jan. 1897), 12.
Hobsbawm, Eric, and Terence Ranger, eds, *The Invention of Tradition* (Cambridge: Cambridge University Press, 1983).
Hodgson, Amanda, 'Defining the Species: Apes, Savages and Humans in Scientific and Literary Writing of the 1890s', *Journal of Victorian Culture* 4 (Autumn 1999), 228–51.
Hogg, James, 'The Mountain-Dew Men by the Ettrick Shepherd', *Fraser's*, 6 (Sept. 1832), 161–70.
Holmes, C. J., 'Hirosage: An Appreciation', *Dome*, 3 (Winter 1897), 63–70.
——, 'Utamaro: An Appreciation', *Dome*, n.s. 1 (Oct. 1898), 21–26.
Hopkin, Deian, 'The Labour Party Press', in *The First Labour Party 1906–14*, ed. K. D. Brown (Beckenham: Croom Helm, 1985), 105–28.
——, 'The Left-Wing Press and the New Journalism', in *Papers for the Millions: The New Journalism in Britain, 1850s–1914*, ed. Joel H. Wiener, 225–41.
Hopper, Nora, 'A Snowdrop Song', *Dome*, n.s. 1 (Oct. 1898), 92.
Housman, Clemence, *The Were-Wolf* (London: Bodley Head, 1891).
Housman, Laurence, 'Blind Love', *Pageant*, 2 (1897), 64–81.
——, 'The Blue Moon', *Butterfly*, n.s. 1 (May 1899), 89–98.
——, *The Blue Moon* (London: John Murray, 1904).
——, 'The Bound Princess', *Parade* (1897), 64–93.
——, 'A Capful of Moonshine', *Dome*, n.s. 1 (Oct. 1898), 7–12.
——, 'The Defence of Farvingdon', *Dome*, n.s. 2 (Jan. 1899), 2–16.
——, *Echo de Paris: A Study from Life* (London: Jonathan Cape, 1923).
——, *An Englishwoman's Love Letters* (London: John Murray, 1900).
——, *A Farm in Fairyland* (London: Kegan Paul, Trench, Trübner, 1894).

——, *The Field of Clover* (London: John Lane, 1898).
——, 'A Gander and his Geese', *Butterfly*, n.s. 2 (Jan. 1900), 228–36.
——, 'The Helping Hands', *Butterfly*, n.s. 1 (July 1899), 220–28.
——, *The House of Joy* (London: Kegan Paul, Trench, Trübner, 1895).
——, 'How Little Duke Jarl Saved the Castle', *Dome*, n.s. 4 (Oct. 1899), 174–78.
——, 'The Poison Tree', *Dome*, 5 (May 1898), 30.
——, *Stories from the Arabian Nights* (London: Hodder and Stoughton, 1907).
——, 'Tales of a Woodcutter', *Butterfly*, n.s. 2 (Feb. 1900), 249–58.
——, *The Unexpected Years* (London: Cape, 1937).
——, 'The Zeit-Geist', *Quarto*, 4 (1898), 17–20.
Housman, Laurence, and W. Somerset Maugham, eds, *The Venture: An Annual of Art and Literature* (London: Baillie, 1903/05).
Howe, Edward, 'The Pit Boys and Their Dogs', *GWY*, 3 (July 1871), 465–67.
[Howman, Knightley], 'The Fauna of the Streets', *MM*, 5 (Jan. 1862), 225–29.
Hughes, Linda K., and Michael Lund, *The Victorian Serial* (Charlottesville: Virginia University Press), 1991.
[Hughes, Thomas, J. M. Ludlow and David Masson], 'Colloquy of the Round Table', *MM*, 1 (Nov. 1859), 72–80.
Humpherys, Anne, 'Popular Narrative and Political Discourse in *Reynolds's Weekly Newspaper*', in *Investigating Victorian Journalism*, ed. Laurel Brake, Aled Jones and Lionel Madden (Basingstoke: Macmillan, 1990), 33–47.
Hunt, Peter, ed., *Children's Literature: An Illustrated History* (Oxford: Oxford University Press, 1995).
——, *An Introduction to Children's Literature* (Oxford: Oxford University Press, 1994).
Hunter, J. Paul, *Before Novels: The Cultural Contexts of Eighteenth Century English Fiction* (New York: Norton, 1990).
Hutton, R. H., *A Victorian Spectator: Uncollected Writings of R. H. Hutton*, ed. Tener, Robert, and Malcolm Woodfield, 2nd edn (Bristol: Bristol Press, 1991).
Huysmans, J.-K., *Against Nature*, trans. Robert Baldick (Penguin: Harmondsworth, 1959).
Image, Selwyn, 'A Lecture on Art: Delivered in London in December 1882', *Century Guild Hobby Horse*, 1 (Apr 1884), 34–70.
Independent Labour Party, *I.L.P. Songbook* (Manchester: Labour Press and Clarion Office, 1897).
Inglis, K. S., *Churches and the Working Classes in Victorian Britain* (London: Routledge and Kegan Paul, 1963)
Irwin, Robert, *The Arabian Nights: A Companion* (London: Allen Lane, 1994).
Jackson, Holbrook, *The 1890s: A Review of Art and Ideas at the Close of Nineteenth Century*, new edn (Hassocks: Harvester Press, 1976).
Jacobs, Joseph, ed., *English Fairy Tales* (London: David Nutt, 1892).
James, Louis, *Fiction for the Working Man, 1830–50* (London: Penguin, 1974).
——, 'Tom Brown's Imperialist Sons', *VS*, 17 (1973), 89–99.
Janzen, Lorraine Kooistra, *Christina Rossetti and Illustration* (Athens: Ohio University Press).
——, *The Artist as Critic: Bitextuality in Fin-de-Siècle Illustrated Books* (Aldershot: Scolar Press, 1995).
Jones, Greta, *Social Darwinism and English Thought: The Interaction between Biological and Social Theory* (Sussex: Harvester, 1980).
Kennedy, Dane, '"Captain Burton's Oriental Muck Heap": *The Book of the Thousand Nights* and the Uses of Orientalism', *Journal of British Studies* 39 (2000), 317–39.

Kincaid, James R., *Child-Loving: The Erotic Child and Victorian Culture* (New York: Routledge, 1992).
Kingsley, Charles, *Glaucus; or, the Wonders of the Shore* (Cambridge, Macmillan, 1855).
——, *His Letters and Memories of His Life*, ed Frances Kingsley. 2 vols (London: King, 1977).
——, 'Madam How and Lady Why, No. VI – "The True Fairy Tale"', *GWY*, 1 (Apr. 1869), 257–62.
——, 'Madam How and Lady Why, No. XI – "The World's End"', *GWY*, 2 (Sept. 1870), 531–39.
——, *The Roman and the Teuton* (Cambridge and London: Macmillan, 1864).
——, *The Water-Babies: A Fairy Tale for a Land-Baby*, *MM*, Aug. 1862 to Mar. 1863.
——, *The Water Babies*, ed. Brian Alderson (Oxford: World's Classics 1995).
——, *The Water-Babies. A Fairy Tale for a Land-Baby*, ed. W. T. Stead, *Books for the Bairns 111* (London: Office of *Books for the Bairns* [May 1905]).
Klaus, H. Gustav, ed., *The Rise of Socialist Fiction 1880–1914* (Sussex: Harvester, 1987).
Knoepflmacher, U. C., 'The Balancing of Child and Adult: An Approach to Victorian Fantasies for Children', *Nineteenth Century Fiction*, 37 (1983), 497–530.
——, *Ventures into Childland: Victorians, Fairy Tales, and Femininity* (Chicago, IL: University of Chicago Press, 1998).
Kotzin, Michael C., *Dickens and the Fairy Tale* (Bowling Green, OH: Bowling Green University Popular Press, 1972).
Kuper, Adam, *The Invention of Primitive Society: Transformations of an Illusion* (London: Routledge, 1988).
Kynaston, David, *King Labour, the British Working Class 1850–1914* (London: Unwin, 1976).
Lane, Edward W., trans., *The Thousand and One Nights, Commonly Called, in England, The Arabian Nights Entertainments: A New Translation from the Arabic with Copious Notes*, 3 vols (London: Charles Knight, 1839–41).
Lang, Andrew, *The Blue Fairy Book* (London: Longmans Green, 1889).
——, 'Fairy Tales', *Illustrated London News*, 3 Dec. 1892, 714.
——, 'Mythology and Fairy Tales', *Fortnightly Review*, n.s. 13 (May 1873), 618–31.
——,*The Red Fairy Book*, ed. Andrew Lang (London: Longman's Green, 1890).
Lang, Marjory, 'Childhood's Champions: Mid-Victorian Children's Periodicals and the Critics', *VPR*, 13 (1980), 17–31.
Lee, Alan J., *The Origins of the Popular Press in England 1855–1914* (London: Croom Helm, 1976).
Le Gallienne, Richard, 'Tree-Worship', *YB*, 1 (Apr. 1894), 57–60.
Lee, Vernon [Violet Paget], 'Prince Alberic and the Snake Lady', *YB*, 10 (July 1896), 289–344.
[——], *Tuscan Fairy Tales: Taken down from the Mouths of the People* (London: Satchell, 1880).
Lenox, George Louis, 'Annette: A Fairy Tale', *Hibernian*, Dec. 1873, 646–48, June 1874, 312–14.
[Lewes, George Henry], 'Studies in Animal Life', *CM*, 1 (Feb. 1860), 199–207.
Lie, Jonas, *Weird Tales from the Northern Seas*, trans. R. Nisbet Bain (London: Kegan Paul, 1893).
Litvack, Leon and Colin Graham, eds, *Ireland and Europe in the Ninteenth-Century*, (Dublin: Four Courts, 2006).
MacDonald, George, 'At the Back of the Northwind', 1 (Nov. 1868 to Oct. 1870).

——, *A Dish of Orts: Chiefly Papers on the Imagination, and on Shakspere* [sic] (London: Sampson Low, 1893).
——, 'The Princess and Curdie', *GT* (Jan. 1877 to June 1877).
——, 'The Princess and the Goblin', *GWY*, 3 (Nov. 1870 to June 1871).
——, 'Ranald Bannerman's Boyhood', *GWY*, 2 (Nov. 1869 to Oct. 1870).
Macdonald, Lizzie, *Cinderella Annual – The Book of the National Cinderella Society* (London: Lizzie Macdonald [1893?]).
Macdonald, W., and J. Arthur Thomson, 'Proem', *Evergreen* (Spring 1895), 9–15.
Macleod, Fiona [William Sharp], 'The Last Night of Artan the Culdee' and 'The Monody of Isla the Singer', *Dome*, n.s. 1 (Oct. 1898), 75–76.
——, 'The Secrets of the Night', *Dome*, n.s. 2 (Jan. 1899), 68–69.
Macleod, Norman, 'Editor's Address', *GWY*, 1 (Oct. 1869), 590.
——, 'Talks with the Boys about India, I', *GWY*, 3 (Dec. 1870), 116–19.
Mackmurdo, Arthur H., M.C.G. [Member of Century Guild], 'The Guild's Flag Unfurling', *Century Guild Hobby Horse*, 1 (Apr. 1884), 2–13.
Macmillan, Hugh, 'A Lump of Coal', *GWY*, 1 (Dec. 1868), 102–05.
MacNicce, Louis, *Varieties of Parable* (Cambridge: Cambridge University Press, 1965).
Maidment, Brian E., 'Magazines of Popular Progress & the Artisans', *VPR*, 17 (1984), 83–94.
[Martineau, Harriet], 'Middle-Class Education in England – Girls', *CM*, 10 (Nov. 1864), 549–68.
Martineau, Jane, ed., *Victorian Fairy Painting* (London: Merrell Holberton, 1997).
Masson, David, 'Gaelic and Norse Popular Tales: An Apology for the Celt', *MM*, 3 (Jan. 1861), 213–24.
Mattar, Sinéad Garrigan, *Primitivism, Science, and the Irish Revival* (Oxford: Oxford University Press, 2004).
Maw, Martin, *Visions of India: Fulfilment Theology, the Aryan Race Theory and the Work of British Protestant Missionaries in Victorian India* (Frankfurt: Lang, 1990).
Maxwell, Christobel, *Mrs Gatty and Mrs Ewing* (London: Constable, 1949).
Mayo, Robert. D. *The English Novel in the Magazines, 1740–1815* (Evanston: Northwestern University Press, 1962).
McGann, Jerome, *The Beauty of Inflections: Literary Investigations in Historical Method and Theory* (Oxford: Clarendon Press, 1985).
McGillis, Roderick, 'Childhood and Growth: George MacDonald and William Wordsworth', *Romanticism and Children's Literature in Nineteenth-Century England* (Athens: University of Georgia Press, 1991), ed. James Holt McGavran Jr, 150–67.
McKenzie, D. F., *Bibliography and the Sociology of Texts: The Panizzi Lectures 1985* (London: British Library, 1986).
[Mew, James], 'The Arabian Nights', *CM*, 32 (Dec. 1875), 711–32.
Milroy, James, *The Language of Gerard Manley Hopkins* (London: André Deutsch, 1977).
Miscellaneous Studies, 3rd edn (London: Macmillan, 1900).
Mitchell, Jack, 'Tendencies in Narrative Fiction in the London-based Socialist Press of the 1880s and 1890s', in *The Rise of Socialist Fiction 1880–1914*, ed. H. Gustav Klaus, 49–72.
Morgan, Kenneth O., *Keir Hardie: Radical and Socialist* (London: Weidenfeld and Nicolson, 1975).
[Morley, Henry], 'Ground in the Mill', *HW*, 22, Apr. 1854, 224–27.
——, 'Little Red Working-Coat', *HW*, 27 Dec. 1851, 324–25.
Morris, G. L. L., 'Notes on Decadence,' *Beam*, 2 (Mar. 1896), 55–59.
Morris, William, *The Ideal Book: Essays and Lectures on the Arts of the Book*, ed. William S. Peterson (Berkeley: University of California Press, 1982), 67–73.

——, 'News from Nowhere: or, An Epoch at Rest. Being Some Chapters from a Utopian Romance', *Commonweal*, 11 Jan. to 4 Oct. 1890.
——, 'Rapunzel', in *The Early Romances of William Morris*, 2nd edn (London: Dent, 1913), 60–71.
Müller, [Friedrich] Max, *Chips from a German Workshop*, 4 vols (London: Longmans, Green, 1867–75), I (1867).
——, 'Introductory Lecture on the Science of Language', *MM*, 7 (Mar. 1863) 337–49.
——, *Lectures on the Science of Language*, 1st and 2nd series (London: Longman, Green, Longman and Roberts 1861–64).
Mutch, Deborah, *English Socialist Periodicals: 1880–1900: A Reference Source* (Aldershot: Ashgate 2005).
Nelson, Claudia, 'Fantasies de Siècle: Sex and Sexuality in the Late-Victorian Fairy Tale', in *Transforming Genres: New Approaches to British Fiction in the 1890s*, ed. Nikki Lee Manos and Meri-Jane Rochelson (Macmillan: Basingstoke, 1994), 87–107.
'Norman', 'My Ogre', *AJM*, 3 (July 1867), 143–46.
Norris, W. E., 'Leslie Stephen, Editor', *CM*, n.s. 28 (Jan. 1910), 46–50.
Norton, Caroline, 'The Angel in the House' and 'The Goblin Market', *MM*, 8 (Sept. 1863), (398–404), 401–03.
[Oldmeadow, Ernest J.], 'The Editor of "The Jonquil"– A short story à la mode', *Dome*, n.s. 1 (Nov. 1898), 167–81.
Ollier, Edmund, 'A Scientific Figment', *HW* (23 Dec. 1854), 453–56.
Onslow, Barbara, *Women and the Press in Nineteenth-Century Britain* (Basingstoke: Macmillan, 2001).
Opie, Iona, and Peter Opie, eds, *The Classic Fairy Tales* (London: Oxford University Press, 1974; repr. London: Paladin, 1984).
Pater, Walter, *Appreciations*, 2nd edn (London: Macmillan, 1890).
——, *The Renaissance: Studies in Art and Poetry, the 1893 Text*, ed. Donald L. Hill (Berkeley: University of California Press, 1980).
Peachey, Caroline, trans., 'Popular Tales from Andalucia, as Told by the Peasantry', *AJM*, 3 (Aug. 1867), 230–34; 3 (Sept. 1867), 283–86; 4 (Feb. 1868), 226–28.
Pelling, Henry, *The Origins of the Labour Party 1880–1900*, 2nd edn (Oxford: Oxford University Press, 1965).
Pennington, John, 'Solar Mythology in George MacDonald's "Little Daylight" and "The Day Boy and the Night Girl"', *Journal of the Fantastic in the Arts*, 10 (1999), 308–20.
Phegley, Jennifer, 'Clearing Away "The Briars and Brambles": The Education and Professionalization of the *Cornhill Magazine*'s Women Readers, 1860–65', *VPR*, 33 (2000), 22–43.
Pierson, Stanley, 'John Trevor and the Labour Church Movement in England, 1891–1900', *Church History*, 29 (Dec. 1960), 463–76.
Plotz, Judith, *Romanticism and the Vocation of Childhood* (Basingstoke: Palgrave Macmillan, 2001).
[Prest, Thomas], 'The String of Pearls', *People's Periodical*, Nov. 1846 to Mar. 1847.
Prichard, T. H., 'An Elm Recounts', *Dome*, n.s. 1 (Oct.1898), 90.
Prickett, Stephen, *Victorian Fantasy* (Sussex: Harvester, 1979).
Purcell, Edward, 'Of Purple Jars', *Pageant*, 2 (1897), 199–220.
Purkiss, Diane, *Troublesome Things: A History of Fairies and Fairy Stories* (London: Penguin, 2000).
Raeper, William, *George MacDonald* (Tring: Lion Publishing, 1987).
Reading Experience Database http://www.open.ac.uk/Arts/reading/
Reed, David, *The Popular Magazine in Britain and the United States 1880–1960* (London: British Library, 1997).

Reid, F., 'Socialist Sunday Schools in Britain 1892–1939', *International Review of Social History*, 11 (1966), 18–47.
Reid, Julia, *Robert Louis Stevenson, Science and the Fin de Siècle* (Basingstoke: Palgrave Macmillan, 2006).
Reynolds, Simon, *The Vision of Simeon Solomon* (Stroud: Catalpa Press, 1984).
Richardson, Alan, *Literature, Education and Romanticism: Reading as Social Practice, 1780–1832* (Cambridge: Cambridge University Press, 1994).
[Ritchie, Anne Thackeray], 'Beauty and the Beast', *CM*, 15 (June 1867), 676–709.
[——], 'Betsinda and her Bun', *CM*, 36 (Sept. 1877), 325–32.
——, *Bluebeard's Keys: And Other Stories* (London: Smith, Elder, 1876).
[——], 'Cinderella', *CM*, 13 (June 1866), 721–42.
——, *Five Old Friends; and A Young Prince* (London: Smith, Elder, 1868).
[——], 'Jack and the Beanstalk', *CM*, 28 (Sept. 1873), 311–34; *CM* 28 (Oct. 1873), 431–56.
[——], 'Maids-of All-Work and Blue Books', *CM*, 30 (Sept. 1874), 281–96.
[——], 'The Sleeping Beauty in the Wood', *CM*, 13 (May 1866), 556–66.
[——], 'Toilers and Spinsters', *CM*, 3 (Mar. 1861), 318–31.
——, *Toilers and Spinsters and other Essays* (London: Smith, Elder, 1876).
——, 'The First Number of "The Cornhill"', *CM*, n.s. 1 (July 1896), 1–16.
——, 'Blackstick Papers: No. V: "Egeria in Brighton"', *CM*, n.s. 10 (June 1901), 722–29.
——, *The Letters of Anne Thackeray Ritchie*, ed. Hester Ritchie (London: John Murray, 1924).
——, *Thackeray's Daughter: Some Recollections of Anne Thackeray Ritchie*, comp. Hester Thackeray Fuller and Violet Hammersley, 2nd edn (Dublin: Euphorion, 1952).
——, *Anne Thackeray Ritchie: Journals and Letters*, ed. Abigail Burnham Bloom and John Maynard, with Biographical Commentary and Notes by Lillian F. Shankman (Columbus, OH: Ohio State University Press, 1994).
Robbins, Ruth, '"A very curious construction": Masculinity and the Poetry of A. E. Housman and Oscar Wilde', in *Cultural Politics at the Fin de Siècle*, ed. Sally Ledger and Scott McCracken (Cambridge: Cambridge University Press, 1995), 137–59.
Robinson, Thomas, 'Odin and His One Eye', *LP*, 5 (Aug. 1896), 132–33.
——, 'The Elves and Fairies' *LP*, 5(Oct. 1896), 165.
——, 'Elfhome. Charlie's Garden', *LP*, 6 (Apr. 1897), 61.
[Rolfe, Frederick, 'Baron Corvo'], 'Stories Toto Told Me IV: "About Beata Beatrice and the Mamma of San Pietro"', *YB*, 9 (Apr. 1896), 93–101.
——, 'Stories Toto Told Me: "About What is Due to Repentance"', *Butterfly*, n.s. 1 (Aug. 1899), 267–75.
[Roscoe, James], 'My After-Dinner Adventures with Peter Schlemihl', *Blackwood's*, 45 (Apr. 1839), 467–80.
Rose, Jonathan, *The Intellectual Life of the British Working Classes* (New Haven, CT: Yale University Press, 2001).
Rossetti, Christina, 'The Fairy Prince who Arrived too Late', *MM* (May 1863), 32.
——, *Poems and Prose*, ed. Jan Marsh (London: Dent, 1994).
Rossetti, Dante, Gabriel, 'Hand and Soul', *Dome*, n.s. 5 (Nov. 1899), 67–80.
Rowe, H. C., 'Socialism in Fiction', *LP*, 4 (June 1895), 81–83.
——, 'Sunday Schools for the Children', *LP*, 2 (Sept. 1894), 121.
——, 'Ways and Means', *LP*, 2 (May 1894), 62.
Runciman, John, 'Neo-Ruskinism: A Protest', *Dome*, n.s. 2 (Feb 1899), 118–24.
Ruskin, John, *The King of the Golden River, or the Black Brothers* (London: John Wiley, 1851).
Sala, George A., 'A Case of Real Distress', *HW*, 14 Jan. 1854, 457–60.

——, 'The Complaint of the Old Magician', *HW*, 4 Feb. 1854, 540–46.
Salveson, Paul, 'Allen Clarke and the Lancashire School of Working-class Novelists', in *The Rise of Socialist Fiction 1880–1914*, ed. H. Gustav Klaus, 172–202.
——, 'Getting Back to the Land. The Daisy Colony Experiment', *North West Labour History*, 10 (1984), 31–36.
Salway, Lance, ed., *A Peculiar Gift – Nineteenth-Century Writing on Books for Children* (Harmondsworth: Penguin, 1976).
Schacker, Jennifer. *National Dreams: The Remaking of Fairy Tales in Nineteenth-Century England* (Philadelphia, PA: University of Pennsylvania Press, 2003).
Schenda, Rudolf, 'Telling Tales – Spreading Tales: Change in the Communicative Forms of a Popular Genre', in *Fairy Tales and Society: Illusion, Allusion and Paradigm*, ed. Ruth B. Bottigheimer (Philadelphia, PA: University of Pennsylvania Press, 1986), 75–94.
Schmidt, Barbara Quinn. 'Introduction – *The Cornhill Magazine*: Celebrating Success', *VPR*, 32 (1999), 202–08.
Schweizer, Niklaus R., 'Kahaunani: "Snowwhite" in Hawaiian: A Study in Acculturation', in *East Meets West – Homage to Edgar C Knowlton, Jnr.*, ed. Roger L Hadlich and J. D. Ellsworth (Hawaii: University of Hawaii, 1988), 283–89.
Sedgwick, Eve Kosovsky, *Between Men: English Literature and Male Homosocial Desire* (New York: Columbia University Press, 1985).
Sharp, Evelyn, *All the Way to Fairyland* (London: John Lane, 1898).
——, *Fairy Tales: As They Are, as They Were, as They Should Be* (Brighton: D. B. Friend, 1889).
——, *Round the World to Wympland* (London: John Lane, 1902).
——, *Wymps and Other Tales* (London: John Lane, 1897).
Shattock, Joanne, ed., *The Cambridge Bibliography of English Literature*, 3rd edn, IV (Cambridge University Press: 1999).
Showalter, Elaine, ed., *Daughters of Decadence* (London: Virago, 1993), 1–5.
Shuttleworth, Sally, 'The Psychology of Childhood in Victorian Literature and Medicine', in *Literature, Science and Psychoanalysis 1830–1870 – Essays in Honour of Gillian Beer*, ed. Helen Small and Trudi Tate (Oxford: Oxford University Press, 2003) 86–101.
Silver, Carole G., *Strange and Secret Peoples: Fairies and Victorian Consciousness* (New York: Oxford University Press, 1999).
Sinfield, Alan, *The Wilde Century*: *Effeminacy, Oscar Wilde, and the Queer Moment* (New York: Columbia University Press, 1994).
Smith, Charles C., 'Fairies at Ilkley Well', *Folk-Lore Record*, 1 (London: Folk-Lore Society, 1878), 229–31.
Stead, W. T., ed., *Cinderella, and Other Fairy-Tales. Books for the Bairns 7*. 'Review of Reviews' Office [Sept. 1896], 3.
——, ed., *The Frog Prince and Other Stories from Grimm's* [sic] *Fairy Tales. Books for the Bairns 13* (London: Review of Review's Office [Mar. 1897]).
Steedman, Carolyn, *Strange Dislocations: Childhood and the Idea of Human Interiority, 1780–1930* (London: Virago, 1995), 81–95.
[Stevens, Charles], 'The Editor's Address', *Boys of England*, 24 Nov. 1866, 16.
Stewart, *Crimes of Writing: Problems of Representation and Containment* (Oxford: Oxford University, Press, 1991).
Stitt, Megan Perigoe, *Metaphors of Change in the Language of Nineteenth-Century Fiction* (Oxford: Clarendon, 1998).
Stocking, George W. Jr, *Victorian Anthropology* (New York: Macmillan, 1987).

Stokes, John, *Oscar Wilde: Myths, Miracles and Imitations* (Cambridge: Cambridge University Press, 1996).
Stone, Harry, *Dickens and the Invisible World: Fairy Tales, Fantasy and Novel-Making* (Bloomington, IN: Indiana University Press, 1979). .
Stoneley, Peter, *A Queer History of the Ballet* (London: Routledge, 2006).
[Strahan, Alexander], 'Bad Literature for the Young', *Contemporary Review*, 26 (Nov. 1875), 981–91.
Sturrock, June, 'Establishing Identity: Editorial Correspondence from the Early Years of *The Monthly Packet*', *VPR*, 39 (Fall 2006), 266–79.
Summers, David, 'The Labour Church and Affiliated Movements', (unpublished doctoral thesis, University of Edinburgh, 1958).
Sumpter, Caroline, 'The Cheap Press and the "Reading Crowd" Visualising Mass Culture and Modernity, 1838–1910', *Media History*, 12 (Autumn 2006), 233–52.
——, 'Extending the Parameters of the Text: Anne Thackeray's Fairy Tales in the *Cornhill Magazine*', *Victorian Periodicals Review*, 33:1 (Spring 2000), 65–80.
——, 'Making Socialists, or Murdering to Dissect? Natural History and Child Socialisation in the *Labour Prophet* and *Labour Leader*', in *Culture and Science In the Nineteenth-Century Media*, ed. Louise Henson et al. (Aldershot: Ashgate, 2004), 29–42.
——, 'The Spinster Tale-teller in the Victorian Marketplace', *New Comparison*, 27/28 (Spring–Autumn 1999), 83–97.
Sutherland, John, '*Cornhill's* Sales and Payments: The First Decade,' *VPR*, 19 (Fall 1986), 106–08.
Sutton, Emma, *Aubrey Beardsley and British Wagnerism* (Oxford: Oxford University Press, 2002).
Swinburne, Charles Algernon, 'Simeon Solomon: Notes on his "Vision of Love", and other Studies' (*Dark Blue*), July 1871, 568–77.
Symonds, John Addington, *In the Key of Blue and Other Prose Essays* (London: Elkin Mathews, 1918 edn), 55–86.
——, '*A Problem in Modern Ethics*': Being an Enquiry into the Phenomenon of Sexual Inversion (Davos [n. pub.] [1891]).
Symons, Arthur, 'Ballet, Pantomime and Poetic Drama', *Dome*, n.s. 1 (Oct. 1898), 65–71.
——, *Studies in Seven Arts* (London: Constable, 1906).
——, *The Symbolist Movement in Literature*, 2nd edn (London: Constable, 1908).
Tarpey, J. T. Kingsley, 'The Merrow', *Dome*, n.s. 3 (July 1899), 209–18.
Tatar, Maria, *The Hard Facts of the Grimms' Fairy Tales* (Princeton, NJ: Princeton University Press, 1987).
[Taylor, Edgar] 'German Popular and Traditional Literature: No. 1', *NMM*, 2 (1821), 146–52; 'No. IV', *NMM*, 4 (Apr. 1822) 289–96.
Taylor, Jenny Bourne, 'Between Atavism and Altruism: The Child on the Threshold in Victorian Psychology and Edwardian Children's Fiction', *Children in Culture*, ed. Karín Lenik-Oberstein (Basingstoke: Macmillan, 1998), 88–121.
Tennyson, Alfred, *In Memoriam and Other Poems* (London: Dent, 1994).
[Thackeray, William Makepeace], 'A Grumble About the Christmas-Books', *Fraser's*, 35 (Jan. 1847), 111–26.
[——], *Greek Studies* (London: Macmillan, 1890).
[——], 'On Some Illustrated Children's Books', *Fraser's*, 35 (Apr. 1846), 495–502.
[——], 'Roundabout Papers – No. I: "On a Lazy Idle Boy"', *CM*, 1 (Jan. 1860), 124–28.

Thompson, E. P., *The Struggle for a Free Press* (London: People's Press, 1952).
[Thoms, William, ed.], *Gammer Gurton's Famous Histories of Sir Guy of Warwick, Sir Bevis of Hampton, Tom Hickathrift, Friar Bacon, Robin Hood, and the King and the Cobbler. Newly Revised and Amended by Amb Mer* (London: Joseph Cundall, 1846).
Thomson, J. Arthur, 'Germinal, Floreal, Prairial', *Evergreen* (Spring 1895), 21–25.
Thornton, R. K. R., '"Decadence" in Later Nineteenth-Century England', in *Decadence and the 1890s*, ed. Ian Fletcher, 15–29.
Tieck, Ludwig, 'Pietro D'Abano; A Tale of Enchantment, from the German of Tieck' [trans. James Ferrier], *Blackwood's*, 46 (Aug. 1839), 228–55.
Trench, Richard Chenevix, *The Stuff of Words. Five Lectures*, 8th edn (London: Parker, 1858).
Trevor, John, 'Cinderella Letter', *LP*, 2 (Oct. 1893), 101.
——, trans., 'The Little Fur Slipper: From the French of Charles Perrault', *LP*, 2 (May 1893), 42–43.
——, *My Quest for God* (London: Labour Prophet Office, 1897).
——, 'Our Altered Form', *Prophet*, 1 (Mar. 1894), 1.
Trimmer, Sarah, *The Guardian of Education*, 5 vols (Bristol: Thoemmes, 2002).
Turner, Mark W., 'Time, Periodicals, and Literary Studies', *VPR*, 39 (2006), 309–16.
——, *Trollope and the Magazines: Gendered Issues in Mid-Victorian Britain* (Basingstoke: Macmillan; New York: St. Martin's Press, 2000).
Tylor, E. B., *Primitive Culture: Researches into the Development of Mythology, Philosophy, Language, Religion, Art and Custom*, 2nd edn, 2 vols (London: John Murray, 1873).
Uffelman, Larry, and Patrick Scott, 'Kingsley's Serial Novels, II: The Water-Babies', *VPR*, 19 (1986), 122–30.
VannArsdel, Rosemary T., *Macmillan's Magazine* and the Fair Sex 1859–1874 (II) *VPR*, 34 (2001), 2–15.
Vann, J. Don, and Rosemary VannArsdel, eds, *Victorian Periodicals: A Guide to Research*, 2 vols (New York: Modern Language Association, 1978–1989).
Victoria & Albert Museum, *Penny Dreadfuls and Comics: English Periodicals for Children from Victorian Times to the Present Day* (London: Victoria & Albert Museum, 1983).
Vincent, David, *Literacy and Popular Culture* (Cambridge: Cambridge University Press, 1989), 157.
Voisenon, Abbé de, *Fairy Tales by the Abbé Voisenon*, trans. R. B. Douglas (Athens: Erotica Biblion Society [Leonard Smithers], 1895).
Waller, John O., 'Charles Kingsley and the American Civil War', *Studies in Philology* 60 (July 1963), 554–68.
Ward, J. P., '"Came from yon fountain": Wordsworth's influence on Victorian Educators', *VS*, 29 (1986), 405–36.
Warner, Marina, *From the Beast to the Blonde: On Fairy Tales and Their Tellers* (London: Vintage, 1995).
Waters, Chris, *British Socialists and the Politics of Popular Culture, 1884–1914* (Manchester: Manchester University Press, 1990).
Wawn, Andrew, *The Vikings and the Victorians: Inventing the Old North in Nineteenth-Century Britain* (Cambridge: D. S. Brewer, 2000).
Webb, *The British Working-Class Reader 1790–1848: Literacy and Social Tension* (London: Unwin, 1955).
[Wedgwood, Julia]. 'The Boundaries of Science: A Dialogue I', *MM*, 2 (June 1860), 134–38; II, *MM*, 4 (July 1861), 137–47.
——, 'The Origin of Language: The Imitative Theory and Mr Max Müller's Theory of Phonetic Types', *MM*, 7 (Nov. 1862), 54–60.

——, 'Sir Charles Lyell on the Antiquity of Man', *MM*, 7 (Apr. 1863), 476–87.
Weeks, Jeffrey, *Coming Out: Homosexual Politics in Britain from the Nineteenth Century to the Present*, rev. edn (Quartet Books: London, 1990).
——, *Sex, Politics and Society: The Regulation of Sexuality since 1800* (London: Longman, 1981).
White, Chris, ed., *Nineteenth-Century Writings on Homosexuality: A Sourcebook* (London: Routledge, 1999).
White, Gleeson, 'The Editor's Room', *Studio*, 4–6 (Oct. 1894 to Jan. 1896), xli.
——, 'Sandro Botticelli (Filipepi)', *Dome*, 1 (Spring 1897), 81–87.
Wiener, Joel H., 'How New was the New Journalism?' in *Papers for the Millions: The New Journalism in Britain, 1850s–1914*, ed. Joel H. Wiener (New York: Greenwood Press, 1988), 47–71.
Wilde, Oscar, *The Complete Short Fiction*, ed. Ian Small (London: Penguin, 1994).
——, *Intentions*, 8th edn (London: Methuen, 1913), 153–217.
——, *The Happy Prince and Other Tales* (London: David Nutt, 1888).
——, *A House of Pomegranates* (London: Osgood, McIlvaine, 1891).
——, *Letters of Oscar Wilde*, ed. Rupert Hart Davis (London: Rupert Hart-Davis, 1962).
——, *More Letters of Oscar Wilde*, ed. Rupert Hart-Davis (Oxford: Oxford University Press, 1985).
——, *Plays, Prose Writings and Poems*, ed. Anthony Fothergill (London: Everyman, 1996).
Williams, Raymond. *The Long Revolution* (London: Penguin, 1965).
Wilson, Anita C., 'The Shining Garb of Wonder: The Paradox of Literary Fairy Tales in Mid-Victorian England', *Cahiers Victoriens et Édouardiens*, 37 (1993), 73–93.
Wood, Sally, *W. T. Stead and His Books for the Bairns* (Edinburgh: Salvia, 1987).
Wordsworth, William, *The Poetical Works*, new edn, 6 vols (London: Moxon, 1849–50)
——, *The Five-Book Prelude*, ed. Duncan Wu (Oxford: Blackwell, 1997).
Worth, George J., *Macmillan's Magazine 1859–1907* (Aldershot: Ashgate, 2003).
Wullschläger, Jackie, *Hans Christian Andersen: The Life of a Storyteller* (London: Allen Lane, 2000).
Yeats, W.B, *The Celtic Twilight* (London: Bullen, 1902).
——, 'Dust Hath Closed Helen's Eye', *Dome*, n.s. 4 (Aug. 1899), 162–66.
——, *Fairy and Folk Tales of the Irish Peasantry* (London: Walter Scott, 1888).
——, *Ideas of Good and Evil* (London: Macmillan, 1903) 237–56.
——, *Irish Fairy Tales* (London: Unwin, 1892).
——, *Mythologies*, ed. Warwick Gould and Deidre Toomey (Basingstoke: Palgrave Macmillan, 2005).
——, 'Song of Mongan', *Dome*, n.s. 1 (Oct. 1898), 36.
——, 'A Symbolic Artist and the Coming of Symbolic Art', *Dome*, n.s. 1 (Dec. 1898), 233–37.
——, *Uncollected Prose*, ed. John Frayne and Colton Johnson, 2 vols (Basingstoke: Macmillan, 1970–75).
Yeo, Stephen, 'A New Life: The Religion of Socialism in Britain, 1883–1896', *History Workshop Journal*, 4 (1977), 5–56.
Yonge, Charlotte, 'Children's Literature of the Last Century II: Didactic Fiction', *MM*, 20 (Aug. 1869), 302–10.
——, 'Children's Literature of the Last Century III: Class Literature of the Last Thirty Years', *MM*, 20 (Sept. 1869), 448–56.
——, 'Hints on Reading', *MP*, n.s. 23 (Jan. 1877), 95.
Ziegler, Arthur P. Jr, 'The *Dome* and its Editor Publisher: An Exploration', *American Book Collector*, 15 (1965), 19–21.

Zipes, Jack, *Fairy Tale as Myth Myth as Fairy Tale* (Kentucky: University Press of Kentucky, 1994).
——, *Fairy Tales and the Art of Subversion* (New York: Routledge, 1983).
——, ed., *Victorian Fairy Tales: The Revolt of the Fairies and the Elves* (New York: Methuen, 1987; repr. New York, Routledge, 1991).
——, *When Dreams Came True: Classical Fairy Tales and Their Tradition* (Routledge: New York, 1999).
——, *Why Fairy Tales Stick: The Evolution and Relevance of a Genre* (London: Routledge, 2006).

Index

Illustrations are marked in **bold**.

Adventures of Musul; or, The Three Gifts, 14
Aesop's Fables, 14, 118
aestheticism, 134, 136, 137, 139, 141, 148–50, 155–6, 160
   see also decadence, Symbolism
Africa, 49, 157
Ainger, Alfred, 39
Alderson, Brian, 80
All the Year Round, 1, 3, 4, 25
Altick, Richard, 184 n.26, 188 n.101
'Ambrose Merton', *see under* Thoms
American Civil War, 73, 85, 188 n.33
American Journal of Psychology, 166
Andersen, Hans Christian, 6, 48, 181 n.21
   autobiographies of, 52–3
   fairy tales by, 6, 11, 19, 32–3, 52–5, 61, 137, 140
   socialist appropriations of, 102, 104–5, 115–16, 123
   individual works: 'The Daisy', 181 n.20; 'The Darning Needle', 116; 'The Dying Child', 54; 'The Galoshes of Happiness', 59; 'The Harebell's Sermon', 116; 'The Little Match-Girl', 55, 80, 104–5; 'The Little Mermaid', 6; 'The Little Ugly Duck', 181 n.20; 'The Red Shoes', 56, 181 n.20; 'The Snow Queen', 162; 'There was a Difference', 115–16; 'What the Goodman does is Sure to be Right', 61; 'What the Whole Family Said', 52
Anderson, Benedict, 178
androgyny, 156, 160–62, 164, **165**, 166–7, **168**, 169
Anon!, 63
Ansani, Antonella, 5
anthropology, 9, 30–31, 34–5, 41, 49–52, 70–0, 103–0, 143, 156–7, 176–8
   see also Clodd; Darwin; evolution; Lang; race; Tylor; McLennan
anthropomorphism, 11, 122

antiquarianism, 15–16, 24, 46–7
   see also comparative mythology; folklore; folktale; Indo-European; philology
Apo, Satu, 24
Arabian Nights, 3, 11, 24, 27, 79, 130, 131–2
   anthropology and, 51–2, 68–9, 157
   decadence and, 150, 156–7, 160–1
   homosexuality and, 156–7, 160, 162–3
   socialist appropriations of, 96, **97**, 98
   see also Burton; Galland; Housman, Laurence; Lane; Wilde, Oscar
Arnold, Matthew,
   'The Study of Celtic Literature', 70–1
'Art for Art's sake', 134, 136, 140–42, 150–51
   see also aestheticism; decadence; Symbolism
Arthurian romance, 39, 67, 137, 147, 148
Artist and Journal of Home Culture, 154, 163, 172
Arts and Crafts Exhibition Society, 137
Arts and Crafts movement, 7, 131, 135–7, **138**, 139–41, 144–5, 148, 153
Aryan *see under* Indo-European
Asbjørnsen, Peter Christen, 45
   see also Dasent
Ashbee, Charles Robert, 163–4
Ashbee, Henry Spencer ['Pisanus Fraxi'], 216 n.131
Ashton, John, 24
Asia,
   as origin of fairy tales, 16–17, 42–3
   and 'Sotadic Zone', 157
   see also Orientalism
Athenæum, 6, 9, 18–19, 178
Atkinson, Rev. J. C., 46, 47, 50
Auerbach, Nina, 7, 182 n.31–2, 201 n.86
Aulnoy, Marie-Cathérine le Jumel de Barneville de la Motte, Countess d', 32
   'The Green Serpent', 157
   Tales of Mother Bunch, 11

Aunt Judy's Magazine, 7, 34–9, 43–9, 52–66, 117, 176
Aurevilly, Jules Barbey, d', 148
Austin, Sarah, 18

'Back to the Land movement', 105–13
  see also socialism
ballads, 16, 22
  see also chapbooks
Barlow, Jane,
  The End of Elfin-Town, 164, **165**
Barnacle, 64
Barrie, James M.,
  Peter Pan, 141
Batten, John D., 136
Bayes, Alfred Walter, 55, **56**
Beam, 133, 140–1, 154
Beardsley, Aubrey, 149, 158
  and *Yellow Book*, 131, 132, 134–5
  'The Slippers of Cinderella', 131, 209 n.4
  Under the Hill, 164
  'The Woman in the Moon' (*Salome*), 161
'Beauty and the Beast', 12, 67, 81, **159**
Bechstein, Ludwig, 48
Beckett, R. A., 91
Bede, Cuthbert, 2
Beer, Gillian, 74, 87, 218 n.6
Beerbohm, Max, 131,
  'Be it Cosiness', 149
  'Yai and the Moon', 161
Beetham, Margaret, 65
Belgravia, 2, 4
Bell, Edward, 52
Bell, George, 38
Benjamin, Walter, 175–6
Bennett, Tony, 8
Bentley's Miscellany, 6
Berkeley, Bishop George, 79–80, 153
Bernhardt, Sarah, 167
Bevir, Mark, 113
Birmingham Guild of Handicraft, 135, 137, 139
Birmingham School of Art, 133, 137
Blackwood's Edinburgh Magazine, 18, 25
Blake, William,
  'A Little Girl Lost', 151–2
  and Symbolism, 151–3

Blatchford, Robert [Peel Glanville],
  and Cinderella clubs, 102–5
  and *Clarion*, 88, 89, 91–4, 96, 100–103, 125
  and fairy tales, 102–5, 111, 120, 127–30
  and *Labour Prophet*, 104, 125
  and 'religion of socialism', 100–101, 106–7
  Altruism, 102
  Fantasias, 92
  God and My Neighbour, 100
  Merrie England, 92, 96
  The New Religion, 107
  The Sorcery Shop, 107
'Bluebeard', 14, 22, 25, 137
Bodichon, Barbara,
  'A Dull Life', 85
Böhl de Faber, Cecilia, 44, 195 n.126
Book-Lover's Magazine, 162
Booth, William, 52
Botticelli, Sandro, 142
Bottigheimer, Ruth B., 4, 12, 181 n.14
Bourdieu, Pierre, 134
Bourke, Angela, 24
Bown, Nicola, 9, 181 n.15, 182 n.36, 194 n.94, 197 n.12
Boys of England, 34, 37–8
Boys Own Magazine, 189 n.6
Brake, Laurel, 163, 181 n.25, 197 n.8, 210 n.23, 215 n.129, 202 n.20
Brett, Edmund, 37
Brierley, Benjamin, 7
Bristow, Joseph, 215 n.111, n.127; 216. n.129, n.139
British Magazine and Review, 13
British Quarterly Review, 40
British Society for the Study of Sex Psychology (BSSP), 166
Brocklehurst, Frederick, 93
Brooke, Emma, 93–4
Broomfield, Andrea, 83
Browne, Mathew, 64
Browning, Elizabeth Barrett, 114, 135
Bunbury, Sir Charles, 73
Burke, Peter, 12, 185, n.37
Burne-Jones, Sir Edward, 154, 167
Burnett, Mary G., 98, 111
Burton, Sir Richard
  The Book of the Thousand Nights and a Night, 131, 172
  homosexuality and, 156–7, 162–3

see also Arabian Nights; Order of Chæronea
Butterfly, 132–4, 139, 143–4, 155, 157, 160, 167, 169

Cadogan, Mary, 54
Calaïs, 162
Caldecott, Randolph, 57, **60**, 96
Campbell, J. F.
  Popular Tales of the West Highlands, 69, 71
Canepa, Nancy L., 5
cannibalism, 25–6, 31, 72, 122–3, 187 n.71
capitalism,
  as destroyer of folk belief, 109–10, 139, 175–6
Carlill, James Briggs, 69
Carlow Morning Post, 20
Carlyle, Thomas, 73, 95, 107, 118
Carpenter, Edward, 166
Carroll, Lewis [Charles Ludwidge Dodgson], 10
  Alice's Adventures in Wonderland, 5, 32, 68, 122
  'Bruno's Revenge', 39
Catholic Emancipation, 23
celestial mythology *see under* solar mythology
Celtic Revival, 7, 131, 136, 145–8
  see also Irish Revival; Yeats
Celticism, 68–73, *see also* Ireland, race
Century Guild Hobby Horse, 133, 134–6, 146, 153, 156, 167
Certeau, Michel, de, 6
Chaillu, Paul Belloni Du,
  Explorations and Adventures in Equatorial Africa, 73–4
Chamberlain, Joseph, 98
Chambers, Robert, 21
  Vestiges of the Natural History of Creation, 77
Chambers, William, 21
Chambers's Edinburgh Journal, 2, 6, 21–4, 70, 103
Chamisso, Adelbert von,
  Peter Schlemihl, 18
chapbooks, 3, 4, 13–21, 176
chapmen, 12, 22
Chatterbox, 38, 52–3, 57, **58**
Chaucer, Geoffrey, 68
Chauncey, George, 166

Chavannes, Puvis de, 133
cheap press
  and folk culture, 11–13, 15–6, 19–26, 52–3, 57, **59**, 96–129, 175–6
Chermside, Richard, 76
child correspondents and writers, 13, 36, 62–5, 118–26
child, constructions of, 3, 8, 9, 13, 14, 16–18, 25–9, 32, 35–49, 50–1, 53–4, 56–7, **58–60**, 62–5, 71–72, 75–8, 96, 101–27, 139–44, 147–51, 152–4, 174
'childhood of the race', *see under* recapitulation thesis; *see also* primitivism
chivalry, 147
  and homosexuality, 148, 163–4, 172
Christian socialism, 75–8, 87
  see also Labour Church
Christianity, 35, 36–7, 42, 48, 52, 53, 64–65, 69, 72, 74–6, 79–80, 83, 86, 87, 89, 100, 153, 170–1, 176
Church Quarterly Review, 10, 36
Churchman's Last Shift, 11
'Cinderella', 30, 32, 67, 75, 80–1, 131, 148
  socialist appropriations of, 105, 111–12, 114–118, 126
  Cinderella clubs, 101–5, 111, 117, 125, 176
  Cinderella schools, 102, 104, 114, 117
circulating libraries, 15
  Mudie's, 3, 10
Clarion field clubs, 112
Clarion, 88–94, 96, 103, 107, 111–12, 125, 130
Clarke, [Charles] Alan, 45, 110
  'A Talk About Fairies', 88, 108–9
  'Little Red Riding Hood', 110
Clarke, Erskine, 38
Clayton, Joseph, 111–13
Cleary, Bridget, 24
Clodd, Edward,
  socialist appropriations of, 105–6
  Fairy Tales from Hans Andersen, 10, 19
  The Childhood of Religions, 96, 106
  The Childhood of the World, 106
  'The Philosophy of Rumpelstiltskin', 25
  Tom Tit Tot: An Essay on Savage Philosophy in Folk-Tale, 106

242   Index

Cobbe, Frances Power, 83
Cohen, Francis, 46
  'Antiquities of Nursery Literature', 15–16
Cole, Sir Henry, 19, 29
Coleridge, Samuel Taylor, 13, 42, 191 n.44
Collins, Charles Alston, 76
Collins, Wilkie, 26
Comic Cuts, 102
'communications circuit', 4, 180 n.12
comparative mythology, 8–9, 29–31, 34–5, 42–52, 66, 68–7 105–7, 148, 158, 177–8
  see also antiquarianism; anthropology; folktale; folklore
Comte, [Isidore] Auguste [Marie Francois Xavier], 69
Cornhill Magazine, 8, 11, 29, 35, 67–70, 77–9, 81–2, 84–7
correspondence columns, 7, 35–6, 96, 98, 100, 118–26
Cox, George, 69
Cox, Mabel, 153–4, 156, 172
Craig, Patricia, 54
Craik, Dinah Mulock
  The Fairy Book, 5, 28, 32
  'The Last News of the Fairies', 34, 39, 44–5
Crane, Walter, 136–7
Croker, Thomas Crofton,
  and newspapers, 23–4
  Fairy Legends and Traditions of the South of Ireland, 23–4, 31–2
  see also Yeats; folktales, Irish
Cross, Victoria, 157, 214 n.102
cross-dressing, 166–7
Cruikshank, George,
  and *Aunt Judy's Magazine*, 57, **58**
  Gammer Grethel's Fairy Tales see under Housman, Laurence
  George Cruikshank's Fairy Library, 27–9, 33
  German Popular Stories, 27–9, 136, 142
  see also Grimms' fairy tales
Cundall, Joseph,
  Home Treasury, 19, 29
Cunningham, Valentine, 68, 80

d'Arch Smith, Timothy, 163, 172
Daily Mail, 134
dandy, the, 148–50

Dark Blue, 155
Darwin, Charles, 41, 87, 129–30, 177
  Origin of Species, 8, 68, 72, 75–80, 87, 106–7, 177
  see also anthropology; degeneration; evolution; race; social darwinism
Dasent, George Webbe,
  Tales from the Norse, 31, 45–6, 69, 71
Dawson, Julia, 108
Dearmer, Mabel, 140
decadence, 7, 131, 133, 139, 140–2, 145–9, 154, **159**, 160, 172, 174
  see also aestheticism, Symbolism
Defoe, Daniel, 11
degeneration (biological), 51, 72, 74, 146–8
  see also Darwin; decadence; evolution
Dellamora, Richard, 156, 215 n.127
Depping, G. B., 17
Dial, 133, 135, 157
Dicey, E. D., 73
Dickens, Charles, 25–8, 32
  and 'fancy', 1, 4, 26–7, 175–6
  'Frauds on the Fairies', 3, 27–8, 32, 33
  Hard Times, 26–7
  'Nurse's Stories', 25
  'On Strike', 187 n.78
  'The Thousand and One Humbugs', 27, 96
  see also All the Year Round, Household Words
Dixon, E. S., 78
Dome, 132–6, 139, 142–6, 152–3, 155, 158, **159**, 167, 170,
Dorson, Richard M., 9, 31
Douglas, Lord Alfred, 174
  'Prince Charming', 172
Dowling, Linda, 132, 163, 212 n.65
Drotner, Kirsten, 36, 64
Dublin and London Magazine, 20–23
Dublin Evening Mail, 23
Dublin University Magazine, 20
Duffy, James, 22
Duffy's Sixpenny Magazine, 20
Dulac, Edmund,
  Stories from the Arabian Nights, 132, 157
Dumfries and Galloway Courier, 22

Earls, Brian, 20, 22, 23
Eden, H. K. F., *see under* Gatty, H. K. F.

Edgeworth, Maria,
  'Purple Jars', 150
education,
  as destroyer of folklore, 2, 9, 45,
    109–10
  child, 93–6, 101–5, 108–27
  female, 54, 59–60, 84–6, 195 n.121
  socialist, 88, 92–6, 98, 101–29
Egoff, Sheila, 35
Ellis, Havelock, 160
  Sexual Inversion, 166, 216 n.136
Emerson, Ralph Waldo, 46, 100, 107,
  189 n.4
Emmett, George, 37
Emmett, William Laurence, 37
Empire, 23–4, 35, 48–9, 65, 70, 176
Eros, and coded homosexual discourse,
  162–4, **165**
ethnology, see anthropology
'Ettrick Shepherd', *see under* Hogg, James
eugenics, 147–8
euhemerism, 49, 50
Evergreen, 146–8
evolution, 9, 34, 39, 41–52, 59, 68–80,
  87, 107, 143, 158, 177–8
  and socialism, 89, 99, 100, 102,
    105–13, 127, 129
  see also anthropology; Darwin;
    degeneration; philology
Ewing, Juliana Horatia (J. H.),
  and *Aunt Judy's Magazine*, 9, 10, 34,
    37–9, 45–7, 54–7, 61–3, 66
  and debt to the Grimms, 45, 48, 60
  and gender 54, 61–3
  and class, 47, 56–7, 62
  and manuscript magazines, 62, 195
    n.132
  'Amelia and the Dwarts', 55
  'The Brownies: A Fairy Story', 46–7
  'The Kyrekegrim Turned Preacher', 47
  The Story of a Short Life, 39–40, 54
  Jackanapes, 39–40
  Lob Lie-by-the-Fire, 193 n.68
  'Old-fashioned Fairy Tales' 45, 47,
    54–5, 60–1
  'Timothy's Shoes', 56–7
  see also Gatty, H. K. F.; Gatty,
    Margaret; *Aunt Judy's Magazine*
exotic, constructions of, 156–81
  see also Orientalism

Fabian socialism, 89, 94, 102, 114, 129
  see also socialism
fables, 14, 34, 45
Fairies, 1–2, 9, 18, 23, 31, 39, 40, 46, 47
  49, 67, 71, 81, 87, 88, 141, 151–2,
  164, 166, 169–71, 144
  departure of, 2, 9, 44–5, 108–13
  socialist appropriations of, 88, 108–9,
    111–12, 115–17 (*see also* giants)
  homosexual appropriations of, 160–4,
    165, 166–7, 170–4
  fairy and folkloric types:
    brownies, 46–7; dryads, 170;
    dwarves, 50, 79, 81; elves, 28, 46,
    49, 117–18, 141; giants, 64,
    119–27, 147; goblins, 39, 50–1;
    hobs, 46; leprechauns, 20;
    mermaids/merrows 141, 146;
    gnomes, 50; kobolds, 50; niss, 47;
    ogres, 27, 49, 61, 64; púca, 20;
    sidhe, 20; trolls, 49–50, 71;
    scratlings, 49
Fairy ballet, 5, 181 n.15
Fairy pantomime, 32, 181 n.15
fairy tales:
  definitions of 4, 31–3, 195 n.116
  canon formation and, 13, 27–9,
    32–3
  debates over origin and diffusion of,
    8–9, 16–19, 30–31, 42–50, 69–70,
    106–9, 143–8, 177–8
  morality and, 14, 17, 30, 33, 50–5, 65,
    72–3, 75, 78, 80–1, 83, 86, 102.
    114–16, 118, 123, 126, 132,
    141–52, 163, 172–4
  class and, 2–4 6–9, 13–16, 18–29,
    32–3, 34–5, 44, 47, 48 9, 58–55,
    57–60, 62, 68, 72, 75, 78–81, 87,
    96–130, 139–40, 146, 172
  gender and sexuality and, 7–8, 54–66,
    82–7, 107–8, 141, 147–8, 151–3,
    156–74
  see also antiquarianism; evolution;
    folklore; folktales; comparative
    mythology; philology;
    primitivism; race; individual
    authors and titles
famine, Irish, 24
Farrar, F. W., 41
Fay, E. F., 92, 125

Index

'Felix Summerly' fairy tales, *see under* Cole, Sir Henry
feminism, 8, 58–62, 82–6, 93, 132, 152, 157
Fenton, John, 143
'Fernán Caballero', *see under* Böhl de Faber, Cecilia
Fielding, Sarah
  The Governess, 2, 14
Flaubert, Gustave, 157
Fletcher, Ian, 132, 163, 167, 171
'folk', constructions of, 2, 4, 12, 15–16, 18–20, 32, 41–9, 55–7, 69–71, 105–113, 138–48, 160, 175–6
Folk-Lore Journal, 20, 143
Folk-Lore Record, 20, 25, 39
Folk-Lore Society, 10, 20
Folk-Lore, 4
Folklore:
  definitions of, 8–9, 19, 24
  see also anthropology; comparative mythology; fairy tales; folktales
folktales, 1–4, 8–9, 15–25, 23–5, 29–31, 34, 39, 42–51, 50, 53, 55–7, 69–71, 87, 105–113, 117–29, 140–1, 143, 146–7
  and authenticity, 12–13, 15, 20, 176, 183 n.10–11
  by nation/region:
    Andalucian, 42, 44, 48, 61, 195 n.126; Breton, 44; Celtic, 69–71, 136, 145–7 (*see also* Irish, Scottish); English, 2–4, 15–17, 19, 22, 25, 46–7; 123, German 16–18, 24, 45, 47, 57 (*see also* Grimms' fairy tales); Hawaiian, 24; Indian, 17, 32, 53; Irish, 4, 19–24, 44, 47, 56, 145–6; Manx, 108; Scandinavian, 24, 45–47, 69, 70–71, 117–18; Scottish, 2, 22, 46–7, 69, 70–71, 145; Tuscan, 141
  see also antiquarianism; chapbooks; folklore; comparative mythology; fairy tales; philology
Forman, H. Buxton, 59–60
Forster, John, 25
Fortnightly Review, 140, 142
Fox, Charles, 37
Fraser, Alexander Campbell, 79–80
Fraser's Magazine, 6, 18, 29, 76

Frere, Mary,
  Old Deccan Days, 32, 53
Froude, Anthony, 72

Gagnier, Regenia, 161
Galland, Antoine,
  Thousand and One Nights, 11
  see also Arabian Nights
Galton, Arthur, 156
Garrett Anderson, Elizabeth, 83, 84, 86
Garrett Fawcett, Millicent, 83
Gaskell, Elizabeth, 11
  Cranford, 86
Gaskin, H. J., 137
Gatty, Horatia Katharine Frances (H. K. F.)
  and *Aunt Judy's Magazine*, 37, 54
  see also Gatty, Margaret; Ewing, J. H.,
Gatty, Margaret, (Mrs Alfred),
  and *Aunt Judy's Magazine* 36–9, 45, 54, 56–7, 60, 195 n.121
  and child correspondents, 62–5
  Aunt Judy's Letters, 63
  Parables from Nature, 36, 60
  see also Ewing, Juliana Horatia; Gatty, H. K. F.
Gatty, Stephen. H.,
  'The Galoshes of Happiness', 59–60
Gay discourse/subculture, *see under* homosexuality
Gay's Fables, 14
Geddes, Patrick, 147–8
General Election (1895), **97**, **99**, 123
geology
  and parallels with philology, 34, 41–2, 177
Germ, 155
Gibbon, Edward, 71
Gidley, S. M., 48
Gilbert, R. A., 31
Gilbert, William,
  'Sinbad in England', 51–2, 68
Girl's Own Paper, 66
Goethe, Johann Wolfgang von,
  'The Tale', 18
Goldney, S., 43, 48
Golsworthy, Arnold, 133
Gomme, Laurence, 30
Good Things for the Young see under Good Words for the Young
Good Words for the Young, 34, 35, 37, 38–45, 48–52, 64, 71

Good Words, 35, 67
Goody Two-Shoes, 56, 194 n.114
Gordon, Jan B., 148–9
gorillas, 72–3, see also Chaillu
Gosse, Edmund, 148
Gosse, Philip Henry, 77
Gothic fiction, 15, n.141, 146
Gould, F. J., 110–11, 191 n.40
Gould, Peter C., 113
Gould, Sabine Baring, 193 n.82
Gould, Stephen Jay, 41, 191 n.40, see also recapitulation thesis
Graves, Clotilde, 157
Gray, John, 133
'The Great Worm', 157–8, 160
Greek myth, 43
 coded homosexual discourse and, 162–7
Greg, Percy, 76
Grimm, Jacob,
 Teutonic Mythology, 45–6
 with Grimm, Wilhelm,
 Grimms' fairy tales, 4, 12–13, 16–18, 24, 26, 28–33, 45, 48, 60, 137, 140, 160, 169
 socialist appropriations of, 102, 123, 127
 editions (books):
 Gammer Grethel's Fairy Tales
  see under Housman, Laurence
 Kinder und Haus Märchen, 13, 16
 Grimm's Goblins, 26, 29, 32, 82–3
 Grimms' Household Tales, 213 n.87
 German Popular Stories, 17, 27–9
 individual tales:
 'The Elves and the Shoemaker', 46;
 'Faithful Henry', 129; 'The Girl without Hands', 155, 213 87n.;
 'Hans in Luck', 61; 'The Ragamuffins', 105; 'Rapunzel', 137, **138**; 'Rumpelstiltskin', 105;
 'The Seven Swans', 129; 'The King of the Golden Mountain', 129;
 'Snow White', 25, 155; 'The Twelve Brothers', 24
Gunpowder Plot, 63

Haeckel, Ernst, 41
 Haekel's biogenic law see under recapitulation thesis
Halfpenny Journal, 26

Halliday, Andrew, 3
Harcourt, Sir William, 98
Hardie, [James] Keir, 4, 6
 and *Labour Leader*, 88, 90, 92–6, **97**, 98–101, 106, 109, 113, 117–29
 children's columns, 109–13, 118–26, 176
 'The History of a Giant', 120, 122
 'Jack Clearhead. A Fairy Tale for Crusaders', 88, 113, 119–24, 126, 129
 see also Blatchford; Morris; Independent Labour Party; socialism; Trevor
Harland, Henry, 134
Harper's Magazine, 154
Harries, Elizabeth Wanning, 12–13, 188 n.94
Hartland, Edwin Sidney,
 The Science of Fairy Tales, 31
Hearn, Michael Patrick, 8
Herder, Johann Gottfried, 13
Hibernian Magazine, 20
'Hibernian Tales', 19
Hincks, J. G., 42
Hinduism, 48–9, see also India
Hinton, James,
 'The Fairy Land of Science', 68–9
Hirosage, Utagowa, 158
'The History of Cock Robin', 3
Hitch, Jessie, 118–19
Hodgson, Amanda, 74
Hogg, James, 18, 185 n.35
Hokusai, Katsushika, 158
Holmes, C. J., 158
Home Rule (Ireland), 24, 97
homosexuality
 coded discourse and, 7, 157, 160–64, **165**, 166–7, **168**, 169–72, **173**, 174
Hopkin, Deian, 89, 91
Hopper, Nora, 124
'A Snowdrop Song', 145
Household Words, 1–3, 11, 26–7, 70, 187 n.78
Housman, Clemence, 218 n.165
Housman, Laurence, 4, 33
 and Arts and Crafts, 135–6, 139–40, 143–5, 153
 and coded homosexual discourse, 156–8, 160–74, 176

Housman, Laurence (*Contd.*)
  and decadence, 132, 139–40, 149, 160–61, 172–4
  and feminism 132, 152
  and little magazines, 131–3, 135–6, 139, 142–5, 149, 151–6, 160–64, 166–7 **168**, 169–172, **173**
  and Symbolism, 139, 140, 151–2, 151–4, 166, 169
  'Blind Love', 151–2, 154, 161, 172, **173**
  'The Blue Moon', 157–8, 160–2, 164
  'The Bound Princess', 210 n. 29
  'A Capful of Moonshine', 135, 143–5, 151, 161
  'Death and the Bather', 169
  'The Defence of Farvingdon', 143
  Echo de Paris: a Study from Life, 171
  The End of Elfin-Town, 164, **165**
  An Englishwoman's Love Letters, 218, n.164
  A Farm in Fairyland, 136, 160, 164
  The Field of Clover, 136, 164
  Gammer Grethel's Fairy Tales, 131, 132, 142, 153, 169, 174
  'A Gander and his Geese', 143–44, 151
  'The Helping Hands', 155
  The House of Joy, 164
  'How Little Duke Jarl Saved the Castle', 135, 143
  'The Invisible Princess' (from 'Blind Love'), **173**
  'The Poison Tree', 170
  'Puss in Winter', 162
  'The Reflected Faun', 167, **168**
  'The Rooted Lover', 160
  Stories from the Arabian Nights, 132, 157
  'Tales of a Woodcutter', 169–72
  The Unexpected Years, 136
  'The Zeit-Geist', 149
Howe, Edward, 50–1
Howitt, Mary, 6
Howitt's Journal, 6
Howman, Knightley,
  'The Fauna of the Streets', 77–8
Hughes, Linda K., 8
Hughes, Thomas, 75
Humpherys, Anne, 120
Hunter, J. Paul, 12–13
Hutton, Richard Holt, 28

Huxley, Thomas Henry, 74, 79, 87
Huysmans, Joris-Karl,
  À Rebours, 150
Hyndman, Henry Mayers, 90

Illustrated London News, 31
Image, Selwyn, 136
Independent Labour Party (ILP), 89, 93–4, 98–9, 108, 112, 117, 122–7
India, 16–17, 43, 48–9
Indo-European:
  family of languages, 16, 42–9, 69–70
  thesis of mythological diffusion 16, 30–1, 42–9, 69–70, 107, 148, 177
  and India, 16–17, 48–9
  and Celticism, 69–70
  see also fairy tales; philology; Müller; solar mythology
Inquirer, 28
Ipswich Journal, 25
Iran, 43
Ireland, 3, 4, 6, 8, 18–24, 45, 46, 47, 69–73, 80, 146
Irish Penny Magazine, 21–2
Irish Revival, 4, 9, 19–20, 23–4, 145–6, 153, 178
  see also Celtic revival; folktales; Yeats
Irish Times, 23
'Islamic Orient', 157–8
Ives, George Cecil, 163

'Jack and the Beanstalk', 67
'Jack the Giant-Killer', 3, 22, 68, 147
  socialist appropriations of, 88, 113, 119–24, 126, 129
Jackson, Holbrook, 132, 133
Jacobs, Joseph, 30
  English Fairy Tales, 4
  More Celtic Fairy Tales, 136
James, Henry,
  'The Turn of the Screw', 143
James, Louis, 22
Janzen, Lorraine Kooistra, 161
Japan, 133, 158–60
  see also Orientalism
Jefferies, Richard, 107
Jones, Sir William, 16, 48
  see also Asia; India; Indo-European
Justice, 90, 92, 94

Kains-Jackson, Charles, 162–4, 172, 174
  see also chivalry, Order of Chæronea
'Kama Shastra Society', 157
Keightley, Thomas, 46, 47
Kelmscott Press, 139, 158
Kincaid, James R., 42
King, K. Douglas, 141
Kingsley, Charles, 4, 9, 34, 45, 198 n.33
  and *Good Words for the Young*, 39–40, 42, 44, 49–51, 66, 71
  and *Macmillan's Magazine*, 5, 8, 67–9, 71–5, 78–80, 85–7, 197 n.11
  and religion, 42–3, 72, 74–5, 78–80, 87, 177
  and race, 68, 71–8, 80
  and Ireland, 71–2, 74, 80
  and Darwin, 71–8, 198 n.26, 27
  and Max Muller, 42, 44, 45, 71, 74
  Madam How and Lady Why, 5, 39, 42, 44, 49–50, 69, 71–2
  The Heroes; or Greek Fairy Tales for my Children, 5
  The Roman and the Teuton, 71–2
  The Water-Babies, 5, 8, 32, 51, 67–8, 71–6, 78–83, 86–7, 103, 176
  'Women and Politics', 86–7
Klaus, H. Gustav, 94
Knight, Charles, 21
Knoepflmacher, U. C., 8, 40, 56
Kotzin, Michael C., 27

L'Héritier, Marie-Jeanne de Vallandon,
  'The Wary Princess, or the Adventures of Finette', 11
Labour Church, 89–96, 98, 99–118, 125–6
Labour Crusaders, 118–27
  see also Hardie; *Labour Leader*
Labour Leader, 7, 88, 90, 92–101, 108–112, 117, 119–22, 124–9, 118–26
Labour Prophet, 88–9, 90–120, 23, 126–7
Lamb, Charles, 13
Lambeth School of Art, 133
Lane, Edward W.,
  The Thousand and One Nights, 203 n.48
  see also *Arabian Nights*
Lane, John, 134, 140, 141, 167, 169
Lang, Andrew,
  and dispute with Müller over folktale origin, 30–1

  and the press, 11, 30–1, 149, 177–8,
  and 'savage survivals', 30–1, 49, 177
  Blue Fairy Book, 11
  Red Fairy Book, 30, 177
Le Cachet, 63
Le Gallienne, Richard, 169
  'Tree-Worship'
Lee, Vernon [Violet Paget], 131
  'Prince Alberic and the Snake Lady', 141–2
  Tuscan Fairy Tales, 141
'Legends of the Fairies', 19
legends, 19, 39
Leisure Hour, 23
Lenox, George Louis,
  'Annette: A Fairy Tale', 13
Lewes, George Henry,
  'Studies in Animal Life', 77
Liberalism, 98
Lilliputian Magazine, 13
Linton, Eliza Lynn, 62
literacy, 4, 5, 12, 20–3, 39, 44–5, 109–10, 176–7, 186 n.59, 188 n.101
  see also oral storytelling, readerships
Literary Gazette, 25
Little Folks, 64
Little Red Riding Hood', 19
  appropriations of in *Household Words*, 27
  socialist appropriations of, 19, 96, 98, 99, 110,
Lloyd, Edward, 187 n.71
  Arabian Nights Entertainments, 26, 33
  People's Periodical, 26
Locke, John, 14, 65
London Clipper, 38
London Journal, 6
Lover, Samuel, 21, 24
Ludlow, J. M., 73, 75
Lund, Michael, 8
Lyell, Sir Charles, 74

MacDonald, George, 9, 10, 32, 48, 191 n.39
  and *Good Words for the Young*, 9, 34–5, 38–40, 42, 44, 50–1, 66
  At the Back of the North Wind, 5, 39, 40, 42, 44
  Dealings with Fairies, 40

248 Index

MacDonald, George (*Contd.*)
   The Princess and the Goblin, 5, 39,
     50–1, 66
   The Princess and Curdie, 5, 51
   Ranald Bannerman's Boyhood, 40
   see also Kingsley
Macdonald, Lizzie, 103
Macdonald, W., 147
Mackmurdo, Arthur Heygate, 133–4
Macleod, Fiona *see under* William Sharp
Macleod, Norman
   and *Good Words for the Young*, 35, 37,
     48–9
Macmillan (publishing house), 5
Macmillan, Alexander, 67, 74, 75, 79,
   82–3, 196 n.8
Macmillan, Hugh, 41–2
Macmillan's Magazine, 5, 8, 28, 31–2
MacNiece, Louis, 68
Malthus, Thomas Robert, 78
Mann, Tom, 118
'march of the intellect', 2, 24, *see also*
   education
Marshall, John, 16
Martineau, Harriet, 73, 84
'Marty's Escape', 64
Marvellous Magazine, 15
Marx, Karl, 107
Marxism, 89–90 *see also* socialism
Masson, David,
   and Celticism, 69–73
   and *Macmillan's Magazine*, 69–73, 75
Mattar, Sinéad Garrigan, 9, 24, 70, 178
Maugham, W. Somerset, 132
Maurice, Frederick Denison, 75
Mayhew, Henry, 52
Mayo, Robert, 15
Mazzini, Giuseppe, 107
McArthur, Archie, 127
McLennan, J.F., 52, 194 n.97
medievalism, 110, 129, 137, **138**, 139,
   141, **159**, 179
Mélusine myth, 141
Meteyard, Sidney,
   'Rapunzel', 137, **138**
Mew, James, 11
Mill, John Stuart, 60, 86
Mirror, 25
Mitchell, Jack, 94
Moe, Jørgen, 45 *see also* Dasent

monogenesis, 72
Monthly Packet, 4, 34–8, 42–8, 50, 54, 55,
   64, 66
Moreau, Gustave, 133, 167
Morley, Henry,
   'Ground in the Mill', 187 n.78
   'Little Red Working-Coat', 27
   see also Dickens and fancy; *Household*
     Words
Morning Chronicle, 92
Morning Post, 24
Morris, G.L.L., 154
Morris, Jane, 137, 155
Morris, William, 123
   and Arts and Crafts, 136–7, 139, 145
   and socialism, 90, 92–3, 103, 107,
     110–11, 123, 129, 137–9, 145
   and *Commonweal*, 90, 92
   A Dream of John Ball, 92
   The Ideal Book, 138–9
   News from Nowhere, 93, 103, 107, 110,
     129
   The Pilgrims of Hope, 92
   'Rapunzel', 137, **138**
'Mother Goose', 11, 14, 20, 57, **59**, **60**, 64
   see also Perrault, Charles
Mudie's, *see under* circulating libraries
Müller, [Friedrich] Max, 30–31, 197 n.20
   and child readerships, 41–6
   and the 'disease of language', 43
   and Charles Kingsley, 42, 44, 45, 71, 74
   and Indo-European thesis of
     mythological diffusion, 30–1,
     41–6, 49, 69–70, 107, 148, 177
   Chips from a German Workshop, 30,
     42–4, 46, 69–71
   Lectures on the Science of Language, 199
     n.41
   Sacred Books of the East, 107
   see also comparative mythology;
     Indo-European; philology
Mulock, Dinah, *see under* Dinah Mulock
   Craik
Musäus, Johann Karl August, 13
   'Rubezaal; or The Wizard of the
     Mountains', 116
mysticism, 145–6, 152–4, 166–7, 175
mythology *see under* comparative
   mythology; Indo-European; fairy
   tale; Greek myth

National Art Training School, 133
nationalism, 4, 19–23, 145–6, 147
Native Americans, 49, 71
natural history, 36, 41–2, 75–8, 80
　socialist, 107–13, 177
natural theology, see under nature
nature,
　and spiritual belief, 9, 24, 30, 42–3, 46, 69–70, 75, 77–80, 87, 100–101, 105–113, 117–18, 145, 176
　see also Labour Church
New Journalism, 5, 10, 89, 91–2, 95, 102, 134, 135
New Monthly Magazine, 17
New Novelists' Magazine, 15
'new philology', see philology
New Woman, 93, 157
New York,
　homosexual subculture in, 166
Newbery, John, 13
Newry Magazine, 20
newspaper stamp, 16, 24
newspapers, 1–9, 11–16, 20–25, 33, 87, 88–130, 134
　and destruction of folk culture, 1–4, 9, 16–17, 23–4, 175–6
　see also cheap press; Benjamin; Yeats and journalism; individual titles
Niebelungen Lied, 68
Norton, Caroline, 83
Notes and Queries, 19
novels:
　'novel of circulation', 11, 176
　novelettes, 14–15. (see also gothic fiction)
　sensation novels, 38
　socialist novels, 94
'Nunquam', see Blatchford
nursery fictions, see folktales
Nutt, David, 136

Odin, 117–18
Oldmeadow, Ernest J., 135
oral story-telling, 2, 12–13, 15, 18–25, 39, 47, 57, 59, 60, 61, 63, 199 n.62, 102, 171, 176–7
　see also folklore
Order of Chæronea, 163–4
　see also homosexuality
Orientalism 16–17, 157–8, 159, 160–1

Original London Post, 11
Orpheus, 162
Owen, Sir Richard, 74

Pagan Review, 134
Pageant, 132, 139, 148–53, 161, 167, 169, 172, **173**
Pall Mall Gazette, 25
Pantheism, see under nature
Parade, 290 n.9
Parker's London News, 11
Pater, Walter, 140, 142, 149
　and coded homoerotic discourse, 145, 148, 155, 167, 172
　'The Age of Athletic Prizemen', 167
　'The Child in the House', 149–51
　'The Myth of Demeter and Persephone', 148
　'Dante Gabriel Rossetti', 155
　'Wordsworth', 142–3
　The Renaissance, 145, 148
Patmore, Coventry,
　The Angel In the House, 83
Patton, Sir Noel
　'A Midsummer Night's Dream', 121
Paul Greenhalgh, 166
Peachey, Caroline, 44
peasantry, see under 'folk', constructions of
pederasty, 157
Péladan, Sâr Joséphin, 166
penny dreadfuls, 37–8, 190 n.21
Penny Journal, 20
Penny Magazine, 2, 21
People's Periodical
Perrault, Charles,
　fairy tales, 11, 14, 31, 32, 104, 137
　Histories, or Tales of Past Times (Tales of Mother Goose), 11
personification, 44, 122–3
Phegley, Jennifer, 84
philanthropy, 48, 53–54, 57, 61, 79, 87, 93, 100–3, 114, 116, 176
philology, 9, 16, 34–5, 41–9, 69–71, 107, 143, 177
　see also Grimm, Jacob and Wilhelm; Müller; Indo-European
Pioneer, 160
Plato, and coded homosexual discourse, 163, 170–1
Playboy, 83

Police News, 38
pornography, 157, 162–4
popular tales, *see under* folktales
Pre-Raphaelitism, 132, 137, 140, 154–6, 158, 164, 167
Prichard, James,
  The Eastern Origin of the Celtic Nations, 70
Prichard, T. H.,
  'An Elm Recounts', 170
primitivism, 9–10, 12–13, 39–45, 69–74, 77, 105–13, 129–30, 137, 139–55, 157–8, 175–8
  see also savagery
Prince de Beaumont, Jeanne-Marie le,
  The Young Misses Magazine, 12, 14
print, technological innovations in, 22
Printer's Register, 43
Prophet, 90–1 *see Labour Prophet*
psychology,
  and the child, 41, 143, 191 n.40
  and homosexuality, 166
Punch, 6,
  'Monkeyana', 74,
  'The Missing Link', 74
  see also gorillas, Chaillu
Purcell, Edward
  'Of Purple Jars', 149–51
'Puss In Boots', 3, 30

Quarterly Review, 15–16, 25
Quarto, 133, 134, 137, 149
Quelch, Harry, 94
Quest, 133, 135–7, **138**, 139, 158

race, 34–35, 39, 44, 45, 48–52, 68–74, 76, 85, 106, 143, 158, 177
Radcliffe, Ann,
  The Mysteries of Udolpho, 15
  see also gothic romance
railways, 2, 109
rationalism, 14, 16, 17, 68–9, 177
readers and reading communities, 6–8
  adult, 6, 11–33, 35–7, 39–41, 44, 45, 65, 67–87, 131–74, 175–8
  child and teenaged, 3, 5, 6–7, 9, 12–14, 17–18, 25–26, 28–33, 34–66, 80, 88, 91–2, 93, 96, 101–6, 108–28, 136, 176
  homosexual, 156–74, 148
  Irish, 3–6, 19–25

middle-class, 1–9, 11–20, 24–8, 29–33, 67–87, 88, 90, 94, 95, 103, 134–5, 149, 177
working-class, 2–8, 12, 13, 15–26, 32–3, 37–8, 52–3, 57–8, **59**, 88–96, 98–130, 176
female, 7, 35–7, 92, 93, 94 95, 115, 119, 123, 125, 126, 127
coterie, 131–74
  see also correspondence columns, child correspondents and writers
realism, 26–7, 67, 81, 92–4, 104
Recapitulation thesis, 34, 39–45, 52, 77–8, 108–113, 142–3, 175–7
'religion of socialism', 87, 89, 100–1
  see also Labour Church
'Reynard the Fox', 45, 118
Reynold's Weekly Newspaper, 120
Richardson, Alan, 14
Ricketts, Charles, 132, 133, 157, 161, 167
Ritchie, Anne Thackeray, 4, 6, 196 n.2
  and *Cornhill Magazine*, 67, 78–9, 81–2, 84–6
  childhood reading of fairy tales, 29
  and class, 78–9, 81, 176
  and gender, 78–9, 81–2, 84–6
  'Beauty and the Beast', 67, 81
  'Betsinda and her Bun', 78–9
  'Blackstick Papers', 86
  'Cinderella', 67, 81
  'The First Number of "The Cornhill"', 196 n.7
  'Jack and the Beanstalk', 67
  'Maids-of All-Work and Blue Books', 81
  'The Sleeping Beauty in the Wood', 84–5
  'Toilers and Spinsters', 85 and n
Robinson, A. Mary F., 114
Robinson, Thomas, 117–18
Rolfe, Frederick, ['Baron Corvo']
  'Stories Toto Told Me', 167
Romanticism, 3, 12–13, 15–19, 35, 39–45, 41–6, 54–5, 70, 101–15, 139–44, 147–54, 177, 191 n.35
  see also child and folk, constructions of; Müller; Grimm
Roscoe, William Caldwell, 28
Rose + Croix school, 166

Rose, Jonathan, 7
Rosebery, Lord [Archibald Philip Primrose], 97–8
Rossetti, Christina
  'The Fairy Prince who Arrived too Late', 82–7
  'Goblin Market', 82–3, 132
Rossetti, Dante, Gabriel, 82, 135
  'Hand and Soul', 154–5
Rothenstein, William, 150
Rowe, H. C., 91, 93, 94, 114
'Royal Fairy Tales', 19
Runciman, John, 145
Ruskin, John, 28, 107, 111, 144, 145, 190n
  The King of the Golden River, 45
  German Popular Stories, 28, 45, 139, 174
Russell, George (AE), 146, 153

Sala, George Augustus,
  'The Complaint of the Old Magician', 1–2
  'A Case of Real Distress', 1–2
  see also Dickens; *Household Words*
Samber, Robert,
  Histories, or Tales of Past Times (Perrault), 11
'savage survivals', 31, 39–52, 72, 177
  see also anthropology, Kingsley; Lang; Tylor; McLennan
savagery, 9–10, 30–31, 34, 44, 49–52, 71–2, 106–7, 143, 177
  see also primitivism
Savoy, 153, 164
Schacker, Jennifer, 4
Scheherezade, 11, 157
  see also *Arabian Nights*
Schenda, Rudolf, 7
Schiller, Friedrich, 18
Schreiner, Olive, 104
science, 4, 8–10, 29–31, 41–6, 48–52, 59, 66, 67–79, 87, 96, 102, 106–7, 110–13, 143, 147, 166, 176–8
  see also comparative mythology; Darwin; evolution; geology; natural history; philology; recapitulation thesis
Scott, Patrick, 73
Scott, Sir Walter, 17, 81
  Minstrelsy of the Scottish Border, 46

'serial time', 6
Shannon, Charles, 133, 150, 167
Sharp, Evelyn, 131, 140
Sharp, Willam (Fiona Macleod), 134, 145, 147
Shaw, [John] Byam [Liston], 135, 158, **159**
Sherwood, Martha Mary, 39
Shuttleworth, Sally, 143
Silver, Carole G., 9
Sime, S. H., 167
Slade, the, 133
slavery, 73–4, 85
'Sleeping Beauty', 43, 61, 82, 84–5, 82–7
  and decadence, 151
  and women's rights, 129
  socialist appropriations of, 128–9
  see also Ewing; Ritchie; Rossetti
Small, Ian, 156
Smiles, Samuel
  Self-Help, 8, 76
Smithers, Leonard, 156
  Fairy Tales by the Abbé Voisenon, 164
  Harlequin: A Romance, 164
  Aglae, an Erotic Fairy Tale, 164
  see also Burton, *A Thousand Nights and a Night, Savoy*
social darwinism, 72–8
  see also Darwin, evolution
Social Democrat, 94
Social Democratic Federation, 89, 90, 99
socialism, 88–130, 137–140, 144
  socialist fairy tales, 88, 96, **97**, **99**, 101, 128, **129**, 30, 137–40, 144, 176
  socialist fiction, 92–99
  socialist Sunday schools, 102, 104, 105, 109, 113–17, 125–7 see also fairies; Cinderella schools; Christian socialism,
Socialist League, 90
Socialist penny press, 5, 10, 88–130
Society for the Diffusion of Useful Knowledge (S.D.U.K.), 2
solar mythology, 30, 43, 148, 212 n.67
  see also Müller; Indo-European

Solomon, Simeon, 163, 167, 172
  'Baccus', 167
  'The Bride, The Bridegroom and Sad Love', 162
  'Love among the Schoolboys', 156
  'Love in Autumn', 162
  A Vision of Love Revealed in Sleep, 155
  see also homosexuality; Housman, Laurence; Pater
'Sotadic' sexuality, 157, 162–3, *see also* homosexuality
Southall, Joseph, 137
Spectator, 28
Spencer, Herbert, 41, 76, 78, 106
Stead, Estelle, 33
Stead, W. T.
  Books for the Bairns, 32–3
Steedman, Carolyn, 142
Stenbock, Count Eric, 174, 218 n.165
Stephen, Laura, 29
Stephen, Leslie, 196 n.8
Stevens, Charles, 34
Stevenson, Robert Louis, 142
Stewart, Susan, 15
Stocking, George W., 52
Strahan, Alexander, 35
Strand, 134–5
Studio, 164
Summers, David, 106
Sunday Chronicle, 93, 102
superstitions, *see under* fairies
Swedenborg, 153
Sweeney Todd, 26
Swinburne, Algernon Charles, 155–6
Symbolism, 7, 131, 132, 133, 137, 139, 140, 145–6, 152–4, 166, 169
Symonds, John Addington,
  and coded homosexual discourse, 163–4
Symons, Arthur, 134
  on decadence, 149, 154
  on Symbolism, 145, 153–4
  and androgyny, 167
synaesthesia, 155

Tabart, Benjamin, 14
  Fairy Tales: or the Lilliputian Cabinet, 15
Tarpey, J. T. Kingsley,
  'The Merrow', 146

Taylor, Edgar, 46
  and Grimms' fairy tales:
  'German Popular and Traditionary Literature', 17–18
  Gammer Grethel's Fairy Tales,
    see under Housman, Laurence
  German Popular Stories, 17, 45, 57
Taylor, Harriet, 83
Taylor, Jenny Bourne, 143
Teleny, 164
Tell-Tale, 15
temperance movement, 119
Tennyson, Alfred Lord, 79
  In Memoriam, 100
Terrific Register, 25
Teutonic mythology,
  see Indo-European
Teutons, 71
Thackeray, Anne, *see under* Thackeray Ritchie, Anne
Thackeray, William Makepeace, 6,
  and *Cornhill Magazine* 67, 196 n.8
  fairy-tale reviews, 29
  'Half a Crown's Worth of Cheap Knowledge', 52
  'Roundabout Papers', 67
  The Rose and the Ring, 79, 86
Thompson, A.M., 92, 111
Thompson, Francis, 167, 169
Thoms, William John,
  Gammer Gurton's Story Books, 19
Thomson, J. Arthur, 147–8
Thoreau, 100, 107
Thousand and One Nights see under Arabian Nights
Tieck, Ludwig
  'Pietro D'Abano: A Tale of Enchantment', 18
Tillett, Benjamin, 92, 118
The Times, 6, 67
Titbits, 92, 103
Tolstoy, Leo, 107
'Tom Thumb', 12, 13, 18, 147
trade unionism, 89, 92, 99, 118
Tree of Life, 170
Trench, Richard Chenevix, 46, 189 n.4
Trevor, John, 113
  and evolution, 100, 106, 108, 110, 129

and *Labour Prophet*, 88–94, 98–101
  and *Cinderella Supplement*, 101–5, 114, 126–7
  and Labour Church Movement, 88–91, 101, 107, 113
  My Quest for God, 108
  see also socialism, religion of, and *Labour Prophet*
Trimmer, Sarah, 65
  Guardian of Education, 14
Turner, Mark W., 35
Tylor, Edward Burnett,
  and comparative method, 49, 106, 158, 193 n.83
  Researches into the Early History of Mankind, 49
  Primitive Culture, 30, 49, 74
  see also anthropology; Lang; Clodd; McLennan

Uffelman, Larry, 73
Ulrichs, Karl, 166
Universal Spectator, 11
Unstamped press, 183 n.26
'Urianian' subculture, see under homosexuality
Utamaro, Kitagawa, 158
utopianism, 10, 105–113, 118–20, 122–3, 126–7, **128**, 129–30, 140, 175–7

'Valentine and Orson', 18
Vanke, Francesca, 157
Venture, 132, 133, 164
Vickers, George,
  Grimm's Goblins, 26, 29, 32, 82–3
Volksbuch, 18, 185 n.37 see also chapbooks

Waldegrave, A. J., 106
Washington, Samuel, 92
Watts, George Frederick, 150
Webb, R. K., 22
Wedgwood, Julia
  'The Boundaries of Science: A Dialogue', 75, 79–80, 87
  'The Origin of Language', 69, 74, 177
  'Sir Charles Lyell on the Antiquity of Man', 69, 74
  see also evolution; philology; primitivism; savagery

Wedmore, Frederick, 167
Weeks, Jeffrey, 163
Wells, Herbert George,
  A Modern Utopia, 129
  The Time Machine, 78
Whistler, James MacNeill, 133, 158
White, Gleeson, 142, 164
  see also Order of Chæronea
Whitman, Walt, 100, 107, 140
Wieland, Christoph Martin, 13
Wiener, Joel H., 91
Wilde Oscar, 10, 33, 88, 132, 158
  and coded homosexual discourse, 156–7, 160–1, 166–7, 16–71
  and constructions of the child, 140, 149
  trials of, 135, 160, 163, 170–2
  'The Critic as Artist', 151
  The Happy Prince and other Tales, 136, 149
  'The Nightingale and the Rose', 158; 'The Selfish Giant', 144, 171; 'The Devoted Friend', 151, 169
  A House of Pomegranates, 131, 161
  'The Fisherman and his Soul', 141, 157
  The Picture of Dorian Gray, 131, 141, 144, 148
  Salome, 157, 61
  'The Soul of Man Under Socialism', 140, 144
Wilde, Lady Jane Francesca Agnes, ['Speranza']
  Ancient Legends of Ireland, 146
Wilde, Sir William, 20
Wilson, Edgar, 160
Women's columns (socialist press), 93, 95
Women's Social and Political Union, 152
women's suffrage, 85–6, 152 see also feminism
wonder tales, see fairy tales, 4
Wonder, 103
Wood, Ghislaine, 166
Wordsworth, William, 13,
  and childhood, 17, 41, 43–4, 142–3, 192 n.54–55
  Five-Book Prelude, 17

Workman's Times, 93
Worth, George J., 73

Yeats, William Butler,
   and journalism, 4, 20, 134–5, 145, 152–3, 175, 178, 185 n.44, 186 n.58
   and Irish folk belief, 4, 19–20, 24, 31, 45, 145–6, 175, 178
   and nationalism, 4, 19–20, 23–24, 31
   and symbolism, 135, 145, 146, 152–3, 166, 170
   Celtic Twilight, 23, 145
   'Dust Hath Closed Helen's Eye', 145
   Fairy and Folk Tales of the Irish Peasantry, 4, 19–20, 24
   Ideas of Good and Evil, 4
   Irish Fairy Tales, 185 n.44
   'Song of Mongan', 145
   'A Symbolic Artist and the Coming of Symbolic Art', 152–3
Yellow Book, 131–5, 140–41, 157, 167, **168**, 169, 170
'Yellow Dwarf' *see* Harland, Henry
Yeo, Stephen, 89, 102
Yonge, Charlotte,
   and *Monthly Packet*, 36–8, 64
   and fairy tales, 28, 31–3, 68

Zipes, Jack, 6, 8, 10, 176